Positive Parenting

A Guide to Raising Psychologically Healthy Children

Terence Sheppard and

Margaret Kummerow

Connor Court Publishing Pty Ltd

Published in 2022 by Connor Court Publishing Pty Ltd.

Connor Court Publishing Pty Ltd.
PO Box 7257
Redland Bay QLD 4165
sales@connorcourt.com
www.connorcourt.com

ISBN: 9781922815194

Cover Design by Caroline Robertson/MILCO.

Printed in Australia.

Contents

Dedication

For our children who taught us how to be parents and

For Fergus and Alfie, pioneers of a new generation.

Acknowledgements

It is very encouraging to write a book about children because most people, when they learn what you are doing, want to help. We have received support and contributions from many quarters: friends who have shared stories about their own children, young people who have told us about their lives growing up, colleagues who have recommended scholarly articles and books, and most of all from our patients and their parents who have provided priceless insights into why children turn out the way they do. There are also many others who know who they are whom we also wish to thank for sharing intimate details of their lives.* It is a pleasure to acknowledge the assistance of all these people here.

Others who have provided invaluable help are colleagues from the Thrive Medical Centre in Broken Hill, including psychologists Alex Forner and Nick Chizzoni, as well as occupational therapist and Thrive CEO, Heather Pearce. Felicity Copeland, a midwife working with the UN on children's health in developing countries, read an early draft and her suggestions about the book's structure and content, as well as her enthusiastic encouragement, were crucial in bringing it to a successful conclusion.

Dr Emma Rischbieth, GP and a new mother, provided thoughtful comments on the ideas we have presented here, and Lucy Kummerow, a young friend and relative, was generous in her observations about the challenges facing teenagers growing up in the 21st century. She also in-

* This book contains many stories about young (and older) people we have encountered during our professional and personal lives. Apart from stories about our own children the names and personal details of all the others have been deliberately changed to preserve confidentiality. We have also altered many of the details of their individual circumstances for the same reason. However, all the stories are true and the fundamental facts about each remain accurate.

troduced the authors into the mysteries of how her generation use social media. Dr Elsa Jureidini, a child psychiatrist, very kindly reviewed the final draft and provided expert comment on technical issues.

Our research assistants, provisional psychologist Dr Phoebe Drioli-Phillips and Amelia Winter (both of whom are working mothers) edited numerous drafts and were indefatigable in chasing down references to half remembered research from our undergraduate and postgraduate days. They also rescued us from some of the worst excesses of our personal enthusiasms regarding how children should be raised. We also acknowledge the hard work of our editor, Michael Gilchrist, particularly his tolerance for ongoing changes to the 'finished' manuscript.

Finally, we want to thank our own children, Hugh, Rory, and Megan who generously agreed to appear as themselves, corrected our memory of some of their early adventures, and commented on the text. As much as anything this book is a tribute to what they have given to the authors' lives.

As is always the case any errors remain our own.

About the Authors

Dr Terence Sheppard (B.Ec., B.A. Psych. (Hons), PhD) is a psychologist and his partner, Dr Margaret Kummerow (MBBS, FRACP) is a paediatrician. Following time in academia Terence has spent more than 30 years as a private consultant working in clinical and organisational settings focusing on child and adult mental health as well as leadership and safety in the workplace. Margaret was a GP for 12 years, before qualifying as a paediatrician, and since 2003 has worked exclusively with children and their parents. During this period, they have also raised their own children Hugh, Rory, and Megan, who feature in the book – alongside many other young people – to provide examples for parents of what and what not to do.

This book is the product of countless conversations between the authors about children and their parents and particularly why some youngsters thrive while others struggle. In this book they have combined their clinical experience with current research into child development and youth mental health to give modern parents a useful handbook for the most important job of their lives, raising the next generation.

This book will be of value to all parents whatever your situation – married, single, gay, step or adoptive – and wherever you are on the parenting journey. Whether you are 'beginners' with your first newborn, dealing with 'rowdy' pre-teens, guiding teenagers through the complexities of adolescence or assisting adult children to find a worthwhile life for themselves, there is plenty of advice and encouragement to be found in the pages of 'Positive Parenting'.

Introduction

As the Twig is Bent ...

"As the twig is bent, so grows the tree", Alexander Pope (English poet)

We wrote this book primarily because of our concern – shared by most parents, educators and health professionals – about what can only be described as a crisis in the mental health of teenagers and young adults in Australia and elsewhere.

Unfortunately, there is abundant evidence, reviewed in Chapter 1, that, compared with previous generations, today's young Australians report significantly greater degrees of psychological disorder, particularly anxiety and depression, and record tragically higher levels of suicide, attempted suicide, and self-harm. In Australia suicide is now the most common cause of death among young people aged 15 to 24.[1] A similar picture of youth mental health is emerging in other Western countries, including the US.

What we are seeing is not simply the result of improved reporting or better data capture. Recent US research, which tracked adolescent anxiety and depression between 1938 and 2007, confirms that today these are significantly higher than they have ever been in the past.[2]

In Chapter 1 we also look at data which suggest that young people today, at least in the West, are less confident, more risk averse, and less prepared for adulthood than previous generations at the same age. Whether this is a direct consequence of rising anxiety and depression is hard to say, but something real is happening to our children and it is not good.

The deterioration of mental health in adolescents and young adults in Australia and elsewhere is too sudden and too recent to be explained in terms of DNA. Young people today are genetically the same as those of previous generations who reported significantly lower levels of mental disorder.

How we are raising the next generation – the environment parents create for them to grow up in – is the major contributor to these grim statistics. Children are primarily the product of their parenting: this is the lesson in the quotation from Alexander Pope (see above).

This is important to know because it means we – parents, carers, teachers, and health professionals – can intervene to help children avoid or reverse these ominous trends. But first we need to understand what is going on. Why is it that in a world which is safer, healthier, more prosperous and provides more educational and career opportunities than ever before, are so many young people struggling psychologically?

However, our story is not a pessimistic one. On the contrary, we know that many parents can and do raise happy, psychologically healthy children. How do we know this? The evidence is all around us in the many wonderful young people we meet every day!

We titled this book 'Positive Parenting' because we believe parents can do a great deal to protect their children from the menace of mental illness as well as prepare them to lead successful lives by how they choose to raise them. We define positive parenting as teaching children how to live rather than what to live for. Parents do this by encouraging their children to pursue a life that is rewarding and worthwhile for them, rather than defining their future for them.

It is true that as children grow, others, particularly peers, also influence their development. But it is parents who lay the foundations, particularly between birth and five years of age, which underpin their future personality development.

If we can start young children on the right track, then our next challenge, guiding their later childhood and adolescence, will be much easier.

However, there are no guarantees.

In Part 1 we emphasise that there is no road map or blueprint for raising happy or successful children; every child is unique and so is their path to adulthood. The ongoing interactions between a child's biology and their environment means that no one can predict their destiny with confidence.

The evidence that there is no foolproof system for raising 'successful' children is to be seen in the many parents who are struggling to meet the daily challenge of child rearing, often with unfortunate consequences for their offspring. But while there may be no road map, we do believe there are reliable guidelines for positive parenting, based on experience and research, which can assist us to rear happy, psychologically healthy children.

The fact that each child is unique, and their future unknown, is what makes raising children endlessly fascinating, as well as confusing and distressing at times. It also means parents must make plans for their children (for example, where to send them to school) and make decisions on their behalf without knowing if what they are doing is 'right' for a particular child.

Put simply, there are rarely certain answers to the questions, "What is right?" or "What is best?", when considering options for your children.

In Chapter 2, to address the question, "What is best for my child?", we explore what reasonable expectations parents might have for their children. Having considered common parental aspirations such as, "I want my child to be happy and successful ...", and so on, we conclude that parents are more likely to be satisfied with their efforts if they encourage their children to develop particular personal qualities – what we call accomplishments of character – rather than simply accumulate a list of prizes or achievements. In other words, as suggested above, that they teach children how to live rather than what to live for.

The ten accomplishments of character we recommend for children provide an answer to the question, "What is best?" Together they provide the framework for a model of childrearing to guide parents when deciding in the best interests of a child.

But knowing what is generally 'best' for children and teenagers is the easy part. What is genuinely difficult, in the absence of a proven formula for parenting, is to instil or embed this knowledge into their everyday behaviour. This reality is reflected in the frequent lament of parents: "I know what I want my kids to do, I just can't get them to do it!" In Chapter 3 we explore how to address this daily challenge for parents.

We can't, nor should we try, to monitor our children 24/7 once they are no longer young. Sooner or later, and preferably sooner, we need them to be making wise choices when we are not around. Acting wisely, after all, defines what it means to be a mature adult.

We can assist our children to make wiser choices by creating situations in which, as early as possible, they enjoy a degree of autonomy where they are left to decide for themselves, to choose between a range of (age appropriate) alternatives. By making their own decisions, and accepting the consequences, they will come to learn, firstly, that some options are generally better than others and, secondly, to carefully consider the likely consequences of each before acting, that is, to learn to 'look before they leap.'

However, the benefits of managed autonomy go well beyond learning discretion. Raising autonomous, independently minded children, with the courage to decide for themselves and accept the consequences of their own choices, is central to positive parenting because these qualities are synonymous with psychological health and personal resilience.

We conclude Chapter 3 by discussing a dilemma familiar to all parents, deciding when to intervene in what children are doing or saying and when to refrain; or, to put this another way, when to 'step in' and when to 'hold back.' That is, how to achieve a successful balance between giving children the independence they need to flourish while at the same time protecting them from risk they cannot yet manage.

In Part 2 we summarise the current state of knowledge regarding best practice parenting, which includes lessons from our grandparents as well as insights from the most recent research.

A great deal has been known for a long time about raising confident, happy children, lessons which have stood the test of time because they work. In Chapter 4 we discuss one of these which has been handed down by generations of thoughtful parents and educators: "Prepare the child for the road, not the road for the child." This nugget of timeless wisdom acknowledges that life is not a free ride, and that problems as well as opportunities – large and small – loom ahead for children, most of which they will have to manage on their own.

The alternative is an ultimately futile attempt by parents to anticipate and resolve all obstacles to their children's progress – a favoured tactic of today's so-called 'helicopter' or 'lawn mower' parents. More importantly, it leaves children, raised in this way, incapable of coping independently; the first time they are truly tested on their own they are likely to struggle. (See Story: *Going to School*).

Story: *Going to School*

We recently observed a mother and her two primary school sons on their way to school. It was raining lightly and the two boys were each holding an umbrella. What caught our attention was their mother, who was leading the way without an umbrella while carrying both of her children's back-backs!

We might add that the elder of the two was almost the same size as his mother. What, we wondered, lies ahead for these boys?

If this is how their mother manages the routine task of getting them to school, how will they learn to handle the much greater challenges they will inevitably face in the future?

ꕥꕥꕥ

We will have many occasions to comment on the behaviour of parents and their children in the course of this book, behaviour we have observed ourselves or has been related to us by others.

From the outset we should emphasise that a single interaction

between a parent and a child tells us nothing about their parenting style.

What we saw that day in the rain may have been a very unusual incident; a busy parent running late and getting her children to school as quickly as possible so she could go to work. If having their bags carried by their mother was quite uncharacteristic of the way they normally went to school – perhaps they usually walked on their own – this incident means nothing. But if it was the mother's standard procedure then there is cause for concern because it probably reflects how she manages her children in many other situations as well.

Too many experiences of over-caring and over-protective parenting and these boys would be well on their way to learned helplessness – incapable of making their own way in the world as adults without a parent by their side and prey to anxiety or depression due to their inability to manage on their own.

We socialise children via the tens of thousands of interactions we have over the first 15+ years of their life and how we manage these inevitably becomes habitual. If we are not careful, we will engage with our children without reflecting too much about what we are doing or the longer term consequences.

In particular, we may neglect to require them to assume increasing personal responsibility as they grow and continue to regard them as younger than they really are in terms of our expectations of them. In effect, if we are not careful, we will infantilise them: physically they will become adults but psychologically remain children, incapable of looking after themselves, much less others.

All the more reason to think hard about what we want for our children and how we should interact with them now to set them up for a successful and independent future.

We hope that reading this book will give you a chance to reflect on how you are raising your children and to consider, if necessary, making changes to your parenting style that ultimately will be in their best interests.

Part 2 continues with a review of the exciting research into child and adolescent development completed during recent decades, the results of which are only now becoming accessible outside the academic literature.

In Chapter 5 we introduce the intriguing concept of antifragility. Children are not fragile, although babies may certainly appear that way, neither are they robust. Rather they are *antifragile*, which is the true opposite of fragility. Something that is fragile requires constant protection and care; the antifragile child, in contrast, *needs* challenge, and the stress which comes with it, if they are to achieve full physical and psychological maturity. Moreover, shielding a child from the stimulus of adversity may, in fact, *harm* them by not providing the necessary impetus they require to grow into fully fledged adults.

The suggestion that children positively thrive on challenge is encouraging, particularly since the world they are growing up in today is vastly different and more complex than the one their parents remember from their own childhood.

One example of this, which we explore in detail, is internet technology, especially the smartphone. Just 20 years ago a personal communication device was the stuff of science fiction, but today can be found in the hand of almost every teenager in Australia and around the world. The internet – and social media in particular – constitutes a major environmental shift in our children's lives, one with profound implications for their psychological health.

Jean Twenge, a psychologist, notes in her book *iGen* (a major study of US teenagers) that adolescents today are spending less time together in person and more time online. She is adamant: "The results could not be clearer; teens who spend more time on screen activities are more likely to be unhappy and those who spend more time on non-screen activities are more likely to be happy."[3] That said, like them or not, smart phones (and the social media applications that come with them) are here to stay and parents need to have a clear strategy about how and how much their children should use this technology.

In Chapter 6 we learn that mood disorders, like anxiety and depression, are primarily acquired or *learned* as children grow. While it is true that some children appear to inherit a genetic predisposition to these and other unhealthy conditions, such as ADHD or addiction, whether these emerge in their behaviour is fundamentally determined by the circumstances of their childhood – the world they grow up in. In other words, DNA is not destiny. Parents, whatever their circumstances – married, single, divorced, adoptive, gay or straight – can and do make a fundamental difference to the adults their children ultimately become.

And even if a child does develop a mood disorder or other psychological condition as an adolescent or later, how they manage it – successfully or otherwise – is essentially determined *by the character or personality they have acquired while growing up.*

Chapter 7 considers another parenting maxim: "Children need plain food and dull monotony." While we are less concerned with diet we argue strongly for the importance of routine – the modern equivalent of 'dull monotony' – particularly for young children. Predictable routines, which govern their day-to-day activities, inject order and structure into youngster's lives which provide a sense of security and the confidence that goes with this. Routine also provides external boundaries which eventually children internalise as self-discipline or impulse control, necessary for successful independence and personal maturity.

We argue that routine is particularly important for children who experience a family separation early in their lives. Chapter 7 also looks at the particular challenges facing parents who have left their partner and are raising children alone or have become stepparents. We discuss the critical role which daily routine plays in assisting all children, but particularly those whose parents have separated, develop a positive sense of identity, self-confidence, and a fundamental trust in their world; qualities they will need to ultimately stand on their own feet. Routine is necessary in any household but especially so in single parent and blended households where a child may be struggling to adjust to entirely new living arrangements.

Part 3, the core of the book, takes its name from our title: Positive Parenting. The purpose of positive parenting is to equip a child with the accomplishments of character they will need to flourish as adolescents and adults. These qualities are not only synonymous with psychological health but are also those displayed by mature, autonomous adults able to confidently pursue a life of their own choosing. Positive parenting is not merely an antidote to psychological disorder in young people, if it does occur, but provides your best chance of ensuring your children avoid the scourge of mental illness altogether.

Positive parenting begins with the fundamental requirement for parents to respect every child as an autonomous person who has the same privileges and responsibilities as all other human beings. This is true even though they cannot fully exercise their birthright until they are adults.

However, we are aware that the expression 'Respect your child' has been overused to the point where it has lost much of its meaning and value. In Chapter 8, we address this deficit by exploring what respect for a child really means. In particular we consider the important distinction between loving a child and treating them with respect. This is something we believe even conscientious parents may overlook.

Chapter 9 focuses on the use of rules to create a family environment in which all members, parents included, can find love and assistance while pursuing their individual interests and ambitions with minimum disruption to and from others. Ideally our home is somewhere we are happy to go to and (at least slightly) reluctant to leave even when we must. Rules which are reliably implemented are necessary for achieving this desideratum.

Rules, however, are of limited value, unless accompanied by consequences for infringements, which are consistently and impartially applied. This, of course, leads to a discussion of the contentious topic of discipline, which we regard as the central pivot around which positive parenting revolves. In Chapter 10 we explore techniques of effective discipline, backed by love and respect, that are compassionate rather than coercive, and can be used relatively easily by busy parents.

In Chapter 11 we discuss the 'difficult' conversations parents will inevitably have with children, particularly teenagers, if they are serious about promoting their welfare through discipline. We demonstrate how parents can conduct such conversations, including managing conflict, without damaging their relationship with a child or creating lingering resentment. The positive parenting techniques we recommend for influencing children's behaviour are not difficult to understand or to use, they just require a bit of practice – like any other useful skill.

In Chapter 12 we consider the reality that while all children are different, indeed unique, from birth some are 'more different' than others. That is, they may appear unusual, strange or eccentric when compared with their peers and they may need more individual attention and support. Nevertheless, even very different children are normal in the sense that they require the same approach to parenting that we are advocating for their 'mainstream' peers.

'Labelling' a child who is different or unusual, or fails to meet our expectations in some way, as a 'disappointment' or a 'problem' can actually exacerbate the very behaviour which concerns parents in the first place. This, in turn, may lead them to raise their child them quite differently than others regarded as 'normal' which will merely increase the challenges they are facing.

Similarly, a child diagnosed with a non-organic mood, personality, or conduct disorder – or indeed a developmental disorder of some kind – while possibly needing specific support or intervention – requires the same approach to parenting that we advocate for any other child. The emotional and practical tools of positive parenting – love, affection, respect, rules, and discipline – are as important for children who are 'different' as they are for all the others.

Finally, in Chapter 13 we offer what we have called 'tools for the road': skills, knowledge, and accomplishments of character your children will need for their journey to the future, so they can successfully manage the triumphs and joys, as well as the failures and disappointments, that must await them. We have tried to include advice regarding the most common concerns that perplex parents and their children as well as useful tips for preparing young people to travel with competence and confidence.

In summary, what we have tried to provide in these pages is a handbook for enhancing your success as a parent. Specifically, we explain how to instil in your children those qualities – or personality traits – which will minimise their risk of mental disorder, or, if it does emerge, assist them to manage it successfully. In addition, the accomplishments of character we recommend will facilitate their growth as successful, independent people who will become all they can and wish to be.

We have already noted that there are no guarantees when it comes to raising children. You will make mistakes and may well get things spectacularly wrong at times (as did we!). However, we firmly believe that 'Positive Parenting' is a reliable guide for raising psychologically healthy children which will mean they are prepared to forge rewarding and worthwhile lives for themselves and, ultimately, their own families as well. At the same time positive parenting will enhance your joy and satisfaction as a parent.

Time to Get Started

Human babies are the least developed of all newborn mammals. They have by far and away the most growth ahead of them, not least physically and neurologically, to say nothing of the progress they must make psychologically and socially before they can leave home and make their own way in the world.

Our privilege as parents is to assist them on their journey so that one day, sad as it may be to say, they will live very well and, ideally, better without us. And we don't have a lot of time, so we had better get started!

PART 1

There Is No Road Map

"Before I got married, I had six theories about bringing up children; now I have six children and no theories."

John Wilmot (English poet)

Although the real author of this aphorism is in dispute, it points to an important truth: there is no guaranteed formula for raising a child.

It is not possible to explain precisely why some young people emerge from childhood as confident, well integrated adults while others do not. The complex interactions between DNA and environment, or nature and nurture, mean that we cannot predict in advance the adult a particular child will become.

For parents starting out with a newborn this means that there is no definitive guide – no road map – to raising the 'perfect' child, assuming one would want to define what is meant by this word. Quite simply, as psychiatrist Anthony Storr points out, there can be "no blueprint for an 'ideal' upbringing since no two individuals are the same."[1]

But when you think about it, this is not so surprising. The 'product' of parenting – the young adult – is the outcome of literally millions of interactions between their genetic inheritance and the world they grow up in. It would be absurd to suggest that there is a proven model or system which could ensure that these interactions always turn out well or anticipate their longer-term consequences to avoid any negative outcomes.

There is simply no way to ensure that a newborn will enjoy a painless journey through childhood and adolescence. In fact, the odds are strongly against this happening. Moreover, as we argue later, a serene and effortless childhood is not in the best interests of any child.

Anyway, the notion that we could program a child's development according to someone else's notion of an 'ideal' outcome would be repugnant to any parent. We rightly regard every baby as unique with potentials yet unknown because these are created and emerge as they grow. Children are literally a work in progress, further reinforcing the point that their future can never be known in advance.

So, if there are no perfect solutions to the challenge of parenting, why did we write this book?

Well, even if there is no '5, 10 or 20 Step Plan' for raising the 'ideal' child, and never will be, there is nevertheless a great deal we do know from research and experience which can inform our approach to parenting. It is certainly possible to recommend guidelines for child rearing – what we call positive parenting – which will give your children their best opportunity of becoming confident, resilient, and psychologically healthy adolescents and adults.

The need for positive parenting has never been greater. In Chapter 1 we review alarming evidence which points to a dramatic rise in the incidence of mental disorder and psychological distress in young people in Australia and elsewhere. This increase is too sudden and too recent to be explained in other than environmental terms, that is, how they are being raised in and outside the home.

Our purpose in writing this book was to, firstly, highlight the current crisis in the mental health of young people in Australia and elsewhere, and then to suggest what parents can do to prevent the curse of mental illness from threatening the lives of their own children.

While our proposals do not guarantee a result, they offer a reliable guide, based on research and the experience of previous generations of parents, for raising children which, we believe, will maximise their chances of achieving happy, healthy and rewarding lives.

Parents, like their children, are also a work in progress. We continue to grow and change as we age. This means that we can adjust our parenting style, regardless of the age of our children, including when they are adults. We never cease being parents, no matter where we are on the parenting journey. We can always choose to modify how we interact with our children today in order to influence their future behaviour in ways we believe will benefit them.

Children are not pre-programmed. Rather, they are dynamic entities who interact with the world around them to become themselves. They inherit genetic predispositions, but their biology and psychology change over time as each interacts with their environment in unique and sometimes unpredictable ways. And, because children never cease to grow and change, parents have the opportunity, at any stage in their lives, to influence their future development. Put simply, it is never too late to exert a positive impact on how your children are travelling.

This book will be of value to all parents, whatever your status or circumstances and wherever your children are on the road to adult independence; whether you are 'beginners' with a new baby, managing rowdy youngsters, guiding teens through the complexities of adolescence, or trying to assist adult children who are struggling to create a worthwhile life for themselves.

Neither the precise path a child will take through life nor their ultimate destiny as an adult can be known in advance. And this is a good thing. Raising a child is not like baking a cake. Rather, it is to take part in a creative project, the outcome of which is uncertain; this, of course, is why it is so exciting, fulfilling and, at times, distressing. But – and this is important – it is the child's project not their parents'. Ultimately, they must plot their own course. To step in too often is to deny a child the right, and obligation to undertake their own search for a fulfilling life and to become the person they need to be.

In summary, how a child develops and the environment they grow up in are beyond anyone's direct control. Parents can influence these – that is the purpose of parenting – but they cannot, nor should they try, to dictate their children's final destination.

1

What Is Happening to Our Children?

"*We see how early childhood experiences are so important to lifelong outcomes, how the early environment literally becomes embedded in the brain and changes its architecture.*" Alan S. Garner (US paediatrician)

Story: *Jane and Oliver*

Jane and Oliver were born in the same year and in the same city. They both have two siblings and grew up in loving families with parents committed to each other and the success of their children. Jane and Oliver went to similar schools and enjoyed a comfortable childhood. They are both now 25 years old.

Jane completed high school, went to university, and is employed as a qualified accountant. She lives with her partner of three years with whom she is planning a family. She remains close to her brothers and parents, particularly her mother, and enjoys a wide circle of friends.

Oliver dropped out of school before completing Year 11. He is a regular drug user, has struggled to find work and remains unemployed. He lives mostly at home, has no stable partner and is financially dependent on his parents.

Regrettably he has difficult relationships with both, particularly his father, and rarely sees his adult brother or sister. He has been in trouble with the police and last week was taken to ED following a drug overdose.

❧❧❧

Two questions immediately arise from the story of Jane and Oliver. Why do two children with such similar backgrounds turn out so differently? And what, if anything, could Oliver's parents have done differently?

One possible answer to the first question is that Jane and Oliver were always destined to be different; it was 'in their DNA' as the saying goes.

But there is considerable evidence to suggest that while temperament, or basic emotional style, is inherited, the subsequent development of our personality – the type of people we become – is substantially mediated by life experience, particularly by how we are raised.[1, 2]

In fact, a major conclusion of the last decades of research in developmental neuroscience is that the infant brain is not fixed from birth but "is designed to be moulded by the environment it encounters".[3] In other words, early childhood experience permanently alters the neurological and psychological development of the growing child.

The suggestion that environment produces permanent neurological change in infants now has widespread support. Cicchetti and Tucker observe: "Environmental experience is now recognized to be critical to the differentiation of brain tissue itself. Nature's potential can be realized only as it is enabled by nurture".[4] This is the point made by Alan Garner in the quotation at the beginning of this chapter.

The process whereby inherited potential can only be unleashed by certain circumstances is particularly apparent in how infants learn to talk. Those denied the stimulus necessary for speech – regular vocal interaction with adults – fail to develop the neurological pathways required.

The ongoing interplay between nature and nurture permanently alters a child. This process determines which parts of their DNA are expressed as they grow, and which remain dormant; the final result is the adult they eventually become.

Jean Twenge, introduced earlier, confirms this point when she notes that among persons genetically predisposed towards depression, only a proportion – those exposed to particular conditions – will display later symptoms of this disorder.[5]

The available research suggests that our initial genetic profile may be less significant for determining who we become than the world we grow up in, particularly the world created by our parents.

The unpredictable interaction between genes and environment means that, even children who have been raised in the same homes, and in essentially the same way, become quite different, indeed unique, adults. You may be able to test this statement by comparing yourself with your own siblings! Interestingly, this appears also to be true for identical twins, even those raised in the same household.[6,7]

As with anxiety and depression some children are genetically predisposed to developing addictive behaviours, such as Alcohol Use Disorder (AUD). However, in 2020 the US National Institute of Alcohol Abuse and Alcoholism website reported:[8]

> Research shows that genes are responsible for about half of the risk for AUD [Alcohol Use Disorder]. Therefore, genes alone do not determine whether someone will develop AUD. Environmental factors, as well as gene and environment interactions, account for the remainder of the risk.

These findings suggest we should be very careful when attributing children's behaviour to their genetic blueprint. The research reported above clearly suggests that genes are only one, and possibly a smaller, part of the story; inherited potential is stimulated or depressed depending on how children are raised.

And even when inherited characteristics such as addiction or depression do emerge, how they impact a person's future life has a great deal to do with the character or personality he or she has acquired or learned while growing up.

Your own experience will tell you that among 'alcoholics', addiction is managed in a variety of ways. Some successfully practise total abstinence (Bob Hawke, who gave up alcohol when he was elected Prime Minister of Australia in 1983, is a good example) while others remain teetotal apart from an occasional lapse. But for some unfortunates it propels them into a personal hell from which they may struggle to emerge.

Whether a genetic predisposition (towards depression or AUD for instance) is realised in a child's behaviour in the first place, and how it impacts their life if it does, can be explained by differences in acquired character – the personality they develop as they grow.

As parents we can't change our children's genetic makeup, and we may have limited influence over the wider world they enter when they are 6+ years of age and start attending school. But we can significantly determine the type of people they become and the character they acquire by how we raise them (particularly in their first 5-6 years) and the environment we create in the family home.

It is character development which primarily determines a child's future success and happiness, and it is character development which is the central focus of positive parenting.

For the second question raised above, "What could Oliver's parents have done differently?", unfortunately there are no simple answers.

Oliver's parents were as committed to their children as Jane's and no doubt tried their best. However, the simple truth is that, because of the complex interactions between genes and environment, loving and conscientious parents may have children who experience mental disorder or addiction as well as other personal challenges. The reverse is also true: resilient children do sometimes emerge from dysfunctional homes in which parents struggle to care for themselves much less their offspring.[9]

However, this does not mean that parents cannot make a positive difference to how their children grow; research confirms the critical impact which their environment has on children's development. Parenting style clearly does matter, and parents do influence the progress of any child. So that even if a teen or young adult does experience a psychological illness, a resilient character acquired through positive parenting will put them in a much better position to manage it successfully.[10, 11]

Adolescents raised via an appropriate combination of what has been called parental 'demandingness' and 'responsiveness' are reported to be generally 'better adjusted' than peers whose parents emphasise one over the other. Demandingness refers to the extent to which parents impose boundaries on their children's behaviour and establish appropriate expectations of maturity as their children grow. Responsiveness refers to the degree of warmth and engagement parents display.[12, 13, 14, 15, 16]

This is important to know and gives us some clues about raising children. But it is insufficient as a practical guide to parenting. Our purpose in writing this book was to explore how, every day, and faced with a myriad of conflicting demands on their time and attention, parents can and do make a positive difference to their children's psychological health, as well as their future success and happiness.

Adolescent Anxiety and Depression

The need for positive parenting has never been greater. Something very concerning is happening to young people in Australia and elsewhere.

Recent investigations into the mental health of young Australians have reported alarmingly high and rising levels of anxiety, depression, and psychological distress.

In 2021, Mission Australia and the Black Dog Institute released the latest results of a nine-year study into the mental wellbeing of young Australians aged 15-19.[17] For this research more than 20,000 participants (a sample reflective of the wider population of Australian teens) completed the Kessler (K6), a widely recognised measure of non-specific psychological distress which is used for detecting symptoms of mood disorders, primarily anxiety and depression.[18, 19]

Participants were divided into 3 groups: low psychological distress (mental disorder unlikely), medium psychological distress (mental disorder possible) and high psychological distress (mental disorder very likely). Those who scored 19 or more on the K6 were classified as experiencing high level of psychological distress and very likely to exhibit symptoms of mental disorder.[20]

Of the sample of young people studied nearly 27% were in this third category; that is, they met the criteria of a probable serious mental disorder, primarily anxiety or depression. Additionally, the proportion of teenagers in this group had increased significantly over the previous nine years, from 18.7% in 2012 to 26.6% in 2020.[21]

While an increase was observed for both genders, the rise for females was significantly greater. Over the nine years from 2012 to 2020 the proportion of teenage girls reporting significant psychological distress increased from over one-fifth (22.4%) to over one-third (34.1%). For males the comparable figures were 12.6% and 15.3%.[22]

This disturbing picture is confirmed by the results of a second major survey of the mental health of Australian young people released in 2015, the Young Minds Matter Report.[23] Using both carer and self-report data, this study concluded that 13.9% (1 in 7) of their sample (aged 4 to 17 years) had met the DSM-IV criteria for a formal diagnosis of a mental disorder in the last 12 months – effectively 560,000 young Australians.[24] When analysed by age, the data revealed that a diagnosis of mental disorder was three times more likely in adolescents (12-17) than children (4-11).

Attention Deficit Hyperactivity Disorder (ADHD) was the most common disorder diagnosed (7.4%), followed by anxiety disorders (social phobia, separation anxiety, generalised anxiety and obsessive-compulsive disorder – 6.9%), major depression (2.8%) and conduct disorder (2.1%).

Data used in the Young Minds Matter Report came from interviews conducted with parents and carers of the children and teenagers in the sample, as well as from the young people themselves (who completed a confidential diagnostic survey).

Interestingly, what young people say about themselves presents a somewhat different picture than the one provided by their parents and carers, particularly with regard to depression. Based on their own self-reports, the incidence of major depressive disorder was nearly double in the 11 to 17 group (7.7%) when compared with parent/carer provided data (4.7%).

Symptoms of depression were also significantly more likely to be self-reported by teenage girls (16-17) than boys in the same age group (20% vs 7.2% respectively). Perhaps even more concerning is that nearly 17% of the same group of females admitted to having self-harmed in the past.

Levels of depression self-reported by 16–17-year-old girls in 2015 in the Young Minds Matter survey are approaching those recorded by the same cohort of girls in the Mission Australia/Black Dog Institute data for the same year, which also used a self-report methodology.

Self-report data should be treated with caution for two reasons: firstly, respondents may be reluctant to reveal the depth of their feelings, even in an anonymous survey (and hence under-report symptoms), or alternatively they may exaggerate their symptoms to present what they believe is an appropriate picture of a 'modern' child or teenager.

While survey results of the kind reported above do not constitute a formal clinical diagnosis of psychological illness, they suggest many young Australians are currently experiencing at least some of the symptoms of serious mental disorder. And the gap between what parents/carers report and their young charges say about themselves suggests that some, at least, may be reluctant to share their feelings with adults.

Two-thirds of those who self-reported a major depressive disorder, but which was not also reported by a parent or carer, believed the adults in their lives knew little or nothing about their feelings. Even among those whose parents and carers were aware they were depressed a majority expressed similar doubts.[25]

The differences between what these youngsters say about themselves and what their parents/caregivers report suggest that what parents see in their children may not always be the whole story.

Perhaps we should not be surprised that adolescents in particular are reluctant to share dark feelings with parents and carers, but these findings should alert us that our children may be less happy than they appear on the surface.

This does not mean that we should rush them off to a psychologist, but rather ensure we stay as close as possible to them. To the extent that we build strong relationships with our children based on love, trust, and mutual respect we will find it easier to communicate with them during the delicate period of adolescence when they transition from dependence on us to an independent life of their own.

To complete this brief summary of the Young Minds Matter study, almost 20% of adolescents also self-reported very high or high levels of psychological distress, as distinct from specific symptoms of mental disorder. Once again, this figure was significantly higher, nearly double in fact, for females (26%) than males (15%).[26] Other Australian research also confirms that significant levels of psychological distress are more common among females than males.[27]

Whether young people are reporting symptoms of probable mental disorder or, more generally, psychological distress, what they are saying should give us pause for thought. At the very least these data suggest that too many young Australians are very unhappy and struggling with the challenges of growing up.

The results of the two major surveys reviewed above support a conclusion that mental illness, particularly anxiety and depression, is a major and growing problem for a significant proportion of young Australians today.

Further evidence that the mental health of young people in Australia continues to deteriorate can be observed in significant increases in Emergency Department (ED) presentations for mental health issues in recent years. A 2018 Australian study examined changes in mental health presentations (specifically for self-harm, suicidal ideation and intentional poisoning) at 115 hospitals in New South Wales between 2010 and 2014.

Presentation rates for mental health issues had increased over the five years in every age group (from 0 to 80+) with the exception of 0 to 9-year-olds. Presentation rates were highest for 15-19-year-olds while the greatest year on year increases in presentation rates (27% pa) for the same period was observed among 10- to 19-year-olds.[28]

Overseas research presents a similar picture. In the US the proportion of teenagers reporting symptoms of a major depressive episode increased by 56% between 2010 and 2015. This data was collected from a nationally representative sample of 17,000 young people who responded anonymously to questions based on DSM-IV criteria (the global standard for diagnosing mental disorder).[29]

This study confirms that a statistically significant increase in mental disorder occurred across all socio-economic and ethnic groups in the US during this period, and was not confined within particular socio-economic classes or cultural groups. As in Australia, the increase observed was even more marked among girls.

The same US survey found that in 2015 nearly 20% of females (12 to 17 years) reported symptoms of a major depressive episode in the previous year, almost double the number describing similar symptoms three years earlier. Among males in the same age group the proportion self-reporting depression rose from 8.5% in 2012 to nearly 13% in 2015. These findings are very similar to results from Australian research reported above.

Unfortunately, higher rates of depression were also accompanied by an increase in teenage self-harm and suicide.[30]

In October 2020 *The Weekend Australian* reported that between 2009 and 2015 in the US, hospital admissions for self-harm among girls aged between 15 and 19 had increased by 62%. For pre-teen girls the rise in the same period was a scarcely credible 189%![31]

Self-Harm and Suicide

Australian data, once again from the Young Minds Matter report, indicates that in 2015 10% of young Australians aged 12-17 years had at some point in their past, self-harmed – some 186,000 young people. Self-harm often takes the form of cutting arms and legs with a knife or razor blade. In older adolescents and young adults, it can also take the form of self-inflicted poisoning or cigarette burns.[32] Self-harm in older females was found to be effectively double that in males (16.8% of girls aged 16 to 17 admitted to self-harm in the previous 12 months) and older adolescents of both genders were twice as likely to report self-harm compared with their younger peers.

The same study also found that 7.5% of 12-17-year-old Australians had seriously considered a suicide attempt and that one in 40 attempted suicide in the previous year. For every youth suicide, there are an estimated 100 to 200 more attempts. Suicidal behaviour is most common in older adolescent girls.

The data for death by suicide in this age group make for grim reading.

In Australia, for the period 2016-2018, suicide was the leading cause of death among people aged 15–24 (37%), followed by land transport accidents (21%). For people aged 25–44, it was also suicide (22%), followed by accidental poisoning (13%).[33]

In Australia about 460 young people aged 15-24 take their own lives every year - more than die on the roads - and this number continues to increase.

Young males are three times more likely to die by suicide than young females because they tend to use more lethal methods, but females report more attempts. In 2018 the suicide rate for 15-24-year-old males was 20.2 per 100,000 people, an increase of nearly 10% on the previous year. For females in the same age group the figure was 6.4 per 100,000 with no discernible increase on the previous year.[34]

Sadly, young people of Aboriginal and Torres Islander descent are significantly overrepresented in these figures.[35] Between 2015 and 2019, one-third (32.4%) of all Aboriginal and Torres Strait Islander deaths between 5-17 years of age were due to suicide.[36]

Issues of Concern for Young People

The Mission Australia/Black Dog Institute survey, referred to above, also asked young people to assess the importance of a range of personal issues. Of some twenty issues which they were asked to consider, the top four they identified as being most important to them were mental health (or depression), stress (or anxiety), body image and school/study problems.[37]

The table opposite presents the proportions of 15-19-year-old Australians who rated these four issues as being of major concern but divided into two groups.

In the left-hand column below are the proportions of those who regarded these issues as being of major concern and who also reported high to very high levels of psychological distress (consistent with a diagnosis of mental disorder). In the right-hand column are the proportions of those who rated these four issues as also being of major concern to them, but who did not report high or very high levels of psychological distress.

Concern	Proportion of 15 to 19-year-olds who reported an issue to be of major concern *who also* reported psychological distress	Proportion of 15 to 19-year-olds who reported an issue to be of major concern *who did not* report psychological distress
Mental health	67.7%	21.8%
Coping with stress	73.1%	31.5%
Body image	59.0%	23.7%
School/study problems	53.6%	24.8%

Not surprisingly, both depression (mental health) and anxiety (coping with stress) are rated as issues of major concern by a majority of young people who also reported high or very high psychological distress (67.7% and 73.1% respectively in the left-hand column). But the numbers in the right-hand column suggest that anxiety in particular (31.5%), as well as depression (21.8%) are significant issues for all Australians teenagers, not merely for those who also report elevated levels of psychological distress.

It should also be noted that responses to these issues varied considerably by gender. Females were much more likely than males to say they were either extremely or very concerned about coping with stress (59.5% compared with 27.0%), mental health (52.8% compared with 25.2%) and body image (47.2% compared with 15.0%).

A comparison of the figures in the left- and right-hand columns of the above table also confirms that the presence of likely mental illness significantly increases the importance and impact of other typical teenage worries, in this case body image and the demands of schoolwork.

It is possible that as anxiety and depression increase normal adolescent concerns, about body image for example, these, in turn, will intensify anxiety and low moods. Thus a vicious cycle may be set up whereby poor mental health lowers young people's confidence in themselves which may then exacerbate their existing symptoms of mental illness. This leads to even lower feelings of self-esteem, thus creating a negative, self-reinforcing loop.

Research in the United States, once again, presents a similar picture. A large majority of American teenagers (70%) not only also cite anxiety and depression as major issues, but they also regard these as being of significantly greater importance than other concerns including bullying, drug addiction, and gangs.[38]

Damaged Lives

It is perhaps too easy to pass over the unpleasant subject of deteriorating mental health in so many young Australians unless we grasp the number of individual lives involved.

In 2020 approximately 735,000 Australians were teenage girls aged 15 to 19 years.[39]

If, as concluded by the Mission Australia/Black Dog Institute study, more than 1 in 3 (34.1%) of these reported symptoms of probable serious mental illness in the same year, we are talking about just on a quarter million of troubled young women and twice that number of parents trying to help them. A similar calculation places well over 100,000 boys of the same age and their parents in a similar situation.

What is worse is evidence that these numbers continue to rise. The personal cost in terms of damaged lives is immeasurable and the financial impact on our already overstrained mental health services immense.

It is worth repeating that the deterioration in young people's mental health reported here and overseas is too recent and too sudden to be explained by anything but environmental factors, notably how they are raised and the conditions under which they grow up.

If, as a nation, we are to do something about the genuine crisis in mental health facing our young people, action must start in the family home when they are young. Any psychologist will tell you that repairing the damage of early anxiety and depression is very difficult and sometimes may be impossible.

The time to address these curses is before they have a chance to take a hold. Prevention is always better than cure. This is why all of us – parents, carers, relatives, mentors and educators – must learn how to nurture psychologically healthy children.

What is going on?

It is not possible to state precisely why anxiety, depression and self-harm are rising among young people in Australia and elsewhere and, in the case of young males, death by suicide as well. Nevertheless, there is a growing body of research pointing to some of the possible causes.

These include overprotective parenting inspired by a modern culture of 'safetyism', increasing numbers of children whose parents separate when they are still young, excessive screen time (particularly devoted to social media) and a decline in the amount of unsupervised time young people spend interacting face to face with peers. We examine each of these possible explanations in detail in later chapters of this book.

But, whatever the causes, there is too much consistent evidence from a variety of sources to dismiss rising mental illness in Australia and elsewhere as purely a result of increased reporting or better data capture. As we noted earlier, something real is happening to our young people and it is not good.

Accompanying these disturbing trends are other reports which suggest that young people in Australia and elsewhere are less prepared to take on the responsibilities of adulthood than previous generations at the same age.

They are leaving home later, often much later,[40] getting married later (and less),[41] entering full-time employment later,[42] having their own children later,[43] and are less likely to hold a driver's licence.[44]

These trends are not necessarily negative and some, at least, can be linked to the recent explosion in post-secondary education in Australia as well as significant increases in the costs of living independently. Nevertheless, to us they also suggest a picture of young people preferring to stay young and avoid the responsibilities of growing up.

To what extent the declining mental health of teens and young adults is contributing to these shifts in their broader behaviour is difficult to say, but it can be argued that the two are causally linked: young adults remaining younger for longer because fewer of them have the self-confidence and optimism required to take off on their own in the same way as previous generations.

We shall also explore these issues in more detail later. For the moment it is sufficient to note that something is going seriously wrong for too many children growing up in the 21st century.

Why, for instance, do so many young people today appear not ready to be adults even though they are old enough to vote, drive a car and fight in the military? Why, when our world is safer, healthier and more prosperous than ever, have anxiety, depression, self-harm and suicide become such threats to our children?

We have already noted that inherited characteristics are only a part, and possibly the smaller part, of an explanation of why children turn out the way they do. The way they are raised and schooled is critically important in determining the adults they become.

From our perspective this is good news. If your child's mental health as a teen and young adult is primarily genetically determined, you would (rightly) think there is little or nothing you can do to influence it. But this is not the case. In fact, parents (together and apart), step-parents and carers play a deciding role in determining children's future psychological health.

One reason for this is that the early years of childhood (0 to 5 in particular) are a biologically critical period during which infants ideally achieve attachment, a fundamental relationship with a primary care-giver (generally their mother), which provides powerful defences against the later development of mental disorder. It is also during this time that children must learn to interact with others so that they are welcomed and nurtured by peers and adults outside their immediate family; to become what psychologists call 'socially desirable', "… to comply gracefully with the expectations of civil society."[45]

Children who are not pleasant or easy to be around are shunned by their peers; even the adults responsible for their care – including their parents – will tend to avoid them. They are just too hard to manage and deal with.

Sustained rejection by others severely compromises a child's psychosocial development (because a strong social network is integral to mental health) and significantly increases the likelihood of them becoming lonely and socially dysfunctional adults.

Let us be clear. Wanting children to be 'socially desirable' does not mean turning them into little sycophants who 'suck up' to people to gain their attention and approval. Nor does it mean that they become robots, simply conforming to the ideas and opinions of whomever they happen to be talking with at the time.

Rather it means to teach them, if necessary with discipline, to interact respectfully with friends as well as strangers so that they can build mutually rewarding relationships. And this includes teaching them how to disagree appropriately with others as well as how to stand up for what they believe even if the weight of opinion is against them.

Secure attachment and being firmly anchored in a social network are both critical requirements for lifelong psychological health, and it is parents and carers who essentially determine whether these are met for children. It is in these early years, when their influence is not diluted by school and friends, that parents make some of their most important contributions to their children's future happiness and psychological health.

Attachment before Independence

"Life is best organised as a series of daring adventures from a secure base."
John Bowlby (English psychologist and psychiatrist)

The first step in preparing a child for the future, and one of the most critical, is to ensure they establish a strong sense of attachment with at least one of their caregivers. This usually will be their mother, but a father or other caregiver can also successfully perform this role. Secure attachment to at least one primary caregiver gives infants an internal sense of security as well as, in John Bowlby's words (see quotation above), "a secure base" from which to explore their world.[46]

Most babies establish secure attachment with their mother in their very early years when she cares for and interacts with them regularly and intimately. It is this bond which provides a fundamental sense of personal security which is the foundation for lifelong psychological health.

Allan Schore has intensively explored the impact of early environment on future mental health. He argues that the quality of a child's "emerging, social, psychological, and biological capacities" – which determine the person they ultimately become – are fundamentally influenced by the nature of their relationship with their primary caregiver.[47]

Schore also emphasises the importance of attachment for a child's capacity to regulate their emotions and, in particular, to manage stress or anxiety. He suggests "… the development of the ability to adaptively cope with stress is directly and significantly influenced by the infant's early interaction with the primary caregiver".[48]

Bessel Van der Kolk[49] explains that we learn to care for ourselves physically and emotionally by how *we* are cared for in our early years. We learn how to manage or regulate our emotions, especially our stress response, from the way our caregivers respond to us. A parent or caregiver who manages an infant's emotional outbursts in a calm and measured manner teaches them to do the same for themselves and to deal with stressors (like minor pain or strangers) in a proportionate way.

Alternatively, if a parent responds to a child's distress with an excess of anxiety, the child will mirror this behaviour and is less likely to acquire a capacity to manage their emotions.

Van der Kolk concludes:

> Mastering the skill of self-regulation depends to a large degree on how harmonious our early interactions with our caregivers are. The more responsive the adult is to the child, the deeper the attachment and the more likely the child will develop healthy ways of responding to the people around him.[50]

Reliable care by a mother or other caregiver, including assistance to manage emotional fluctuations calmly and confidently, provides a child with essential security and teaches them to trust others; to acquire what

Erik Erikson (a prominent psychologist) called "a sense of basic trust".[51]

It is through their interaction with their mother or care giver that a child literally acquires the capacity to self-regulate their feelings. This includes responding in a measured way to stressors, such as novelty and separation, which otherwise can provoke what to parents appear to be wild and disproportionate emotional reactions in a child.

Secure attachment is of fundamental importance to your new child and any disturbance to this first relationship can have profound implications for their future. Anthony Storr, a psychiatrist (introduced earlier), suggests that if the link between mother and child is suddenly and prematurely broken, following the loss of their mother, a child is "... likely to develop a sense of basic distrust with regard to people and an exaggerated anxiety about the arbitrary and unpredictable nature of the world".[52]

Psychiatrist John Bowlby (introduced above) pioneered the now widely accepted thesis that successful attachment between, generally, mother and child, is vital for the later development of self-reliance, impulse control (or self-regulation) and motivation as well as empathy for others. He was first to promote the view that sound attachment provides a solid foundation of security on which a child can build a successful life.[53]

Failure to achieve secure attachment, or the early severing of the fundamental link between caregiver and child can be, in some cases, a precursor for later adolescent and adult mental illness. This is because the child does not develop the necessary neurological coping or regulatory mechanisms to manage the everyday stressors or conditions which may trigger psychological disorder.

Schore's review of clinical research from psychiatry, abnormal psychology, and psychoanalysis, confirms the central link between the quality of a child's early relationships with a primary carer and healthy psychosocial development.[54]

The good news is that a large majority of children (over 60% according to one major study) do achieve secure attachment.[55] Mothers and babies appear to be instinctively programmed to make this happen unless events combine to prevent it. A reliable and responsive daily round of feeding, bathing, holding, hugging, cuddling and soothing, and, particularly, communicating, is enough to ensure secure attachment for a newborn. You don't have to be a child development expert. You just need to love your child!

The first thing working in parents' favour is that children have an innate need to attach – it is a survival mechanism which facilitates their successful passage through infancy and childhood. The second is that, as Donald Winnicott (paediatrician and early student of attachment theory) points out, it does not require uncommon talent to be what he calls a 'good enough mother'; that is, a parent who achieves successful attachment with their child.[56]

The primary requirement for successful attachment is (what Winnicott and others have called) 'attunement', that is, getting on the same 'wavelength' as your child. A large majority of parents achieve this automatically as they respond to or 'tune into' their baby both physically and emotionally. They do this by responding to how their child is feeling, inferred from his or her facial and vocal expressions. If a child is happy a parent responds appropriately and if they are upset, they display empathy and concern while immediately seeking to address the problem by feeding, cleaning, cuddling, soothing and so on.

What does a child learn during this process as a caregiver addresses their problems and helps to calm them down? That bad experiences don't last, that even intense anxiety can be resolved, and that their world is fundamentally secure and relatively predictable.

Through reliable care and responsive parenting an infant learns to associate sensations such as pain, hunger, or fear, with feelings of mastery and competence rather than intense distress or a sense of being unable to cope. The child learns that unpleasant sensations can be managed and resolved, consequently they develop adaptive responses to common stressors.

Just as a carer 'tunes into' a child so the child 'tunes in' to their carer and learns to imitate their physical and emotional responses. From a calm but responsive and empathic carer, a child learns to moderate their responses to unpleasant sensations and to regulate their feelings in healthy, beneficial ways.

Anthony Storr (mentioned above), in his book *Churchill's Black Dog and other Essays*, contrasts the outcomes for children who achieve secure attachment with those who do not:

> A child who is wanted, loved, played with, cuddled, will incorporate within himself a lively sense of his own value; and will therefore surmount the inevitable setbacks and disappointments of childhood with no more than temporary sorrow, secure in the belief that the world is predominantly a happy place and that he has a secure place in it. And this pattern will generally persist throughout his life. A child on the other hand, who is unwanted, rejected, or disapproved of will gain no such conviction. Although such a child may experience periods of both success and happiness these will neither convince him that he is lovable nor finally prove to him that life is worthwhile.[57]

In this passage Storr is referring specifically to Winston Churchill, who, despite his enormous achievements, including leading the fight against Nazi Germany and winning the Nobel Prize for Literature, suffered from depression for much of his life and ended it as a sad, lonely man convinced that he had done nothing of value.

It is painful to relate that Churchill's early years provide almost a textbook account of how a child can fail to establish a secure pattern of attachment. It is worth noting, however, that Churchill's story also provides clear proof that inadequate attachment, however undesirable, is not necessarily a barrier to outstanding achievement or future success, even though it may compromise fundamental happiness.

Circle of Security

Achieving secure attachment requires more than cuddling and playing with an infant as well soothing their distress or resolving their discomfort. It also extends to enabling a child to enter their world with assurance as they take their first steps towards independence.

Three psychotherapists, Bert Powell, Ken Hoffman and Glen Cooper, developed a Circle of Security model (reproduced below) to demonstrate this process.[58] Their model describes how thoughtful parents provide their children with two things: a secure base from which to explore, and a safe haven to return to whenever anxiety or stress threaten to overwhelm them.

As we shall see in the next chapter, children are attracted to and indeed *need* the challenge (and risks) of independent play alone and with peers. They are more likely to pursue these necessary and normal activities when their parents provide a safe place for them to step out from and to which they can return when they are frightened or feel unable to cope.

Parents create a secure base from which to leave, and a safe haven to return to, through their own behaviour. Ideally, they are (in the words of Cooper et al.) "bigger, stronger, wiser, and kind", and remain attuned to their child's needs so that they can take over when necessary.

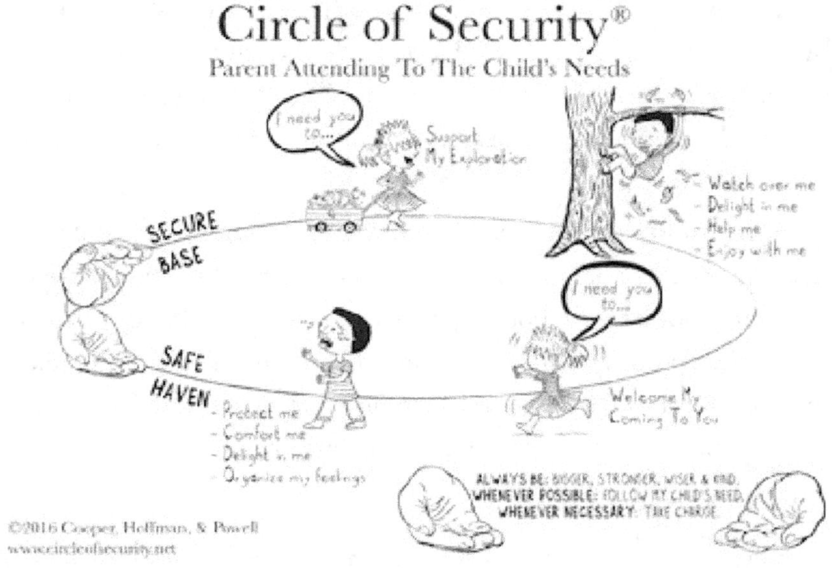

Reproduced with permission

A secure base gives children the courage to explore, to experiment and to make mistakes, as well as to learn from these. A safe haven to return to for support and comfort teaches them to trust others and that their world is fundamentally benign.

The need for attachment continues throughout a child's life. While they must ultimately take off on their own to build their own life, they will (just like their parents) continue to need the support of family and friends. And, while early attachment is clearly preferable, parents can promote feelings of security and confidence in their children at any age.

Ideally, throughout their children's lives, parents continue to provide them with a safe place to return to if necessary. Just as the attachment process is never finished, so our role as parents is never over. At every stage in their journey, we can provide support to strengthen a child's self-confidence, while encouraging them to meet the challenges of independence.

Successful Relationships

Successful attachment does more than create a sense of basic trust and personal security in a child as well as a willingness to venture into the world. Bessel Van der Kolk argues that secure attachment also forms a template for children's relationships with others. What he means is that because securely attached children have learned through their carers' example to be trusting and empathic towards others, they are better able to build fruitful relationships for themselves.[59]

They also, interestingly, appear more adept at 'reading' people, particularly those who may be frauds or not have their best interests at heart. For children for whom attachment is unsuccessful or at best uncertain, future relationships are more likely to be troubled by misunderstandings, a lack of trust, and disappointment.

Van der Kolk cites longitudinal studies (which follow children from birth to early adulthood) which suggest that early maternal emotional withdrawal – even more so than outright maternal hostility – is a significant predictor of future mental illness in children, characterised by an inadequate sense of self, emotional instability, self-harm, and suicidal behaviour.

He concludes "…the quality of early caregiving is critically important in preventing mental health problems, independent of other traumas".[60] What he is saying is that the legacies of secure attachment are twofold: firstly, it insulates a child, from future psychological illness; and secondly, maintains their emotional equilibrium even if they subsequently experience trauma which threatens their mental health.

Put simply, the best indication of successful attachment is resilience in the face of stress.[61]

But once again, it should be emphasised that, regardless of a child's early experience, parents can assist them to develop psychological resilience throughout their childhood and adolescence and, indeed, into adulthood.

The First Two Years

Current thinking suggests that primary attachment takes place during the first 1,000 days of life, including time in utero, which brings us to approximately two years of age. This period coincides with a rapid acceleration in brain growth between the third trimester of pregnancy and between 18 and 24 months of age, during which the infant brain essentially doubles in size.[62]

During this period, as we have seen, children need the comforting physical and psychological presence of a parent or carer, particularly when they are confronted with pain or insecurity created by something strange or new. Issues that to adults may appear relatively minor can assume massive proportions for a baby or toddler and produce spectacular emotional eruptions often described as 'meltdowns'.

A child in this condition is consumed by inconsolable grief and/or anger which a distraught parent may struggle to calm or resolve. In these cases, most parenting authorities recommend acknowledging the child's feelings while soothing them physically and emotionally until they recover.

While a 'meltdown' can be a challenge for parents unused to them, it is important to remember that they are quite normal in young children and nothing to worry about. Because their world is strange and, at times, threatening or painful, it is quite understandable that they will 'lose it' from time to time until they become more familiar with their new surroundings and confident that they can cope.

Managing a 'Meltdown'

Dealing with 'meltdowns' effectively, which is necessary for successful attachment, is a two-part process. Firstly, as mentioned, it is important to validate the emotions a child is experiencing by naming and accepting them. A parent might say, "I understand that you are upset because you fell off the swing, but you'll feel better very soon."

Secondly, by soothing them physically and emotionally, which helps them to recover as quickly as possible, they learn, as we have seen, to self-regulate their responses; they come to understand that their emotions are under their control and need not threaten to take charge.

Managing a 'meltdown' in this way can take up to 30 minutes, which will try the patience of the most devoted parent, but is necessary if the child is to learn to self-regulate their emotions while retaining their basic sense of trust in their world – both of which are fundamental to later mental health.

Please note that assisting your children to manage their emotions does not, nor should it, cease at two to three years of age. While the early years are important, this is not the only period during which children learn emotional management and develop confidence in their world. You can continue to assist your children to self-regulate their emotions in healthy, adaptive ways as they grow. (For a discussion of teaching children and adolescents emotional control see Chapter 6.)

Whatever their age, validation of a child's feelings as well as comfort and support will help them, not only to bring these outbursts under control more quickly, but also to reduce their intensity in the future. In this way, parents can teach their children how to respond proportionately to the mishaps and dramas which inevitably will come their way.

What we are saying is that, despite an uncertain start, a child can achieve attachment through loving and conscientious parents later in their lives. This suggestion is supported by Allan Schore, who confirms that even for those whose early attachment was inadequate or disrupted it is possible to achieve what he calls "earned secure attachment" later in life.[63]

This is important to know, particularly for parents and carers (including stepparents and adoptive parents) whose children's early years may have been difficult. It tells us that attachment is *not* an either/or matter which can only happen early if it is to happen at all.

Story: *Jacinta*

A young woman, Jacinta, was referred to a colleague for assistance with unspecified pains in her arms and legs and intermittent tiredness. She came for her appointment accompanied by her mother.

Jacinta had consulted various specialists for her pain and fatigue with little success. Her pain symptoms were inconsistent with a diagnosis of arthritis, and chronic fatigue syndrome was ruled out because although she frequently felt tired, she rarely required bed rest.

She was a successful professional with a job as editor for a publishing house. However, her symptoms were sufficiently disabling for her to have recently changed to a part time role. She had also stopped driving a car because this caused her anxiety, and she was uncertain about the future of her relationship with her partner.

Her background was not especially unusual, except that, as a child and adolescent, she had a history of relatively frequent emotional 'meltdowns' during which she would scream and hyperventilate for minutes at a time.

Apparently, these could be provoked by quite trivial issues, her brother poking her for example. Her 'meltdowns' became less frequent as she got older, but she remained an unusually anxious person subject to regular panic attacks.

Her history also revealed that she was the youngest child in a blended family of six children; both her parents had two older children from their previous relationships as well Jacinta and her brother, so she had been born into a very busy household. Furthermore, around the time of her birth her parents had been trying to assist one of their older boys who was struggling with serious mental health and drug related issues.

While her mother was adamant that Jacinta had received the same care and attention as a baby and toddler as her older siblings, our colleague was less sure. He wondered whether the demands of earning a living and running a hectic home, plus helping their son, who had been diagnosed with schizophrenia, meant that meeting Jacinta's early needs may have been something of an afterthought for both parents.

He was confident that her pain and fatigue were likely to be the product of anxiety (which might, in turn, be related back to insecure attachment), rather than due to any organic cause.

❧❧❧

It is probable that Jacinta's symptoms of pain and tiredness were psychosomatic. In other words, they were an unconscious response to the anxiety she experienced managing the challenges of being an adult – working in a busy professional role, managing an intimate relationship, and even driving a car. Her pain and fatigue meant she could reduce her work commitments and avoid driving without necessarily addressing the underlying psychological cause of her symptoms.

While we cannot be certain, it is quite possible that the circumstances surrounding her birth, plus the persistence of emotional meltdowns well into adolescence, point to inadequate or ambivalent early attachment. Her elevated anxiety and uncertainty regarding her relationship with her partner, as well as her chronic hypochrondia, support this suggestion.

Psychotherapy can help Jacinta to manage her anxiety and, ideally, return to a full personal and professional life. In addition, it can also be expected to relieve the symptoms of pain and chronic tiredness for which she originally sought assistance.

It is never too late to assist a child whose first years may have been less than ideal. Committed parenting in later childhood can address, if not entirely ameliorate, the impact of imperfect beginnings. Many people, with or without professional assistance, have, at least partly, recovered from the effects of insecure attachment.

Jacinta's story should, however, alert new parents to the primary importance of ensuring a newborn achieves a secure pattern of attachment during their first two to three years. The research clearly indicates that if sound attachment does not occur during this critical period, then a child is at risk of developing mental illness in the future. This suggests that prospective parents need to plan ahead to ensure they have the time and resources necessary to devote to this key responsibility.

However, please note the research does *not* indicate that mental illness is an automatic consequence of inadequate attachment; it tells us what happens within groups of children, but not about outcomes for individuals, including your child (see following Cautionary Note, page 42). Positive parenting, focused on building accomplishments of character, can reduce if not completely eliminate the impact of even the worst start in life. Parents continue to influence the development of children at any age; with care, engagement, and discipline they can maximise any child's chances of enjoying a happy and fulfilling future.

The circumstances of a child's birth are not always conducive to secure attachment. All the more reason for busy parents to be aware of the need to invest time, love and regular attention to the needs of their newborn. Mothers and fathers who suspend successful careers after a baby arrives are aware of the importance of their early care for providing the best start in life he or she can get.

Giving a baby to grandparents, a nanny or an older sibling to take care of from time to time is fine, and good for all of them, but is not a substitute for parental engagement.

One solution for busy parents is to bind a baby to them, as is more common in some non-Western cultures, while they go about their business so that he/she is securely held and literally touching their body, rather than placing them in a pusher or pram. Babies carried like this can feel the parent moving and hear them speaking and generally are perfectly content – while secure attachment takes place as a matter of course.

As an aside we found a great way to sooth anxious babies was to place them on our lap sitting up and facing us, with one of our arms around them to keep them in place while we made phone calls, dictated letters or worked on the computer. The sound of our voice and closeness of our body was soothing and often sent them to sleep so that they could be transferred straight to bed. It was also very nice for us as well!

The real challenge, of course, comes when your 3+-year-old still regularly indulges in meltdowns and you are starting to wonder if they will ever grow out of them.

The subheading introducing this section, "Attachment Before Independence", reminds us that children ultimately must learn to function successfully, independently of their parents. Having a meltdown at school, or worse, later in the workplace, is not a helpful strategy for achieving social desirability or independence (see Story: *Jacinta*).

It is for this reason that once your child is around 3+ years of age and has achieved attachment, we recommend you adjust how you manage their emotional responses to the reality that not everything will always go their way. It is at this point that we believe you would be wise to introduce, as required, disciplinary procedures, in particular, the time out technique we discuss in detail in Chapter 10.

Watching an adolescent or an adult have a 'meltdown' is not a pretty sight and something all parents would wish to avoid for their own children. You can help them overcome this bad habit when they are still young by talking calmly to them when they are disinclined to do what you wish.

For example, if it is time to leave the playground and they proceed to disagree violently with this plan, you can calmly say, "I understand that you have been enjoying yourself and wish to stay and are upset that we need to leave. However, it is time to go home for your tea now. But we will come back tomorrow (or the next day) and you can play some more. You can also keep playing when you get home."

New mothers of our acquaintance attest to the sometimes miraculous effect of words like this. It is not uncommon for their children to settle down quickly and willingly return to the car. If, however, they continue to scream, pick them up and put them in the car while repeating your earlier message. If they continue in this vein on the way home ignore them until they calm down and, if necessary, use time out when you get there (see Chapter 10).

While it is important to acknowledge and validate how a child is feeling, it is also necessary to be aware that helping them overcome strong emotion, once they are older, is not the same as acquiescing with their wishes. Hence, if it's time to go home, it's time to go home, and they need to learn that however much fuss they make will not induce you to change your mind. Your children need to learn as early as possible that you mean what you say in matters of their behaviour and that no amount of protests will lead you to fall in with their preferences when other priorities take precedence.

Cautionary Note

Whatever the circumstances of your child's early years, it would be a mistake to conclude that their personality and behaviour are irrevocably fixed from two to three years of age. While the attachment process is clearly important, they still have a lot to learn about managing their emotions and relations with others.

Even if their first few years have been difficult, this does *not,* as we have already emphasised, automatically condemn them to later mental disorder. How do we know this? Well, we have seen too many children progress from early disadvantage to future success and happiness to doubt that this can and does happen.

The research findings indicate that on average children for whom attachment is inadequate or ambivalent are more at risk of experiencing psychological problems; that is, they refer to aggregates, or groups, of children, not to individuals.

Compromised mental health in children who have a difficult start to life is by no means a certainty, and need not happen to your child if, as they grow, you assist them to manage their emotions and behaviour effectively.

Conclusion

While all is not going well for young people in Australia and elsewhere, particularly with regard to their mental health, the good news is that the family environment, created by their parents (particularly when they are young) predominantly determines the type of adolescent and adult they eventually become.

Accumulating research now confirms the crucial importance of the first two to three years of a child's life. It is during this period that secure attachment – which provides the foundation for later self-confidence, resilience, and independence – largely takes place.

But attachment is not an either/or issue. Some children experience uncertain early attachment, but this does not constitute a guarantee that their future lives will be clouded by mental disorder or relationship difficulties. This is particularly true if as they grow their parents remain focused on assisting them to manage their emotional responses in healthy ways.

Parents, whether they are biological, single, step, relatives or foster parents or carers, and whether they are gay or straight, make the key difference to any child's life. That is why we wrote this book. We know (and experience and research support this) that parents and carers can significantly enhance their children's chances of enjoying success and happiness now and in the future. In addition, they can help them avoid many of the hazards that might derail their progress as well as detect the early signs that all is not going well and intervene to do something about it.

Summary

- The available evidence suggests that most indicators of mental disorder in young Australians, including anxiety, depression, self-harm, attempted suicide and suicide, have increased significantly in recent years and, in most cases, are continuing to rise.
- These trends are too sudden and too recent to be explained by DNA alone. They must be the product of environment, particularly how children are raised.
- Genetic factors play only a part and, possibly, the smaller part, in determining the type of adults children become.
- Young Australians appear to be growing up more slowly than earlier generations; they are staying at home longer, marrying later, are older when they become parents themselves and delaying entry to full time employment. This, to us, suggests that they may be less confident about managing the challenges of independence than previous generations.
- Parents, stepparents and carers are the critical influence in their children's early lives. They create their children's primary environment which determines the quality of attachment they achieve which, in turn, influences the future course of their personality development.
- Whatever the circumstances of a child's first years, positive parenting as they grow can significantly reduce any risk of mental illness which may flow from initial experience.

2

Ten Accomplishments of Character: A Model for Positive Parenting

"The hand that rocks the cradle rules the world."
William Ross Wallace (Scottish poet)

"You who are on the road
Must have a code that you can live by
And so become yourself"
Crosby, Stills, Nash and Young, "Teach Your Children." (US musicians)

Raising the next generation is our greatest responsibility since it determines what the future for all of us will look like including the world that we, as parents, will grow old in. This is true whether the children in your care are born to you, adopted or stepchildren, or you are their primary carer (such as a grandparent or foster parent). Parenting can be frustrating and depressing, as well as exhilarating and deeply satisfying. It can also at times be extremely stressful not to mention deadly boring. But there is no doubting its significance – that is the meaning of William Wallace's observation quoted above.

Parents themselves agree. A 2015 survey of parents conducted in the United States reported that while, 91% said parenting was their greatest joy, 73% also found it to be their greatest challenge. Sixty-nine per cent of those surveyed also agreed that if they knew more positive parenting strategies they would use them, and 54% wished they had more information about how to be a better parent.[1]

So, yes, parenting is both joyous and demanding, and it appears many parents want to learn more about it, which is a good thing. Yet how often do we stop and ask ourselves, "What is best for my children?" or, "What should I be trying to achieve as a parent?" Or to ask the same questions in a different way: "What is the purpose of parenting?"

Parents have only limited opportunities to practise trial and error with their children, to try one thing and, if that doesn't work, to start again and attempt something else. We must respond, act, and decide on behalf of our children in real time, with incomplete information and without fully understanding the longer-term consequences of much of what we are doing.

Your answer to the question, "What is the purpose of parenting?", is clearly important because it determines how you will influence your children through the countless interactions you have with them as they grow, and the choices you make when deciding for them.

Without a satisfactory answer to this question, which you are confident will provide a reliable guide when seeking the best outcomes for a child, your performance as a parent is likely to be less than satisfactory.

It makes sense then to consider deeply what it is you are trying to achieve and to develop strategies, if not guaranteed formulas, for getting there. In this chapter, we present a model of parenting which seeks to answer the questions posed above.

We believe the model of positive parenting we propose will significantly reduce the risk that your children will be threatened by mental disorder. It will also assist them to better manage this or other challenges, such as addiction, if these do arise. Just as important, it will also maximise their chances of becoming confident, autonomous individuals who can choose a life which is right for them and, in the process, become all they can and wish to be.

When asked about their aspirations for their children, most parents are likely to give one or more of the following replies: "I want my children to be happy"; "I want my children to be my friends"; or "I want my children to be successful." There are issues with each of these answers. Let us start with happiness.

"I want my children to be happy"

"*Happiness is a by-product of character. In people who are developing a strong character, there is a dramatically higher level of happiness than in those who live to chase after the next good time.*" Pat Holt and Grace Ketterman (US authors)

Wanting children to be happy is a noble aim, but we need to exercise care in how we help them achieve happiness.

As the quotation above suggests, the direct pursuit of happiness – either by giving children everything they ask for or removing anything painful or difficult in their way – will end in disappointment. Genuine happiness cannot be directly achieved.

A never-ending series of material possessions or good times quickly loses its appeal; children in this situation become increasingly demanding for more of the same while, at the same time, progressively dissatisfied with what they have and what they get.

Another lesson from this quotation is that happiness is a predictable by-product of character, of who we are, *not* what we have. Happiness comes from within rather than outside us; it is something each of us creates for ourselves. It may come from mastery of a desired skill, being promoted at work, or solving a difficult problem, but each of these requires personal qualities such as patience, perseverance and courage, as well as raw talent.

Talent or intelligence alone, which we may be fortunate enough to develop, is not enough to guarantee happiness or, indeed, success. Too many talented people remain disappointed with themselves and their world no matter how well they perform or how high they climb. This is because they believe happiness requires a never-ending accumulation of 'successes' or 'good times' which quickly lose their appeal with repetition and ultimately fail to deliver lasting satisfaction.

There are also legions of very smart people who remain disappointed with themselves for a different reason: they have never developed the qualities of character required to turn their gifts into genuine competencies, which are the true source of lasting contentment because they provide an enduring sense of fulfillment.

Success defined in terms of status or achievements alone will not make us happy, if only because there is always someone out there who is more important than us, richer than us, or better known than us. Whether *any* level of achievement makes us happy or not depends on our personality, not on what we own, or how high we climb on the ladder of 'success'.

One key to happiness is being content with our accomplishments, however modest, even though we may continue to strive for improvement. This requires us to learn to think about ourselves and others in a certain way.

For example, if I think that, in order to be happy, "I *must* be the best tennis player in the club and if I am not, it is very bad and I am a failure", chances are I will be disappointed. And it gets worse because, even if I am the best in my club, there will always be better players elsewhere.

Alternatively, I could say to myself, "It is nice to be a successful tennis player and, while I prefer to win, it is not the end of the world to be beaten by a better player, provided I have done my best." If this is the way I think, then my experience of tennis and my opinion of myself will be a lot more positive.

The idea that what we think or believe determines how we feel is a central premise of Stoicism, a school of philosophy founded by Zeno of Citium (early third century BCE).

The Stoics taught that it is not our circumstances which determine our emotional wellbeing but rather how we choose to think about and react to them. They argued that, while external events may be outside our control or direct influence, we have complete autonomy over how we decide to respond to them. And how we respond is determined by what we believe or think about ourselves as well as the events themselves. Much of modern psychotherapy, such as Cognitive Behavioural Therapy (CBT), is based on this fundamental principle. Teaching this to children, that *to think is to feel,* is an important part of positive parenting.

Distinguishing between what they can and cannot control and developing beliefs which allow them to (relatively) comfortably ride the inevitable ups and downs of life, are important lessons which children must learn. Thinking in this way is an important hallmark of adult maturity as well as being critical for psychological health.

How they think and what they believe will ultimately dictate how happy children are. We return to the vital subjects of thinking, believing, and feeling in Chapter 6. For now, let us simply note we are suggesting that parents should teach children how, not what to think.

Like us, you want your children to be happy, and you can help them achieve genuine happiness. But if you approach the goal of 'happy kids' in a straight line by simply providing a series of pleasant experiences or by removing or shielding them from all sources of unpleasantness, you and they, as we have suggested, will be disappointed.

An absence of obstacles or challenges, or a plethora of material possessions and 'good' times, does not equate to active happiness. To reiterate happiness is self-created, something children must achieve for themselves. In fact, as we shall see in Chapter 5, removing problems from a child's path and making it as pleasant as possible can impair their capacity to achieve independence, confidence, *and* happiness by denying them the opportunity to struggle and deal with (not always successfully) the known and unknown obstacles that life will throw their way.

"I want my children to be my friends"

Parents who believe their purpose is to be friends with their children will also struggle to raise happy or successful offspring. This is because friendship is a relationship between independent equals and not the same as the bond a parent has with their child. Children, particularly when they are young, need direction because they simply do not know what is best for them in most situations.

In addition, they are vulnerable to risks – physical and psychological – and need protection. This recedes as they get older, but most parents continue to advise and caution their children throughout their adolescence and well into adulthood. And so they should, provided that when they are adults your children specifically request your input. Providing gratuitous or unasked for advice to an adult child is a great way to start an argument!

While you may overlook aspects of a friend's behaviour, which you disapprove of, you cannot do this with your children, not least when they are young; you are responsible for them in a way you are not responsible for a friend.

Friendship is a voluntary association while the relationship between parent and child is not – they didn't choose to live with you. Friends may need direction and be vulnerable, but as adults they have a right and responsibility to make their own decisions. You can offer guidance – which they may accept or ignore – but ultimately, they must decide. You cannot nor should you insist that friends follow your direction in the way that, at times, you must do with your own children while they are children.

This is not to say that even youngsters should never make their own decisions and live with the consequences of these, but parents ultimately determine the boundaries within which their children can act autonomously.

Friends have minimal authority to correct each other's behaviour. As parents, you must be prepared to discipline and to override your children's wishes, when you believe this to be in their (and/or others') best interests. You must also be prepared to manage philosophically the hostility that this may attract.

This is something most friends will not accept. Their response will be to find a new friend. Parents don't have this option; your children can't replace you. For this reason, Jordan Peterson, a psychologist, notes: "… parents are more, not less, than friends."[2]

One way of thinking about your relationship with children is to consider them, if you like, as honoured guests who come to live with you for a period of time before they leave to create their own lives. Like any other guests, they have both rights and obligations which, although initially they may not be able to understand or exercise, remain their birthright nonetheless.

At the same time, however, they are more than guests because, having invited them into your home without their consent, you have specific responsibilities towards them that you wouldn't acknowledge or accept for anyone else.

Specifically, these are to assist them navigate their early years so that when they do leave, as they must, they are properly prepared to claim their inheritance (with all its benefits and burdens) as full members of adult society. Or, to put it another way, parents are responsible for teaching children how to be successful human beings, something they would never contemplate taking on for a friend.

If your desire to be friends with your children means that you are unwilling to exert legitimate authority over them you are, in effect, reneging on a principal responsibility of parenting to provide them with compassionate, equitable and reliable discipline, based on love and respect. The potentially disastrous consequences of not doing this are discussed in Chapter 10.

When your children become adults your relationship with them will change, whether you like it or not. In fact, it must change if you wish to keep them in your life. Ideally it will become closer to an adult friendship, but it will never be quite the same.

As discussed earlier, giving a friend what may be well meant advice can be a quick way to lose them as a friend. But no matter how difficult your relationship with your children may become you never 'lose' them in quite the same way. Parents always remain 'more than friends'. We advise you to be content with that.

"I want my children to be successful"

Let us now consider what is, perhaps, the most common reply parents make when asked what they desire for their children: "I want my children to be successful."

This is hard to argue with – most parents want the same thing – and it is a reasonable definition of what parenting is all about. However, a lot depends on what we mean by 'success'.

If we define success in purely material terms – like winning a coveted award, getting the 'right' job, or marrying the 'right' partner – once again, we, and they, are likely to be disappointed, if only because a regular accumulation of prizes (like the pure pursuit of happiness) cannot be repeated indefinitely; some failure is inevitable. Furthermore, no amount of material achievement on its own, however significant, translates into sustained feelings of contentment or fulfilment.

To understand why material success does not equate to lasting success or happiness, we need to understand the difference between extrinsic and intrinsic goals. Intrinsic goals are directly linked to the activities and personal qualities required to achieve them, such as learning to play the piano. Developing competence at the piano can be a powerful source of satisfaction for a child; it becomes part of who they are because any progress they make generates an increased sense of personal mastery or control, regardless of the level of excellence they achieve.

Extrinsic goals, on the other hand, like becoming 'rich', are much less closely related to what must be done to achieve them, which means we identify less closely with them. In fact we may find that what we must do to achieve an extrinsic goal becomes boring or indeed repugnant. It may, in fact, conflict with our personal values. Lack of identification with extrinsic goals becomes doubly true for children, if these are not chosen personally but imposed by the expectations of parents, friends, or broader society.

For these reasons, achievement of extrinsic goals is less likely to bring lasting satisfaction of the kind experienced when pursuing those of an intrinsic variety. Indeed, an ongoing repetition of extrinsic 'success' may not only lose its appeal, but become a source of active dissatisfaction.

This can be observed in adults who dislike their work but remain in it because it is financially rewarding. Under these conditions they may find it difficult to stay motivated so that genuine job satisfaction remains elusive.

The millionaire, relentlessly seeking wealth and status (not unlike the hedonist devoted to endless 'good times'), while simultaneously lamenting their bitterness and disappointment, is a common, but nevertheless very real cliché.

Ironically, the reverse – removing all reference to individual accomplishment or achievement – is not the road to true success either.

Parents can, if they choose, create an environment in which a child always 'succeeds'. This can be done by placing them in classes where there is no assessment, in sports teams where results are not scored, and in competitions where everyone 'wins' a prize.

Children in these situations will experience a period of 'success'. But are these children truly successful; and what happens to them when their parents are no longer available to create a 'winning' environment in this way?

This is not what most parents really mean when they say they want their children to succeed, and most children can see through it as well!

What is worse, as we shall see, is that overlong exposure to this type of 'success' can seriously impede a child achieving genuine success or happiness as an adult, simply because they never fail. As a result they never learn to persist in the face of difficulty and temporary failure while pursuing goals of importance to them.

So, if true success is neither a remorseless pursuit of 'prizes' nor the elimination of achievement altogether, what is it?

It is not our job to define success for your children in the sense that we should dictate how they spend their lives. In the following sections we explain what we believe parents, who want their children to enjoy sound mental health and genuinely happy and successful lives, should be aiming for.

"I wish..."

While pondering on the nature of true success and happiness ourselves we came across a lovely book by Bronnie Ware, *The Top Five Regrets of the Dying: A Life Transformed by the Dearly Departing.*[3]

Ware is an Australian nurse who worked for many years in palliative care, providing counselling for terminally ill patients, many with only weeks or days to live.

Many of her patients were in their eighties or older who, looking back on their lives, often expressed regrets for neglected opportunities or relationships lost. Ware identified the five most common regrets expressed by people facing the reality of death:

1. "I wish I had pursued my dreams and aspirations, and not the life others expected of me."
2. "I wish I didn't work so hard."
3. "I wish I had the courage to express my feelings and speak my mind."
4. "I wish I had stayed in touch with my friends."
5. "I wish I had let myself be happy."

What is interesting about these regrets is that none of them are concerned with extrinsic achievement. "I wish I had been more important" or "I wish I had been richer" do not appear in her list. Rather, the regrets expressed by her patients focus on the choices they made about *how* they lived while they had the chance.

The realisation that happiness is a choice available to us all, regardless of our material circumstances, underlines the point made above that happiness is, as the saying goes, an 'inside job' and not (and never can be) the direct consequence of endless good times or the relentless achievement of material or status goals.

Reading the first regret in Ware's list, it is sad to reflect that too many people realise, too late, that they did not create the life for themselves they really wanted; that they did not become a person who had lived a braver life on their own terms rather than simply 'fitting in' with the dictates of parents, friends, and society. From the perspective of this book, it is important to note that, in some cases at least, parents themselves were a primary obstacle to their children pursuing their dreams and achieving ultimate happiness.

But what is most striking about these five regrets is that they highlight an absence or insufficiency of personal qualities, courage for example. A different character would have enabled Ware's patients to forge their own path and express their true selves, so that they lived a more authentic life they chose themselves rather than one selected for them. This argues that it is the personal qualities we develop in our first 15-20 years which primarily determines how, and how well, life unfolds for each of us whatever the circumstances of our birth.

We believe this insight is most useful for parents when considering the questions, "What should I want for my children?" or "What is the purpose of parenting?" To us it suggests that the primary purpose of parenting is to equip children with qualities of character, particularly confidence, courage and persistence, necessary for building a life they personally choose, rather than one dictated by others. By focusing on your children's character development, you will assist them not only to create genuine success and happiness on their own terms but also help them to avoid, for the most part, the doleful legacies of regret described by Ware.

A similar message, we believe, can be found in the opening lines of the Crosby, Stills, Nash and Young hit song, "Teach Your Children", quoted at the beginning of this chapter. They are suggesting that children need a code or guide for how to live along the road of life.

What is even more interesting is that they regard such a code as indispensable for 'becoming' ourselves, that living is a creative process and that our most important creation is what we make of ourselves. This is something that many of Bronnie Ware's patients discovered too late. Furthermore, the song's title reminds us that children need to be taught such a code, that they won't come to it on their own.

We believe these few words capture the essence of positive parenting; teaching children *how* to live, rather than *what* to live for, in the sense of career or material achievement, so that they become everything they are capable of being and wish to be.

Defining success for children

When you read our definition of success you will note that it has nothing to do with status or material achievement. Rather, it focuses on the qualities of character children need to follow their own star and become their own person rather than simply slotting into others' preferences regarding who or what they should be.

For us it is accomplishments of character that provide the code or guide for living that Crosby, Stills, Nash and Young sing about.

If you are to assist your children find true success and happiness, we believe your emphasis should be on the type of people they become, rather than ensuring they get the 'right' job, the 'right' friends or the 'right' house in the 'right' suburb and so on.

If they succeed in terms of temperament or character, the rest, material rewards and recognition, will generally come of their own accord.

There is nothing wrong with wanting, achieving, and enjoying a high-status role, material wealth or the recognition that comes with winning a prestigious award. These are worthwhile accomplishments and should be celebrated, but they are the *by-products* of what really constitutes genuine and lasting success for children and adults, which is character or personality.

Character development is the true purpose of positive parenting.

It is the accomplishments of character that parents instil in their children which will see them navigate the highs and lows of their life without losing faith in themselves or their family and friends, nor a strong belief that a worthwhile and meaningful life is available to them as much as anyone else. In addition, these qualities will also minimise the risk of them becoming prey to mental disorder or psychological distress as well as assisting them to manage these effectively if they do occur.

We are all far too familiar with stories of sports stars, media celebrities and other 'high achieving' individuals who struggle with drugs, relationship issues and/or their mental health and seem incapable of being happy.

Their inability to enjoy their achievements suggests that something is missing, that they didn't learn how to truly succeed or be happy while they were growing up (See Story: *The Rower*).

Story: *The Rower*

Some years ago, one of us saw a mother and her 17-year-old son. Physically he was a large boy, taller than most, and obviously very fit. Nevertheless, he appeared embarrassed and reluctant to talk. Eventually we learned, primarily from his mother, that he had difficulties controlling his temper.

He was verbally abusive towards her and his sister and contemptuous of requests to treat them with respect. His mother had made their appointment because during their most recent argument he had struck her, and she was now concerned for her own and her daughter's safety.

Discussion revealed that he was a very talented rower. He rowed stroke (the most important position in the boat) for his school's highly successful First VIII rowing crew. He had also been offered a place in an elite rowing program at the Australian Institute of Sport which grooms future Olympic rowers.

Not surprisingly, he was treated as something of a hero at school by his friends and highly regarded by his sports teachers. In many Australian schools, rowing is a very prestigious sport and winning the 'Head of the River' trophy a highly prized accomplishment.

Their son's success was also a source of great pride to his parents who had sacrificed much to promote his rowing career, including sending him to an expensive private school. One sensed that having an Olympian athlete in the family was their overriding priority which would amply compensate them for all their sacrifices, including putting up with his appalling behaviour.

To be fair to the boy, he was as horrified by what he had done as his mother. We discussed anger management techniques, as well as the need for significant consequences if any abuse was repeated. We proposed that if, in the future, he abused his parents or sister verbally (physical abuse would be referred to the police) he would miss one week of rowing races. Multiple incidences would see him withdrawn from rowing for the rest of the season.

Mother and son both agreed to these proposals and left.

The next day his rowing coach called. He was concerned that his best rower had been upset, potentially threatening the success of the whole crew in a big race which was coming up that week.

Although he understood our concerns about the boy's behaviour (and its implications for his future) he seemed unable to grasp that the character of his crew was much more important than how many races they won or how ultimately these are directly linked. In the end we agreed to disagree.

We include this story because it highlights what can happen when parents (and teachers) emphasise goal achievement at the expense of character development. During the rowing season, training and preparation were prioritised over all other activities, including schoolwork, and parents were encouraged to ensure that their boys' home lives were as smooth as possible.

Essentially this meant that they were relieved of their normal household responsibilities, assuming they had any, and unreasonable behaviour would be excused because they were under pressure to succeed.

Teaching a child that they are not required to respect others and that they can ignore courtesy and good manners while neglecting their share of household chores – in other words, that their welfare should override the needs of everyone else – is about the worst preparation for adult life that one could imagine.

Just because a child is pursuing challenging goals, an excellent thing in its own right, this should never be made an excuse for them avoiding the obligations they owe to family and others.

The inevitable result will be to deprive them of the character or temperament required for lasting success and happiness.

Ten Accomplishments of Character

The pure pursuit of material or status goals, even if successful, will not alone deliver a lifelong experience of contentment, fulfilment and sense of purpose. True success and happiness are the consequence of personality or temperament; what is critical is *how* we achieve, not what or how much.

From this perspective we define success for children in terms of the following ten accomplishments of character:

1. **Self-Confidence**: They are self-assured and independent, and can tackle challenges on their own; they have the courage to stand up for themselves and what they believe in.
2. **Persistence**: They demonstrate tenacity and grit when solving problems or learning new skills; they do not give up easily when confronted with obstacles and handle failure with confidence.
3. **Maturity**: Their conduct is characterised by prudence and thoughtfulness for others; they tell the truth, keep their promises, and accept personal responsibility for the consequences of their words and deeds.
4. **Grace**: They are modest in success and acknowledge the efforts of those less fortunate than themselves; they are cheerful in defeat.
5. **Respect**: They respect themselves as well as others, and they promote the rights of others as well as their own; they are courteous and apologise when they are in the wrong.
6. **Emotional Control**: They manage their feelings to enhance their experience of happiness and contentment, while minimising negative emotions including anger, anxiety, depression, envy, jealousy and resentment.
7. **Positive Identity**: They have a strong sense of who they are, of being a person in their own right, which is reflected in powerful feelings of personal control. They have clear values which they use to think for themselves, act with integrity and decide independently, even in the face of criticism.

8. **Competence**: They pursue personal and professional activities which are meaningful and rewarding and provide a lifelong experience of mastery and competence.
9. **Empathy**: They understand and respond to the feelings of others; they develop strong friendships and lasting relationships – most importantly with an intimate partner – characterised by love, respect, trust, and empathy.
10. **Resilience**: They manage hardship and disappointment without losing confidence in themselves, the love of those close to them, or a firm belief that success and happiness are achievable. They use failure as a spur for improvement, not a reason for despair; in a word, they are resilient.

You may wish to make your own improvements to this list, but we believe that, overall, these ten accomplishments of character provide worthwhile aspirations for parents who wish genuine success and happiness for their children. We also argue strongly that they will protect children from psychological illness, including mood disorders such as anxiety and depression, as well as insulate them from other destructive emotions, including anger, envy, jealousy and resentment.

In addition, even if a child or adolescent does develop symptoms of mental disorder or addiction, the accomplishments of character we advocate will significantly enhance their chances of managing and overcoming these successfully.

Consistent with our definition of success, the ten accomplishments of character emphasise personal qualities and behaviours rather than achievement of specific goals. To reiterate, they provide a guide for how to live not what to live for.

Wanting a child to be a professional footballer, or an accountant, is not merely futile but dangerous. You neither know what strengths or talents your children will develop nor what careers will be available in the future. Furthermore, the harder you press a child towards a specific career the more likely they are to push back or give up trying altogether.

Please note, defining success in this way does not mean that setting and pursuing goals is not important. Far from it. Teaching a child to persist and tolerate some failure in pursuit of cherished ambitions (especially those of an intrinsic variety) is priceless. But it is the lessons in persistence and competency development that are important, not so much the objective itself or the standard of excellence achieved.

Goals and skills needed to achieve them will change over time – think how your own aspirations have changed – but a capacity to persist cheerfully in the face of initial failure and ongoing obstacles lasts a lifetime.

We will return to each of these accomplishments of character throughout this book as we explain how you can realise each of them in your own children.

A Model for Positive Parenting

The ten accomplishments of character presented above provide the framework for a model for positive parenting, which offers clear answers to questions such as, “What should I want for my children?”, or “What is the purpose of parenting?” By describing a mature, resilient adult they set clear goals for raising psychologically healthy, successful children.

A better understanding of where you are heading and why with your children makes it easier for you to respond consistently to the many “What is best for my child?” dilemmas which confront parents every day. By remaining focused on the personal qualities, or accomplishments of character, you wish your children to develop, as well as the current issue, you can respond to both a child’s present and future needs.

In some cases these will clash, and the conscientious parent may sometimes need to discount a child’s immediate preferences in favour of their future welfare. But clearly knowing what you are trying to achieve will give you the confidence to intervene or decide on their behalf and to persevere even in the face of tears and recriminations.

Having clear goals for how you wish children to develop, is, of course, only one component of a useful model for parenting; achieving these is the larger part. Parents also need to know how to embed preferred personal behaviours into the daily conduct of their children so that they become well learned habits – habits which are characteristic of competent, mature adults capable of pursuing successful lives they have chosen for themselves.

The principles and techniques of positive parenting presented in the rest of this book explain how parents, despite the distractions of everyday living, can instil the ten accomplishments of character into their own children. Every interaction you have with a child provides opportunities to promote desired personal qualities. Every decision you make on their behalf can be guided by an understanding of the type of person you wish them to become. Provided you remain clearly focused on children's character development, positive parenting can be usefully applied by any parent or carer, whatever their situation.

The Purpose of Parents

We commenced this chapter by posing the question, "What is the purpose of parenting?" We will now give you our answer:

The purpose of parents is not to deliver children to a specific destination, but to help them develop the personal qualities or accomplishments of character they need to successfully find their own way to their own future, one which is rewarding and meaningful for them.

This answer highlights three important elements of positive parenting: firstly, a child's character development should be parents' primary focus; secondly, while parents can assist, it is a child's responsibility to create their own future (if only because they may resist one which is imposed on them); and, thirdly, everyone – parents as well as children – need to decide for themselves what is a purposeful and worthwhile life.

One implication of our model of positive parenting is that children raised in this way are quite likely to pursue alternate lives, and hold different ideas or beliefs than those their parents might expect, or indeed would prefer.

A mother of our acquaintance expressed a strong desire that her children would be just as committed to 'social justice' as she and her partner are. It is inevitable, and indeed desirable, that we harbour hopes of this kind for our children. Other parents, for example, may desire that their children commit to their particular religious convictions.

This mother's children may well develop similar values to her own simply because of the authentic commitment to social and economic equality displayed by both their parents, as well as her vigorous encouragement that they commit to redressing injustice whenever they see it. As she herself pointed out, this is consistent with our definition of self-confidence offered above: children need to be taught to stand up for what they believe in.

This is fine. Parents should express clearly to their children what they believe in and why. They can also encourage them to follow suit. However, it is most important that children are also given every opportunity to develop their own values without sustained pressure to adhere to a specific set of beliefs advocated by parents, teachers, or others. Trying to make our children in our own image is contrary to the model of positive parenting and futile in any case. As you are well aware, pushing your children to adhere to your beliefs is probably the best way to get them to profess (if not necessarily believe) the polar opposites. It can also irrevocably damage your relationship with them at the same time.

Raising children in the manner advocated in this book – encouraging and indeed requiring them to think for themselves – may well mean that they come to hold quite different, but nevertheless genuinely held, beliefs than their parents. What is important is that this is just as welcome to parents as having children who agree with them on all important issues. Differences of this kind are clear evidence that you have raised children who *can* think for themselves and have developed their own values – as part of a positive identity – not merely assumed those of their parents.

It would be disappointing and unnecessary if parents, whose children's beliefs and values vary from their own, consider themselves to have 'failed' in some way, or struggle to remain close to them, simply because of honest and legitimate differences of opinion. Such parents clearly haven't failed. They have nurtured thoughtful people who have the courage to maintain what they believe, even in the face of vigorous disagreement. In this context, it is important to distinguish between disagreement and disapproval: disagreeing with our children is healthy and often necessary, disapproving of them because they don't agree with us is not.

This last point highlights a fundamental premise of positive parenting: although you create your children, you do not own them. They are not your property to mould in any way that you think fit, regardless of their ambitions or preferences.

In this context, we note Steve Biddulph's comment that most parenting books contain the hidden assumption that "... the world in which we live in is just fine, and our job is to fit our kids into the passing parade", when the truth, as he sees it, is that the earth is terminally threatened and that it will be our children's and grandchildren's task to save it. He concludes: "Clearly, we don't need kids who fit in. We need HEROES."[4] (emphasis in original).

We agree, insofar as we believe the purpose of parents is to enable children to create their own future rather than simply plugging them in to some existing status quo, characterised by the 'right' job, the 'right' partner, or the 'right' life, and so on. We also agree that wanting our children to be committed to a particular social cause (or causes) is, as suggested earlier, fine, provided they arrive at this ambition for themselves. Otherwise, there is a risk that wanting a child to be a 'hero' is to pigeonhole them in the same way as wanting them to be a lawyer simply because "... your father/or grandfather is/was a lawyer".

How your children choose to live – as heroes or otherwise – is up to them. Preparing them to succeed in the life they choose is up to you. The big question, of course, is how to go about it? The rest of this book is essentially our attempt to answer this question.

On another note, we have been at pains to emphasise character development over material achievement as central to positive parenting.

However, no parent wants their children living in poverty or subsisting on social welfare. Neither did we. Some level of affluence is a necessary precondition for them for building the life they want.

But we strongly believe two things: first, character development as defined above is as good a guarantee of career success for a child as you can get; and, second, without the requisite temperament, material wealth is hard to achieve and even tougher to keep (see Story: *The Builder*).

Story: *The Builder*

Randolph left school early and became a carpenter. He then started a small building company building residential homes which flourished. He was a rather driven man who tended to focus almost exclusively on his own concerns and through sheer focus and effort built a successful business. Unfortunately, in the process he neglected his partner and particularly his children.

His eldest reached adulthood relatively unscathed, possibly because she was the first and attracted more of his time and attention when she was young. Also, in these early years he was still employed as a carpenter and less distracted by the demands of running a small business.

His second two children, however, and especially his younger son, displayed many of the inappropriate behaviours neglected children use to attract the attention of a too absent parent. Both dropped out of high school, even though they were more than capable of finishing, and followed the all too familiar path of drugs, unemployment, and failure to find a meaningful life for themselves.

For the second boy this led to serious mental illness and a very hard time indeed. Even then Randolph regarded him as more of a distraction from the real business of business rather than a child in dire need of help from his father.

Randolph also experienced a difficult relationship with his partner who felt sidelined despite the material comfort which his success provided.

Unfortunately, worse was to come. Randolph embarked on a major building development against the advice of his advisors and colleagues.

This was to be the crowning achievement of his business career and establish him as a major 'player'. But he became financially overstretched, and his company was put into administration. When the dust settled, Randolph had lost his home and business as well as other investments. He and his family were left with virtually nothing but a few personal possessions.

At one level this is a cautionary tale about the dangers of pursuing material achievement at the expense of accomplishments of character. But it also highlights the impact this can have on other people, not least, children, in the process. Randolph not only failed to hold on to financial success but badly neglected his family at the same time.

Are business and family success compatible?

Certainly! The evidence for this can be found in the hundreds of thousands of successful businesspeople in Australia who also raise outstanding children and enjoy a happy home life.

In fact, there is some evidence to suggest that the two go hand in hand; that the personal qualities required for lasting achievement in the commercial world are also those essential for creating a lifelong relationship with an intimate partner and raising happy, healthy kids. Intuitively this makes sense; success in business is about building lasting relationships and so is success at home.

The lesson from this story for people who are ambitious – an admirable quality in itself – and also have a family is to ensure you focus on accomplishments of character, for yourself and your children, and maintain a healthy balance between work and home in terms of your time and attention. It needn't be a case of either/or, so why not have both?

What Is 'The Good Life'?

Finally, it is worth trying to answer two questions: "What is a worthwhile and meaningful life for me?" and, "How will I know it when I see it?", if only because your children may demand answers.

Our suggestion is to follow the advice of Rolf Dobelli, author of *The Art of the Good Life* (Sceptre, 2017), which we would encourage everyone to read. His 260 pages are full of wise and practical ideas for living happily and successfully.

In the last sentence of his book, he defines the good life in terms which also answer our two questions. He states, "So that would be the definition of the *good life*: someone hands you a few million, and you don't change anything at all."[5] (emphasis in the original).

Perhaps he is overstating this a little. You might pay off a few debts or buy or new car, but his point is that you wouldn't change anything fundamental or substantial about your life. A good example of a person who has achieved a life like this, Dobelli suggests, is the legendary investor and billionaire Warren Buffett. This man, who can literally buy anything he wants, still lives in the same house with the same wife that he and she moved into when they got married.

Conclusion

Wanting children to be happy and successful, on their own terms, are worthwhile goals shared by pretty much every thoughtful parent. Wanting our children to befriend us should not be.

Neither happiness nor success can be achieved in a straight line, either by pursuing a life that is as pleasurable and smooth as possible, or one fixated on material or status achievement. Lasting happiness and success are the inevitable by-products of character.

The true purpose of parents is to equip children with the personal qualities or accomplishments of character they will need to become mature, psychologically resilient adults, capable of pursuing the life they choose for themselves, rather than fervent accumulators of wealth, status, or good times.

The ten accomplishments of character presented in this chapter provide a framework for a model of positive parenting which offers clear answers to questions such as "What is my role as a parent?" and "What is best for my child?". Positive parenting offers a guide for assisting children pursue a life that is happy and successful on their terms rather than one imposed on them by parents. In addition, the accomplishments of character we recommend will minimise their chances of developing mental illness and, even if they do, of managing its impact as effectively as possible.

Summary

- Sustained happiness is a by-product of character rather than simply the avoidance of hardship or the pursuit of pleasure.
- Parents are more than friends to their children and always will be. You can replace friends, but families are bonded for life. Don't try to be friends with your children.
- The pure pursuit of material or extrinsic goals will not deliver lasting satisfaction or fulfilment. True success for children is best defined as accomplishments of character rather than accumulation of prizes.
- Character development is the best guarantee of material success, psychological wellbeing and lifelong happiness for your children as you are likely to find.
- The ten accomplishments of character presented in this chapter provide the framework for a model of parenting which offers answers to questions such as "What should I want for my children?" and "What is the purpose of parents?"
- The true purpose of parents is not to deliver children to a specific destination but to help them develop the personal qualities – accomplishments of character – they need to successfully find their own way to their own future, one which is rewarding and purposeful for them.
- Positive parenting means to give children the time, space and opportunities they need to create their own life rather than seek to plug them into the 'passing parade' with the 'right' job, the right 'partner', the 'right' friends and so on.

3

"I Know What I Want My Kids To Do, I Just Can't Get Them To Do It!"

"Play is the work of the child."
Maria Montessori (Italian educator and philosopher)

"The best way to make children good is to make them happy."
Oscar Wilde (Irish poet and playwright)

In the previous chapter we suggested that the purpose of parents is not to deliver our children to a specific destination, but to help them develop the personal qualities or character they need to successfully pursue their own life.

So far so good, but the key question is "How?"

More specifically, how, in the absence of a road map, can parents assist children develop maturity and forge a successful path to the future while, at the same time, protect them from risks which they cannot yet manage on their own?

This question is reflected in the title of this chapter. As we have suggested, most parents know in broad terms what they want for their children – enduring success and contentment – but they are not always sure how to get them there.

To answer this question, it is worth considering Maria Montessori's comment (quoted above) that "play is the work of the child". She was the founder of the Montessori school movement and a profound student of child psychology. What did she mean by this observation? To find out we will take a quick look at the nature of adult work to see what it can tell us about helping children achieve psychological health and find a life that is right for them.

The Nature of Work

Although there is a major body of literature about what people do at work and why, strangely enough, there is relatively little agreement about the nature of work itself. Macdonald et al. observe that despite the many books written about work, "… it is rare to find a clear definition".[1]

Perhaps even more important than a lack of clarity, these authors also note that most definitions of work miss entirely its dynamic, transformational nature.

Macdonald and his co-authors define work as "turning intention into reality" to address this deficit.[2] They describe work as a human activity which requires decision-making and the exercise of discretion to transform plans or concepts (intentions) into concrete outcomes (reality).

Further, they recognise that just as work transforms ideas and raw materials into products and services, it also transforms, for better or worse, the people doing the work. It is in both these senses that work is a dynamic or transformational process.

Meaningful work has long been recognised as being critical to mental health. As Sigmund Freud observed, work "gives a secure place in a portion of reality".[3]

At its best work provides purpose to our lives as well as promoting a positive sense of identity and feelings of personal mastery and self-esteem. But Macdonald et al. point out that these benefits only accrue when three conditions are met:

- Those doing the work understand and support its purpose.
- They are allowed to exercise their *own discretion.*
- Their contribution is properly recognised.

In the absence of any these, a worker is likely to become frustrated and alienated. In addition, their sense of individuality, or identity, is damaged. Macdonald and his co-authors conclude: "Thus work is essential to our wellbeing. It is potentially a creative expression of ourselves, especially when recognition is given accurately and appropriately."[4]

This is why we derive a sense of meaning and self-worth from well-designed work – it becomes part of who we are. It also plays a vital role in us becoming valued individuals in our own eyes and those of the world.

... and Play

What has all this got to do with raising children?

Well, interestingly, from the perspective of this book, Macdonald et al. also make the point that the importance of work for psychological wellbeing is not confined to adult employment.

They suggest that the same benefits can be observed when:

> We see small children working extremely hard (adults call it play), applying intense concentration and effort, experiencing immense frustration and joyful success – processes we continue throughout our lives if we are to enjoy a positive identity.[5]

Thus, regular opportunities to engage in purposeful activity, which offers room for creative decision making and the exercise of personal discretion, are just as important – and deliver similar benefits – for children at play as much as for adults at work. This is the meaning of Maria Montessori's observation quoted earlier.

For play to be fully beneficial, children should be given autonomy to decide what to do, how to do it, and in what order their 'work' should be done. The opportunity to exercise discretion when playing delivers two important benefits: a child develops creativity by applying their knowledge and skills as they see fit, and they develop a sense of individuality – what we have called a positive identity – by solving problems independently and plotting their own, unique, path to their goal.

'Free' Play

"*Play is the shortest route between children and their creative calling.*"
Vince Gowmon (US author)

The value of largely unsupervised or 'free' play for children's physical and psychological development has been appreciated for centuries even if, until recently, the reasons why it is so important have been unclear.

One authority on this subject, Peter Gray, defines free play as "activity that is freely chosen and directed by the participants and undertaken for its own sake, not consciously pursued to achieve ends that are distinct from the activity itself".[6]

Playing on their own and, particularly with others, appears to have value for children in and of itself *regardless* of what they are doing; it is the fact that they are playing independently, not what they are doing, that is important. Gray here stresses the value of unsupervised play outdoors with other children. He cites evidence that this is also children's preferred leisure activity even compared with television or other screen-based activities. Unfortunately, at the same time, he also documents the precipitous decline in the amount of unsupervised play time children enjoy today compared with 50 or even 20 years ago.

Gray notes that between 1981 and 1997 there was a 25% decrease in the amount of free play (both indoors and outdoors) enjoyed by six-to-eight-year-olds in the US. By 1997 this had declined to just over eleven hours per week. Similar findings are reported for the UK. Gray also makes the point that the recent decline in free play has been even more significant due to the rise in popularity of computer-based activities since the middle to late '90s. Similar trends can be observed in Australia.

Free play is clearly important for children. According to Macdonald et al., it benefits and transforms the child in a manner similar to how meaningful work benefits and transforms the adult worker.

Research in evolutionary biology is beginning to reveal why. Young mammals are born with a range of genetic potentialities, but require practice to realise these as the knowledge and skills they need to survive – to hunt, to fight and to flee.[7] They get this practice by playing with one another, their parents and other adults. Puppies in a group are one illustration of this.

An even better example of turning latency into competency is the development of human speech. Human babies are born with the potential for speech but not the capacity. They only learn to talk through constant vocal interaction, first with parents and later with others, so that their early babble becomes intelligible conversation.

Young children 'play' at talking, something they obviously enjoy, by interacting with parents and copying what they say. In doing so, they learn to speak. A child deprived of the opportunity to interact vocally in their early years never learns to speak properly.

Interestingly, the vast majority of children learn to talk – probably our single most complex human achievement – with no formal instruction whatsoever. We participate by talking to them and responding to their sounds, sometimes by repeating the words we think they are trying to say. But they decide what to say and when to say it, as well as how much or how little to speak, with no direct instruction from us.

What a remarkable achievement, and one which highlights the need to give them time and space to apply themselves at their own discretion!

The importance of allowing children to exercise similar discretion (within age related boundaries) during free play cannot be over emphasised. It is not only central to the development of inherited potential, but is also directly linked to healthy social and psychological development.

Children who regularly engage in unstructured play are much more likely to develop a sense of personal mastery or control. This gives them a firm sense that they can significantly influence what happens to them and that they can chart their own course in life.

Julian Rotter, a psychologist, contrasts what he calls internal and external "locus of control". Locus of control essentially refers to where a person believes control of their life resides.[8] Those with an external locus of control tend to believe that how you do in life is a result of others' behaviour, that they are the victims of fate, luck, or chance. Consequently, they do not take full responsibility for themselves or their lives. In contrast, those with an internal locus of control believe that they are self-directed, that they can work independently, are accountable for their actions, and believe that they do exert a significant influence over what happens in their lives.

Perhaps, not surprisingly, people with an external locus of control are more likely to report higher levels of mental disorder.[9] Because they believe outside forces direct their lives they are more likely to be wary of others, apprehensive about the future and uncertain about their chances of achieving success or happiness.

By making their own decisions, solving their own problems and fixing their own mistakes during free play, children are much more likely to develop an internal locus of control or sense of individual mastery, a belief that they can significantly influence, if not completely determine, what happens to them. Both research and clinical experience confirm that depression and anxiety are causally linked to a lack of sense of personal control, which is key to the development of a positive identity as an accomplishment of character.

Gray, mentioned above, notes: "Those who believe that they are master of their own fate are much less likely to become anxious or depressed than those who believe that they are victims of circumstances beyond their control."[10] He argues that there is a causal relationship between the decline of unsupervised play over the past 50 years and the well documented increase in anxiety and depression among children and adolescents in the West.

Recent Australian research reported that young people who self-reported psychological distress were nine times more likely to indicate feeling as though they had no control over their lives than young people without similar symptoms. Interestingly, this relationship was more than twice as strong for teenage boys than girls.[11]

But the benefits of free play for children go well beyond learning to exercise discretion and encouraging a sense of personal control or mastery. Gray also cites evidence which suggests that playing with other children without adult supervision teaches children to regulate their emotions; they want to play with others, but are excluded if they won't fit in and cooperate. They also learn that they are not special, that the rules apply to them as much as anyone else and that they must wait their turn if they wish to participate. In this way they learn how to get along with others as equals and to make friends. In the process they acquire a range of accomplishments of character including self-confidence, maturity, respect, positive identity, emotional control and empathy.

In short, free play makes children happy while an absence of free play makes them unhappy. Yet, as parents, we are in danger of depriving them of one of the most important activities which contribute directly to their psychological wellbeing. By deliberately reducing their access to free play, due to concerns about their personal safety, we may, in fact, be exposing them to even greater risks as far as their mental health and social development are concerned.

Risk and Play

"*The more risks you allow your children to take, the better they learn to look after themselves.*" Roald Dahl (English author)

Your own observation will tell you that playing children are not always gentle. They can be rough with one another, physically and emotionally, and will take risks we would rather not watch. They appear to intentionally expose themselves to at least moderate degrees of danger when left alone to play, like climbing trees or jumping off jetties, as if to teach themselves how to manage the physical and emotional stress involved.

The enthusiasm with which children engage in what to an adult onlooker can appear a pointless and, at times, dangerous, waste of energy is enough to tell us that it is vitally necessary for them, that they are driven to do it in order to become neurologically, physically and psychologically mature.

And as Roald Dahl suggests in the above quotation, we would be wise to let them.

Sandseter and Kennair (2011) suggest that risky play is a necessary part of children's normal development.[12] They cite considerable evidence that a large proportion of normal children, when left unsupervised, will explore their environment and engage in risky forms of play, including play fighting, to test their physical strength and courage. They do this despite the possibility of being hurt.

These authors consider risky play to have an evolutionary benefit in preparing children for adulthood and, most importantly, assisting them overcome normal childhood anxieties (like fear of heights), which otherwise would persist into maturity. They conclude, "we may observe an increased neuroticism or psychopathology in society if children are hindered from partaking in age adequate risky play".[13] (See Story: *Swimming with Sharks*).

Story: *Swimming with Sharks*

A friend of ours who grew up in the West Indies has told us how he and his friends would ride their bicycles across the surface of naturally occurring tarpits. The surface of a pit is slightly harder than the semi-liquid tar underneath. The trick was to keep going fast enough to get to the other side without sinking and possibly drowning in tar!

However, in terms of risk, this didn't compare with their other game which was to dive from a 20-foot cliff into the sea and try to catch one of the (non-aggressive) 'lemon' sharks which basked in the water under the cliff. If they were successful, the shark would give them a free ride under water as it attempted to escape!

Their parents tried to dissuade them from engaging in both of these activities, apparently with little success.

ꕥꕥꕥ

This story is a perfect example of how, when left to their own devices, children will voluntarily expose themselves to risk. They seem to do it because they *have* to, because it is vital to their healthy physical and psychological development.

As noted in the text, research suggests that they are driven to it by their genetic inheritance, presumably to prepare themselves for the practical and emotional challenges they will encounter as adults.

We can see the same thing occurring every day on a suburban skateboard ramp as well as in every playground.

ꕥꕥꕥ

So there is considerable research which attests to the critical benefits of free play for the acquisition of physical and social skills, confidence and independence. This, of course, is consistent with our observation that the exercise of discretion within appropriate constraints – another term for free play – is necessary for the development of what Macdonald et al. term a positive identity, something we also regard as an important accomplishment of character (see Story: *Tarzan and Jane*).

Story: *Tarzan and Jane*

When she was about 13 years old our daughter Megan had a group of friends over for the day.

After lunch they decided to go outside where they found an old rope hanging from a tree in a remote part of our garden. Inevitably they started swinging on it. Then they decided to all swing from it together and, you guessed it, the rope broke!

The result of their combined tumble was a few bruises and one girl, Angela, with a damaged ankle which was later found to have a hairline fracture. They arrived back at the house carrying their friend and all laughing (Angela included) about their adventure. They then proceeded to have afternoon tea.

We of course rang Angela's parents who fortunately were extremely understanding, and when she had finished her tea, we, plus the whole gang, took Angela to hospital. She received a plaster cast which her friends soon covered in humorous comments and best wishes. They also made a plan that when her plaster came off, they would go to a beauty salon together and get their legs waxed!

&&&

To us this is another example of young teens enthusiastically engaging in what to parents may appear a pointless and dangerous activity. But more than that, apart from our concern for Angela, what impressed us was how easily and cheerfully they managed the dramatic and painful end to their game of Tarzan and Jane. To them it was an integral part of their play and nothing to be particularly concerned about.

What is even more interesting was how much they enjoyed their adventure and how their shared experience seemed to bring them

closer together creating stronger friendships between them. It was obviously meaningful and important for them. To this day Megan will occasionally reminisce about this incident and laugh.

Obviously, we would have preferred that Angela had not hurt herself, although thankfully she recovered quickly and completely, and we discussed with all the girls what they had learned about swinging from a rope without knowing its condition beforehand. But perhaps in retrospect a cracked ankle was a small price to pay for the benefits they all took away with them.

Sphere of Autonomy

Babies are born with no awareness of themselves as individuals distinct from other people or indeed objects around them. They develop an identity, a sense of independent selfhood, as they grow and explore their surrounding environment. But this is much less likely to happen if they are given no room to work out who they are, find their own path and develop a sense of personal autonomy. This is the essence of positive identity – a key accomplishment of character.

They will acquire this by plotting their own course as much as possible, making their own decisions and fixing their own mistakes. If they can do this in a relatively risk-free manner while they are growing up, they will continue in a similar fashion when they are older and expected to do it for themselves.

It is during this period that positive parenting provides a circle of security: a secure base for children to step out from and the safe haven they need to return to when their adventures threaten their self-confidence (see Chapter 1). They are more likely to test themselves in risky situations, something they need to do, when they know that they have a reliable source of parental love and support close at hand.

It is worth repeating that making up their own mind and learning to correct their own errors are critical for developing children's self-esteem, a solid sense of self, and a belief that they can, to an important extent, influence, if not fully control, what happens to them.

Without the confidence that comes from a positive identity – knowing that they have a secure place in the world and the capacity to manage independently – they risk becoming prey to anxiety and depression.

When children lack belief in themselves, they worry about their capacity to succeed when, for example, they are required to address something new or difficult. Their default response is to look outside for help, which can leave them sad and disappointed with themselves as well as resentful of assistance provided by others. Such feelings create fertile ground for the development of mental disorder.

Parents have a key role to play here, not least by providing opportunities for self-direction within a *sphere of autonomy* where a child can become themselves. We call this aspect of positive parenting 'benign neglect', regularly leaving children to their own devices within boundaries set to protect them from their own worst impulses but with plenty of room to 'do their thing' free of parental interference.

Benign neglect, by the way, is not the same as 'fire and forget' – there is still plenty for you to do.

When your child is contemplating a project or activity of some kind you can discuss their options with them, including some of the risks which you have left for them to manage within the constraints you have set up.* You may allow your son or daughter to cook with all the tools in the kitchen except the sharpest knives and devices which use electricity (except the oven). Another constraint should be that they clear up any mess they make.

---

* In this context it is worth distinguishing between hazards and risk. Hazards are sources of risk of which children are unaware and either should be removed or explained so that they recognise the risks involved. Risk, on the other hand, is a known quantity; children are aware of it and will adjust their behaviour accordingly albeit with the possibility of the odd mishap. The job of parents is to remove unacceptable risk in the form of hazards children are currently unable to manage as well as ensure they understand the risks which remain within the sphere of autonomy which you believe that they can handle. What you should not do is remove all risk from their free play which deprives them of the opportunity to develop physical, cognitive, and social competencies as well as master their fears.

By all means discuss their options with children. You might even make suggestions but avoid taking over their 'work' yourself. When they are confronted with a problem and ask for help use open questions – What? Why? How? – to encourage them to, once again, review alternatives but leave them to make and implement their own decisions.

They may get it wrong and have to try again. No problem! Learning from errors and persevering in the face of difficulties are important accomplishments of character including self-confidence, persistence, competence and resilience.

By failing and trying again (if necessary, with some discreet encouragement from parents) children develop the sense of mastery or personal control which is so vital to their mental health. Even small improvements in their performance signal to them that they can impose their 'will' on the world, that they can replace chaos with order and bend future outcomes in their favour.

Repeated experiences like these give a child the solid self-confidence to tackle even greater challenges in the future; a capacity to manage initial failure with enthusiasm, indeed enjoyment, and a genuine sense of being an active, autonomous agent in their world.

Making Wiser Choices

"*Children learn how to make good decisions by making decisions, not by following directions.*" Alfie Kohn (US author and lecturer)

What is also going on during this process is that children are learning 'what is generally best' in a range of situations.

For example, blaming a friend for the failure of a homemade skateboard or for losing at netball may mean losing the friend, at least for a while. Or hitting a nail too hard will merely bend the nail while hurting a thumb or finger. In both cases, provided they are left to manage the consequences, they will reflect on better alternatives, and next time try something different.

Once again, this is more likely to happen if parents encourage a discussion about what happened and why. Repeated experiences of this kind, in which a child experiments, reflects on their progress and, when necessary, changes direction will develop their sense of what works and what doesn't in a wide range of scenarios before they come up against them in the real world. These lessons will be even more powerful if one or both parents recognises their efforts, particularly when they make wiser choices.

The last point addresses an issue confronting all parents: how, with no road map to guide us, do we teach children how to self-manage their lives in ways that are generally beneficial to them and others. We have already suggested that this challenge may be heard in the title of this chapter: "I know what I want my kids to do, I just can't get them to do it!"

While parents often know what they want for a child, what is genuinely difficult is to realise or embed 'what is generally best' into their daily, unsupervised activity. Your task is to get them to the point where they can make 'good' decisions on their own without the need for parental guidance or intervention. And we have reflected that making wise choices is a useful description of a mature adult.

You can assist your children learn to make better decisions for themselves – to become successful self-managers – by, once again, creating situations in which, as early as possible, they enjoy a degree of independence to decide for themselves. This is the point made by Alfie Kohn in the quotation at the beginning of this section. Regular experiences of this kind nurture feelings of autonomy and personal mastery reflected in positive identity, self-confidence, and competence.

They also teach children, often by trial and error what works and what doesn't – whether this be when planning a project, fixing a wheel to a buggy or offering help to a friend – and to live with the consequences of their own decisions.

The lessons they will eventually learn in this way include that what works best for them in most situations also works better for others; that most problems or conflicts are best resolved in a collaborative manner, in which the interests and contributions of all parties involved are recognised; and that generally there is more satisfaction to be gained from helping others rather than simply helping oneself.

As always, judicious praise and recognition from parents will reinforce this process. And we need not emphasise how priceless this learning is for their future happiness and success.

In particular, it will assist them acquire the accomplishment of character that is maturity: their conduct will become characterised by prudence and thoughtfulness for others. They will also learn the value of speaking the truth, keeping their promises, and accepting personal responsibility for the consequences of their words and deeds.

The alternative is to simply tell your children what they should be doing, which may work provided they are listening. But it certainly won't when you are not there to tell them. Of course, we all give 'what is best' advice to our children on a range of subjects and so we should. But let's not kid ourselves that this is a reliable substitute for learning to decide for themselves.

At best, 'telling children' will only reinforce the painful lessons which personal experience teaches them. Better that they learn these early rather than late, when the consequences of unwise decisions are much more serious.

To summarise, children are happier when they are managing their own affairs. As Oscar Wilde points out, in the quotation at the beginning of this chapter, if we want them to be 'good', that is to do what 'we want them to do', it is important to ensure they are happy.

Holding Back vs Stepping In

Let us now return to the question we posed at the beginning of this chapter:

How, in the absence of a road map, can parents assist children develop maturity and forge a successful path to adulthood while, at the same time, protect them from risks which they cannot yet manage on their own?

Our earlier discussion about the relationship between work and mental health emphasised that children, as much as adults, need non-supervised space and time to play or 'work' on their own, to exercise discretion and make their own decisions in pursuit of worthwhile objectives.

This, as we have learned, is important for the development of a secure identity and personal maturity, each of which is necessary for mental health.

Part of an answer to the question posed above then is to create what we have called a sphere of autonomy in which children can become themselves. You should allow, indeed require, your children to consistently exercise their discretion, free from adult interference, while at the same time protecting them from unacceptable risk by placing age related constraints on their independence.

This will promote their development as mature, resilient individuals while, at the same time, shield them from hazards they are currently unable to manage. Here, it is particularly effective if you regularly and publicly acknowledge the emergence of 'wiser choices' and maturity in their behaviour.

As children become more competent, aim to expand and eventually remove all boundaries placed on their activities, other than those imposed on all adults. A useful habit for parents is to regularly (say monthly) reflect on the degrees of independence and personal responsibility they place on their children and to progressively widen these, up to and a little beyond that which they can currently manage.

The alternative is to continue doing too much for too long, well past the time they should be flying more or less solo. This puts them at risk of becoming infantilised and incapable of managing their own affairs, even when this is desirable and, indeed, necessary.

A sphere of autonomy within which children are expected to plan their own 'work', make their own decisions, solve their own problems, and rectify their own errors is one of the best preparation for a psychologically healthy adolescence and adulthood that parents can provide. By working alone and with others they will learn, sometimes painfully, what is the best way to achieve important goals and get things done. In the process they will come to realise that sharing, cooperating, and persisting are generally the best ways forward.

The contribution of parents, as we have suggested, is to support and encourage but not take over. In particular, look for *any* sign that your children are learning 'what is generally best', such as when they help a younger sibling, and recognise this through praise and encouragement.

Parents need to step lightly, if at all, when intervening to solve their children's problems for them. In the next chapter we review research which identifies overprotective parenting as positively harmful for children and likely to be a major factor contributing to the unprecedented increase in anxiety and depression reported by today's teens and young adults.

Unless you provide time and space for your children to exercise discretion and develop a genuine sense of autonomy, you will leave them vulnerable to developing the same conditions.

Perhaps with smaller children it is easier to hold back, because we are less anxious about the outcomes of their free play time. Because we are not concerned about what they are 'achieving', we are content to give them a few toys and leave them to it – in the same way that we let them schedule how they learn to talk.

As they get older, however, the danger is that we may be tempted to exert too much control over what they are doing and how they are doing it. Our desire for academic success for our children, for example, may lead us to intervene too much and too often in their schoolwork.

Every parent does this from time to time, including one of the authors of this book who dictated a Year 12 Business Studies essay for our son Rory, the night before it was due for assessment – desperate times call for desperate measures!

The trick is to not make this a habit with obvious consequences for your children.

How to Hold Back

'Holding back' from taking over a child's life starts with goal setting.

Some goals they should set and execute entirely on their own. This is what happens when they play independently, alone, and with others.

Other goals parents and educators will determine for them, particularly when they are young.

Children will not always choose to eat healthy foods, therefore parents need to provide them with a nutritious diet. This is no different from the work environment where organisational goals, and constraints or limits of discretion are generally decided by senior management.

Whatever the age of a child, however, it is important to involve them in discussing goals, even if the final decision remains with parents. Talking with them about the goals you wish them to adopt will increase their understanding of why particular achievements are important as well as their willingness to engage with them.

As much as possible try to acknowledge their concerns and incorporate their preferences into the final outcome. This will make for better decisions and happier children and parents. It also underscores the fundamental point that positive parenting is something we do *with* children rather than *to* them.

By treating parenting as a *team* activity in this way you will be less likely to simply take over. More importantly, your children will learn from an early age how to engage with others to negotiate preferred outcomes for themselves. They will also learn that sometimes they have no choice but to cheerfully conform with the wishes of those in authority, something we all need to do from time to time.

What is clear from the world of adult work is that it is not necessary for people to set all or even most of their goals. What *is* necessary is that they identify with them so that they understand their importance and thus pursue them seriously.

Through discussion, encouragement and negotiation many of your intentions for your children will become their own. This is another way of saying that they learn to incorporate what is generally best – what experience teaches is the better option – into their own independent behaviour.

Helping children identify goals that are worthwhile and to seriously commit to their achievement is an important job for parents. One thing is certain: if parents do not consider a goal to be important (like completing Year 12) it is far less likely that their children will.

The opposite can also be true: just because a parent embraces certain outcomes for a child does not automatically mean their child will do likewise. This should sound a note of warning to parents who seek to fill a child's waking hours with a raft of school and extracurricular activities without first ensuring they have genuine 'buy in' from their child. Unless he or she adopts the purpose of these activities as their own, they will resist engagement, become alienated from what they are doing and possibly also from their parents.

Of course, children won't adopt all our goals and plans for them, and neither should they. In this book we are at pains to emphasise the need for young people to find their own way to a fulfilling future. But there is no doubt that they are more likely to pursue activities which will reap benefits for them later if we are there at the beginning to support and encourage.

Goal Orientation

While parents may continue to have specific aspirations for children, what is more important is that, by engaging them early in discussions about the future, they are more likely to become goal oriented, preferably towards intrinsic goals, which promote personal mastery and happiness, as well as providing career opportunities. Being goal-oriented means that a child becomes familiar and relaxed about planning for the future. Similarly they will come to regard the temporary degree of discomfort or apprehension associated with learning new skills and solving new problems – on their way to achieving worthwhile aims – as normal and appropriate.

Children will become goal-oriented if their early attempts to master skills and complete tasks – primarily determined by parents and teachers – are recognised and encouraged. Consequently, when they are older, they will have already acquired the confidence to contemplate more significant achievements, as well as the persistence required, to accomplish larger objectives they set for themselves.

This is more likely to occur if they are given, as soon as possible, a sphere of autonomy within which they have frequent opportunities to engage in free play and any competency improvement they display is consistently and publicly praised. What they are achieving is less important than that they become relaxed about the business of achievement itself. They are learning critical accomplishments of character – including self-confidence, persistence, and resilience – which will be invaluable to them in the future when they may choose or be required to change career paths or acquire a new sets of competencies.

Being goal-orientated becomes increasingly important as children get older and start to create their own life. Having their offspring follow them into the family business may be highly desirable for parents but may not suit a particular son or daughter. But if they have not been taught to achieve more broadly, they may struggle to find an alternative future for themselves.

To avoid an impasse of this kind, children need to be comfortable with the *process* of achievement itself, including the focus and persistence required. They also need the confidence to make independent choices regarding what they wish to accomplish. Parents can make their search easier, of course, provided they are supportive rather than disappointed that their children want to go their own way.

An absence of goal orientation becomes most apparent if, for some reason, they don't complete high school. Adolescents in this situation appear to fall into two groups. Some simply hang around at home and appear clueless about what to do next despite parental efforts to get them 'launched'. The others, those who have learned how to achieve independently, quickly turn their attention to something which genuinely interests them and calmly get on with their lives. They may get a job and start saving to go travelling or pursue alternative training. Either way they are able to forge a satisfactory future for themselves (see Story: *Jennifer*).

Story: *Jennifer*

Jennifer's parents were so anxious for her to attend higher education that they promised to pay her a significant sum of money on the day she graduated from high school on the condition that she would go on to complete a university degree. She duly enrolled but dropped out after two years because she was there for the wrong reason – she was fulfilling her parents' ambition rather than her own. They promptly demanded repayment of their money.

Fortunately, they had raised her to be goal oriented and to accept the consequences of her own decisions. She entered a trade course and became a successful chef. Once she was earning, she repaid her debt and today is running her own successful restaurant.

ॐॐॐ

To us this story emphasises the importance of children being goal oriented, that is, confident and capable of selecting and pursuing ambitions they select for themselves. Initial failure did not curb Jennifer's enthusiasm for learning, rather, it assisted her to identify the life she wanted for herself and what she had to do to get there. Importantly, she took responsibility for her failure to complete university rather than blaming her parents for 'making' her do it. Growing up she clearly had acquired the accomplishments of character required to create a satisfactory life despite her initial failure which also imposed a significant financial burden on her. Both she and her parents deserve credit for the ultimate success she achieved.

ॐॐॐ

Once goals are agreed, for work of any kind to be beneficial, the people doing it, young or old, as we have emphasised, must be allowed to get on with it unimpeded. This requires parents to be 'hands off' as much as possible to allow their children to decide how they will plan and execute a particular task – not always an easy thing to do!

This dilemma for parents – wanting to help but knowing they should back off – reminds us of the saying: "One of the hardest things in the world is to stand back and watch without comment someone do something which you know you can do twice as well and twice as quickly!"

But this is what you must do if your children are to learn how to plan, how to decide, how to problem solve, how to experiment and how to persevere, in other words, how to succeed.

Just as important, through this process they develop an independent sense of self or, in Macdonald's words, "to identify themselves as an active agent in the world". This last, as we have argued, is a core component of mental health.[14]

The worst thing a parent can do is step in and 'fix' something for a child unless they are endangering themselves. Sometimes this is the right and correct thing to do (see Story: *On the Roof*). Even then, how you intervene is important.

Getting angry because a child takes excessive risks is understandable although rarely useful. Better to calmly discuss what they were doing and why it was dangerous, or inappropriate, and ask for their commitment not to do the same thing in the future.

You might have to make some practical changes in the yard or garden, like putting a better lock on the pool gate, but simply becoming angry or distressed and issuing a strict edict forbidding any repetition is not helpful. The child may be confused if they are still unaware of the danger they were exposed to, and a barked instruction is less likely to change their behaviour than a quiet, structured conversation. We provide a simple model for discussions of this type (the 4Is) in Chapter 11.

Story: *On the Roof*

Many years ago, we were called by a very anxious lady from next door who had just observed two of our neighbours' children (a sister and brother) sitting on top of the roof of their house.

We hurried outside to see for ourselves. There they were (they were about 9 or 10 years old) laughing and talking and when asked if they were okay replied, "Fine thank you!" They had crawled up there while their parents were out and seemed to be having a whale of a time enjoying the view and waving at startled passers-by.

While concerned for their safety, we were also impressed with their courage to climb on the roof in the first place, and their obvious confidence in their ability to get back down again in one piece. We encouraged them to do this, which they did, still laughing and talking, although not without a few tricky moments, just as their parents arrived home.

What then happened impressed us further. Rather than fly into a rage or become overly distressed, both parents greeted their children happily and, while obviously relieved they had come to no harm, proceeded to have a calm and rational conversation with them about their escapade.

The parents briefly outlined the dangers involved and asked each child not to climb on the roof again. They also listened carefully to what their children had to say. The conversation was over in a few minutes, concluding with the children's agreement not to repeat their adventure.

There was no shouting, no disrespect displayed by either party and, as far as we could see, no loss of love between parents and children. We came away having learned an important lesson about raising happy children.

ꕥꕥꕥ

We observed the family more closely, following this event. What we noticed was that both children had a great deal of personal autonomy; they rode their bikes all over the neighbourhood, went shopping together without their parents and caught the bus to school on their own.

They also had regular household responsibilities, which included putting out the rubbish and working in their garden. Most notable for us was their enthusiasm and courtesy when talking to adults either when we passed in the street or when they were looking for odd jobs to earn some pocket money.

They were polite and respectful, but also very self-assured. When we left the suburb, they looked set for a happy and rewarding future.

To us the parents of these children provide an object lesson in positive parenting. Whether they planned it that way or not they seemed to be giving them the best possible chance of becoming successful, psychologically healthy adults. They gave each child genuine autonomy and responsibility and had obviously taught them how to interact with all manner of people respectfully but assertively, ac-

complishments of character which include self-confidence, respect, grace, positive identity and empathy.

The impact of their upbringing was apparent in the courage and confidence they both displayed when climbing on the roof. Even if that incident was a case of a bit too much too soon it gives a clear indication of how they were likely to tackle challenges and obstacles in the future.

❧❧❧

Apart from when children are genuinely in danger, parents should exercise caution when tempted to take over. Even if they ask for help, rather than simply doing something for them, ask questions and make suggestions but let them remain in charge.

You should also regularly recognise their efforts to improve or to 'do the right thing' (see The Importance of Recognition below). But as much as possible refrain from doing those things for them that they need to learn for themselves.

What Do Children Learn when Parents 'Step in'?

When a parent intervenes to assist with a task a child can complete for themselves, however imperfectly, or before they have given it their best shot, three things happen.

First, they are deprived of the opportunity to persist and work something out for themselves, which contribute to their development of positive identity.

Second, when you take responsibility away from children, you teach them that they are not capable of managing on their own, thereby lowering their self-confidence.

Finally, if you do take over, with or without being asked, they will learn to expect, indeed demand, help whenever they are confronted with difficulty or challenge; and the more help you provide the more they will seek. By taking over you are literally training them to take the easier option – to expect, and look for, external help whenever a problem arises. This is not helpful for someone preparing to be an adult.

It is worth reflecting on the cumulative impact of a parental strategy of 'stepping in' on children's future mental health. We are arguing that requiring children to exercise discretion, to tackle problems on their own and to persist in the face of difficulties, are necessary preparations for them to develop a robust sense of self-worth and the confidence required to live independently.

There is increasing evidence, which we review in the next chapter, that denying them this opportunity, by stepping in and taking over whenever the going gets even slightly tough, is to leave children at the risk of developing symptoms of anxiety and depression when they are teenagers or adults (see Story: *On The Phone*).

Story: *On The Phone*

One of us consulted the parents of a 40-year-old man who unfortunately appeared to be struggling to make a satisfactory life for himself.

From his parents' description he was obviously intelligent, having completed university and gone into business for himself. Unfortunately, his career had been punctuated by a series of failed enterprises, each of which his parents had rescued him from, at significant financial cost to themselves.

The primary reason for his successive failures appeared to be that, after an initial burst of enthusiasm, he would lose interest in the daily grind of meeting client needs, neglect his costs which soon got out of control, and essentially walk away leaving his parents to sort out the mess.

In addition, his personal life had been punctuated by failed relationships and he had developed dependencies on prescription medication and alcohol.

Our concern that he had remained too dependent on his parents was confirmed by the fact that he would ring his mother at least five or six times a day, and sometimes many more, asking for advice or assistance. This apparently had been going on since he was a young teenager.

She, as a loving parent, would always respond to his requests for help often by jumping in her car and going to see him with food, money or whatever else he required.

Unfortunately, this had not resulted in a close mutually supportive relationship between mother and son. Not surprisingly, he bitterly resented his state of dependence, even though he did nothing to end it because he was unable to.

His hostile behaviour towards his parents, especially his mother, had led them to seek professional help.

ꕥꕥꕥ

What had happened here? Essentially, mother and son, although the father was not blameless, had established a relationship of mutual dependency which dated from when he was a little boy.

He had learned early that asking for help always produced the desired result, particularly from his mother; she invariably stepped in without hesitation to fix his problems and without requiring him to learn the grit and persistence required by all successful small business owners, indeed all successful people. And this pattern of parenting had continued throughout the son's adolescence and adult life.

In short, his mother, in particular, had never learned to hold back and let him sort out his own problems and experience the consequences of his own decisions, even when he was long past the age where he should have been required to do just that. His father was also a contributor to this fiasco by continuing to not only bail him out of his business failures but also fund his lifestyle while he was unemployed.

Both parents were engaging in what psychologists call 'enabling' behaviour. Essentially this means to shield another person from the normal or 'natural' consequences of their actions, so they are not required to take responsibility for, live with or learn from the 'fall-out'. To enable someone in this way is simply to reinforce their inappropriate or maladaptive responses to setbacks until these become bad habits. That this had happened was apparent in the way the son had learned to walk away from his business responsibilities and his immature reliance on his mother and father.

These parents had literally infantilised their son, that is, they had encouraged him to continue to behave as a dependent child even though he was a grown man.

The consequences for the man's mother were just as depressing as they were for him. She relied on his constant requests for assistance to provide her life with relevance and purpose in the same way that he needed her to manage his.

Any suggestion that she needed to step back and let him learn, even at this late stage, to stand on his own feet was met with distress mixed with hostility. As much as she loved him and wanted him to be happy, stepping back would threaten her role as a caring and supportive mother. Of course, she was also aware that stepping back now could result in much more calamitous consequences for her son than would have been the case when he was younger.

She was sure that someone had a 'cure' for his behaviour which they could administer to 'fix' his 'problem' without requiring her to modify her own actions in any way – in fact she struggled to accept any responsibility for what was happening.

As far as she was concerned, she was only doing what was 'right' and necessary. From our last contact it appeared likely that the current state of affairs within this dysfunctional family would continue indefinitely.

Setting Limits of Discretion

Earlier we recognised the need for parents to protect children from harm, particularly when they are young, by removing or managing risk they can't handle on their own.

In this regard, you would not let a 5-year-old walk to the shops alone, although you should encourage them to make an agreed purchase on their own, and you expect a 15-year-old to be home at an agreed hour or to inform you if they are delayed.

Constraints should be age-related to reflect a child's knowledge and competence as well as their size and strength and the nature of the task they are engaged in. As they grow in skill, confidence and maturity, limits of discretion should be widened to allow them to continue to learn and develop. The key thing is that they have time and space of their own, free of adult interference, in which to explore, experiment and to learn to fail as well as succeed.

As your children grow, aim to first broaden and later remove constraints altogether. If you don't, they will ultimately break free from these anyway and not always in ways you would wish.

This should be a continuous process, matched to a child's growing competencies, so that ultimately they can live independently within the limits placed on all adults. To fail in this is to perform a major disservice to children. It is to literally infantilise them – to ensure they remain in a state of near childhood, unwilling to grow up because they are unable to do so. (See Story: *The Lunch Box*).

Positive parenting means to be proactive in widening the constraints placed on children by providing more freedom and opportunity, preferably *before* they request it. This is subject, of course, to your observation of your child's progress.

Encouraging children to take more responsibility and accept more autonomy is a great boost to their self-confidence and increases their willingness to take charge in more areas of their lives.

Story: *The Lunch Box*

Many years ago, one of us was consulted by a mother who was concerned that her son's memory was faulty, that he kept forgetting things. She was right about the second, as he did keep forgetting things, but not the first – there was nothing wrong with his memory.

When asked to provide an example of his 'faulty' memory, she said that on most schooldays he left his lunch at home. When asked what she did about this she said, "Well, I take his lunch box to school and give it to his teacher of course!" She seemed surprised that she needed to explain what to her was obvious and what any good mother would do in the same situation.

Testing of the son's short- and long-term memories confirmed these were normal and it was suggested that the quickest way to fix his memory 'problem' was to stop remembering things for him; that a couple of days without lunch would ensure he did not forget it in the future. She was a little taken aback, and we never learned whether she applied this advice or not.

ॐॐॐ

This story provides an example of what can happen when parents fail to progressively increase a child's responsibilities (i.e., widen their limits of discretion) and let them experience the consequences of their own mistakes.

This lady was a devoted mother but her love for her son was encouraging in him at least two bad habits which could have more serious consequences when he was older: firstly, learning to 'forget' things (remember there was nothing wrong with his memory); and, secondly, relying on others, indeed expecting them, to do things he should be doing for himself.

Children Who Are Anxious

There are some children who, due to the interaction of DNA and environment, are less confident and prefer their parents to remain in control. Anxiety about growing up is quite normal but needs to be addressed. Unfortunately, too often parents regard such anxiety either as permanent and normal, or as evidence that their children are not ready or, worse, unable to grow up.

In Chapter 1, we reviewed data that indicate unhealthy anxiety is increasingly prevalent among young people. One of the reasons for this, we believe, is that some parents regard anxiety in their children as an innate condition, like blonde hair or blue eyes, something to be accepted rather than addressed while they are young. Unfortunately, a diagnosis by a psychologist or psychiatrist that their child has an anxiety disorder may mistakenly reinforce this belief.

A minimum level of alertness is a survival mechanism built into our nature, but beyond a normal 'resting' level it can become debilitating anxiety which inhibits a child's development. Elevated anxiety need not be permanent and can be reduced to a normal level in many cases. But, for this to occur, concerned parents need to recognise that their own behaviour, their over-concern, or being overly protective, if you like, is a major contributing factor to their child's anxiety. For a child to change, parents must change first.

Parents of anxious children tend do more for their children than they should and step in too often when they should hold back. This prevents their child from learning to master anxiety by engaging with its causes, such as meeting new people.

Observation of anxiety in children suggests that

> ... anxious children may elicit overprotective behaviour from others, particularly parents and caregivers, and that reinforces a child's perception of threat and decreases their perception of controlling the danger. Overprotection might thus result in exaggerated levels of anxiety.[15]

So, overprotection may well increase a child's anxiety. It may also mean that the anxious child avoids responsibilities they should be accepting for themselves. The inevitable result is that children who have not been assisted to reduce their 'resting' level of anxiety when young are more likely to be anxious and less capable adolescents and adults. Their inability to cope will further exacerbate their anxiety, which in turn reduces their confidence in themselves and their willingness to grow up. In this way a self-reinforcing negative loop may be set up with mournful consequences for their future.

How often have you heard a parent excuse a child's lack of courtesy, and silent exit to another room when you arrive, with a laugh and a comment like, "Oh she's very shy, she doesn't like meeting new people"? Their words and tone send two messages to their child: firstly, that this is just the way he/she is and there is nothing to be done about it; and, secondly, that ignoring visitors is acceptable and appropriate.

Too many parents regard shyness – which itself is a normal type of anxiety – as a permanent condition which does not require their attention or intervention. However, while shyness *is* normal it need not be permanent.

Childhood shyness, if left unaddressed, can morph into adolescent and adult awkwardness which seriously impairs a person's capacity to mix comfortably with others in professional or social settings. It will also inhibit their acquisition of empathy, the capacity to understand and respond to others' feelings as well as develop sound friendships and lasting relationships.

Courtesy towards others, although desirable, is not the issue here. What is important is what the child learns when she is not expected to welcome a visitor to her home, or she hears a parent's comment such as the one above.

What she learns is that shyness is an acceptable excuse for not greeting people appropriately whether you know them or not. Thus, a valuable opportunity is lost to assist the child to learn to reduce, if not eliminate, her quite natural shyness by coaching her in how to interact with strangers. As a consequence, she may fail to learn to treat others with appropriate respect, an accomplishment of character which will be critical to her future success as an adult.

To reiterate, shyness in children is quite normal and a degree of shyness may persist into adolescence and, later, despite parents' best efforts. What is not desirable is that shyness is left to morph into adult anxiety or accepted as an excuse for not treating others with respect or avoiding social responsibilities (see Story: *The Visitors*).

Story: *The Visitors*

We remember visiting the house of an acquaintance to organise a social event at the sports club all our children played for.

We followed him into the lounge where his three teenage children were sitting intently engaged with their screens. None of them, whom we knew slightly, acknowledged our presence, either with a word or a glance, as we made our way through to the kitchen.

Their father said nothing; we concluded our business and left.

What surprised us at the time was not so much the children's behaviour – let's be fair, this is not unusual for teenagers – but that their father made no attempt to ask them to welcome visitors to their home. He seemed to regard them ignoring us as entirely normal and unworthy of comment.

Here was a perfect opportunity missed for them to learn how to interact respectfully with others, particularly strangers, and to learn to gain the support they would need in the future from others outside their home. He could have asked them to stand up and briefly greet us before going back to what they were doing, but he didn't.

Later, when we were gone, he could also have used this episode to discuss ways of interacting with visitors and why it is a useful skill for the future, such as at their first serious job interview.

We know we shouldn't be influenced by first impressions when meeting people for the first time, but that is exactly what happens. We are impressed by those, and especially young people, who are confident and courteous, who can hold our gaze and engage in thoughtful conversation. And we are more likely to employ them.

Human resource managers will attest to the importance of the first impression a young interviewee makes by how they manage an employment interview – whether they are confident and well prepared or nervous and disorganised. They are not expected to know a great deal or to have much relevant experience. All the more reason for them to leave a lasting and positive personal impact if they want to get the job.

Self-Directed Learning

A good way to assist children who lack confidence is to provide them with opportunities for self-directed learning. This combines a sphere of autonomy with some structure from you to give them direction and get them started.

If you have a project at home or work you can delegate particular tasks to them which are within their competence, but which still require independent decision making and problem solving. Sorting tools into groups of the same type (when you are organising the shed), or putting books into alphabetical order, are examples of this. For older children, it might be to paint the hull of a dinghy, design the cover of a report you are preparing for work or put together a play list for your next party. The list is endless, and tasks can be adjusted to suit their interests and competencies.

So rather than saying, “Please pass me the big wooden spoon”, you might try, “We're going to cook a chocolate cake. Please get the ingredients and cooking utensils we'll need out on the bench for me, here's the recipe.” Then leave them to it. You can coach and encourage as required (maybe by helping them to read parts of the recipe) but as much as possible let them sort it out.

It is most important not to correct or criticise (which will only increase their reluctance), but rather ask questions to help them identify something they may have missed. You might say, “I wonder if that bowl will be big enough to hold half a litre of water. Could you check its capacity?” They will then learn how to use a measuring jug to work it out for themselves.

Praise for their efforts, however minimal these may be, will encourage them to keep going and increase their belief that they can succeed independently. Also, as we have already emphasised, you should seek to widen their sphere of autonomy as their skills and confidence grow. In this way you can assist an anxious child to develop a positive identity, persistence and self-confidence as accomplishments of character.

For children who are shy or nervous among strangers, particularly adults, asking them to help serve food and non-alcoholic drinks at social gatherings is a great opportunity for self-directed learning. It gives their interaction with new people a purpose and structure – they don't have to think of topics for conversation – and helps them become more comfortable mixing with others.

It need not be said that working together with one or more of your children on a project in this way is also a great way to get to know them better and to find out what they are truly interested in as well as what may be troubling them.

The Importance of Recognition

You will recall that in the earlier discussion of adult work Macdonald et al. emphasised the importance of recognising a worker's input. These authors suggest:

> The affirmation of our contribution to the process and outcome of work, especially when positive, recognises that we exist and that the output of our thinking has genuine worth; it encourages us to use and develop our capabilities.[16]

These authors stress that recognition is not simply about acknowledging success but should embrace a person's entire effort regardless of the results; recognition of this kind will leave them less downhearted by failure but rather encourage them to use it as a platform to persist.

In addition, recognition, particularly of determination and perseverance, not only promotes the accomplishments of character of positive identity, self-confidence, and persistence, but is also crucial for encouraging children to commit to goals you select for them – like attending a certain school.

As noted earlier, your intentions for your children are more likely to become theirs if you recognise and encourage their earliest attempts at engagement and mastery, however small.

To take one example. If you speak enthusiastically of the advantages of completing high school, take an active interest in their progress, and recognise their efforts, *regardless of their level of success,* they are much more likely to stick at school and embrace graduation as a goal.

Recognition is a key tool for encouraging the development of desired accomplishments of character. Whenever you see one of your children displaying behaviours you wish them to acquire permanently it is important to take the time to acknowledge and praise, or, as a psychologist would say, to 'reinforce' these. Approval and encouragement of specific behaviours or qualities you desire in your children increases the likelihood that these will be repeated in the future until they become permanent habits.

Acknowledgement of qualities you want to encourage in your children is central to positive parenting. Targeted praise should become an automatic habit for you and your partner to ensure your children acquire the accomplishments of character they will need on their journey to becoming successful adults.

Don't Underestimate Your Influence

It often comes as a surprise to us how parents, particularly of teenagers, discount their importance in the lives of their children and their capacity to shape their behaviour. The danger is that the more you mark down your potential influence as a parent the less likely you are to exert it for your children's benefit.

Parents play a much more important role in children's lives than they often give themselves credit for. This is true, as long as you focus on three things: modelling (setting the right example), setting limits of discretion, and praise or recognition for desired behaviour. For the most part, parents should avoid direct instruction (except when coaching children in a specific skill), and criticism which children tend to ignore.

An important factor working in your favour is the innate need all humans have for the attention of others. Children and adolescents crave recognition from their parents, even if their response to praise does not always suggest this.

A child who rejects praise is not telling you that they don't like or want it. What they are signalling is that they lack the confidence necessary to accept it gracefully, that they need more of your attention, not less, in order to become comfortable with it. Recognition is critical to a child believing that they are worthwhile, that they are a valued person in their own right. (This powerful tool for encouraging a child to develop preferred accomplishments of character is discussed in more detail in Chapters 5 and 10).

We have already mentioned the importance of children becoming socially desirable, that is, they are welcomed by others and attract their support. To this desideratum we would add social competence: the capacity to manage themselves confidently and respectfully among others so that they can take advantage of available opportunities, to profit from social desirability if you like.

There are endless occasions to assist your children learn social competence, to engage confidently with the world, simply by bringing them with you whenever you can and asking them to help you in whatever you are doing.

When they are younger, they particularly enjoy being with their parents and helping out. Don't assume that they will find whatever you are doing will be boring and prefer to be at home.

They will learn a lot a more going with you to the golf club working bee, or to buy a new drill, or simply into the office for 20 minutes than sitting at home looking at a screen. This is particularly true if you are explaining what you are doing and encouraging their active involvement.

Developing Accomplishments of Character

When discussing character development in Chapter 2 we suggested that what children are doing or achieving, while significant, is less important than *how* they conduct themselves in the process.

For example,

- Are they gracious or arrogant when successful and does failure leave them grumpy or cheerful?
- When they encounter problems, do they remain calm and willing to persevere or do they become angry, tearful or give up?
- Do they blame others when things go wrong or accept appropriate personal responsibility?
- Do they display care and empathy or are they selfish and neglect the needs of siblings and friends?

- When involved in a disagreement are they respectful towards others, or do they become aggressive or simply withdraw?
- Are they excited by the challenges of growing up or lack confidence in their ability to succeed?
- Are they shy and avoid interaction with strangers or pleasant and respectful?
- Are they surly and truculent when they don't get their own way, or do they accept cheerfully and gracefully that sometimes that is how life goes?

We could continue with a longer list of similar questions, but you get the point!

There are at least eight ways to assist your children develop the ten accomplishments of character which we argue will help them achieve genuine success and happiness, as well as psychological health:

1. From birth, respect your child as an autonomous person with the same rights and obligations as every other human being, even though initially they are unable to fully understand or exercise these (see Chapters 8 and 12).
2. Provide an appropriate role model (or example), yourself, of the personal qualities and behaviours you wish them to display, *particularly when you are under pressure* (see Chapters 6, 8 and 13).
3. Create a sphere of autonomy from the very beginning in which they learn to become their own person (see Chapters 3, 4 and 5).
4. Provide regular opportunities for self-directed learning (see Chapter 3).
5. Use targeted public recognition – praise and encouragement – to highlight and reinforce the specific behaviours and personal qualities (the accomplishments of character) you wish them to develop as permanent habits (see Chapters 3, 5 and 10).

6. Deliver regular coaching sessions to directly teach them techniques and skills (particularly emotional control) as well as how to manage anxiety associated with tackling new activities and projects (see Chapters 6, 8 and 13).
7. Develop agreed family rules to introduce routine, security and self-discipline into their lives (see Chapters 7 and 9).
8. When necessary, intervene directly to discipline their behaviour and guide their character development (see Chapters 10 and 11).

By applying these tools of positive parenting, you can use almost any activity or interaction with your children to influence their development. We explore these in greater detail in each of the chapters indicated above, and explain how to use each to assist children establish the accomplishments of character which define a mature, psychologically resilient adult.

Every day there are multiple opportunities to influence children, to change their behaviour in ways beneficial to them and others. But we don't always grasp them.

Why are we reluctant to have these discussions even when we see the need?

Well sometimes we will be tired or late for work. But perhaps a bigger part of our unwillingness is because none of us enjoy what we expect to be a 'difficult' conversation. We may also lack the necessary skills; we are not sure how to encourage change and improvement in our children's behaviour without starting a war of words which simply damages our relationship with them while producing no discernible benefit. With practice comes confidence, but we need the skills first. How to manage 'difficult' conversations with children and teenagers, and the conflict which these may entail, are explored in detail in Chapter 11.

Conclusion

Children of any age need a sphere of autonomy, a space free of adult interference, to exercise their own discretion and achieve a sense of mastery. An example of this is free play during which they learn to manage reasonable risk and develop a positive identity by doing things their own way, solving their own problems, and live with the consequences of their own mistakes.

Parents need to exercise caution before stepping in to do things for children which they must learn for themselves.

The boundaries or constraints you place on children's behaviour to protect them from some (but not all) risk should be progressively relaxed as they grow so they learn risk management and know you trust them. This builds their self-confidence and increases the likelihood that they will learn to regulate their own behaviour and to accept personal responsibility. Providing increasing autonomy also assists children to understand 'what is best' in more situations and to make wiser decisions when parents are elsewhere.

Stepping in when you should hold back deprives a child of significant developmental opportunities. It can literally infantilise them, rendering them incapable of maturing into adults who are confident of their place in the world and can build a worthwhile life for themselves.

Summary

- Just as meaningful work is essential to adult mental health so too is free play for children's healthy psychological development; it helps them acquire a positive identity, learn social skills, and gain the confidence to manage risk and tackle problems on their own.
- For play to be beneficial, it is vital to provide sufficient time and space – a sphere of autonomy – to allow children to exercise their discretion and engage in a degree of age-related risk taking.
- Giving children autonomy assists them to learn what is generally best, to make wise decisions which are on the whole beneficial for themselves and others; in this way they acquire the thoughtfulness and prudence characteristic of mature adults.

- Loosening and then removing constraints as children grow sends them the affirming message that you trust them to act responsibly, increases their confidence in themselves, and encourages them to take charge in more areas of their lives.
- Positive parenting is as much about holding back as stepping in. Taking over when children should be left to manage on their own is to infantilise them, to undermine their belief in themselves and deprive them of the opportunity to achieve independent responsibility.
- A lack of confidence associated with shyness or unnecessary anxiety are quite common in children but should be addressed while they are growing to ensure these do not progress to become permanent features of their adult personality.
- Every interaction with a child provides parents with an opportunity to develop and strengthen accomplishments of character. We have suggested eight approaches to achieving this.

PART 2

What We Do Know

"Children learn what they live."
Dorothy Nolte (US author)

We have reviewed the current crisis in child and adolescent mental health and discussed two key challenges facing parents: firstly, that there is no road map to a perfect future for any child and, secondly, ensuring they make wise decisions and do 'what is generally best' when we are not there to guide them.

But while there may be no guarantees for successful parenting, there is a great deal we do know about raising happy, psychologically healthy children, established knowledge which still provides vital lessons for modern parents (for example, the importance of 'free' play, discussed in the previous chapter).

In Chapter 4 we revisit a widely quoted piece of parenting wisdom: 'Prepare the child for the road not the road for the child' and discuss what this means for successfully raising the next generation.

In the context of this statement, we consider some recent changes in modern society, including a rising culture of 'safetyism' most evident in Western countries and, in response to this, the emergence of what has been called 'paranoid' parenting.

But perhaps the biggest change in children's lives in the past 15 to 20 years has been the arrival of internet-based technology, evident in the proliferation of smart phones, and the astonishing growth of social media platforms such as Facebook, Snapchat, Instagram and TikTok. Going 'online' is now the most common waking activity for far too many children and teenagers, and the consequences of too much screen time for their psychological and physical health do not look encouraging.

The internet is here to stay and is a major vehicle for learning so simply banning it from your home is not a useful option. But parents need to know much more about its effects to help children use it wisely, if only because social media is becoming a fertile ground for cyber bullying, a modern version of the traditional face to face variety.

We review data on bullying in schools, which confirm it is a serious and growing problem, and discuss why children become victims of bullying as well as how to teach them to deal with bullies confidently and assertively.

In addition to what we can learn from the past, there is also a considerable body of recent research into child development which sheds light on why children grow in certain ways and the conditions which may impair their mental health, a central concern of this book.

Chapter 5 introduces one of the more intriguing insights into the nature of the growing child – antifragility. Despite appearances small children are not fragile, neither are they robust. Rather they are antifragile, which is the true opposite of fragility. Something that is fragile is in constant need of care and protection. In contrast, the antifragile child needs challenge and stimulus as well as the stress which flows from these, to achieve full physical, neurological, and psychological maturity. Indeed, an absence of adversity, in age related doses, is positively harmful for a child. The implications of this statement for parenting are profound and we make some suggestions for raising antifragile children.

To know that children require a degree of pressure – and the stress that comes with it – to develop peoperly is useful because both are normal aspects of everyday life. We can't shield them from most of the conditions or stressors that may (not will) trigger debilitating anxiety or depression because these are part of growing up – like facing a major exam, being rejected by a cherished friend or losing a grand final by a whisker.

But what we can do is to teach them how to respond to everyday stressors in healthier, more adaptive ways, in particular to the inevitable disappointments that lie ahead, so that these do not produce chronic unhappiness, or worse, mental disorder. In Chapter 6 we explore the principles and techniques of modern psychotherapy, particularly Cognitive Behavioural Therapy (CBT), which provide powerful tools for helping young people manage their emotions more effectively.

The core principle of CBT is that feeling is the product of thinking. Emotions, good or bad, are not beyond our control but, in fact, are determined by us, specifically by how we have learned to interpret or think about what happens to us, not least, 'bad' events.

CBT advocates that it is not our external circumstances which create our emotions but rather how we choose to 'read' or understand these. Teaching children to think about or 'read' events adaptively, so that they understand and manage their feelings more effectively, is one of the greatest gifts of positive parenting because it is the key to emotional control.

In Chapter 7 we reflect on the once common rule of parenting that children need 'plain food and dull monotony'. While we are less concerned with diet, we argue strongly for the inestimable benefits of routine, the modern equivalent of 'dull monotony', particularly for younger children. Daily routine is critical for assisting children to introduce structure and order into their lives which, in turn, contribute to their sense of personal security and ultimately promotes self-discipline or self-regulation.

The need for routine and the security it provides is most acute for children whose parents have separated and who divide their time between different households. In Chapter 7 we also discuss what is known about raising happy and healthy children living in this situation.

Dorothy Nolte suggests that children "learn what they live" (see quotation at the beginning of this section). What she means, as we have already suggested, is that children learn how to live – how to think, how to feel and how to behave – for better or worse, from the conditions they grow up in, the world created for them by parents and others. This fundamental truth applies to all children but especially so to those whose parents part company early in their lives.

4

Prepare the Child for the Road Not the Road for the Child

"It is not what you do for your children, but what you have taught them to do for themselves that will make them successful human beings." Anne Landers (US columnist)

"The more we shelter children from every disappointment, the more devastating future disappointments will be." Fred G. Gosman (US author)

The recommendation, "Prepare the child for the road not the road for the child", has been passed down by generations of thoughtful parents and remains relevant for those of today because it has stood the test of time. It also captures the true essence of positive parenting.

If we accept there is no road map to follow, we must admit that we don't know exactly what lies ahead for our children. We can provide opportunities, advise, and encourage, but we cannot predict their destiny with any accuracy. For the most part they must find their own way to their own future and that is how it should be.

What we do know, however, is that, along with success, our children will inevitably meet with some disappointment, failure, and hardship. These are endemic to our world and soon there will come a day when they must face these alone.

Does it not make sense then to assist them learn to manage challenges and problems for themselves now, to prepare them for the road ahead while we can, rather than, by over protecting or neglecting them, leave them ill-equipped to cope with the future?

We believe that it does. This, also, is what Anne Landers is saying in the quotation at the beginning of this chapter.

Even if this means leaving a child to struggle with a task which they have been taught, but have yet to fully master, rather than complete it for them, no matter how tempting this may be and despite their complaints or tears. We are not suggesting that you ignore your children when they are clearly out of their depth, but rather ensure they learn how to persist, and at times to fail, with confidence rather than make their progress unnecessarily easy.

Parents can do this by teaching a child a new skill and then encourage them to keep practising until it becomes an established habit. This is clearly preferable to simply taking over and thereby encouraging them to automatically look for help whenever things get a bit tricky.

This is what it means to prepare the child for the road, rather than the road for the child; assisting them to acquire the accomplishments of character – the competence, values, confidence, and maturity – they will need to navigate their future lives independently and successfully.

Although the wisdom contained in this simple statement has been recognised for a long time, it appears necessary to keep repeating it. Why? Partly because it is counter intuitive – it does not make immediate sense. Our 'natural' response as a parent is to want to protect our children and make things easier for them, not leave them to struggle on their own.

This understandable impulse stems from the 24/7 care we must provide for newborns. It also explains the origin of the 'helicopter' or 'lawnmower' parent we hear so much about in the media.

However, even the most conscientious parent cannot protect a child from all of life's hazards, even if they keep them permanently at home. In fact, overprotective parents can themselves become a primary threat to a child's future happiness.

That this may occur is reflected in the major first regret of Bronnie Ware's dying patients, that they failed to follow their dreams and live the life they would have preferred, sometimes at least because of the influence of their parents.

We can see the consequences of this emerging in the sometimes bitter and unresolved conflicts between parents and their adult children which can last a lifetime.

Preparing a child for the road requires parents in age related stages to leave children to sort out their own 'dramas' rather than to step in and fix them. However, this suggestion can provoke quite a hostile response from some parents.

To hold back rather than step in appears to deny them the very role that they cherish. This is because they misunderstand the purpose of parenting, which is not to smooth their children's immediate path, but rather to prepare them for the future – to teach them how to take charge of their own lives and to confront obstacles rather than avoid them. The alternative is to leave them dependant on the uncertain charity of others.

In short, preparing a child for the road is to equip them with the accomplishments of character presented in Chapter 2 and to ensure that you keep this priority clearly in mind during every interaction you have with them and when making decisions on their behalf.

It also gets back to providing a sphere of autonomy for children discussed in the previous chapter. It means to provide them with as much discretion as possible to solve their own problems – be these with their homework or the neighbour's kids – without getting involved.

Of course, parents protect children from significant harm (which does *not* include, say, a bit of 'rough and tumble' with others of a similar age and size or falling off their bike, provided they are wearing a helmet); and obviously you should step in when things really are getting out of control or they clearly require assistance.

Apart from this, it is far better for their psychological health (and yours) to let them resolve things for themselves as much as possible. By doing this you are teaching them to handle anxiety, manage conflict, confront bullies, compromise when necessary and experience the pride we all feel when standing on our own feet.

A childhood like this will automatically equip adolescents with many of the accomplishments of character we have used to define adult maturity, notably self-confidence, emotional control, positive identity, competence, and resilience.

It will also produce young adults familiar and comfortable with the moderate (and normal) degree of temporary uneasiness or anxiety we all feel when confronted with something new or difficult, managing risk or taking personal responsibility. Having experienced such feelings many times before when young, they will not be discouraged by these when they are older because they know that if they press on their initial apprehension will quickly disappear.

The alternative – to step in – leaves parents making excuses to teachers because a project is not completed, adjudicating childish squabbles, and fixing all the minor complications that make up a child's normal day. This is both time consuming and irritating for parents, but the consequences are more serious for children.

Firstly, as we have seen, they learn to accept, then expect and ultimately demand, assistance to manage every setback that comes their way as this is the only approach to problem solving that they know.

Secondly, and worse still, they may never learn the vital lesson that the best way to permanently eliminate most anxiety and stress is to address the source of these unpleasant feelings through personal action rather than letting someone else take over.

Finally, when parents do take over a child's responsibilities, he or she is less likely to learn that their actions have consequences, for example, that failure to complete homework may result in a 'detention' period, and to modify their behaviour in the future.

Ultimately, they will have to face the consequences of their choices without their parents to shield them. It makes sense then for them to learn early that what they do or don't do today may have repercussions tomorrow and to adjust their choices accordingly; in other words, to learn 'what is generally best' in most situations. (See story: *Freddy Michaels*).

Story: *Freddy Michaels*

One of our contemporaries, Freddy Michaels, was the most talented boy in school when we were in Years 11 and 12. He excelled academically and was a leading footballer and cricketer. As far as his future was concerned the sky appeared to be the limit.

Unfortunately, his father was one of the most meddling, interfering, and fussy parents we have ever known. Even back then, we recognised that Fred's father was a pain to have around. He was constantly in and out of the school talking to Fred's teachers about his son's progress and always there after school to collect him.

He clearly admired – indeed worshipped – his son and was present at every school activity which involved Fred. But he was not content to stand back and watch. He was constantly making sure Fred had everything he needed, that his footy boots were clean and his water bottle full and so on.

He even attended team meetings and, at times, contributed his own thoughts. He irritated the rest of us and drove Fred to distraction, who unfortunately treated him with a level of disrespect bordering on contempt. His father appeared to accept this without comment.

The longer-term impact on Fred of his father's constant 'stepping in' became painfully apparent midway through Year 12 when he was not at school one Monday and did not appear for another week.

When he returned he had a stitched lip and a plate to replace two lost front teeth. He had been in a fight in a poolroom late on a Sunday evening before school and someone threw a pool ball in his face.

He struggled academically for the remainder of the year and, although he went to university, his heart wasn't in it and he dropped out midway. He appeared to have little motivation or self-confidence and subsequently drifted through a life marked by fighting, drinking, failed relationships and serial unemployment.

❧❧❧

The consequences for Fred of his father's behaviour is a clear lesson about the dangers of parents stepping in too much and too often.

Fred was given little room to use his undoubted talents to forge his own identity by tackling life on his own. His father was too concerned that everything go right on what he believed to be Fred's preordained path to adult success to let him alone.

Perhaps it was inevitable that Fred reacted by rejecting the person his father wished him to be by becoming someone very different.

Worse still, Fred's difficulties were exacerbated by his father's failure to insist that he display respect towards him and, by extension, other people. His admiration for his son blinded him to Fred's need, through discipline when required, to acquire those accomplishments of character essential for building successful relationships with others, particularly grace, respect and empathy.

In this sense his father, although he loved, indeed, as we have noted, worshipped his son, nevertheless failed to respect Fred as an autonomous human being with the right and obligation to find a worthwhile and meaningful life for himself.

The importance of respecting as well as loving children is discussed in Chapter 8.

Learned Helplessness

There will be times when stepping in to assist children is clearly the right thing to do, mainly when a child is in danger of being seriously hurt or when they are obviously unable to manage on their own.

Psychologists Martin Seligman and Steven Maier discovered something very interesting when experimenting with dogs. They found that a majority of dogs, who had previously received mild electric shocks, which they could not avoid, made no attempt to escape similar shocks in later experiments, even when they could easily have done so.[1]

Subsequent experiments demonstrated that dogs with no previous experience of shocks quickly learned to evade them when possible. But the random and inevitable nature of the shocks administered in earlier experiments to the first group of dogs appeared, in many cases, to have removed their motivation to escape even when they could.

It was as if they had learned to passively accept discomfort and believed there was nothing they could do to stop or avoid it. Seligman and Maier named this phenomenon "learned helplessness".

Learned helplessness can also be observed in children who are neglected by carers or do not receive reliable help when they genuinely need it, either with tasks that are beyond them or when they are clearly distressed.

A child for whom this is a regular experience, who is frequently left to struggle beyond his or her capacity to manage, can come to distrust their capacity to cope more generally. They learn to accept that there is nothing they can do to control what happens to them and thus tend to be passive rather than proactive in the face of everyday challenges.

Learned helplessness can persist into adulthood with predictable consequences. Hence it is not surprising that learned helplessness in children and adults has been associated with symptoms of mental disorder, including anxiety, depression and a variety of phobias.[2]

So yes, there are times when we must step in. But, remember, learned helplessness can cut both ways. Children who receive too much assistance, for whom the path has been made too smooth, will also struggle to think and act independently, and feel similarly threatened by growing up, as those who receive too little.

As we have seen, the danger of stepping in too often is that children come to expect and then demand help even at an age when they should be able to manage for themselves. We would suggest that for a majority of readers of a book like this – conscientious parents who want the best for their children – doing too much is a more likely trap than doing too little (see Story: *Helping With Exams*).

Story: *Helping With Exams*

A mother of our acquaintance told us she was taking three weeks' leave from work.

"Excellent", we replied, "Where are you going for your holidays?" "Oh", she said "I'm staying home to help my two boys with their exams."

This seemed a reasonable use of her time until we learned that her sons were 25 and 30 years old, respectively. We then assumed that she was merely going to take some meals over to where they lived and perhaps do some washing for them given their extra work loads.

But we were wrong. Both men – and they are adult men – still lived at home, looked after by their parents, and relied on them to directly assist with organising their revision programs and completing practice exams.

At that point we became speechless.

ॐॐॐ

This is not an unusual story, at least with regard to the fact that two adult sons were still living with their parents. Research confirms that, today, more and more young adults are staying in their family home for longer. Between 2001 and 2017, the proportion of men aged 18 to 29 living with one or both parents, increased from 47% to 56%. The increase for women in the same age group was even more marked, up from 36% to 54% in the same period.

Staying at home for longer is especially true of women in their early to mid-20s. In 2001, 30% of women aged between 22 and 25 were still living at home, while by 2017, this proportion had almost doubled to 58%.[3]

The HILDA survey explored a range of factors which may lead to young adults to remain at home for longer. These included the cost of renting or buying housing, the growth of casual, less secure employment, particularly for younger workers, and an increase in the length of time this cohort remains in full time education.

The authors of this survey concede that it is difficult to tease out the relative importance of economic factors compared with the personal preferences of adult children in their decision to stay at home.

However, they raise another factor which is often overlooked in discussions of this kind. They point out, "… one thing is clear: it could not happen *without the capacity and willingness of parents to accommodate their adult children*. So perhaps, ultimately, we should be looking to their parents for an explanation of this trend." (emphasis added)

This is a striking statement and one which, we believe, points to relatively recent changes in parental attitudes and behaviour towards adult children.

Our own conversations with many parents of young adults suggest that they are indeed reluctant to let them go for the simple reason that, in many ways, they *still* are children and woefully unprepared to leave home.

This observation is consistent with other findings reviewed in Chapter 1 which also indicate that young people today are growing up more slowly and are less ready for adulthood than earlier generations at the same age.

Getting The Balance Right

Trying to steer a path between doing 'too much' or 'too little' for children can be confusing.

On one hand, as we explore in the next chapter, children need to experience challenge and a degree of stress if they are to flourish, while, on the other, there are times when they require direction and guidance to manage tasks and situations which are clearly beyond them. In these cases, failing to assist can put them at risk of developing learned helplessness.

With younger children, the need for intervention is perhaps more obvious, but as they get older the most appropriate response by a parent may be less clear. Nevertheless, with practice you will learn when your children genuinely need help and when to let them be.

A good rule of thumb, as they grow, is to at least wait until they ask for help. However, at any age, how you intervene is important.

Simply stepping in and fixing a child's problem is not helpful since, as we have seen, they learn nothing of value themselves. At times, you may have no alternative – you may be running late – but try not to make it a habit.

Better options are to intervene to offer help with a specific task, such as carrying heavy materials, or opening a tin of paint, as well as to discuss alternative ways of achieving what they are trying to do.

You might discuss with them different approaches to designing a school project, but still let them decide which one they will choose. The important thing is that you don't take responsibility for planning and completion away from the child. This will reduce them to the status of junior assistant at best and likely to see them lose interest in their own project.

They should retain their exercise of discretion, but your engagement signals clearly that you are interested in how they are getting on.

Some of the most important interventions parents make are those which take the form of mini coaching sessions to help a child complete a current task and better prepare them for future ones. You might show them how to tie a shoelace or use a hammer, and then encourage them to try for themselves.

What you shouldn't do is take over, by simply tying their shoes or fixing their go cart and leaving it at that, because this reduces their opportunity to acquire accomplishments of character they will require to live as independent adults – self-confidence, persistence, competence and resilience. (See Story: *In The Bathroom*).

The lessons they learn from coaching sessions of this kind are priceless and will set them up for a more rewarding and independent future. This aspect of positive parenting is captured in the well-worn observation: "Give a man a fish and you feed him for a day, teach him how to fish and you feed him for a lifetime."

However, if they don't want coaching, that's fine. Leave them to it but make it clear that you are happy to help them at another time. Try not to be offended because they reject your well-meant offer, rather be proud that they prefer to stick at it on their own.

Story: *In The Bathroom*

A little boy of eight years and his mother recently consulted one of us regarding his rapid weight gain and also because he was becoming increasingly angry and verbally aggressive, particularly towards her.

He was a healthy, intelligent boy, with two loving parents, who was doing well at school, so on the surface it was difficult to see what he had to be unhappy about.

His weight gain was explained by the fact that he ate fast food on most nights of the week, which it was suggested would need to change.

More discussion revealed that his mother, a caring but clearly anxious lady, still wiped his bottom when he went to the bathroom at home and cut up all his food for him so that "he made less mess".

What was even more surprising was the difficulty he had getting off the examination couch unaided, even though his feet were dangling less than 40 cm from the floor. He was tempted to jump off like most children do but was clearly hesitant. His mother immediately organised the steps for him but when encouraged to get down on his own he found this simple physical task quite awkward.

What we learned was that he had never engaged in any organised physical activity, due to his parents' concerns for his safety, and had yet to develop basic physical coordination.

His mother left with some rather clear recommendations:

1. *Fast food on only one evening per week, as a 'treat', provided he was respectful towards his mother and father.*
2. *Leave him to his own devices in the bathroom and require him to clean up any mess. (He was apparently managing perfectly well at school).*
3. *Require him to cut up his own food and, once again, clear up his own mess.*
4. *Enrol him in swimming classes immediately so that he could develop physical coordination.*

Time will tell how successful these are.

ঌঌঌ

Why was this boy becoming angrier and more resentful towards his mother?

Well, primarily because overprotective parenting was preventing him from growing up and putting him at risk of acquiring learned helplessness.

He had become aware of this, notably his physical awkwardness,

by comparing himself with his peers at school. He was becoming increasingly unhappy with his inability to keep up with his schoolmates and his hostility, as is often the case, was directed at his parents.

What is also interesting about this story is his mother's answer to the question, "Do you still expect to be wiping his bottom when he is 18 years old?" Her response, not surprisingly, was, "Of course not!", but she struggled with the notion that if nothing changed now that is exactly what might happen.

This lady is a loving and caring mother but has still to learn that if parents want children to grow up then they must continually adjust their expectations of them to promote age appropriate behaviours and a willingness to accept increased personal responsibility.

'Paranoid' Parents

We have emphasised the merits of parents holding back rather than stepping in when children encounter difficulties. Unfortunately, there are signs of a growing tendency among parents to do just the opposite.

The authors of *The Coddling of the American Mind*, Greg Lukianoff and Jonathan Haidt, review some disturbing trends in the United States today. They highlight the growth, especially among middle class parents, of what they call "paranoid parenting".[4]

'Paranoid' parents regard their children as being permanently at risk and in need of constant protection, even though children in the US (and Australia) are now measurably physically safer than they have ever been, and certainly safer than their parents were at the same age.

Lukianoff and Haidt suggest paranoid parenting is a response to a cultural development in the US which they call "safetyism", one which can also be observed in other Western countries, once again including Australia. In Lukianoff and Haidt's words, a culture of safetyism is one which:

> … encourages people to systematically protect one another from the very experiences embedded in daily life that *they need in order to become strong and healthy*. (emphasis added).[5]

'Safetyism' is characterised by a concern for personal safety which has expanded beyond protecting people from purely physical harm (like wearing seat belts in cars) to include shielding them from emotional discomfort or distress. This may be created by ideas different from their own or the behaviour of others which they perceive to be 'unfair' or 'intimidating'.

A desire for emotional or 'psychological safety' among teens and young adults is reflected in the development of 'safe spaces' and 'trigger warnings' in universities in Australia and overseas, especially in the US and the UK. Safe spaces are havens for students to go to when they feel threatened or intimidated by campus life. Trigger warnings are placed in recommended literature to alert readers that these contain ideas which may spark a traumatic response or revive past trauma (like domestic violence). While these initiatives may be beneficial for individuals at risk, the broader implications of growing safetyism for our society appear less healthy.

Lukianoff and Haidt observe:

> When children are raised in a culture of safetyism, which teaches them to stay 'emotionally safe' while protecting them from every imaginable danger, it may set up a feedback loop; kids become more fragile and less resilient, which signals to adults that they need more protection, which then makes them even more fragile and less resilient.[6]

What they are suggesting is that parents, by stepping in too often to protect their children rather than holding back to let them learn independence, are unwittingly leaving them less able to manage the road ahead.

Lukianoff and Haidt argue that paranoid parenting and a creeping culture of safetyism, together with a decline in the amount of free play children enjoy, are among the root causes of the significant increase in anxiety and depression among young people observed in the US, Australia and elsewhere. Having read this far, their conclusion regarding the mental health benefits of free play will not surprise you.

iGen

The data reported in Chapter 1 on the decline in mental health among young people in the United States is taken from the book, *iGen*, by psychologist, Jean Twenge. The full title of her book is worth quoting: *iGen: Why Today's Super Connected Kids Are Growing Up Less Rebellious, More Tolerant, Less Happy – And Completely Unprepared for Adulthood (and What that Means for the Rest of Us).*[7]

That is quite a title, but what really caught our attention was her suggestion that too many of what she calls iGen or the "internet generation" (children born from 1995) are not ready to be adults, even though the oldest of them today are in their mid- to late-twenties. Her conclusion, that young adults in the US are less prepared for the future than earlier generations, is consistent with our argument that young Australians are also becoming more reluctant to embrace adulthood.

Twenge notes that smartphones first came on the market in 2007 when the first iGen'ers were turning thirteen. They are, she points out, "the first generation to enter adolescence with smartphones already in their hands".[8] It is safe to say, and the data support this, that teenagers everywhere have taken to these devices like ducks to water.

In 2020, the Pew Research Centre in the US reported that YouTube, Instagram and Snapchat are the most popular online platforms among teens (13-17). This data also indicate that 95% of US teens have access to a smartphone, and that 45% say they are online "almost constantly".[9]

Lukianoff and Haidt cite research indicating that unsupervised teenagers will average nine hours screen time per day. The same number for 8 to 12-year-olds is six hours. This is *in addition to* the time they spend on screens at school.[10] They also note accumulating evidence that excessive screen use may be associated with negative social and psychological outcomes for children.

Recent Australian data suggest that 77% of young Australians (15-19) spend more than five hours per day on screens and over half (55.9%) use their screens for entertainment for two or more hours each day (in addition to schoolwork) which, in many cases, exceeds the Australian government recommendation of a maximum of two hours per day for recreation.[11]

Twenge explains her findings of declining mental health among US teenagers in terms not dissimilar to those used by Lukianoff and Haidt, but with a particular emphasis on the pervasive use of screens and smart phones among this age group. She points out that iGen'ers spend more time alone with screens as well as less unsupervised time interacting with peers, than previous generations.

Twenge also identifies sleep deprivation as an additional risk factor for depression, occasioned, in part at least, by the late-night use of phones. She reports that teens who average less than seven hours sleep per night are more depressed and 68% more likely to report at least one risk factor for suicide than those who regularly get more.[12]

In Australia, sleep deprivation among teenagers has also been associated with psychological distress; 41.4% of those reporting levels of distress, consistent with symptoms of mental disorder, also reported sleeping (on average) six hours or less per night.[13]

Chronic sleep deprivation is also associated with concentration and memory difficulties, shortened attention span, poor decision-making and fluctuations in mood.[14]

Which causes which is difficult to say and there may be other mediating factors involved. But these data suggest parents need to do their best to ensure that their children are getting the eight to 10 hours of uninterrupted sleep per night recommended by the Australian Department of Health.[15]

Twenge's analysis also reveals that iGen teenagers in the US are spending less time on homework, paid work, volunteering and extracurricular activities compared with previous generations. She demonstrates conclusively that much of the extra time they have created is being spent alone using an internet device, most often a smartphone.

Regarding total screen time, her conclusion mirrors that of Lukianoff and Haidt. She reports that in 2015 senior US high school students were spending on average six hours a day (not including schoolwork) on screen-based activities. This included texting (28%), internet (24%), gaming (18%), TV (24%) and video chat (5%).[16]

Twenge's data suggest that approximately half of US teenagers' daily recreational screen time (three hours per day) is spent using social media; and the situation in Australia is very similar.

The ABS (Australian Bureau of Statistics) reports that Australian teenagers between the ages of 15 and 17 are the biggest users of the internet among all age groups. 98% of this cohort will spend up to 18 hours per week using the internet, predominantly accessing social media. This is in addition to screen time at school.[17]

Screen Time and Mental Health

On the basis of her meticulous investigation, Twenge argues for a causative link between increased screen time and the sudden deterioration observed in the mental health of teenagers. She notes:

> … experiments that randomly assign people to experience more or less screen time and those that track behaviour over time have both found that more screen time causes more anxiety, depression, loneliness and less emotional connection. It seems clear that at least some of the sudden and large increase in depression has been caused by teens spending more time with screens.[18]

Additional recent research in Australia and elsewhere also reports negative relationships between screen hours and children's (5-17 years) physical and psychosocial health.[19, 20, 21]

Twenge concludes that a direct causal relationship between screen time and mental illness is "distressingly clear" citing evidence that teenagers who spend more than three hours per day using smartphones and similar devices are 35% more likely to display at least one suicide risk factor.[22]

As we noted in the Introduction, she baldly states, "The results could not be clearer: teens who spend more time on screen activities are more likely to be unhappy and those who spend more time on non-screen activities are more likely to be happy."[23]

Here, it should also be noted that there are other studies which report little or no relationship between screen time and depression, anxiety and other symptoms of mental disorder. In the light of these findings, some researchers question whether the effects of screen time are sufficiently strong to be a major contributor to the recent increase in mental health issues among young people.[24]

Most authors emphasise the complex nature of this research. They note the many variables in addition to screen time which can be expected to influence mental health in children and adolescents, including, for example, the quality of their home life and the strength of their relationships with peers. Establishing the short and longer term relationships between screen time and young people's psychological wellbeing is extremely difficult. Clearly much more research is required.

But enough is already known for most authorities on the subject – including government agencies – to advocate careful management of how and how much young people access this technology. We strongly support this recommendation. While there may not yet be a complete picture, there is sufficient evidence to suggest that unrestricted use of screens is clearly not in the best interests of children and teenagers, physically, psychologically or socially.

We have already reviewed evidence to support the direct beneficial impact on children's mental health of unsupervised play, alone and with other children, and noted the dramatic decline of 'free' play in recent decades. The data presented by Twenge as well as Lukianoff and Haidt suggest a powerful two factor explanation for why unsupervised play among children has declined so quickly: 'paranoid' parenting encouraged by a culture of 'safetyism' – which keeps children at home – being reinforced by the attractive alternative for children of looking at a screen.

The sad irony is that, while their parents believe they are keeping their children 'safe' by leaving them in their bedroom with a screen, they may well be exposing them to perils worse than anything they are likely to meet in the neighbourhood park on a sunny afternoon.

Social media appears to be especially effective in triggering feelings of anxiety as well as depression among young teenagers already predisposed to either condition. Because it is interactive, it not only encourages vulnerable teens to compare themselves with idealised versions of other people but also facilitates cyberbullying.[25, 26]

Most teenagers tend to be concerned about what they look like and what others think of them. When they post something on a social media platform, like a 'selfie', they are more likely than a mature adult to be concerned about the reaction this may produce from friends and others.

A minimal response, in the form of few or no 'likes', or a negative response, possibly in the form of cyber bullying, can trigger further anxiety, not least when they see others being electronically celebrated. Repeated experiences of a similar kind may lead to lowered self-esteem and, in those already susceptible, chronic anxiety and depression.

To quote from Twenge once more: "… the split between screen and non-screen activities is unmistakable: teens who spend more time on screens are more likely to be depressed, and those who spend more time on non-screen activities are less likely to be depressed."[27]

In summary, a significant body of recent research suggests that children and teenagers are better off spending more time face to face with friends free from parental supervision, more time reading print media, more time playing sport or exercising and less time looking at a screen.

Managing Children's Screen Time

With regard to screen time the solution is not for parents to ban the use of internet technology altogether but to start managing more carefully how and how much their children use it.

Lukianoff and Haidt recommend a maximum of two hours of screen time per day for older children, including schoolwork, and suggest parents ban the use of smartphones during the week for their younger siblings.[28] (See Story: *The Whiz Kid*)

We should include a caveat here regarding our emphasis on the need for parents to hold back from too much interference in their children's lives. Excessive and uncontrolled use of screens in general, and social media in particular, is clearly an exception to this rule. A young teenager sitting alone in their bedroom fixated on Snapchat or Instagram without adult guidance is neither becoming psychologically resilient nor learning to exercise discretion or 'what is generally best' for themselves and others.

Screen time, and social media use in particular, should be the topic of frequent conversations between you and your children and addressed directly in your family's rules for living together (see Chapter 9).

There are many technologies, including electricity and motor vehicles, that pose both benefits and risks for children. Teaching young people to use these, and especially the internet, in ways that advantage themselves and others, while avoiding the harm they have the potential to cause, is clearly an important part of positive parenting.

A young mother of our acquaintance highlighted the importance of parental example when managing children's use of devices, particularly smartphones. She admitted that as a Gen Y parent she too is guilty of overusing her phone and pointed out, "There is no use encouraging my son to reduce his screen time when he sees me regularly looking at my phone!" As in all other aspects of parenting, the example or model you provide is critical for gaining traction when trying to influence your children's behaviour.

Story: *The Whiz Kid*

Ahmed is an internet gaming prodigy. At nine years of age he is creating content for new games and earns money for his product! As you might expect he is a very clever boy who is breezing through school.

Once he finishes his homework and chores each afternoon he settles down at his screen to talk to his online 'friends'.

His parents consulted one of us because they were concerned that he was becoming 'addicted' (their term) to gaming and neglecting the rest of his life. In addition, he had started to dislike school and was becoming less willing to participate in any activity outside his hobby.

Assessment of Ahmed's intelligence confirmed that he was bored at school and needed a lot of extension material to stretch him intellectually and keep him engaged. Bright kids who are underchallenged at school are not uncommon, but the fact that this was the case with Ahmed was not related to his gaming 'habit'.

Using the research cited in the text as a guide, we suggested that gaming activities be kept to 30 minutes each weekday afternoon and two hours per day on the weekends. We also suggested that the time he saved could be devoted to learning a musical instrument which fortunately he was attracted to doing anyway. It was agreed that we would revisit screen time when he entered high school.

On our last contact with Ahmed he had settled into his new routine relatively comfortably. He was enjoying school more and was still in demand as a gaming expert even though he was less available for consultations.

ॐॐॐ

This story highlights the potentially addictive nature of screen-based activities.

Fortunately, Ahmed's parents had done a great job in raising him so that he had a regular daily routine and was contributing to household chores as well as completing his homework every evening.

Also, he was loved and secure and had a happy and mutually respectful relationship with his parents who both attended his appointment. Consequently, Ahmed had other sources of recognition and approval available to him other than that which he received from his online 'friends'.

All of these factors meant that encouraging him to reduce his screen time, that is to change his routine, was a much easier process than it otherwise might have been.

A child in less advantageous circumstances is clearly more likely to continue to be exposed to excessive screen time with the attendant risk of future mental disorder which this may entail.

Avoiding Hurt Feelings

Young people raised by 'paranoid' parents appear unable to cope with the normal requirements of adult life. As we have seen, they are staying at home longer – with their parents' acquiescence – partly, at least, because they are deterred by the challenge of living independently.

These young people are reluctant to leave home because they have not been taught to be self-sufficient when they were growing up. Unwittingly, by stepping in too often their parents have left them incapable of coping, much less thriving, on their own. Whenever they were confronted with a situation that caused them even mild discomfort or anxiety their parents acted to ameliorate or, if possible, remove the source of their uneasiness.

Situations which caused them embarrassment or hurt feelings – which constitute valuable learning opportunities for acquiring accomplishments of character including self-confidence and resilience – were regarded by their parents, and hence also by them, as bad and to be avoided (see Story: *The Birthday Present*).

It is understandable to want to protect children from danger, but today the real danger is that parental concern for their wellbeing may be inflating their fears and reducing their willingness to address risks, however small. Worse still, over-protective parents are in danger of permanently infantilising their children to the point where they are incapable of becoming competent adults.

The research reported earlier clearly indicates that parents, carers and educators are primarily responsible for rising levels of mental health disorders in adolescents and young adults.

Parents, in particular, decide how much autonomy and responsibility to give children and how they spend their discretionary time. They also determine the levels of risk they perceive around them by how *they* choose to interpret 'threat' and 'risk' for themselves and, therefore, for their children.

We can't blame smartphones either. These are merely inanimate objects that require a human to operate them. How and how much children and teenagers use their screens is up to parents and teachers.

The conclusion, that what happens at home as well as elsewhere, is primarily responsible for the recent and rapid deterioration in the mental health of children and adolescents, is supported by further research by Jean Twenge and her associates. They found no relationship between levels of anxiety and depression in young people and other factors sometimes used to explain fluctuations in mental health, such as economic change, wars and other major world events. Twenge et al. report that anxiety and depression among young people were much lower during the last century (including periods covering the Great Depression, World War II and the Cold War) than they are today.[29]

Commenting on these findings, Peter Gray (introduced earlier) observes that the dramatic decline in the mental health of young people seems "… to have much more to do with the way [they] view the world than with the way the world actually is".[30] Once again, how children view the world is predominantly determined by how their parents, carers and teachers present it to them, rather than by factors outside adult control.

This, naturally, is good news, which confirms our earlier comments, that the psychological wellbeing of children is something parents can significantly enhance, specifically via their parenting style.

To reiterate, children's future mental health is directly influenced by how parents choose to raise them.

Positive parenting, as we define it, is essentially a set of strategies for preparing children for the road ahead. The strategies we recommend will maximise your chances of rearing happy, healthy and psychologically resilient children, who will become adults able to create a successful and fulfilling life for themselves and their own families.

Current trends in parenting are not helping children and where does this leave them? Clearly less able to navigate their world confidently and to achieve the rewarding future we so fervently desire for them.

Story: *The Birthday Present*

Years ago, our elder son Hugh attended a birthday party for a school friend. When we arrived, we asked Hugh to greet his friend and give him his birthday present, a jigsaw.

The friend's father, who was with his son, took one look and in a crest-fallen voice said, "Oh! He's already got that one", in a tone of voice which suggested that receiving a duplicate gift was clearly upsetting, and that he and by extension his son were disappointed.

His words and body language all conveyed that this was a bad thing which should not have happened, and which should result in him and his son being unhappy. His son looked suitably dissatisfied and turned away, without accepting the present or thanking Hugh.

ấấấ

This is a classic example of a parent trying to prepare the road for his child rather than the other way around.

Here was an opportunity for a father to help his son ignore a minor setback or disappointment, similar to many he will encounter in the future, to smile and thank his friend who, through no fault of his own, had brought a duplicate jigsaw. In other words, to display the courtesy expected of a successful host. Such behaviours, which reflect respect and genuine empathy for others, are important accomplishments of character which this boy would need to successfully manage interactions with others when he was an adult.

Instead, what did he learn?

1. **To feel bad about anything, however trivial, that impacts, however slightly, on his wellbeing; in other words, that even a small setback should automatically be associated with negative emotions.**
2. **That his emotions are the result of others' words and actions rather than choices he makes for himself.**
3. **That his feelings take automatic precedence over those of others, the gift giver's embarrassment, for example.**

4. **That it is acceptable to be discourteous and disregard others if he has been disappointed in some way.**

That is a lot of unhelpful lessons to take from a 30 second interaction!

All his father had to do was smile and, ignoring the mix up, encourage his son to simply accept the present, say 'Thank you" and invite our boy to join the party. Unfortunately, he did none of these things.

As we have mentioned before, provided this was an isolated incident and uncharacteristic of how the father and son normally responded to a minor 'bump' in the road it would not be worth mentioning. But repeated lessons of this kind will leave a child vulnerable to mental illness because every minor setback – not to mention major ones – is regarded as a 'problem' which must inevitably arouse distressing emotions. In addition, their failure to learn empathy for others will mean that future interactions are likely to be more difficult than they need to be, further contributing to their unhappiness.

You may that think that we are reading far too much into what was, after all, a very trivial incident. But this is the stuff our lives are made up of. Genuine life, or rather, character changing events are few and far between. Rather character or personality is moulded over time through countless experiences of this kind and, in particular, how children are taught to handle them.

Just because they happen all the time doesn't mean they are unimportant. In fact, they are priceless opportunities to influence how your child grows – to assist them develop the accomplishments of character most likely to bring them true happiness and success in the future.

Bullying and Intimidation

As we have noted, hurt feelings and disappointments are increasingly regarded by parents and educators as evils to be avoided rather than lessons in living.

Too often what used to be considered as childish disputes – to be resolved by children themselves – are now labelled as incidents of 'bullying' or 'intimidation' to be reported to the relevant authorities and addressed via a formal review process. These are not healthy developments.

We are not implying that real bullying does not occur nor that it should be ignored. What we are suggesting is that overusing this approach to unpleasant, but normal, interactions between children, will artificially raise their awareness of 'risk' in their world and the level of anxiety they experience as a result. It may also encourage them to believe that almost any hurt or upset should be reported to and addressed by a third party rather than being resolved by themselves.

While there is considerable disagreement in the literature regarding the prevalence of peer on peer bullying and intimidation in schools, it is recognised as a serious and worldwide problem. And so it should be.

Bullying and its modern variant cyber bullying can produce short and long-term impacts for perpetrators as well as victims. These include lower school attendance and performance as well increased risk of psychological illness, suicide and criminal offending.[31] Everyone, children and teenagers included, should have the right to attend school or go anywhere else without being harassed or victimised.

What is Bullying?

Bullying is generally defined as aggressive, intentional acts – verbal, physical or social – which occur repeatedly with the intent to harm a victim or victims who cannot easily defend themselves.

Traditionally bullying has been face to face but with the rise of internet technology cyber bullying is now also recognised as a serious issue.

Three conditions are necessary in order to define aggressive behaviour as bullying: repetition, intentionality and an imbalance of power between bully and victim.

Behaviours that do *not* constitute bullying include:

- Mutual arguments and disagreements (where there is no power imbalance).
- Not liking someone or a single act of social rejection.

- One-off acts of meanness or spite.
- Isolated incidents of aggression, intimidation or violence.[32]

When we look at what constitutes bullying and what doesn't it is easy to understand why children, and many parents, are unsure whether or not to report a specific incident and why the available data should be treated with caution.

Certainly, it is important that children understand that bullying is targeted aggression against one or more people, which is repeated over time and directed particularly at those less powerful than the perpetrator(s).

If they understand these basic points, they will find it easier to distinguish between acts of genuine bullying which are beyond their capacity to address, and should be reported, and the far greater number of individual incidents of nastiness (of the type listed above) which occur daily in schools.

However, it is notoriously difficult to establish accurate data regarding the incidence of bullying, either because children are reluctant to report being bullied or because they report behaviours which don't fit the definition of bullying. Either way the data become skewed.

One of the most comprehensive data sets available (US National Centre for Education Statistics) estimates that in 2016-17 about 20% of US school children (12-17) were bullied.[33]

In contrast, one meta-analysis of 80 studies found that the proportion of students who reported being bullied at school ranged between 9% and 98%! The same study estimated that the average rate of bullying in schools was 35% for the face to face variety and 15% for cyber bullying.[34]

The wide range in the incidence of bullying in different schools reported in this study suggests we should exercise caution when interpreting the results of available research.

Perhaps, not surprisingly, the Australian data also present a mixed picture.

Hymel & Swearer (2015) estimate that 32% of Year 5 and 29% of Year 8 students experience frequent bullying (every few weeks) in Australian schools. They also note that bullying peaks between the ages of 12 and 15 and then tends to decrease by the end of high school.[35]

Data from another recent study suggest that bullying in Australian schools may be less prevalent.

The Young Lives Matter Report, introduced in Chapter 1, asked Australian children and adolescents to confidentially share their experience of bullying. Just under 25% of 11- to 17-year-olds reported being bullied every few months or less often while a further 10% said they were bullied every few weeks or more. Once again younger teens (11-15) were more likely to have experienced being bullied than their older peers (16-17).[36]

The Australian Government website, Bullying No Way!, a joint initiative of State and Federal governments, as well as Catholic and Independent schools, rightly urges caution when looking at data on this topic. The authors emphasise that the prevalence of bullying can be artificially inflated by over-reporting just as it can be underestimated if children who are genuinely bullied are reluctant to report it.[37]

Exaggerated Perceptions of Risk

Understanding the true incidence of genuine bullying is vital, otherwise there is a real danger that children (and their parents) will over-report the prevalence of bullying and thereby unrealistically inflate their perceptions of risk in their school environment.

We have already highlighted the influence of safetyism in Western nations, which may lead parents of iGen children to be unnecessarily risk averse and to reduce rather than expand the degree of autonomy and independence they are willing to afford even older teenagers. And we have also discussed the baleful consequences of this trend for children's psychological health.

The impact of safetyism may also be leading iGen children and their parents to be oversensitive to the risk of them being bullied at school, in the same way that fears for children's wider safety have grown even though our cities and towns have become demonstrably safer.

This, in turn, may encourage over-reporting because children and their parents confuse occasional disagreements, random spitefulness, or even ongoing aggression, where there is no imbalance of power, with genuine bullying.

The potential for over-reporting becomes even more apparent when we look at a breakdown of bullying behaviours.

Australian data report hurtful teasing as the most common form of bullying followed by spiteful rumour spreading.[38] This is consistent with data provided by the US National Centre for Education Statistics which indicate that in 2016-17, 13% of US students reported being made fun of, called names or insulted, 13% being the subject of rumours, 5% being pushed, shoved, tripped, or spat on, and 5% being excluded from activities on purpose.

A slightly higher percentage of boys report physical aggression (6%) than girls (4%), whereas the reverse is true for rumour mongering (18% vs. 9%) and social exclusion (7% vs. 4%).[39]

We know that children are not always very nice to each other. Regular arguments, insults and malice are common features of school life. Learning to manage these on their own or with peers, without adult intervention, teaches children self-confidence as well as how to at least tolerate people they don't like.

The varied nature of verbal abuse, both in terms of frequency and intensity, can make it very difficult to clearly distinguish between what is genuine bullying and what is unexceptional, if unpleasant, child and adolescent behaviour.

The definition provided above allows us to identify clear cut examples of bullying, but there is also a rather large grey within which the distinction between genuine bullying and non-bullying aggression can be confused, most commonly among younger and/or anxious children.

Our concern is that, within a growing culture of safetyism, there is a danger that in some schools at least the incidence of bullying is being systematically over-reported. This may then lead to unnecessarily heightened anxiety and excessive 'risk' aversion among children and their parents.

Once again, let us be clear. We are certainly not denying that bullying in schools is a real and present problem.

Victims of bullying report having fewer friends and lower peer acceptance. They also, not surprisingly, record higher levels of depression and anxiety together with lowered self-esteem.[40, 41]

Schools around the world are mounting major bullying prevention programs and research supporting these is beginning to identify major risk factors for children who are bullied.

Essentially, children who are shy, more anxious, and more socially isolated – who lack a strong friendship network – are predominantly the target of genuine bullying.

Interestingly, a major review of studies of victims' backgrounds suggests that they are more likely to regard their home as being warm but also *overprotective* (italics added).[42]

This last finding is consistent with the argument made earlier that overprotective parents can leave their children more anxious and risk averse and less able to cope successfully, especially when faced with challenges or threats outside the home. This deficit becomes most apparent in the responses of such children to aggressive behaviour from peers, whether this is defined as bullying or not.

Being less confident, they find it more difficult to shrug off unintentional or deliberate rudeness, either with a smile or a retort, and are less able to assert themselves when engaged in common childhood disputes. Their very diffidence makes them more vulnerable to being targeted in the first place and their likely passive response may encourage the perpetrator to persist, thereby turning an isolated incident of harassment into real bullying.

Victims are not responsible for what is happening, but their social isolation and anxiety increase their chance of being harassed and, worse still, for this to continue.

How Parents Can Respond

As parents we can do a great deal to ensure that our children are not victims of bullying and have the confidence and courage to protect themselves and others. Once again this means providing a widening sphere of autonomy within which they develop the accomplishments of character which will enable them to successfully manage bullies on their own.

Among these are self-confidence, which includes the capacity to stand up for themselves without the need for adult assistance, respect for themselves, which means they do not accept a bully's assessment of them, and emotional control, which allows them to handle a difficult situation without resorting to abuse or violence.

Parents can also provide coaching lessons on how to respond to aggression respectfully but assertively. By practising these skills at home and using them at school they will quickly learn that bullies prefer 'softer' targets and at least leave them alone. It will also give them the confidence and skills to protect their less secure peers.

When considering verbal abuse from others, which is the most common form of bullying behaviour, it is tempting to reprise the oft repeated mantra from our own childhood: "Sticks and stones may break my bones, but names can never hurt me!"

This is true, provided parents teach children how to think about themselves and others in healthy, adaptive ways.

If your daughter desperately needs Mary's approval, but Mary is regularly rude to her, then what Mary says can hurt her deeply. If, on the other hand, her response to Mary's discourtesy is more nuanced she is more likely to manage Mary's rejection comfortably. She might say to herself and others, "I would prefer Mary to like me but if she doesn't that's okay. I am a valuable and worthwhile person whose happiness does not depend on what unpleasant people like Mary say about me." Or even better, "I feel sorry for Mary. To abuse other people like she does indicates she is unhappy herself. Maybe I can help her by trying to be friends, but if she rejects my offer that's okay too."

Your first reaction may be that these responses are too sophisticated for younger or even older teenagers to understand and use. You may be right, but we think you may also be underestimating your children's capacity to think adaptively, in ways beneficial to themselves and others. Why not try it and see? We discuss adaptive thinking in detail in Chapter 6.

Cyber bullying is both easier and harder to deal with. The easy way is to simply turn off the phone, but that is to deny children the positive benefits of staying in touch with their friends. It also does not necessarily mean that the bullying will cease. Online bullying may well continue and the victim, even if they have turned their phone off, will become aware of this when they see their friends at school or meet the perpetrator in person.

The best alternative is to instruct your children to ignore bullying by refusing to acknowledge or respond to it and by blocking or 'defriending' the bully wherever possible until they apologise publicly online.

From the perspective of this book, bullying or intimidation at school (or work) is just one of many challenges that your children may face along the road. Our review of the literature has reinforced an important theme of this work: overprotective parenting leaves a child more vulnerable to risk (real or perceived) and less able to achieve genuine independence. It also appears to increase the likelihood that they will be bullied.

Stepping in too often to protect children from 'harm', disappointment, or disapproval, rather than letting them plug away on their own for a bit longer, is to leave them ill-equipped to stand up for themselves now and in the future.

Removing minor bumps in their road when they are young is to fail to prepare them for the more significant obstacles they will encounter when they are older – and you are not around – and the consequences of not coping are more serious.

A Useful Habit

Here is a useful habit to promote positive parenting. Before you engage with your child or decide on their behalf – in other words before stepping in – ask yourself two questions: "Is what I am doing preparing my child for the road ahead" and "or simply smoothing their path to make their next few steps unnecessarily easy?"

If your answers to these questions are "No" and "Yes", respectively, or "Not sure", then defer your action until you can answer "Yes" and "No" with confidence. Also remember that preparing a child for the future may conflict with their immediate wishes and desires thereby producing a predictable response from them.

Managing these quite normal disputes calmly and confidently is yet another skill of positive parenting which is covered in Chapter 11.

Conclusion

Recent research has identified a number of factors which appear to be contributing to the documented increase in anxiety, depression and psychological distress in young people today in Australia and elsewhere.

These include 'paranoid' parenting, which reduces opportunities for them to learn independence, a culture of 'safetyism' which encourages a heightened and exaggerated awareness of 'risk', insufficient unsupervised time spent interacting face to face with friends, and excessive unsupervised use of screens.

Given that adults, and parents in particular, can influence all of these in a child's favour, it is fair to conclude that how we are raising our children is the root cause of most of their troubles.

Preparing a child for the road ahead means to equip them with the accomplishments of character they will require to successfully handle problems, adversity and disappointment (as well as success) on their own.

By making their current lives easier than necessary parents may be setting them up for a difficult future. They are literally robbing them of the capacity to embrace adult independence successfully. What is worse, a childhood like this may also increase the risk of them being bullied and/or developing one or more mental disorders.

Summary

- Shielding children from anything difficult or unpleasant which they can and should manage independently, or with a little help, is to infantilise them, to ensure they continue to behave like small children even as they grow. This, in turn, renders them incapable of managing adult independence.
- When parents step in too often, rather than hold back, children learn to expect and, indeed, demand, assistance when they should be managing on their own.
- When parents hold back, their children learn two important lessons: firstly, that some anxiety associated with trying something new on their own is normal and can best be overcome by pushing on; and secondly that their actions have consequences and to modify their future behaviour to anticipate and avoid most of the negative ones.
- Learned helplessness is the result of abandoning children in situations which are beyond their capacity to manage successfully. Wise parents are alert to the need to modify their responses in terms of stepping in or holding back according to the needs of the child and the nature of the task they are working on.
- A significant body of research suggests that much of the recent rise in teenage mental illness can be attributed to overprotective or 'paranoid' parenting, insufficient (unsupervised) time spent face to face with peers and overuse of screens.
- Social media appears to be unfortunately effective in triggering feelings of anxiety and depression among young teenagers. Because it is interactive, it facilitates cyber bullying and also encourages vulnerable teens to compare themselves negatively with idealised versions of others.

- How and how much children and adolescents use their screens should be the subject of regular discussion with parents. This is one area of parenting which requires close supervision from parents alert to the dangers of too much screen time.
- Overprotective parenting can leave children vulnerable to bullying by making them more anxious, more risk averse and less able to stand up for themselves.

5

Children Are Antifragile

"Don't handicap your children by making their lives easy."
Robert A. Heinlein (US author)

"It is easier to build strong children than to repair broken adults."
Frederick Douglass (African-American social reformer)

Antifragile is a brilliant concept developed by Nassim Nicholas Taleb in his book of the same title.[1] He suggests that everything can be divided into three categories: those which are fragile and easily broken and therefore must be protected; those which are resilient or robust and immune to hard usage; and ones which are antifragile, that literally *require struggle and adversity in order to develop to their full potential.* In other words, something that is antifragile actually profits from a degree of pressure and the stress that comes with it.

Children are in the third category: both physically and psychologically, they are antifragile.

Taleb highlights the common misconception that the opposite of something fragile is robust. He emphasises that the true opposite of something that is fragile is not robust but antifragile.

A fragile object, such as a wine glass, is vulnerable to stress and must be cared for, while something that is robust is not affected by stress either way – neither damaged nor improved – like a plastic cup. Anything that *benefits* from stress, on the other hand, is antifragile. Furthermore, and this is important, while fragile items are at their best when protected, antifragile ones *suffer* from overprotection and an absence of challenge.

This means that for the antifragile child, some modest degree of adversity or even harm is actually *good* for them and 'paranoid' parenting which wraps them in cotton wool is positively bad.

The human immune system is anti-fragile. Through repeated exposures to viruses we develop antibodies which builds our resistance; by fighting infection we become stronger. This is also the principle of vaccination; a small dose of pathogens creates a mild infection to build immunity which protects against a major bout of illness.

Lukianoff and Haidt, introduced earlier, emphasise that anything antifragile "requires stressors and challenges in order to learn, adapt and grow".[2]

These authors are adamant that treating children as if they are fragile – like a delicate cut glass ornament requiring constant protection and supervision – is a root cause of adolescent anxiety and depression. They conclude:

> Children are antifragile … [they] must be exposed to challenges and stressors (within limits, and in age-appropriate ways) or they will fail to mature into strong and capable adults able to engage productively with people and ideas that challenge their beliefs and moral convictions.[3]

We agree. Our previous discussion (in Chapter 3) about how children, when left to play unsupervised, deliberately seek out risk, suggests that intuitively they understand this as well. Children are antifragile and this has important implications for how they should be raised.

It suggests that rather than protect children from all hardship because of fears for their safety, parents should deliberately expose them to moderate levels of age related risk and the stress associated with it. Such exposure should be increased as they become older and more capable. In this way they will grow stronger and healthier, mentally and physically.

By using terms like stress or adversity we are obviously not suggesting that children should be verbally or physically abused, or deliberately harmed. In this context it is better to think of these terms as the moderate degree of physical strain associated with regular exercise and active play and the normal apprehension or uncertainty we all experience when entering a new situation, learning a new skill or solving a problem on our own.

Antifragility in Children

Most parents would agree that they want their children to be 'robust' or 'resilient'. But newborn babies are clearly neither of these. They must be protected from all manner of harm. While this is true, there is the danger that because they are not robust, we assume they are fragile, being unaware of the third category of antifragility.

A simple example of why this is important is how we respond to a crying child. If we regard them as fragile we believe that whenever they cry they must be hurting in some way and immediately try to sooth them, even if it is 3am and we have to be at work in five hours.

If, on the other hand, we understand that they are antifragile we can respond to a screaming child in their cot in a different way. If they are fed, dry and well then it is much more likely that they are crying because they are protesting (in the only way they know how) at being left alone, when they would rather be wrapped in a parent's arms, rather than because they are genuinely hurting in some way. In other words, they are grumpy rather than distressed.

Recognising children are antifragile means to understand their need for the discomfort of learning to sleep alone in order to grow towards independence and resilience, not merely because they can't sleep with their parents forever. This should give parents confidence to more often leave children to cry until they fall asleep, as they generally will, unless there is something genuinely wrong with them.

The alternatives are to either walk the floor with them half the night or allow them to continue to sleep with you well past the age when they need to have developed the confidence to sleep in another room, safe in the knowledge that their parents are close by and all is well.

We are not suggesting that you should never pick up a crying or screaming child. We discussed the need to address 'meltdowns' to ensure babies achieve secure attachment in Chapter 1. They need reassurance that they have not been abandoned.

But, once again, you need to steer a middle course between over and under protection. Once you have reassured yourself and your child that all is well then allowing them to cry themselves to sleep (particularly after the age of 2½-3) is an appropriate recognition that they are antifragile and need a degree of stress to continue to develop normally. With experience you will learn to distinguish between the cries of a child who is merely grumpy with those of one who is genuinely suffering.

If they are apprehensive about sleeping alone by the time they are due to attend pre-school, be ready for some spectacular displays of separation anxiety when you drop them off.

If your child does display separation anxiety – a degree of which is normal – when you, say, go out to a well-earned dinner with friends, the solution is (a) to acknowledge that they are anxious; (b) reassure them that they will be fine with their babysitter; (c) that you will be back later; and (d) leave. They will overcome their fears with the help of a good carer and very quickly begin to enjoy time apart from their parents.

If you are not careful, the consequence of continuing to regard your children as fragile, rather than antifragile, even as they grow, is to omit to expose them to challenges – and the stress that comes with these – that they need to flourish. We have met many parents who continue to do pretty much everything for their children long past the age where they could and should be managing for themselves.

Whether this is from habit or reflects their own need to remain 'relevant' to their offspring is not the point. What they are doing can have disastrous consequences for their children now and in the future.

A child who does not learn to manage their normal anxiety about trying something different or being in new surroundings, for example, is more likely to grow into an anxious and needy adolescent and adult.

Robustness and fragility are static qualities. Something fragile is permanently at risk from harm and something robust is impervious to harm, up to an extreme limit. Antifragility, on the other hand, is a dynamic quality.

Understanding that they are dynamic is the key to comprehending the true nature of children; they are designed to change, to struggle, and to grow as they interact with their world. But, like a plant, they can't grow properly unless they are nurtured in the right environment.

Unfortunately, too many parents regard the 'right' environment for a child as one which is devoid of expectations and responsibility and in which their path to the future should be kept as easy as possible. But the antifragile child *needs* (and benefits from) the progressive testing of their capacities because the experience of reasonable challenge *permanently* changes their nature for the *better* – they become physically and psychologically more resilient, a key accomplishment of character.

We have already reviewed research (see Chapter 1) suggesting that a child's environment will permanently change their neurological status. Discussing the impact of the interaction between the infant's rapidly developing brain and their environment, Cairns and Stoff conclude:

> It is necessary to go beyond the conventional notion that biological variables not only influence behavior and environment to the more modern notion that behavioral and environmental variables also impact on biology.[4]

In other words, it not simply inherited characteristics which determine how children respond to the world around them. Their environment, particularly how they are raised, permanently alters their physical and neurological development to determine which genetic predispositions (to depression or addiction say) emerge and which remain dormant. Their changed biology, in turn, influences their subsequent development in an ongoing reciprocal process.

An absence of challenge or, indeed, adversity in its environment means that something which is antifragile, including a child, will suffer a permanent loss of capacity. As Nassim Taleb emphasises, what is best for something fragile, avoidance of all difficulty and stress, is precisely the worst thing one can do with something that is antifragile.

What this means is that parents permanently weaken, even damage, the antifragile child by failing to expose them to age-related levels of expectation and associated discomfort as they grow (see story: '*I Can Jump Puddles*').

Story: *I Can Jump Puddles*

I Can Jump Puddles *is the title of an autobiographical novel written by Australian author Alan Marshall who was born in rural Victoria in the early 1900s. As a young child he contracted polio which left him partially crippled. His story is an inspiring account of his determination to lead a normal childhood, which included climbing trees, riding ponies, swimming, playing and laughing – as well as fighting – with his friends.*

Having not been told he was unable to do any of these things he went ahead and did them anyway, despite his disability. The role his parents played in this process, notably in their expectation that he would lead as normal a life as possible, was critical to his success and acknowledged in his book

His father built him a wheelchair and crutches and lifted him in and out of carts when he was young, but that was about it. He rode a horse to school, did his share of family chores and if he had a disagreement with another boy, he was expected to sort it out for himself.

In those days a disagreement between boys more often than not became a physical fight and young Alan was expected to fend for himself, despite needing a crutch to stand up.

In the light of the arguments already presented in this book, perhaps we should not be surprised that he grew up to be a highly competent and independent adult. His disability, because of the way it was managed by his parents, became a springboard for his career as a successful author, husband and father.

We can be confident that Alan Marshall's parents had never heard of the term antifragility, but they certainly knew how to raise an antifragile child!

The key point for us from this story is that Alan's parents accepted and respected their son as he was and then, with a few modifications, proceeded to place exactly the same expectations on him as they did on their other children. The fact that he was disabled was effectively irrelevant, as far as his family and hence his friends were concerned. He was not defined in terms of his disability, but treated pretty much as any other child. That this was priceless for him developing into a confident and popular adolescent is clear from his book.

These are lessons all parents can take from this story to apply to their own children: firstly, accept and respect children as they are; secondly, avoid defining them in terms of (what you perceive to be) their shortcomings or 'disabilities', so that you treat your whole child as a 'problem' to be 'managed' or 'solved'; and, thirdly, regardless of where they are starting from, continue to expect and encourage them to become all they are capable of. We return to this important discussion in Chapter 12.

The suggestion that children are antifragile is consistent with our earlier recommendation that they be given time and space to wrestle with a reasonable level of challenge and risk without adult intervention. It is the struggle itself, regardless of the outcome, which enables a child to develop accomplishments of character – a positive identity, self-confidence, emotional control and resilience – which are integral to mental health and required for success as an adult.

By providing limits of discretion, or a sphere of autonomy, within which children are encouraged, indeed required, to act independently, you will provide the stimulus their antifragile nature requires for them to achieve resilience and realise their true potential as people. This point cannot be overemphasised.

In the absence of ill health, children are neither delicate nor fragile, but nor are they robust. They are antifragile. If they are to develop into mature, competent and resilient adults they *must* experience the pressures and discomforts associated with learning new skills, solving problems and meeting deadlines on their own.

Just as the test of regular exercise is vital for healthy physical development, normal psychological growth requires them to experience the temporary and mild unease or tension that comes from coping with the difficult or unfamiliar.

An important skill of positive parenting is to expose children to both types of expectation without allowing them to become overwhelmed.

Physical Health

The benefits of physical exercise are well established. Inactive children are more likely to become inactive, overweight adults, putting them at risk of developing life-threatening conditions, including heart disease, diabetes and cancer.

But the payback from regular exercise goes well beyond physical health. It is also associated with better concentration, improved academic performance, lower stress and greater self-confidence.[5, 6]

In addition, team sports teach children how to socialise and how to cooperate with and, indeed, respect, people they may not particularly like. We don't need to remind you that these accomplishments of character – grace, respect and empathy – are also useful attributes for working in a modern organisation.

Unfortunately, there is evidence that modern parents need to lift their game with regard to children's physical health.

The Australian Institute for Health and Wellbeing reports that, in 2017-18, 25% of Australian children and teens (aged 2-17) were either overweight or obese. What is more interesting is the trend data. When we look at changes since 1995 we see that something surprising has happened.

Between 1995 and 2007-08, the incidence of overweight or obese children in the 5 to 14 age group increased from 20% to 25% before flattening out to remain at 25%. In other words, the chances of children in this age group being overweight or obese increased by a quarter in 14 years and then remained constant.[7] What is going on here?

Factors likely to have contributed to the rapid increase between 1995 and 2007-08 include a diet biased towards excessive fat and sugar plus an unhealthy balance between physical and sedentary activities. That no further increases since 2007-08 appear to have occurred in this cohort (5-14) suggests that parents and schools are beginning to push back a little.

But when we look at the data for Australians between 15 and 24, we see a slightly different story. This older group were also more likely to be overweight or obese in 2007-08 than they were in 1995, just like the 5 to 14-year-olds. However, unlike their younger peers, they *continued* to put on weight between 2007-08 and 2017-18. For the former (5-14), as noted above, no further increase was recorded after 2007-8.[8] Why the difference?

This older cohort, adolescents and young adults aged 15-24, of course, represents the first wave of iGen'ers. The youngest of them, born in 1995, reached fifteen years of age in 2010 and entered adolescence as internet-based technology became widely available and a smart phone a must have possession for every teenager.

You will recall that US data cited by Jean Twenge confirm that iGen adolescents spend less time on homework, paid work, volunteering, sports and extra-curricular activities than earlier generations. In addition, the bulk of the time saved is devoted to their screens, in particular social media. It is quite likely that a similar picture emerged in Australia at the same time.

If this is the case, then it is tempting to postulate a causal link between the continued weight gain of 15 to 24-year-old Australians between 2007-08 and 2017-18 and a decrease in physical exercise in this age group occasioned by the growing popularity of screen-based activities.

Also, overweight teenagers and adults may find it harder to lose weight if they were also overweight children.

We can only speculate why a similar increase between 2007-08 and 2017-18 was not observed among younger children aged 5-14. The most likely reason is that by 2008 the parents of these children (and their schools) were more alert to the dangers of childhood obesity, having been exposed for longer to concerns expressed in the media and elsewhere, as more data became available.

In recent years, Australian schools have made considerable progress introducing healthier food options and more exercise on campus. Parents of the older cohort may have been similarly aware of the need to act, but it is easier to manage a child's weight than a teenager's because parents can exert greater control over what younger children eat and drink.

Nevertheless, it is important that you persevere in encouraging children at any age to remain active and maintain a balanced diet. You can continue to influence these while they are at home through your own example, as well as by closely monitoring the food available to them in the fridge and limiting the amount of money they have to spend at fast food outlets.

Not only is this important for their future physical wellbeing as adults but, as we have seen, physical and mental health are two sides of the same coin; to be fully psychologically healthy children must also be physically fit.

Raising Antifragile Children

Without an opportunity to struggle with the difficult, the unfamiliar or the risky (qualified by age), children remain immature; unwilling, because they are unable, to tackle problems and setbacks on their own and hence frightened to grow up. And such children are also more at risk of being bullied at school and developing symptoms of mental disorder.

With the passage of time they become immature adults who need constant reassurance and are afraid of the future. They refuse to accept the responsibilities of adulthood, although they may well demand the privileges. To complete this dismal picture, they may often blame others, especially their parents, for their situation.

Having never learned to cope independently, they take it for granted that someone else, their partner for example, is responsible for their happiness and wellbeing and for smoothing the road in front of them.

In this context, Nassim Taleb is most critical of overprotective parents who shield their children from risk of any kind. He concludes, "... those trying to help are often hurting us the most."[9]

It is the responsibility of parents to ensure children experience age-related levels of physical and psychological pressure in measured doses. You need to steer a middle path between being overprotective, which denies them the freedom to stretch and test themselves, while avoiding overwhelming them with unrealistic performance expectations.

You will not always get this right. There will be times when you will take over, or step in unnecessarily, perhaps when you have limited time or are tired or distracted. There will also be occasions when you expect too much and overestimate a child's current levels of competence.

But, as a rule, it is better to err on the side of expecting too much rather than too little, provided you remain alert to the danger of overloading which can lead to learned helplessness.

Understanding that your children are antifragile and raising them accordingly will go a long way to ensuring they develop the accomplishments of character presented in Chapter 2, including self-confidence, persistence, positive identity, competence and resilience.

We have already discussed one of the key tools for raising antifragile children: creating a sphere of autonomy within age-related constraints in which they are expected to exercise their discretion free of adult interference.

As we have seen, a good example of creating a sphere of autonomy is 'free' play. This provides regular opportunities to interact with peers on their own (preferably outdoors) during which they decide what to do, make their own rules and resolve their own squabbles and so on.

As they get older, 'free' play becomes going shopping or to the movies with groups of friends. It can also include all day hiking or overnight camping without parents, or indeed any adult, provided they are capable. You might drop them off and agree on a pickup place and time as well as emergency procedures, but after that leave them to it.

Once again, adventures like hiking and camping can be offered in measured doses starting with simple and safe tracks of short duration accompanied by a parent, before proceeding in stages to genuine independent bush trekking.

Positive parenting aims to nurture the antifragile child by continuing to extend their capacity to manage independence competently without an adult having to be there all the time to keep them out of trouble. And you can do this by regularly broadening the constraints you place on their autonomy. In the process they will also acquire maturity as an accomplishment of character, to make wise choices and to do 'what is generally best' when you are not around.

'I Don't Like Arguing'

Raising an antifragile child also extends to teaching them how to interact effectively with others.

How often have you met an adult whose response to a conversation in which even mildly differing points of view are expressed is either to become anxious or refuse to engage in such discussions altogether?

One of us has observed this often in seminars – participants who become anxious when asked a question and are reluctant to express their opinion about even relatively uncontentious subjects. A minority even become hostile when asked to comment, which suggests that they are insecure in some way. Why is this?

We believe it is because they have never learned how to engage in respectful debate, to be comfortable with civil disagreement, and to express their opinions calmly and confidently while exploring another person's point of view with thoughtful questions and comments.

Having little experience of civilised discussion, they confuse it with 'arguing' – a bad thing characterised by negative emotions and perhaps personal abuse – and become uncomfortable when points of view alternative to their own are exchanged.

If this has been their only exposure to disagreement as a child, perhaps it is not surprising that they prefer to avoid it altogether. And if they have been raised in a family and schools in which they have been insulated from 'offensive' ideas or behaviours, they may also become anxious when confronted by confident people who speak their mind and express opinions that differ from their own.

What is worse, as we have suggested, is that their anxiety may be expressed as hostility; they may become intolerant of others' preferences or points of view.

A person who regards as offensive any comment or behaviour, however respectful or thoughtfully expressed, but which falls outside what they have been taught to believe is 'acceptable' or 'right', will be seriously disadvantaged as an adult. At work they may be less willing to listen without interrupting or to express their disagreement appropriately when required.

In addition if they are disinclined to listen, while also insisting on their right to express an opinion, they are in danger of becoming a bigot (see story: "*You're Racist!*").

Story: "*You're Racist!*"

A father of our acquaintance was having dinner at the home of his adult son and Vietnamese Australian daughter-in-law. A highlight of the meal was phÕ (beef noodle soup) with cold rolls, both common Vietnamese dishes.

When offered a serving our acquaintance refused the soup saying he had had it before and didn't like it. Whereupon his son literally said to him, "You're racist"! The son's wife, interestingly, was not in the least offended.

The son's comment of course provoked furious denials from his father and the meal finished quickly in an awkward silence.

It is hard to know how to respond to this story, which has been changed in many of the details but in essence is correct. If we didn't happen to know that it is true, we would never have believed it.

Here we have a perfectly intelligent adult man using one of the worst types of insults to describe his father simply for expressing his culinary preferences!

To say the son's comments were lazy and ignorant doesn't even begin to properly describe them. However, they are an indication of where failure to raise children in an atmosphere of respectful and open disagreement can lead.

You may argue that there were other aspects of the father's behaviour, perhaps displayed in different circumstances, which concerned his son and were reflected in his exasperation. You may be correct, but we are unaware of any. Either way this does not alter the inappropriate and offensive nature of the son's comment within the context in which it was made.

A society in which people are unable to express their personal thoughts and preferences in a respectful manner without being abused can hardly be described as civilised. Hopefully this incident was isolated and unusual, but there are disturbing signs that they are becoming commonplace in Australia, particularly in the anonymous world of Twitter and other social media platforms.

As an addendum to this story, one of us recently consulted a mother and her little boy who busied himself colouring in a square while his mother described his symptoms. The colour he chose was black. When he had finished he showed his mother and asked, much to her and our astonishment, "Is this racist?"

Once again if we couldn't personally vouch for the truth of this story we would not believe it. To us these stories suggest that pejorative adjectives like 'racist', which were originally used to describe a very specific set of attitudes and behaviours, are now applied indiscriminately and completely inaccurately, even in junior primary school. The prospects for civilised discourse in the future are not promising.

Important to raising an antifragile child is to engage them, as early as possible, in robust conversations in which they are encouraged to express their own opinions as clearly as they can as while also listening respectfully to what other people are saying.

The only rules should be no shouting, no personal abuse and no interruptions when another person is speaking. Everyone in the family, from the youngest to the oldest, should be given opportunities to speak without fear of being ridiculed or shouted down.

And when children do speak up it is important to recognise their contribution regardless of whether you agree with them or not. This will encourage them to continue to engage in current as well as future discussions.

We have already noted a rising culture of safetyism in Australia and elsewhere which has expanded to include protecting children from emotional discomfort or distress caused by ideas different from their own. Quite obviously, if children are 'rattled' by people who disagree with them, this will be a major impediment to their future progress at school and work.

This will not occur if they have become used to holding their own in discussions around the family dinner table. This is precious time when, free of the distractions of phones and laptops, the whole family discusses the topics of the day.

If you disagree with or are concerned by the opinions expressed by your children, you can encourage them to examine their own point of view by asking further questions and clearly stating what you believe and why.

This will assist them clarify their own values and beliefs and contribute to their capacity for independent thinking, an accomplishment of character which is part of a positive identity.

However, insisting your children agree with you is futile and likely to stifle further discussion. By challenging their ideas respectfully, you will help them develop their own and broaden their understanding of any issue, even if you never get them to agree with you.

If the conversation becomes disrespectful it is time to intervene and insist on courteous disagreement. What your children believe and say is less important (they may well believe something else tomorrow) than that they learn two things.

These are, firstly, to feel comfortable in an environment of conflicting ideas and forthright opinions and, secondly, to be able to respectfully express their opinion, even if the rest of the room disagrees with them – accomplishments of character which include self-confidence, respect, positive identity and emotional control.

Why is this important? Well, for several reasons, the first of which is that thinking hard about what they want to say and how best to present their case is exactly the type of cognitive pressure antifragile children need to develop intellectually as far as they can go.

Secondly, they will also learn more by carefully listening to ideas different from their own. Thirdly, they will avoid the trap of believing that only they can be right and that no one else has anything useful to contribute to problem solving or decision making – insights characteristic of mature adults.

Finally, good employers value staff who are not afraid to contribute to a professional debate without becoming angry or abusive.

"I Wish I Had the Courage to Speak My Mind"

But perhaps the most important reason for encouraging children to speak up confidently comes from Bronnie Ware, whom we introduced earlier.[10] You will recall that she recorded the five most important regrets her dying patients confided to her during their last days. Number three on her list is: "I wish I had the courage to express my feelings and speak my mind."

This suggests that too many people have spent their lives censoring their own thoughts and words in order not to 'offend' others. In the process they have sacrificed the opportunity to become the person they would have preferred to be. The best time for us to learn the courage and skills to speak our mind is at home when we are children.

Parents can do a great deal to ensure that their children don't have this regret. If we encourage them to speak up, they may have more disagreements with others, and lose a few friends along the way, but they will also live more fulfilling and satisfying lives.

We are not suggesting that you turn your evening dinner into a seminar, although this can be fun. The key point is that all family members are encouraged and expected to participate in conversations about the affairs of the day and to contribute their own thoughts.

We found a good way to help get a conversation started was to ask each of our children what they had learned that day and what the others thought about it. To reiterate the topic under discussion is less important than getting everyone engaged.

Who is the best popular music star, and why, are likely to be of more interest to children and teens than what the Treasurer had to say about the economy on TV, that discussion can come later.

It goes without saying that you will want your children to do most of the talking; you will probably have done more than enough at work. The worst thing you can do is to subject them to a monologue about your favourite 'hobby horse', the contents of which they will ignore, but a bad habit which they may well acquire themselves.

You can also reinforce these lessons from home by encouraging them to participate in debating and public speaking activities at school or, if they prefer, acting. These are all activities which build a willingness to speak up, no matter who is listening – accomplishments of character which include self-confidence and positive identity.

Coaching

In making the case that the antifragile child needs to stand on their own feet, we are *not* proposing that you should never help your children or that there will not be times when it makes sense for you to take over and act or decide for them.

Your aim should be to have them independently manage a task or problem to the limit of – and a little beyond – their current abilities before you step in.

You can do this by encouraging them to keep persisting until it is clear they require more training or confidence, or even the required physical strength to manage successfully on their own. Then target where they are struggling with a coaching session.

For example, they may know how to make a phone call but be unsure how to hold a conversation with an adult to make an appointment or ask for information. You can address this by role playing a series of 'telephone calls' in which they 'make the call' while you play being the person at 'the other end'. Then ask them to make a real call with you on hand to coach them further if necessary.

During coaching sessions of this kind, children learn some enduring life lessons: that anxiety associated with trying something new quickly fades if they tackle it with enthusiasm; that the disappointment that comes with 'failure' is temporary, provided they persist; and that successive 'failures' are the only true way to independent success.

The word 'failure' should be handled with caution, hence our use of inverted commas. Thomas Edison (a famous inventor and founder of the US firm General Electric) pointed out that when an experiment 'failed', he merely succeeded in learning what didn't work!

Ideally your children will come to understand failure in the same way, merely as stepping stones to ultimate success. Persistence, or persevering at something difficult but worthwhile, is an accomplishment of character that all children need, if only because it is the only way for human beings to ultimately become the people they are capable of being.

If they do learn persistence, then over time your children will genuinely surprise you with what they can achieve, but only if you give them a chance, only if you provide gradually expanding limits of discretion and praise their efforts while leaving them to cope on their own as much as possible.

To repeat, stepping in and taking over from children, while they have further capacity to go on alone, ignores the fact that they are antifragile and robs them of a vital opportunity to achieve resilience. Unfortunately, taking over, in things large and small, is an easy habit for parents to acquire – time pressure alone will push you in this direction – and a hard one to lose.

As noted earlier, the best defence against stepping in or taking over unnecessarily is to keep asking yourself the questions, "Is what I am doing now really preparing my child for the road ahead or merely making their next few steps unnecessarily easy?"

More Useful Habits

Another is to develop habits of your own which will reinforce your preference for your children to take increasing responsibility for their own lives.

For example, as parents we found a useful response to a child wanting us to spell a word for them was to simply spell out the word 'dictionary' and leave it at that. This, of course, was in the days before spell check, but the point remains valid.

Other useful habits, in this case to reinforce good manners and respect for others, are to not respond to a request until they say "please" or let go of something they ask for until they remember to say "thank you". Once they understand the process, there is no need for you to speak; let them work out what is required for themselves. A searching glance from you will generally serve as a reminder.

Yet another is to respond with a question whenever your children come to you for help. Rather than simply fix their problem, ask them what they think they should do. This can be done by simply saying, "I'm not sure. What do you think?" You can then discuss the pros and cons of different courses of action and encourage them to decide. As well, when relevant, you can ask them to consider what would be best for others as well as themselves before they act.

The more you do this the less they will depend on you to sort out their own issues. As they got older, our children often declined to ask for help simply to avoid the inevitable conversation they knew this would entail! Eventually they came to us only when they were genuinely at a loss.

This saves you time but, more importantly, is necessary for them. Ultimately they will only seek help with major problems that they simply cannot resolve themselves. Try not to be disappointed that they no longer rely on you, rather be proud that they are becoming independent people.

We should also point out that asking children to step up and tackle life's challenges does not mean they cannot be happy. In fact, children are happiest when they are aware that they are learning new skills, creating new things and standing on their own feet.

Having fun with children is one of the great joys of being a parent and you should grab every opportunity. A great way to have fun is to put them in charge of a project, like cooking the dinner, while you become their assistant. Let them make the decisions and give you instructions rather than the other way around. You can even dress up in costumes suitable to your roles.

Time consuming? Yes! Messy? Yes! But also lots and lots of fun. A kitchen can be cleaned in minutes, but the memories of that evening and others like them will last all your lives. Experiences like this, in effect, 'teach' a child how to be happy.

So please don't think that what we are advocating is a succession of stressful interactions with your child, which leave you both miserable as they try but fail to perform everyday tasks or solve an endless succession of problems on their own. On the contrary. Being happy and taking personal responsibility are not mutually exclusive, rather they go hand in hand.

Because children are antifragile, genuine happiness or contentment can only come through sustained effort as they tackle new challenges. For example, the effort to master a difficult skill, to face and manage situations which are new or intimidating, and to make decisions which they know to be right for them but may disappoint others, including their parents.

In the process they will develop accomplishments of character which include self-confidence, persistence, positive identity, emotional control, maturity and resilience.

Paying Attention

In the earlier discussion of work and play (Chapter 3) we emphasised the importance of public recognition.

Children and teenagers crave our attention, not least our praise. If they are not praised, they will get our attention in less attractive ways. A great deal of misbehaviour is precisely that, a child's unsophisticated attempts to get their parents' attention.

For most of us, attention of any kind, including physical punishment, is preferable to being ignored. Bessel Van der Kolk (introduced in Chapter 1) makes this point when he observes:

> Most human beings simply cannot tolerate being disengaged from others for any length of time. People who cannot connect through work, friendships or family usually find other ways of bonding, as through illnesses, lawsuits and family feuds. Anything is preferable to that godforsaken sense of irrelevance and alienation.[11]

Our lifelong desire to engage with others may well be an extension of our early need for attachment. In this context, we looked at research which suggests that mothers who ignore their babies are more of a threat to them, in terms of their longer-term psychological health, than those who are hostile towards them.[12]

For parents this is a very important insight as you can use children's need to be noticed to influence their behaviour in ways beneficial to them and others.

Attention in the form of praise is a key tool of positive parenting because when they are praised children feel good about themselves (just as we do) and are more likely to conform with your wishes and suggestions.

Praise also encourages them to persist in what they are doing. It helps them, particularly when they are struggling, to know that they are heading in a positive direction and what they are doing is good or right.

In this way, praise is integral to successfully increasing your expectations of children, reflected in widening limits of autonomy. As you encourage a child to try a little harder, praise for persevering, rather than criticism for failing, will preserve their self-esteem and sense of security and strengthen their confidence to keep trying.

Your positive attention and obvious love will inspire them to persist; they will learn the sense of satisfaction and contentment that comes from trying, failing and ultimately succeeding so that persisting in the face of obstacles becomes an accomplishment of their character and a habit for life.

Happy children are not those who have all their difficulties resolved for them, but rather those who receive regular encouragement from their parents and others, for trying to perform a little better, or for facing appropriate risk or challenge, wherever they are on the learning curve.

We have already stressed that carefully targeted praise and attention is an important habit of positive parenting. For instance, when children are contributing to a group task, however ineffectually, trying to master a new skill, whether they are succeeding or not, or simply recognising the needs of others around them.

Attention from parents is critical because it serves to socialise infants into their family and later the wider community. The signals they receive – positive or negative – via the attention of adults and peers are vital for teaching them how to interact successfully and profitably in their world.

Happy children, and this is very important, are also happy because they have been taught, if necessary through discipline, to interact successfully with others. Because of this they have friends, enjoy socialising, and are welcomed into other people's homes. For this reason, attention is more than simply praise.

Positive parenting also requires timely and measured interventions when children are being socially unpleasant or alienating those around them. If parents don't teach children how to attract attention in socially acceptable ways, other people, young and old, will quickly learn to shun them. They will become adults who struggle to develop and maintain mutually rewarding relationships. Even their parents will ultimately find it easier to ignore them.

What is worse, in the absence of positive attention, they will attract the negative variety through anti-social behaviour, the consequences of which – particularly when they are adults – will merely compound their unhappiness.

Children are not always pleasant or respectful towards others which means that appropriate and reliable intervention must also become an established habit for parents who wish the best for their offspring. Compassionate discipline, discussed in Chapter 10, is the core of positive parenting.

Please note that we are not saying that you should never indulge your children with pure pleasure, such as throwing a birthday party where they are the focus, taking them to Disney World or giving them desired possessions. These can be memorable events which both children and parents cherish forever. We are merely saying that a childhood of unalloyed pleasure is as damaging in its own way as one of genuine deprivation, and both are a poor preparation for independent adulthood.

The Narcissistic Personality

We have emphasised the importance of praise and recognition for promoting psychological health in children. However, we have also noted that the recognition you provide should be carefully targeted to promote character development.

Parental praise should be judicious and appropriate. By this we mean that children should be recognised for genuine effort, observable improvement, and consideration for others (for example), not merely told that they are 'wonderful' or 'special' regardless of how they behave.

It is important that children feel special, but this should be achieved by clearly linking the praise they receive to the progress they are making towards acquiring new competencies or achieving personal maturity, rather than providing them with relentless positive affirmation for simply being who they are.

Indiscriminate and unearned approval can be as damaging for children as little or no attention. Parents who put their children 'on a pedestal' and lavish them with undiscerning praise put them at risk of developing narcissistic personality traits, which include an inflated sense of their own importance, feelings of superiority with regard to others, and a tendency to overrate their capacities.[13]

Having received an undiluted diet of admiration from their parents during their childhood, adult narcissists become defensive when criticised, may have difficulty relating to others as equals, and are prone to anxiety and depression when their actual achievements fail to match their exaggerated expectations of themselves.

Unfortunately, there is some evidence, that the incidence of narcissism in young people and adults has been rising inexorably in recent years. One study, conducted by Jean Twenge and a colleague, found that, in 2007, 70% of US college students scored higher in narcissism than the average college student in 1982.[14]

This last finding suggests that modern parents may be falling into two errors: overindulging their children with lavish praise, which is disconnected from how they actually conduct themselves, as well as being less prepared to discipline when necessary.

So praise and recognition are clearly necessary for raising psychologically healthy, happy children. But it is most important that these are used to encourage preferred accomplishments of character rather than being given to children whether they deserve it or not.

Regularly hearing that they are special, as well as more important and/or better than others, for no reason other than the fact they are yours, is to put children at risk of developing a dysfunctional personality and being seriously disadvantaged when they are required to function independently of you.

Conclusion

Children are antifragile; they need pressure, physical and mental, and the stress that comes with it if they are to become all they can and want to be.

An absence of measured adversity can permanently weaken a child psychologically, just as a lack of exercise can permanently weaken them physically. Exposing children to stressors – sources of stress – in age related amounts will maximise their chance of becoming capable and resilient adults and minimise their risk of developing mental illness.

Raising an antifragile child requires parents to continue to widen their sphere of autonomy, to expect him or her to accept increased responsibility and to insist they continue to test the limits of their capacities, even if what they are learning does not come easily.

It also includes encouraging them to express their own point of view respectfully but assertively, even if a majority of listeners may disagree with them.

Praise from parents should be carefully targeted to encourage the accomplishments of character which we have suggested are the keys to genuine happiness and lasting success for children. Indiscriminate praise can be unhelpful in its own way as no attention at all.

Summary

- Children are antifragile; they require challenge and adversity and the stress associated with these, in order to learn, adapt and achieve true resilience.
- What is best for something fragile, avoidance of all difficulty and pressure, is precisely the worst thing for an antifragile child; they are permanently weakened, indeed damaged, physically and psychologically, when parents fail to provide age relevant levels of expectations in terms of their behaviour and performance.
- Treating children as if they are fragile so that they are not tested and pushed, physically and mentally, as they grow, is a root cause of adolescent anxiety and depression.
- Antifragile children require regular physical and mental exercise if they are to discover what they are capable of and what is important and rewarding for them. Sport, art, part time employment, volunteering, in fact any extracurricular activity except

sitting on their bed looking at a screen, provide opportunities to stretch and strengthen the antifragile child.

- Children crave attention from parents and peers. The signals they receive teach them how to socialise with others effectively. If they don't receive positive attention for appropriate behaviour, they will attract your notice in less desirable ways.
- To be effective, praise and attention should be aimed at encouraging preferred accomplishments of character. Putting children 'on a pedestal' by lavishing them with indiscriminate admiration can lead to narcissism which will impair their chances of enjoying psychological health and future happiness.

6

To Think Is to Feel

"... for there is nothing good or bad but thinking makes it so."
Hamlet, Act 2, Scene 2
Shakespeare (English playwright)

"Children must be taught how to think, not what to think."
Margaret Mead (US cultural anthropologist)

Story: *Robert and Peter go to Gaol*

Robert and Peter, young men in their early 20s, were both gaoled for two years for dealing in illegal drugs.

Robert was an only child who was raised by his mother. He left school halfway through Year 11 and drifted into petty crime after struggling to find steady employment.

Peter was born into a stable two parent household and has a sister. He was a successful university student when he first became involved in drugs and began dealing, as he put it, "For the money." He received constant support from his family throughout his time in gaol and afterwards. During the same period Robert's mother remarried and lost contact with him.

Upon his release, Peter commenced a long period of unemployment interspersed with bouts of psychotherapy – generally unsuccessful – to help him 'cope'. He is a very angry, unhappy, and lonely man whose future looks decidedly bleak. He blames others, mostly his parents, for his predicament and seeks to punish them through his own behaviour for what happened.

In contrast, Robert, within weeks of his release, was self-employed in a new start-up business and moving in with a new girlfriend!

The story of Robert and Peter immediately raises an important question. Why should two young men react so differently to essentially the same experience?

On the surface, one would imagine that Peter, with his better education and family support, should have handled the experience of prison more easily than Robert, who was left to his own apparently limited resources. But the reverse is true. Why is this and what does it tell us about raising children?

One of us interviewed Robert a few weeks after his release. Regular psychotherapy was a condition of his parole. When asked what imprisonment was like his reply was impressive.

He said, "It was the best thing that ever happened to me – it's what I deserved. I learned to behave myself, keep my mouth shut and I got completely clean of drugs. I'm never going back to prison or drugs."

Peter, in contrast, as we have seen, was angry and bitter about his experience. He believed his sentence was 'ridiculous' because drugs 'should' be legal. He also emphasised that being sent to gaol was 'unfair' and that he should have 'got off' because he knew plenty of other people doing the same thing who were not caught. If he was punished so should they be.

He was angry with his parents and blamed them for his predicament because they 'should' have made him stop using drugs. His behaviour towards them is so abusive that they are debating whether to ask him to leave home, even though this would exacerbate his problems.

ঌঌঌ

The contrasting reactions of Robert and Peter to their experience of imprisonment tell us a great deal about how human beings create their own emotional life simply by how they interpret what happens to them.

Peter and Robert feel differently about their gaol experience because they each think differently about it. More specifically, they are using different sets of beliefs to interpret similar events which, in turn, determine their very different emotional responses to them. Quite simply, each is *creating* his own emotional experience and memories of gaol. To think really is to feel.

Learning to think in more adaptive ways, in order to reduce our experience of dysfunctional emotions, such as resentment, anger and envy, as well as anxiety and depression, is the key to achieving emotional control as an accomplishment of character.

In this chapter we explore how to endow children with this quality so that they are much less likely to experience a mood disorder in the first place and also far better equipped to manage effectively if one does emerge.

The Power of Belief

To begin let's examine the different attitudes or beliefs Robert and Peter applied to their time in gaol. Robert accepts that gaol has happened, cannot now be changed and, most importantly, takes personal responsibility for having been sent there.

While admitting he has made a mistake Robert does not regard himself as a failure or a worthless person because of what happened to him.

Peter, on the other hand, refuses to accept any responsibility. He believes that his predicament was the fault of others, that being gaoled wasn't 'fair' and that he has been persecuted because others dealing in drugs were not punished like him.

Because of the way he is thinking there is a real danger that Peter has defined himself in terms of this one, admittedly very difficult, experience. He regards himself as a victim, someone who has been badly treated and can't get an even break. Consequently he has low self-esteem, is distrustful of other people, and frightened of what may happen next.

The point here is not whether it is appropriate or even useful to send drug offenders to gaol (your opinion is as valid as ours) but rather the contrasting beliefs or mental 'frames' each man applied to being imprisoned. More importantly, these beliefs or frames are not inherited via DNA, nor are they fixed or unchangeable. Rather they are *learned* as children grow, first from parents and later teachers and friends, and, if necessary, they can change them.

Because patterns of thinking are learned parents can teach children emotional control, that is to think in healthy, adaptive ways to minimise their experience of negative feelings including anger, fear, anxiety and depression.

The beliefs, attitudes or interpretations we learn to apply to external events determine our emotional response to them. That is why people regularly display contrasting reactions to the same or similar events, getting laid off at work for example – some go to the pub and 'shout' the bar while others go home and sink into a deep depression. The first are excited about the new opportunities created by unemployment while the others obsess about the downsides including potential loss of income or status.

Robert and Peter have each used their pattern of acquired beliefs to create their own memory of custody, patterns which will continue to influence their thoughts, feelings and reactions to other events, particularly setbacks, well into the future.

By applying, consciously or unconsciously, contrasting beliefs to interpret what has happened each man is literally choosing how to feel about it as well. And it is worth repeating that you can teach your children to choose beliefs which produce healthier, less debilitating emotions.

Choosing healthier 'frames' or patterns of beliefs to apply to unpleasant or even disastrous events, in order to moderate how we feel about them, is the core of emotional control as an accomplishment of character. It is also central to adult maturity.

How we think not only determines how we respond emotionally to events but also what we learn from them.

Robert accepts that *he* is responsible for what happened and, therefore, has learned from his mistake ("I am never going back.") which will encourage him to make better choices in the future. Peter, in contrast, has chosen a different set of 'frames'. He blames others (the legal system, his parents etc.) and believes that they were at fault and not him. As a consequence, he appears to have learned very little to help him avoid something similar or worse in the future.

Their differing beliefs about themselves and their past mean that Robert sees himself as an active agent in what occurred whereas Peter regards himself as a victim. You will recall from Chapter 3 the importance to their mental health of children regarding themselves as autonomous individuals who believe that they can influence what happens to them. A sense of personal mastery, as we have seen, is necessary for achieving an internal locus of control and is part of the accomplishment of character we have called positive identity.

Acquiring a sense of personal control is, once again, ultimately a matter of deciding how to think (although it may not seem that way to a distressed teenager). By selecting beliefs (when appropriate) such as "I am responsible" or "That was my mistake and I am prepared to live with the consequences", children benefit in two ways: firstly, they profit from their mistake by learning how to avoid repeating it; and secondly, they develop feelings of genuine mastery, of being in charge of their own lives. In addition they are also less likely to experience chronic mood disorders which inhibit their capacity to recover from setbacks or pursue a happy and fulfilling life.

Accepting personal responsibility for much of what happens to them is liberating and uplifting for children; they feel better about themselves and are more confident that they can cope with whatever life has in store for them.

The Power of Language

Reflecting on the story of Peter and Robert it is also worth examining in detail the language each uses to describe their gaol experience.

Peter's comments are full of negatives and 'should' statements about what other people should or should not have done, that what happened to him was 'unfair', that he was 'victimised', and that prison 'should not' have happened. His language encourages him to believe, once again, that if bad things happen to him someone else is to blame and he has a right to be angry.

He wants to change the past to what he believes 'should' have happened. He also wants to change the present so that people around him do what he believes they 'should' do, in other words, what he wants them to do.

Robert is much less concerned about what others should or should not be thinking or doing. He is aware he has little or no control over these. He is focused on what he can control, namely his own thoughts and beliefs about the past and present, as well as his actions, now and in the future. He doesn't waste time blaming others but accepts responsibility for what he has done and so he can move on.

The contrasting impact of the respective belief patterns and language used by each man, on their current and future emotional lives, is profound.

Robert is ready and able to start a new, more successful, chapter of his life while Peter remains tied to the past by faulty, or maladaptive, language and beliefs and the negative emotions these generate. Consequently he continues to be depressed and angry, unable to start again, while Robert has accepted the past and is grateful for a second chance.

Encouraging Children to Think in Healthy Ways

An obvious question in the context of this book is how do parents encourage children to think (and hence feel) more like Robert and less like Peter?

We know from our discussion of the story of Oliver and Jane in Chapter 1 that we can't simply blame DNA for Peter's predicament and leave it at that. The environment each man grew up in and how they were socialised, will have determined what they now believe and the language they use to think and talk about tough times.

This, of course, gets us back to parenting.

Children are not born with an irrevocable set of beliefs or language to think about themselves or the world around them. They learn these firstly from parents and later teachers and peers. How they think, and therefore, how they feel – anxious or happy, depressed, or optimistic – is a product of what they are taught and how they are raised.

Promoting beliefs and language that are synonymous with emotional control is critical to your children's mental health and hence to positive parenting also. They will learn to use these by listening to your responses to adverse events as well through direct coaching and instruction. You teach children emotional control by encouraging them to select mental frames and language that foster healthy, adaptive responses to difficult experiences as well as by using these yourself.

Coaching should also include persuading them to take responsibility for what they have done or failed to do, accepting the consequences of this, and not allowing failure to define them or their future.

Children also learn emotional control when they are taught that past events, however unfortunate, cannot be changed; that to be content they must come to terms with the past, to be 'okay' with it, to acknowledge their mistakes and leave them behind. This does not mean that they forget what they have done but rather learn what they can from the experience, accept it for what it is, and then lay it to rest in their memory. Learning how to accept what now cannot be changed – "It is what it is and I'm OK with it"– is a crucial lesson of emotional control and fundamental to personal resilience.

The alternative for a child is to regularly revisit past errors and relive all the painful emotions associated with them as if they happened yesterday. This, as any psychologist or psychiatrist will tell you, is a primary cause of chronic anger, anxiety, and depression.

Once acquired, beliefs become unconscious 'frames' or mental habits which automatically channel our thinking and hence emotions in particular ways. This is why emotional responses can often seem to be involuntary, to spring ready made out of nowhere. But this is never the case. Feelings are always preceded by thinking, even though we are not always aware of the cognitive processes involved.

Beliefs and the emotions and behaviours which flow from them form strong self-reinforcing loops that can be very hard to break. When they are positive, they are a powerful force for building mental health and a successful life, but when negative they deliver harmful emotions and needless unhappiness.

Adaptive Thinking

The premise that our emotions, good and bad originate in learned beliefs and patterns of thinking, is central to the work of psychologist William James, a major figure in 20th century psychology.

It is also the foundational principle of most modern behavioural therapies, like Cognitive Behavioural Therapy (CBT) and Rational Emotive Behavioural Therapy (REBT), which are generally regarded as the most effective for treating mood disorders, including anxiety and depression, as well as personality disorders.

William James was a profound student of human emotions. Two of his aphorisms we believe should be pasted on every fridge door and discussed with every child. These are:

> *Thoughts become perceptions; perception becomes reality. Alter your thoughts, alter your reality.*
>
> *Most unhappiness is caused because people listen to themselves instead of talking to themselves.*[1]

The first of these observations essentially sums up what we have been saying about Robert and Peter. These men have each created quite different emotional realities by the way they have chosen to think about their time in prison.

This leads us to William James's second and even more interesting comment. What he is suggesting is that rather than simply listening to our existing internal dialogue (i.e. how we think) we should, where necessary, change it through deliberate self-instruction; that is, by talking to ourselves. By consciously changing how we talk to ourselves, and persevering until our new 'frames' become well learned habits, we come to think in healthier and more adaptive ways.

What children learn from others, particularly parents, may focus too often on negatives, such as fears of failing or being publicly embarrassed. James argues that they can, with your help, replace these negatives with something more useful. It is via their internal dialogue, or, if you prefer, private conversation with themselves, that they create their emotions, good or bad, using language and beliefs learned primarily from you as well as peers and other adults.

If a child believes, for instance, that she or he should be angry or distressed when someone does or says something they disagree with, it is not hard to understand why they would be frequently unhappy and dissatisfied with the world.

In this case, following James's recommendation, a parent would encourage them to replace – through coaching and self-instruction – this particular belief with an alternative that leads to healthier emotional responses.

For example, with your help they could work to replace their unhelpful belief about people who disagree with them with something like: "I believe it is important to listen calmly and respectfully to others' opinions, even when I disagree with them, because I want them to show the same respect towards me. Also I might learn something new."

Once this becomes a child's new default belief when dealing with people who disagree with them, they are likely to have fewer stressful interactions with others and they may well learn something new.

This process must start with parents. You provide children with examples of what to believe and how to respond every time you think 'out loud'. If from an early age your children hear you use adaptive beliefs and proportionate language they will, almost automatically, do the same. By the same token, if what they hear from you are destructive and emotionally charged patterns of thinking, then they will follow suit.

Through coaching you can gently challenge their thinking when you hear them applying unhelpful language and beliefs. At the same time encourage them to begin to talk to themselves and others in healthier ways about what is happening to them.

Irrational Beliefs

Albert Ellis, the founder of Rational Emotive Behavioural Therapy, pioneered the view that irrational (what we have called maladaptive) beliefs are the source of most negative emotions and, more specifically, most mood disorders, such as anxiety and depression. He developed a list of beliefs which, he argued, account for most of the unhappiness that people needlessly create for themselves.[2]

For example, Ellis suggests that to believe, "In order for me to be happy I must be loved and liked by everyone I know and it's awful if I'm not", is irrational because it is impossible to realise.

At least one person (and probably many more out there) does not like you and never will. And yet if you persist in believing that everyone should love or like you then you will be regularly disappointed when confronted with the reality – possibly quite frequently – that most people are indifferent towards you, and at least a few actively dislike you. A lifetime of stressful interactions with others is guaranteed.

Ellis would argue that unless a child learns to exchange a belief like this with something more rational and realistic, they will continue to suffer disappointment, anxiety and possibly depression because the world will consistently fail to deliver what they want. An alternative, more adaptive, belief might be "I would prefer that most people like me and will do my best to stay on good terms with them, but I realise that some won't for their own reasons and I'm okay with that". If this is what they believe they will be much more comfortable that they are not and probably never will be the most popular person in the room.

Children and adolescents (and often anxious adults as well) are particularly concerned about what others think of them. Parents can minimise the pain of rejection or indifference from others by teaching them to think adaptively. In this case the self-talk they must learn is:

"If Jeremy/Jonquil doesn't like me so be it. It's disappointing but I'm okay with it. There are plenty of other people to be friends with." By encouraging them to think in these terms rather than "This is awful/horrible" or "I am hopeless/a 'loser'", they will quickly learn to put unpleasant experiences like being occasionally rebuffed behind them.

A further example of an irrational belief coined by Ellis is "I must be successful at everything I do in order to be happy and feel worthwhile". This is irrational because no one can succeed all the time.

It also explains why, as we suggested in Chapter 2, the direct pursuit of success generally does not deliver happiness. If a child does believe this however, when they inevitably fail at something, they are likely to experience dark times. Not only will they feel sad but worse they will also feel ashamed of themselves since, because they have defined themselves in terms of 'success' alone, they may also believe that they are no longer worthy people.

In addition they may avoid future attempts to achieve something worthwhile because the anxiety they experience when contemplating possible failure is too painful.

Once again, you can help them to think more adaptively by suggesting alternative interpretations of failure such as: "It's nice to succeed, but any real success involves a degree of failure and *I'm okay with that*. I know if I persevere I will get better even if I'm never top of the class or the best gymnast in the school. I enjoy getting better and look forward to improving."

To summarise, a child's emotional experience is ultimately determined by the beliefs and language they choose to interpret their life experience. And their choices will generally be ones they have learned growing up, primarily from their parents. It is critical that they understand that they, and no one else, determines how they feel about what happens to them, regardless of the nature of the events themselves. Put simply they must learn that happiness is a choice in the same way as chronic anxiety and depression are *choices* rather than the product of forces outside their control.

This is true even of children with a genetic predisposition to a mood disorder. While they may experience more 'down' or 'difficult' periods in their life the intensity of any negative feelings they experience will be significantly reduced by their use of adaptive language and beliefs. This is why we argue that how you raise your children will directly impact their capacity to successfully manage mental disorder or psychological distress even if they do experience these. Acquiring emotional control as an accomplishment of character will equip them to better manage a mood or personality disorder as well other negative emotions – including anger, envy, resentment and jealousy– that we are all familiar with.

This is good news. It means that your children need not experience unnecessary fear or despair. You can, when required, change their emotional lives by helping them alter the way they talk to themselves; by teaching them to think differently and encouraging them to do the hard repetitive work (through persistent self-instruction) that is necessary to replace old unhelpful beliefs and language with more constructive alternatives.

"I Wish I Had Let Myself Be Happy"

We have already mentioned the five primary regrets Bronnie Ware learned from her dying patients.[3] The fifth is: "I wish I had let myself be happy."

Sadly, it is not until the very end of their lives that too many people come to realise that happiness is a choice and not something that is delivered through the achievement of wealth or status, or simply the product of luck. In other words, that they could have led happier lives regardless of their personal circumstances.

You can ensure your own children don't fall into this trap as long as you assist them to develop emotional control as an accomplishment of character; that is, to teach them how to manage their emotions by selecting appropriate beliefs and language, particularly when they are faced with difficult times. In effect you can teach them how to 'let themselves be happy'.

Learning Emotional Control

It is interesting to watch small children when they fall or bump themselves. Initially they may cry out from the shock but, if no one else notices or responds, they recover very quickly and continue playing unless they have genuinely hurt themselves. Rapid recovery usually happens when they are playing with peers of their own age who are not all that interested in their welfare but whose approval they desire.

However, if parents are present, especially those who react with an excess of solicitude to a child's every tumble, their response may be quite different. They will be well aware that making a fuss will reward them with a great deal of positive attention. In other words, they have learned how to modify their emotional response depending on who is present.

The danger, obviously, is that too much attentiveness from an overprotective parent will teach them that making a major fuss over every minor discomfort or disappointment is normal and appropriate – an expectation that they may well take with them into the future. This is a very unfortunate habit to teach a child. It also has ominous implications for how they will manage their emotions as teenagers and adults in response to the many minor setbacks and occasional significant disappointments they will encounter along the road.

The example of a playing child demonstrates that feelings, for the most part, are *socially constructed* and not an automatic reaction over which they have no control. We are not suggesting children in this situation are being deceitful. They have simply learned to display alternative responses to the same upset in different contexts.

Adults do exactly the same; our response to 'fluffing' a golf shot may be quite different in the presence of the boss than if we are playing a casual round with friends.

This is important to know because it tells us that we can teach children to respond adaptively to the inevitable ups and, particularly, downs that are part of every life.

Clearly if parents encourage overreaction to relatively unimportant issues, by presenting these as 'bad' or 'awful', which should not have happened and about which a child should feel aggrieved, they will experience more disappointment than those who learn to reserve more powerful language and 'frames', and hence feelings, for the much rarer events which genuinely warrant them.

This is not a matter of simply saying to a child "Toughen up and get over it." Rather it is to teach them to habitually apply adaptive beliefs and language, particularly to minor frustrations, which allow them to move quickly past these with minimal emotional consequences.

Fortunately, very few things are sufficiently 'bad' or 'awful' to deserve being described in this way. But children don't know this. If a father thinks and says "It's very unfair that you haven't been picked for the part in the school play you wanted. I am angry. It's extremely hurtful for you and me" then their son or daughter is very likely to think and feel the same way.

Two things are going on here: firstly, the father is promoting a belief that a trivial disappointment is automatically unfair and hurtful, and secondly, that one should be angry about it. Effectively he is training his children to regard any such minor setback as extremely unpleasant and worthy of feelings of sadness or anger, both of which are precursors of depression.

A more appropriate and mature response from the father would be, "Well, that is disappointing for you I know. But you have got another part and if you perform well in that you may have better luck next time. Either way you are going to have a lot of fun." In this case the child learns how to handle disappointment in a measured way that will make it easier for them to cope with bigger issues in the future.

You may respond by saying, well, missing out on the part wasn't 'trivial', it was a big deal for the child.

If this is the case, we would ask, why is that? Why was it so important that he or she get that part and that part only? The answer comes back to how parent and child have discussed the part in advance.

To the extent that the part has been presented to the child as a 'must have', the greater their disappointment is likely to be. As an aside, if you do think your son or daughter really has been unfairly treated, you can discuss this with their teacher, but this doesn't alter how you should discuss it at home.

Another thing to note about the above example is that the words used by the father to describe this very minor event are completely disproportionate to the incident itself.

Words trigger emotions appropriate to their meaning and children learn to associate language with events from their parents and teachers. If something is described to a child as 'terrible', then they will feel sad about it, no matter how trivial it may be. Similarly, if something is labelled as 'unfair', they are more likely to feel angry. If, on the other hand, inconsequential setbacks are described by parents as merely 'disappointing' or 'surprising', children are less likely to be emotionally disturbed by them.

Misusing words in this way can easily become a habit and by listening to others you will quickly realise how common it is (see Story: *Under The Bus*).

Story: *Under The Bus*

You may think we are exaggerating when we suggest that people use disproportionate language to describe the many minor irritations in their lives.

Well, recently, one of us treated a police officer for anxiety and depression. There is no doubt that this is a difficult job, but the man concerned was not helping himself by the way he described his work.

His favourite expression to describe basically anything inconvenient about his role was, "I was thrown under the bus again".

He had used maladaptive language like this to describe his work and much of his personal life until it had become a well-learned habit. As a consequence, anything at work or elsewhere which didn't suit him, like having his roster changed, was a source of far more concern and disappointment than it should have been.

In addition, this kind of expression also encouraged a perception that his supervisor didn't like him and was deliberately engaged in making his life as difficult for him as possible. No surprise then that he was feeling unhappy about his work, although he resisted suggestions that he might seek a new career.

ꕥꕥꕥ

A major aim of CBT (Cognitive Behavioural Therapy) is to assist patients to reflect on their habitual beliefs and language and to change those that are generating unnecessary negative emotions. As we suggest in the text, this is what William James means when he says we should talk to ourselves to develop a more constructive or adaptive internal dialogue, rather than listen to the maladaptive beliefs we learned as children.

ꕥꕥꕥ

Words are extremely powerful triggers of emotion and should be treated with respect.

Parents should exercise caution when describing a 'bad' situation to ensure the adjectives they use are proportionate to the event. This is, particularly true if children are listening. For example, a plane crash is a genuine catastrophe, a 'bad' day at the office is not.

Fortunately there are a lot more of the latter than the former. However, it is common to meet patients, particularly those suffering from elevated anxiety, who use expressions like 'off the scale' or 'insane' when describing everyday demands, such as the expectations of their boss.

Repeated often enough, phrases like these will become a self-fulfilling prophecy. The person using them will experience events which are routine and ordinary as far more stressful than they really should be.

Parents need to carefully monitor how they describe their lives to their children. Most of life's irritations are not worth the trouble of mentioning, much less complaining about, but it is very easy to inflate minor nuisances into major setbacks by using disproportionate language to describe them.

It is important for parents not to fall into this trap because your children are listening and learning from you how to interpret their own lives. The beliefs and language they acquire in this way become habits which will primarily determine the quality of their emotional lives as teenagers and adults.

How To Be Anxious

As we have seen, language is important because it literally determines how we feel about any situation. A prime example of this is how we use language to create anxiety.

Psychologists distinguish between what they call stressors, conditions which have the potential to cause us anxiety, and stress, our physical and emotional responses to stressors. Stressors of any kind, like losing a job, do *not* in and of themselves cause stress or anxiety. The relationship between stressors (current or past events) and how we feel about them is mediated by the beliefs we have learned to apply to them and the language we use to describe them.

Whether you allow a stressor, pressure from a boss to meet a deadline, for example, to cause you stress or anxiety depends entirely on how you decide to interpret or 'frame' 'pressure from the boss' to yourself and others.

If your reaction to last minute demands from your boss is to say, "This is awful, I'll never get all this done; but if I don't I'll miss my next promotion!" you are likely to feel rising anxiety. On the other hand, you might say, "Well, this is nice, poor planning by someone. Doesn't matter though, I think I can knock this off by removing some of the 'guff' I normally put in these reports. Either way, I'll do my best and talk to the boss tomorrow if I can't get it finished. We also need to discuss how to avoid this happening in the future."

The first reaction will ruin your evening (and possibly your family's as well) and if repeated often enough will become the normal way you (and your children) deal with even minor stressors in the future. The second reaction highlights two things: firstly, you're *okay*

– not upset but not thrilled either – about the situation; and, secondly, you will not allow a tight deadline to create unnecessary worry or anxiety. If it's done, fine, and if not, so be it, it can be sorted out in the morning. This last statement is a perfect example of adaptive thinking.

Simply stated, there is no law that requires someone to become concerned because they have a lot of work on their desk or indeed for any other reason. Certainly some situations in life are worth being deeply anxious about, but fortunately these are a very small minority of the day to day 'dramas' that fill our lives. These latter only become real dramas if you choose this option by the beliefs and language you use to interpret them. Positive parenting includes teaching children these vital lessons.

Understanding the relationship between stressors and stress and how they are linked by beliefs and language explains why social media appears to be such a potent source of anxiety for young people, particularly teenagers, who are already concerned about how they look, how well they fit in, and what others think of them.

Potential stressors are everywhere on the internet in the form of images of happy and successful people leading exciting, rewarding lives. The fact that these images are artificially curated to make the people in them appear attractive and successful is not relevant to a teen who is concerned that he or she may not measure up.

But once again it is what a teen believes and thinks about the content of social media which determines whether it breeds anxiety, not the content itself. Many teens handle social media comfortably, generally because they have been taught how to do this by their parents, while for others it is a source of crippling unease.

If an adolescent firmly believes that success on social media is critical to their happiness and sense of self-worth, and that it would be 'awful' if they were rejected by others, their experience using it is more likely to be stressful. If, on the other hand, they are relaxed about other's responses to their posts and comments, they will regard it as (mostly) harmless fun.

The good news, as we have seen, is that children's experience of most anxiety, like any other emotion, is controlled by them, specifically by how they have learned how to 'read' or interpret what is happening to them. Their feelings are not determined by events themselves – in this case what they see or hear on social media – but rather how they choose to interpret these to themselves and others.

As we know some children have an inherited predisposition towards anxiety. But whether they experience debilitating levels of stress is largely determined by how they have learned to think and talk about the normal stressors of everyday life. It is vital that they learn firstly, the true source of anxiety, and secondly, to manage their anxiety response successfully by thinking in healthier ways. Parents can teach them to do this in three ways: by using themselves as a positive example, by pinpointing the beliefs and language driving their child's emotions, and, when necessary, helping them to change these.

You may need to intervene at school or with parents of their friends in situations that are beyond their capacity to manage. However, this doesn't alter the simple truth that, with parents either helping or hindering, children create their own feelings about whatever happens to them at school or elsewhere. They literally learn how to feel as they grow until these lessons become well-established habits, and most of what they learn comes from their parents.

The above comments are not meant in any way to belittle the genuine and crippling anxiety that many people experience, which blights their life and robs them of happiness. They need our support as well as professional help. And of course, as we have said, most people – at least occasionally – experience events worthy of deep anxiety.

Nevertheless, far too many children develop extremely poor mental habits when dealing with everyday issues by the way describe these 'problems' to themselves. The result can be chronic, and in many cases, unnecessary anxiety.

How To Be Depressed

So it is for depression. In his famous work, *Man's Search for Meaning*, Victor Frankl argues that we become vulnerable to depression when what we have or who we are diverges too far from what we want or who we wish to be, especially if our current life appears to lack meaning or purpose.[4] Being unable to close this gap, at least in the short term, can leave us feeling sad and despondent.

A desire to be more successful, better appreciated or to feel more purposeful are not uncommon and not a problem in themselves. In fact we would argue that wanting to become a better person is a good thing. For some people, though, not being able to immediately, or possibly ever, improve or change their lives or themselves as they would wish is a source of deep sadness.

It is not surprising that burdens like chronic illness or poverty are often associated with depression. People in these situations see others in much better circumstances than themselves – on TV or social media as well as in real life – and the realisation that they can't ever be like them, or at least not right away, leaves them vulnerable to misery and despair.

Frankl's insight also tells us a great deal about the influence social media may exert over preteens and teenagers, who can be very sensitive about how they measure up to others – peers, movie stars and glamorous models.

An already insecure teenager compares artificially presented images of someone with the 'perfect' life or the 'perfect' partner, and so on, and comes off feeling second best. Even if logic tells them that few people can really achieve the fake looks and lives of those people they see on the 'net', they nevertheless can become prey to feelings of worthlessness, purposelessness, self-loathing, anxiety and depression.

The gap between them and the 'gods' and the 'goddesses' they see on their screen is simply impossible to bridge, so what is the point of trying to emulate them or, indeed, of trying anything at all? There is a short step between chronic feelings of worthlessness and depression.

And there, in a nutshell, is the fundamental problem with social media for far too many adolescents, in particular those who already have a genetic predisposition for depression or anxiety.

Unfortunately, this type of response to social media and the internet in general is not confined to children and teens. Too many adults also respond in a similar fashion. In fact, as a matter of course, when treating anyone for anxiety or depression, young or old, one of our first recommendations is that they give up social media for good. They will still have many other ways of staying in touch with family and friends.

So the conditions conducive to facilitating depression are real enough, just as are the stressors which create the potential for anxiety. But in neither case do they guarantee that a person will become depressed or anxious; we know this simply because not all chronically ill or poor people are depressed, just as not all people under significant pressure become stressed or anxious.

Jim Lovell, commander of Apollo 13 (played by Tom Hanks in the movie of the same name), was the first person to go into space four times and one of only three astronauts to fly to the moon twice (although he never actually landed). NASA kept selecting him, not merely for his skills, but also because of his extraordinary emotional control; he was always calm and focused, even when faced with a life-threatening crisis. His management of the Apollo 13 disaster was acknowledged as a major factor in the safe return to earth of his stricken spacecraft – with all its crew – following a mid-flight explosion.

Victor Frankl noted similar examples of emotional control when he was a prisoner in the Auschwitz extermination camp during World War II; even in this most hopeless of situations, not all inmates succumbed to despair.

As with anxiety, we are not suggesting that depression is not a crushing burden for many unfortunate people confronted with life conditions that are intolerable. But the fact remains that not everyone reacts to the same conditions in the same way, which confirms that depression can sometimes be avoided, or at least alleviated, even in the most disastrous of situations.

In this context, it is humbling and inspiring to meet people permanently disabled by injuries, for which they are not responsible, and in constant pain, but who refuse to allow this to lead them into chronic depression. The mediating factor is belief.

If someone believes that it is 'bad' or 'awful' that they have a chronic injury and that this is the fault of others – bad people who should be punished – anger followed by depression will not be far away. They are also more likely to suffer chronic pain. (See Story: *More Bad News*).

Story: *More Bad News*

Conrad was a patient. He had been referred for pain management following a truly horrendous (the word is appropriate in this context) work accident which nearly cost him his life.

He scythed away part of one thigh down to the bone with an angle grinder which he mistakenly assumed was not connected to the power. It should have been disconnected by the previous user but Conrad also should have checked its status before flicking the 'On' switch.

He was employed in a workshop and the blade of the angle grinder was covered in oil, flakes of paint and metal fragments. As a result his wound triggered a massive infection which compromised many of his other organs.

He nearly died on a number of occasions, including on one memorable day when all his family, including his sister who had rushed back from the UK, gathered around him for his 'last' moments.

Surprisingly Conrad survived and was eventually released from hospital, after multiple operations, but with limited mobility and still in considerable pain.

He also had various other health complications associated with the heavy duty medications used to fight his numerous infections. In addition he could no longer work and was facing a relatively bleak financial future.

Given his case history it would be reasonable to expect him to be angry about what had happened and depressed about future prospects.

Not a bit of it!

Conrad, although clearly in a lot of discomfort from his injury, pre-

sented as a calm, pleasant and relatively cheerful individual. He accepted that what had happened could not be changed and refused to be angry or resentful towards others. He was also actively engaged in rehabilitation programs with his OT and physiotherapist and positive, although realistic, about his prospects for improvement.

Conrad's response to his accident and its consequences provide living proof that our circumstances need not determine our mood. Not surprisingly he also responded extremely well to hypnosis to manage his pain.

Sadly, very soon after, Conrad received more bad news. He was diagnosed with terminal lung cancer, probably caused by an earlier smoking habit. His calm, measured and accepting response to this latest setback was literally incredible and we record it here as a tribute to a truly remarkable man.

He continued with further treatment, but prepared himself for the inevitable and died some months later.

ꕥꕥꕥ

There is really not much to say about this story other than to marvel at what human beings are capable of in terms of managing their emotions when they deliberately chose how to interpret their 'luck' or 'fate' rather than let these dictate how they feel.

No one could have blamed Conrad for being angry, resentful and profoundly depressed about his circumstances, and yet he chose not to be. He provides a standard for us all to aspire to.

Similarly, you will be aware of children with life-threatening illnesses or chronic disabilities who, with the support of parents and therapists, amaze us with their capacity for happiness even in the face of significant handicaps and a very uncertain future.

ꕥꕥꕥ

People who believe that their current circumstances are 'bad' or 'awful' and require immediate remediation, which unfortunately is not available, can descend into a dark place from which they may find it very difficult to emerge.

If they believe their world should be different but can't fix it, at least immediately, they are at risk of becoming chronically depressed. And the more strongly they believe things should be different than they are, even though they can't change them, the more likely it is they will be unhappy.

The chance of experiencing depression is even greater if they also believe (like Peter following his prison term – see Story: *Robert and Peter Go To Gaol*) that they have been cheated or unfairly treated in some way. In this case they will become resentful and angry about their situation but over time, as nothing changes, anger becomes despair.

It is not uncommon in therapy to speak to young adults (generally men) who are furious one moment and in tears the next because something in their life is not as they believe it should be, for example, a partner who 'should' love them because of 'all they have done for them' but who, nevertheless, does not.

However, it need not be like this for your children.

You can help them to think rationally and adaptively about everything that happens in their life so that, for the most part, it is happy and rewarding. Your challenge, when they are confronted by fear, anger, sadness or other debilitating emotions, is to help them understand why they are feeling this way, and how thinking and acting differently can produce more positive feelings.

For example, if your daughter, in response to a friend's unpleasantness says, "Clara's a bitch and I hope she dies!" you can encourage her to replace this first response with something like this: "While I would prefer to be Clara's friend, if she doesn't want to be well, while this is disappointing, it's still okay. She is a nice person who has the right to be friends with whom she chooses just as much as I do. I know that although most people are positive towards me some won't like me regardless of what I do. I'm okay with that. I'll focus my friendship on people who seem to like me."

This is how to embed emotional control in children, something we have already identified as a critical accomplishment of character. A careful discussion with an unhappy child will reveal the beliefs behind their sadness and give you the opportunity to suggest alternatives. Of particular importance is to discourage dislike or hate for others involved who may be genuinely unaware of how your child is feeling.

Through repeated coaching sessions of this kind parents can teach a child to manage their emotions to minimise their experience of anger, despair or anxiety.

It is true that some very significant events, the loss of a loved grandparent for example, can create temporary trauma which is beyond a child's capacity to manage and for which they may need professional guidance. But even in these situations, how you discuss such events with them, will be critical to their rapid recovery.

Conclusion

Modern psychology has taught us a great deal about the origins of feelings and how to practise emotional control. In particular we now understand the links between the beliefs and language we use to think about our current or past circumstances and the emotions these generate.

It is within your power to help your children develop more mature emotional responses to the disappointments and hardships which you know will come their way by encouraging them to think rationally or adaptively.

We know that by encouraging them to strive after worthwhile goals they will experience more than their fair share of 'failure' and feelings of self-doubt. And if they are to persist in the face of setbacks it is imperative that they learn emotional control.

Parents can ensure their children learn to manage their feelings effectively by teaching them to deliberately choose rational beliefs and more measured language to interpret negative events and persisting with these until they become new and healthier mental habits.

Through coaching and encouragement, as well as your own example, you will ensure that these habits become part of their character which automatically channel their thinking and feeling in constructive directions. In doing so you can insulate them from negative emotions such as anger, resentment, jealousy and envy, as well as the twin menaces of anxiety and depression.

Summary

- Emotional responses are neither inherited nor unchangeable. Rather they are learned choices. Parents can teach children to think differently so that they create a healthier and more positive emotional life, whatever their circumstances.
- Mood disorders in children, like anxiety and depression, are created primarily because they have learned from their parents (and elsewhere) to think irrationally; to relentlessly apply maladaptive beliefs and inappropriate language to interpret or 'read' their world.
- When children use rational beliefs and appropriate language their experience of the present as well as memories of the past will generate (mostly) positive or neutral feelings. In this way they will learn to 'let themselves be happy.'
- Words like 'bad', 'awful', 'terrible' and 'unfair' are powerful generators of negative emotions and should be used sparingly.
- The mature alternative – measured language and rational beliefs – allow children to manage even major setbacks, to eventually leave these in the past and to move on without lasting emotional damage.
- If a child does develop a mental disorder parents can assist them to significantly reduce, if not entirely eliminate, its impact by teaching them emotional control.

7

Plain Food and Dull Monotony

"Children are like travellers newly arrived in a strange country of which they know nothing." John Locke (English philosopher and physician)

Victorian author, Mr William Robinson, was not a fan of the romance novel. In *The Philosophy of Human Happiness* (1845), he argued that people who prefer the excitement of fiction over the "dull monotony of actual life" will become dissatisfied with the real world in the same way "as living on confectionary spoils the appetite for plain food."[1]

A prolonged diet of fantasy, he suggests, mars one's capacity for happiness because it creates expectations that can never be matched in real life.

Whether we agree with Mr Robinson is not important. What is interesting is that his ideas have been preserved in the once popular rule for raising children: "Children need plain food and dull monotony." Some readers may recall their grandmothers, if not their mothers, stating this as an article of faith and raising them accordingly.

We have already mentioned we are attracted to ideas about parenting which have endured. Because they have stood the test of time and experience, there is likely to be something in them of value. Admittedly "plain food and dull monotony" is no longer a staple of child rearing but we believe it still retains an important truth which remains relevant in the 21st century, namely the importance of routine – a modern word for 'dull monotony'.

Recent research into human physiology and psychology has emphasised the importance of routine for children, in particular their need for regular eating and sleeping patterns. Jordan Peterson, introduced earlier, states that routine is necessary for the various systems of the body to coordinate effectively 'like a well-rehearsed orchestra'. He argues that everyday activities need to become 'stable and reliable habits' which replace uncertainty and confusion with 'predictability and simplicity'. The benefits of this he suggests:

> … can be perceived most clearly in the case of small children, who are delightful and comical and playful when their sleeping and eating schedules are stable, and horrible and whiny and nasty when not.[2]

We guess that, like us, you have seen both types of children and both types of behaviour!

What is important to note is that either pattern of behaviour can become habitual if the conditions that promote them persist for long enough during childhood. Whiny, not to mention horrible and nasty, people of any age are never happy or popular.

Perhaps then it is not surprising that Peterson argues that anxiety and depression in adults are also exacerbated by an absence of daily routines. So routine is important and especially so for children who have yet to establish consistent personal habits or reliable self-discipline. Once formed, these allow an adult to go 'off piste' for a while in terms of their lifestyle, say while on holiday, without them slipping permanently into personal disorganisation or worse the private chaos of mental illness.

Psychologist William James (whom we introduced in Chapter 6) suggests that to babies the world is "one great blooming, buzzing confusion."[3] They arrive with no knowledge, no skills, and no understanding of their new surroundings or how to navigate them. As John Locke notes (see quotation above) they are like visitors from another planet, who must quickly learn everything about ours from scratch, without knowing anything about us or the language we speak. No wonder they are frequently upset!

Over time routine teaches children that they can trust their world – that it is relatively predictable – and that they can navigate their own way with confidence. It also saves time and energy for everyone by standardising many aspects of family life including eating and sleeping times, who does what chores, how much screen time children are allowed, and so on. In effect routine creates collective habits which make living together easier and more pleasant because, regularly applied, it reduces confusion and conflict.

Most importantly routine leads children to self-discipline and, in particular, emotional self-regulation. Predictability and consistency at home become reflected in their behaviour as they internalise these as personal habits. In this way they acquire a capacity to self-manage their lives and become confident that they can impose a degree of order on what initially was a "blooming, buzzing confusion".

In the absence of reliable routine children are at risk of experiencing a world which is uncertain, capricious and chaotic, all conditions likely to encourage mental disorder, particularly chronic anxiety.

Family rules, which we explore in detail in Chapter 9, are an important tool for establishing the routine children need. A lot of 'acting out' by children is their attempt to find boundaries in their life within which they can feel safe and comfortable. Routine, backed by rules and discipline, provides such boundaries.

Family Breakdown

In clinical settings it is common to meet anxious or depressed adults and teenagers who have been anxious children, a condition which can often be traced to a shock of some kind early in their lives. The sudden breakup of their family when they were very young is commonly the cause.

A trauma of this kind is particularly distressing for a child who has yet to develop a basic trust in their world – that it is a reliable place, despite occasional upheavals – nor the confidence and skills required to manage themselves in a changing environment.

If they are below three years of age, it can also threaten their establishment of secure attachment to a primary caregiver. Secure attachment, as we emphasised in Chapter 1, is particularly important for future mental health and sound relations with others.

A family separation can mean that a young child's life with its comforting routines and familiar faces is turned upside down and replaced with confusion and disorder beyond their capacity to manage. This can trigger debilitating anxiety about what may happen next which can persist into adulthood.

Anxiety about the future can generalise to all areas of a child's life with predictable consequences for their behaviour and performance in and out of school. Family breakdown can also leave lasting feelings of anger, sadness and guilt both in parents and their offspring; a child may display hostility to one or both parents and/or believe that they, in some way, are responsible for their family disintegrating, while parents often feel they have 'failed' their children.

Re-establishing a young person's confidence in their world can be very difficult, particularly if, following family separation, their later years are impacted by further instability.

The 2016 Census reported that 959,000 families in Australia were single parent ones, of which a majority (82%) had children living with their mother as the sole parent. Single parent families have also become more common in Australia, increasing from 6.5% of all families in 1976 to 10.2% in 2016.[4]

It should be noted that only 65% of single parent families included dependent children. The remainder are those in which one or more adult children live with a parent.[5]

In addition, in 2016, 6.4% of Australian families with two parents plus children were step-families (one biological parent and their children plus a new partner) and 3.7% were blended families (a new relationship in which each partner brings children into the family).[6]

The number of single parent families in Australia is expected to continue to rise in the future. The Australian Bureau of Statistics projects that single female parent families alone will make up to 14% of all families by 2041 and that these will still represent approximately 80% of all single-parent families. The remainder, single male parent families, are projected to increase faster than any other family type, increasing to 127,000 families by 2041.[7] These increases are likely to be mirrored by a proportionate growth in step and blended families.

A recent comment by one of our patients brought home to us how family separation is becoming increasingly common for more and more children.

In response to a question about her childhood she said, "Oh mine was pretty normal actually, my parents stayed together until I was 18."

Family breakdown in Australia and elsewhere in the Western world is an unfortunate fact of life. In this country in 2010 it was estimated that almost 50,000 children were impacted by their parents' divorce each year and that number is rising.[8]

Desertion by a partner or domestic violence, as well as other forms of deprivation, continue to lead desperate parents, primarily mothers, to leave and create a new home for their children. But these are becoming less prevalent as reasons for why families break up.

In the future single parent families will continue to increase because what are called 'low conflict' relationships will be more likely to terminate prematurely. In the past only extremely dysfunctional marriages or partnerships ended in separation (initiated by one partner or the other) but today it is increasingly common for parents in less fraught relationships to part company by mutual consent.[9]

To add to the emotional stress occasioned by separation, single-parent families are also among the most financially disadvantaged in Australia. The median income for single-parent families in 2016 was $974 per week, almost half the national average.[10] Essentially, this means that most single parent families are financially worse off than any other type of family in Australia, further adding to the burdens carried by the heads of these households.

A considerable body of research suggests that the future consequences for children whose parents separate can be significant.

A recent Australian survey of modern marriage notes:

> A large number of studies have shown that marital disruption has both a short-term and long-term impact on many children. They also demonstrate that this impact often extends into adult life with consequences for health, family life, educational performance and occupational status. In few areas of human endeavour has the evidence been so compelling ...[11]

One example of this research concluded that (US) children growing up with both (married) biological parents "are about twice as likely to graduate from high school" compared with those raised by single or divorced parents.[12]

A submission by some one hundred researchers of marriage and family to the US Supreme Court in 2015 concluded:

> Compared with children of man-woman couples raised in any other environments, children raised by their two biological parents in a married family are less likely to commit crimes, experience teen pregnancy, have multiple abortions, engage in substance abuse, suffer from mental illness or do poorly at school, and more likely to support themselves and their children successfully in the future.[13]

Summarising available research, US sociologist David Popenoe concludes: "Few propositions have more empirical support in the social sciences than this one: compared to all other family forms, families headed by married biological parents are best for children."[14]

What is most interesting about this research that it is the presence of *both* biological parents in a household, more than other variables including finances and quality of their parenting style, which appears to be the primary factor in determining outcomes for their children when compared with those from other family arrangements.

The authors of a study of the impact of family structure on child development concluded: "… it is not simply the presence of two parents, as some have assumed, but the presence of two biological parents that seems to support children's development."[15]

Even after controlling for other factors, including socio-economic status and the mental health of parents, researchers have found significantly higher incidences of mental illness and suicide behaviour in children and adolescents from non-traditional families than those living with married biological parents.

A Swedish study of almost one million children (which also controlled for the impact of other variables) concluded that girls with single parents were more than twice as likely to commit suicide and more than three times as likely to die from addiction as were girls living with both their parents. For boys, the risk of dying was 50% greater for those living in single parent families.[16]

At this point we should emphasise that the research reviewed deals in aggregates rather than individuals; if you are a single parent with children, the disadvantages identified above do *not* necessarily apply to your children. Conclusions based on averages tell us a great deal about what goes on in larger groups of children but these consequences do not automatically occur in individual cases (see following Cautionary Note).

The influence of both biological parents appears to be qualitatively different than that of any other two adults, such as a biological mother and stepfather. Essentially the research suggests that children, *on average*, are better off, in terms of future outcomes, with both married biological parents at home, even if the parenting they receive is less than ideal.

What really matters it seems is biological kinship, being with your own flesh and blood. The most dedicated stepparent or single parent simply cannot fully replace this vital element in a child's life.

Why this is so remains unclear, but it must have something to do with the development of a child's identity. Growing up with one's immediate family appears to create a fundamental sense of belonging in children, that there is a unique place for them within a biological kinship group which only they can fill.

Once a kinship group is broken, this visceral or intuitive feeling of belonging may be damaged because it is dependent on the continued presence of each biological member of the group (especially parents), none of whom can be replaced because each is unique to a particular child.

Earlier in this book, we emphasised the importance of positive identity as an accomplishment of character and its role in underpinning the psychological health of children, adolescents and adults. The research reviewed above suggests that identity development is at least partly instinctual – it is pre-programmed – and requires the presence of both biological parents to run the program properly.

If this is the case, the impact of the loss of one or both biological parents on a child's sense of security in an uncertain world cannot be entirely redressed, no matter how loving and supportive those are who replace them. A tragedy that robs a child of one of their natural parents leaves a hole in their life that can never be completely filled.

So, even if we don't fully understand them, there is no denying the special bonds we sense with our own family. In fact, these bonds can be so strong that they may, at times, cloud a parent's judgement and prevent them from doing what is sometimes in the best interests of their children.

We are not fans of the expression 'tough love', but it highlights the need to sometimes make decisions for our children that neither we nor they would prefer. Even though we may understand at a conscious level that our children should suffer the consequences of their misbehaviour, the tug of biology can make it hard for us to follow through.

As consultants, we regularly see parents, both married and single, who tolerate simply awful behaviour from their children (including those who are adults), which they wouldn't accept for a moment from anyone else.

Less often, but still too regularly, we meet parents who have shielded their adolescent and (sometimes) adult children from the legal consequences of their actions. In effect they have broken the law themselves to protect their offspring, something, once again, they would never contemplate doing for others. You don't have to be a psychologist to know that this cannot end well for either child or parent. We discuss the doleful consequences of inadequate discipline for children's longer term welfare in Chapter 10.

Let us be clear. None of the above discussion is meant in any way to denigrate the efforts of the many devoted single and step-parents who, due to a range of circumstances beyond their control, find themselves raising their own child alone or with step siblings when they form a new relationship.

They deserve our admiration and support. These committed souls bring everything they have to the business of parenting.

Nor does it mean that single and step-parents can't make a difference to the quality of outcomes that children in their care will enjoy. A compassionate, loving stepfather is clearly superior to a biological father who is a drunken brute, and a caring, devoted single mother will deliver infinitely better outcomes for her children than a married one who can't look after herself, much less them.

Cautionary Note

If you are a single parent or a step-parent it is important that you read the following piece. As noted above, the research cited in the previous section tells us that, *on average*, children from biologically intact families experience better outcomes as adolescents and adults than those brought up in different circumstances.

However, and this is critical, it says little about individual cases, including your children. What this means is that there are many instances, literally hundreds of thousands, of young people living in single, step or blended families, who significantly outperform and go on to lead happier lives than those who grow up with both biological parents.

Mark Regnerus, a US sociologist, conducted a large scale study of outcomes for children from different family backgrounds, including those raised by lesbian mothers and gay fathers. Reflecting the findings discussed earlier, his data confirm that on average children are more successful as adults, across a range of outcomes, when they grow up with married biological parents.

However, he also makes the following important point:

> Do children need a married mother and father to turn out well as adults? No, if we observe many anecdotal accounts with which Americans are familiar. Moreover there are many cases in [the data] where respondents have proved resilient and prevailed as adults in spite of numerous transitions, be they death, divorce, additional or diverse romantic partners, or remarriage.[17]

This confirms our earlier comment that parents of all kinds, single or step, gay or straight, and so on, can and do make a positive difference to their children's future. Regardless of your particular circumstances, the research results *do not* condemn your child to a second class life or permanent disadvantage. They *do not* mean that your children cannot succeed as happy, successful adults.

The research simply reminds us of something we already know that there are many cases where single and stepparents, despite their best efforts, find the pressures of raising children alone (or with a new partner) too much to manage as well as they would wish. But this need not include you and your children.

Just as positive parenting by informed and loving parents makes a real difference to how children turn out in a biologically intact family, the same is true of parents and their children in any other situation, including those in single parent, step-parent, same-sex parent, adoptive and blended families. The lessons of this book are relevant for all parents and primary carers, irrespective of their family arrangements, not merely for those in a 'traditional' family set up. Biology is important but, as we already know, it is not the whole story (see Story: *Gerald*).

Story: *Gerald*

Gerald was adopted by a childless couple in the days before it was considered important for contact to be maintained between a child and their biological parents. As their only son, he was cherished by his adoptive parents, who ensured he received a first class education as well as their unwavering love and support. He was also fully accepted into their wider family, particularly by his cousins, with whom he spent a lot of his childhood.

When he was 9 or 10, his parents told him that he was adopted because they could not have children and his single teenage mother had been unable to keep him. Once again, because of attitudes which prevailed at the time, no attempt was made to locate her.

Indeed, the fact that he was even told when relatively young that he was adopted was quite rare back then and a tribute to his stepparents.

Gerald continued at school and university where he pursued a career as an engineer. Eventually he married and had his own children. He retired as a highly respected site manager of a gold mine in Western Australia.

Gerald eventually located his mother, after his adoptive parents died. It was lovely to see his face light up as he described the whole new family of relations he had discovered and with whom he remained in close contact.

Interestingly, when one of his own daughters had two children while she was still a teenager, Gerald and his wife raised their grandchildren in the family home while their mother finished high school.

He had obviously learned an important lesson about biological kinship from his own experience.

❧❧❧

There are at least two lessons to be drawn from Gerald's story.

Perhaps the most important, as difficult as this may be for adoptive parents, is to ensure that their children learn about their origins as soon as possible and to facilitate regular access between them and their biological parents, assuming this is possible.

This may need to be qualified, depending on the circumstances of the biological parents, but we know that participating in their own biological network is important for children, even if we don't quite understand why.

Recognising a child's right to know where they come from, as early as possible, is also part of displaying a genuine respect for them, a subject we explore in detail in the next chapter. While we understand that this may be distressing for adoptive parents and involve a fear that they may 'lose' a child, nevertheless, the overriding priority for any parent should be the immediate, as well as longer term welfare of the children in their care.

A second lesson from Gerald's story is the overwhelmingly positive impact which his adoptive parents clearly had on his life. Their devotion to Gerald and determination that he would have every opportunity was decisive for his later successful career.

To us his story reinforces the point stressed earlier in the main text that loving and conscientious parents, whatever their relationship to a child, can and do make a vital difference to his or her future.

Guilt in Children

Guilt is a very destructive emotion – for both children and parents – which, as noted earlier, often accompanies family breakdown.

Children may feel guilty because they believe, however wrongly, that they are the cause of their family's separation. This can induce feelings of self-loathing and anxiety which impact other parts of their life, including their relationships with peers and their school performance.

When parents decide to part, it is critically important to have respectful and cordial discussions, involving the whole family, in which both parents explain their decision and emphasise to their children two things: firstly, that their children are in no way responsible for what has happened and, secondly, that they will always have two parents who love and cherish them.

During these discussions children should be encouraged to express their fears and concerns so that these can be identified and addressed as much as possible. It may also be necessary to philosophically accept the anger they display and avoid reacting negatively to this.

When talking with your children, try to avoid expressions like 'break up' and 'separation', which can raise understandable childish fears of an irrevocable loss of one or possibly both parents.

While you understand what is meant by these terms, it is better when talking to children to use 'living apart' or 'living in different houses', and so on. The aim of this is to minimise any sense of harm or loss on their part and to emphasise that for them a parting of the ways is mainly about changed living arrangements, that they will continue to see both their parents as well as their grandparents on a regular basis (where possible), and that both parents will remain intimately involved in their lives.

Also, rather than focus on the negatives such as, "Mummy and Daddy don't love each other any more", try to use positive language like, "We believe we'll all be happier, you as well, if we live in separate houses"; or, "While we are not going to live together any more, we will still be friends and will always love and support you."

Children don't understand, and aren't particularly interested in, the nuances of adult emotions, but they are acutely sensitive to hostility between parents or any other threat to their fundamental security.

The emphasis, therefore, when discussing the new state of affairs with them must be on the unbreakable bonds between them and their parents as well as your shared commitment to their future.

For conversations of this kind to work, it goes without saying that parents should display respect and, preferably, goodwill towards each other when together and apart. Criticising your ex-partner in front of your children is, firstly, bad manners (which they will pick up), secondly, self-indulgent (which harms your character) and, thirdly, makes their adjustment to the 'new normal' that much harder.

It is sufficiently distressing for children to have to come to terms with a family breakup, given that most will feel torn between the love and loyalty they feel for each of their parents (despite what they say), without it being accompanied by acrimonious communication between Mum and Dad.

No matter what has passed between you and your ex-partner, you are both responsible for minimising the effect this has on your children. It also should not really need to be said that using your children as bargaining chips in negotiations with your ex-partner about finance or access is reprehensible. Unless he/she is a bona fide threat to your children's safety and welfare, access should be shared as equally as possible.

Ideally you will seek to provide as close to equal access as is practical until your children are old enough to decide how much time they wish to spend with each parent. Then let them decide. The implication of this recommendation is that parents – separated or not – must earn the right to be with their teenage children by being people their children want to spend time with. Time with our children is not something we should take for granted.

Guilt in Parents

Parental guilt about breaking up can be fed by a range of concerns. Parents worry that their children will be stigmatised at school or suffer disadvantage following a separation. They may also be concerned that their friends or their parents, especially if the latter have had a long and successful marriage, will judge them harshly.

Most of all, from our experience, guilt in ex-partners is driven by the feeling that, by exposing them to the trauma of separation, they have 'let their children down'. This, we believe, reflects an instinctual understanding that the best situation for children is living in one home with their married biological parents.

It is also important to note that some parental guilt regarding separation can be misplaced, in the sense it concerns issues outside one parent's control or sphere of responsibility. For instance, we meet many parents who feel 'guilty' because of their ex-partner's lack of engagement with their children following separation. Clearly this is inappropriate; one parent is not responsible for the behaviour of the other, and certainly can do little about it.

Nevertheless, unnecessary or misplaced guilt can be just as damaging as the genuine kind. If guilt concerning leaving a marriage or partner is distressing you, we recommend that you seek professional advice.

Feeling guilty is not helpful once you have decided to part company; better to let go of it. If you don't 'park' it, guilt regarding your own or others' behaviour will continue to upset you and, by extension, your children. Moreover, there is a real danger that it will intrude on your behaviour as a parent, and not in a good way.

For a start, guilty parents are miserable and not much fun for their children to be around. For your children to be happy, you must be happy as well. They will learn the habit of 'happiness' from being around parents (living together or apart) who are consistently cheerful and upbeat, despite the inevitable 'ups and downs' of life. Through watching and listening, this will also become their default response to most situations they find themselves in.

Secondly, too many estranged parents compensate for their feelings of guilt by failing to provide the discipline or boundaries children require if they are to grow into mature adults.

We both have consulted separated parents, fathers and mothers, literally in tears because one or more of their children were running wild, but who were reluctant to intervene because of guilt. They felt sorry for what they had done to their children and didn't want to cause them further unhappiness by disciplining them, even though they knew they should.

This realisation merely compounded their original feelings of guilt and distress which in turn led to more tears and naughtier children! (See Story: *Back To Canada?*)

Story: *Back To Canada?*

Lorenzo met a beautiful Canadian backpacker, Maureen, while she was taking a gap year in Australia. They returned to Canada together, got married and had two daughters.

Unfortunately, their marriage was unhappy, not least because Maureen became a heavy user of alcohol. Eventually Lorenzo returned to Australia with both girls because their mother found it increasingly difficult to take care of herself, much less them.

Once in Australia, the younger daughter, who was nine years old, appeared to settle down at school and formed a close relationship with her paternal grandmother. In contrast, the elder daughter (14 years) became increasingly difficult at home and school.

She was openly defiant towards her father and teachers, refusing to comply with their requests, and regularly stole money from her grandmother. She was a desperately unhappy girl who kept insisting that she wished to return to her mother in Canada.

Lorenzo was not keen on this because he knew that his ex-wife's situation had not improved and that if his daughter went back she would have to be cared for by her Canadian relatives.

At his wit's end, he came to see one of us. He was in tears because his daughter was effectively out of control and he feared for her physical safety when she stayed out late without telling him where she was. He was also concerned about the impact her behaviour was having on her younger sister.

However, his guilt about splitting up the family meant that he was reluctant to discipline her, something of course she was taking full advantage of. In discussion it became apparent that his own mental health was also at risk.

Quite obviously the current state of affairs was untenable and had got to the point where before long Lorenzo would be unable to work (he was currently on stress leave), thus putting everyone's – his own and his daughters' – future at risk.

There are no easy solutions in this type of situation, but Lorenzo agreed to impose clear rules regarding the behaviour of both daughters at home and school and to enforce these, if necessary, with the removal of privileges, chiefly access to a smart phone and pocket money.

His elder daughter was to be told that she had a choice; she could stay in Australia under the new conditions, or return to her mother in Canada.

At his next appointment, Lorenzo was literally a changed man. He felt his life was once more under control and that he was now able to provide a stable environment for his younger daughter at least. He was back at work and enjoying his job once more. Interestingly, his elder daughter, for the time being at least, had opted to stay with her father.

She had spoken to her mother and other relatives in Canada and was now not sure if going back was her best option. She had submitted grudgingly to the new rules and was still by no means a model child, but clearly life at home had been transformed and Lorenzo was hopeful that the future would be better for everyone. Time will tell how this particular family drama unfolds.

ஃஃஃ

This story highlights the danger of allowing guilt regarding separation to impact how children are managed. By neglecting to impose boundaries on the behaviour of his elder daughter, Lorenzo was not only putting her at risk, but also himself and his other daughter, as far as their future wellbeing and mental health were concerned.

Returning to Canada was unlikely to be in the best interests of his elder daughter and maybe she had come to this conclusion herself. But giving her the option was the price he had to pay to achieve stability for the rest of his family.

One Mother's Experience

A recent conversation with a single mother highlighted for us the impact feelings of guilt can have on post-separation parenting styles.

She and her ex-partner clearly have maintained a solid relationship, motivated by their shared desire that separation will not overshadow their children's future. She admitted, however, echoing our concerns above, that feelings of guilt can tempt her to 'soft pedal' when the question of disciplining her children arises. The way she handles this is very insightful.

She asks herself two questions: "If I and my partner were still together, what would I do?" And, "Is there any reason to act differently now?"

Invariably she has found that her answer to the second question is a clear "No". In other words, whether she is single or married is not relevant to how she should respond if her children are misbehaving. We strongly recommend other parents in the same situation to use the same questions whenever they feel similarly tempted to overlook unacceptable behaviour in their children.

She also recognises that guilt, if she is not alert, means she tries to do too much for her children rather than expecting them to take responsibility for themselves when they can and should. She recognises that the feeling of having 'let her children down' or that they are 'disadvantaged' in some way because she is now single can lead her to try to redress the balance by overcompensating – doing more for her children than she knows she should.

It is important to note that overcompensating in this way is, once again, a reflection of misguided guilt. Estranged parents find themselves doing things for their children which they should and need to be doing for themselves if they are to become competent adults.

Parents do this because they want children (and themselves) to 'feel good' about their new situation and/or to recompense them in some way for what has happened.

This gets us back to the challenge that all parents face: deciding between stepping in and holding back when children are tackling something on their own. And from this lady's comments it would appear that this issue is of particular importance for single parents.

To reprise our earlier conclusion, doing more than you really need to do for children is to effectively infantilise them, to leave them less able to thrive independently. This is just as true for children from separated families as it is for any others.

As we have noted, most estranged parents are very concerned that separation will not affect their children's future, and rightly so. Our advice, as it is to all parents, is prepare your child for the road and not the other way around.

You do this by insisting that they accept increasing responsibility as they grow older; that they always do their chores, no matter what else is going on, that they respect other people, and step up to challenges rather than being allowed to 'wimp out' because you feel sorry for them.

This is quite simply the best preparation for the future that you can give any child, regardless of their family situation. If you are a single or step-parent it is also the best way to minimise the consequences that separation may have on their lives.

How do we know this? Well we have met too many happy, well-adjusted, successful young adults from 'broken' homes who were blessed with parents who adopted this approach to raising them, for this to be simply a coincidence.

Remember, the research reports averages only. It does not highlight the hundreds of thousands of outstanding young people who emerge successfully from a family separation.

The Upsides of Separation

While we're on the good news let us share two positive consequences of separation for which we are also indebted to the lady introduced above. The first is that the requirements of moving regularly between two households have meant her children have had to become more organised when preparing for school and extracurricular activities.

Initially she would take forgotten items over to their father's house. Then she reflected that this was another form of doing 'too much' and stopped. As a consequence, they very quickly started to think about what they would need during their week with their father and now pack accordingly.

The second upside of separation she mentions is more significant. Her children now spend more time with their father than ever before and he plans his work schedule to ensure he has time with them, including picking them up from school and taking them on camping holidays. This is clearly an unalloyed positive and research confirms that the active involvement of non-resident fathers has lasting beneficial consequences for children.[18]

Fathers and mothers, together or apart, make different but equally important contributions to their children's healthy development. Separation should not be a reason for either parent to disengage from their children's lives, and both parents need to work hard to ensure this does not happen.

It is not uncommon, even in 'intact' households, for the burden of parenting to fall more heavily on one parent or the other, generally the mother. This may often be for practical reasons, if, say, there is only one breadwinner, but there is no doubt that both children, and their too often absent parent, pay a price for this arrangement.

It is certainly a reminder to parents, whatever their situation, to share the parenting role more evenly and to actively engage with their children while they can.

"I Wish I Hadn't Worked so Hard"

Bronnie Ware, an Australian nurse and counsellor in palliative care, whom we introduced earlier, recorded the common regrets of her dying patients. One expressed by many male patients she nursed is: "I wish I hadn't worked so hard."[19]

Men who were dying, in particular often regretted that, because of the time they devoted to their careers, they had missed too much of the lives of their children when they were growing up, as well as the love and companionship of their partner.

They did not regret working but realised too late that they could have simplified their lifestyle and made different choices so that, although possibly earning less, they would have spent more time with those who meant most to them.

Children, as you are well aware, grow up very quickly and will soon come to prefer hanging out with their friends rather than you. This is normal and desirable but sad for parents when we realise we are no longer the centre of their lives.

So grab the opportunity while you can, when your children are not yet older teenagers, to be fully involved in their lives. The relationships you build with them in their early years will encourage accomplishments of character, including self-confidence, respect, positive identity and empathy, which will last a lifetime and assist them successfully manage whatever their future holds.

Sound relations with your adult children will also make your later years more fulfilling and rewarding.

Children need parental engagement. Moreover, when we reflect on the regrets of the dying (men most of all), it is clear that parents need to be close to their children as well.

Managing Separated Families

While the absence of one or both biological parents means something is missing from the family home, this does not mean, as we have emphasised, that single, adoptive and step-parents can do nothing to redress the balance; not least they can ensure that children have regular and amicable access to their absent (biological) parent(s) provided this is possible.

In the rest of this chapter we look at further challenges facing parents who have parted company and make some suggestions for minimising the impact of divorce or separation on their children's future.

We can agree that a family separation can be extremely disturbing for children and which, despite the love of a single parent or step-parents, may leave them with heightened levels of anxiety which they carry forward into adulthood. But there is no doubt that in many cases separating is the only sensible option.

A hostile home in which two parents are locked in bitter conflict, and which spills over onto their the children, is unhealthy for them and certainly no place to raise a happy child. In Chapter 9 we review research from the Young Lives Matter Report which clearly demonstrates the negative impact of family dysfunction on children's mental health.

Deciding to leave is never easy but, sometimes, as noted, it is clearly the right thing to do. Nonetheless, all loving parents who take this step, while knowing it is right for them personally, have severe apprehensions about how it will rebound on their children and, importantly, their future wellbeing. You probably know yourself couples who have deliberately decided to stay together amicably until their children complete high school to minimise this risk.

Their courage and commitment demand our respect and admiration. But this is simply not possible in all cases. Separation also takes courage. Step-parents and single parents who strive to give their children the best life possible should also attract our esteem and support.

If you have left the father or mother of your children there are some important points to keep in mind when setting out to manage your new family. Perhaps the most vital thing to remember is that you, your children, and their father/mother are still part of a family or biological network, and always will be, although you don't all live in the same household.

This means that, as much as possible, both parents should participate in all significant events which involve their children, such as birthdays, wider family gatherings, and school events. Children can adapt to a myriad of family arrangements; they are remarkably flexible in this regard, *provided they feel secure.* What is more important than who lives where for your children's wellbeing is clear evidence that they are loved and supported by both their parents and their wider family, wherever they happen to reside.

A second point, already emphasised, is that children from separated families need discipline in the same way as those living with both parents. All parents and carers have a duty to provide discipline which is compassionate, consistent and fair. To leave children to their own devices because of guilt regarding separation is simply a dereliction of one's duty as a parent.

Why are we tempted to back off?

Well, firstly, as we have suggested, separated parents are disinclined to make their children's lives any tougher than they already are – they are trying, albeit in a misguided way, to recompense them for what they have done. Secondly, they may be trying to make themselves feel better by being 'nice' to their children.

If parents fail to discipline in order to compensate their children, or themselves, for the guilt they feel following separation, they are merely exacerbating any negative legacies of leaving. Whatever the consequences of moving on, you will make these worse by neglecting to discipline your children.

As we emphasise in Chapter 10, discipline is a gift of love conscientious parents bestow on their children. The irony is that it is also love which drives the guilt that estranged parents feel, and which may mean they disregard this primary responsibility of positive parenting. Be careful that misplaced love doesn't take you down the same path.

We should also point out that failing to discipline is not a fault confined only to some parents who are divorced or apart. Those living together with their own offspring can also fall into the same trap of equating love with a licence for children to behave as they wish.

The Wider Family

Another point to remember is that the focus of all your dealings with your ex-partner and their family should be on your children's wellbeing. You may not particularly like your ex-mother-in-law, but she is your children's grandmother and they need her love unclouded by hostility between you and her. So, if necessary, bite your tongue, smile, and make small talk about the weather.

Similarly, if your children enjoy playing with their cousins, let them, even though you may find your ex-brother-in-law to be a bit much. All of their relations, grandparents, uncles and aunts and cousins, are an integral part of your children's family, part of the biological network that is so important to their sense of positive identity and security.

To deprive them of regular opportunities to see family, simply because you don't like one or two individuals, is selfish and petty, and certainly not the act of a loving parent. More importantly, it deprives them of access to a web of relationships which otherwise would be a powerful defence against the worst impact of difficult times in the future, including mental illness.

So family gatherings, as uncomfortable as some of these may be, need to continue until your children are older teenagers and make their own decision to attend or not, although preferably they will continue to do so.

Our observation, when our children were young, was that they and their cousins thoroughly enjoyed big family gatherings. They obviously gained something valuable from getting together, even if some of the adults present could barely tolerate these events (see Story: "*Who Wants To Play Footy?*").

Story: "*Who Wants To Play Footy?*"

We recall one memorable occasion, a 70th birthday for one of our children's grandfathers. There were speeches and kind comments from all and sundry, pleasant for the grandfather no doubt but, after a while, tedious for others.

At the end of the speeches, the master of ceremonies asked if anyone else would like to say something. Our son Rory, who was about 10 at the time, jumped on to a chair much to our bemusement (we wondered what was coming next) and said, "Yes, I do! Who wants to play footy?"

The day ended with a frantic game of football involving old and young, male and female, which we are sure his grandfather cherished long after the kind speeches had been forgotten.

ꕥꕥꕥ

Family networks matter to children in ways that we do not fully understand. But they do matter. All the more reason to keep wider family interactions going even though you have left your partner. Remember you are attending for your children's benefit not necessarily your own.

Back to Routine

Two other important pieces of advice we learned from our friendly single mum were the importance of consistency between the two homes in which her children live, particularly in terms of agreed rules and routines.

Dividing their time between two homes is disruptive enough for children without them also being required to adjust to different ways of doing things on alternate weeks or however access is arranged.

Similar evening routines, including bedtimes, household chores and screen time, will replace at least some of the stability and security children lose when a family is divided.

Earlier in this chapter we emphasised the importance of routine for promoting mental health and providing the security and predictability children need in their lives, if they are to form a positive identity. This is doubly true for children who divide their time between different homes.

A lack of consistency between households also creates the possibility of conflict, either between parents or between parents and children. Serial arguments about routine ("Dad always lets us stay up later") are helpful for no one and obviously make it harder for children and parents to settle into new arrangements.

It cannot be overemphasised that children, who on the surface may appear resilient, simply don't have the same capacity to understand and adjust to change as adults do. Their resilience is founded on living in a secure and predictable world. For this reason, separated parents must use every tool at their disposal to facilitate their offspring's adjustment to their new life. A lot of things you can't control, but routine is something you can. We advise you to use it.

The potential for conflict in estranged, as well as in other, families, is most acute when parents disagree about how much to give children, whether in the form of pocket money, possessions or 'good times'. What to give children and when should be agreed and stuck to by parents and carers in any situation, so that it ceases to be a source of disagreement.

Gift giving to children can be a form of disguised warfare between parents who are unable or unwilling to resolve differences via respectful discussion. It also confuses children, who unwittingly use gifts as levers to stir up parental guilt ("Look what Mum gave me!") Pocket money should be regular and age-adjusted, while presents outside of birthdays and Christmas should be few and far between.

In this context we are reminded of the following piece of parenting wisdom from Esther Selsdon, an American author: "*If you want your children to turn out well, spend twice the time with them as you think you should and half the amount of money*". We would argue that this advice should be applied to all children in every kind of family.

Conclusion

The benefits of routine – or 'dull monotony' – for growing children have long been recognised. Routine is important for injecting structure and order into their lives, particularly when they are young, which in turn provides the stability they need to develop a sense of personal security, as well as accomplishments of character which include self-confidence, maturity, respect, positive identity and self-discipline.

Over time, as sustained routine becomes internalised, they acquire a capacity for self-direction, which enables them to manage their lives, and their emotions, with less adult assistance. An absence of routine in the early years can produce unpleasant children but, more importantly, leave them at risk of living chaotic lives and developing mental health problems when they are older; an absence of structure, order and self-discipline are important drivers of psychological illness.

Unfortunately, a sudden disruption to their lives and routines –

when families break up, for example – can permanently undermine children's confidence in themselves and their world as well as distort their personality development.

Losing a parent early through accident or separation may also impair a child's sense of attachment, vital for identity development and future mental health. The sudden shock to their apparently secure and stable world may generate anxiety and depression which can persist well into adulthood.

However, and this must be stressed again, survey research deals in aggregates; it tells us what happens on average to children from divided homes. But it does not predict the fate of any individual child. This is easily demonstrated by comparing the many, many children from biologically 'intact' families who have made a disastrous mess of their adult lives with those from 'broken' homes who flourish in their later years.

This is important to know because it means that separation does not condemn the children of estranged parents to sustained disadvantage, provided both are committed to preventing this outcome. And this can include your children if you are in this situation.

All parents, including those in single, step, or same sex parent families and adoptive or blended families – as well as the married biological variety – can and do raise successful, psychologically healthy children.

Summary

- Routine, provided by regular schedules and consistent expectations, provide children with the structure and order they need to achieve a sense of 'basic trust' in their world which is the foundation of positive identity.
- Consistent routines, which replace uncertainty and complexity with predictability and clarity, assist a child to acquire self-discipline, reflected in stable, healthy habits and personal maturity.

- Research confirms that, on average, children grow up best with their married biological parents. However, it says nothing about individual cases. If you are a single parent it is important to remember that many outstanding young people have emerged from 'broken' homes.
- Guilt following separation is of no value to you or your children; when you are happy your children are more likely to be happy also, and when they are cherished by both parents they are less likely to feel guilty themselves.
- After separation try to maintain family traditions, including shared birthdays, Christmas and other wider family events. Remember that engagement with your ex-partner's family is for your children's benefit, not necessarily yours.
- At the very beginning of a separation engage the whole family in cordial respectful discussions about shared rules and routines between households. Get these agreed – children have an input but parents have the final say – and then stick to them. These should also include agreements about pocket money, presents and 'treats'.
- Never forget that countless successful young adults have a background of family separation. Leaving your partner need not condemn your children to a second class life, provided you and your 'ex' are committed to not letting this happen.

PART 3

Positive Parenting

"Ask any child development expert and they will tell you that children do not develop in a straight line. There are no average children. There are no standard children." Cassi Clausen (US educator)

In Part 1 of this book we defined what we believe parents should aim for if they wish to raise psychologically healthy children. We suggested that the purpose of parents is not to deliver children to a specific destination but to help them to successfully find their own way to their own future, one which is rewarding and meaningful for them.

If you accept this as the purpose of parenting, it follows that the emphasis of parents should be on teaching children how to live rather than what to live for. In other words, you should focus on assisting them to develop the temperament – or accomplishments of character – they will need for their journey, rather than encouraging them to simply accumulate a list of achievements or 'prizes'.

In Part 2 we agreed that, while there may be no guaranteed formula or road map for raising children, research and experience provide useful guidelines which will make the challenge of child rearing easier:

1. Prepare the child for the road not the road for the child.
2. Children are antifragile: they need challenges, indeed adversity, and the pressure that goes with these in order to thrive, physically and psychologically, and become all that they are capable of being.
3. Everyone, children included, creates their own emotional life – good or bad. They do this using beliefs and language, which they have learned growing up to interpret or 'read' what happens to them, not least misfortune.

4. Routine is necessary for all children, and young ones in particular, because it introduces structure and order into their lives, which promote feelings of confidence and security and which they later internalise as self-discipline.
5. Every parent and caregiver, whatever their family arrangements and personal circumstances, can make a positive difference to the future of their children.

Part 3, the core of this book, is devoted to what we call positive parenting: raising children in a way that maximises their chances of achieving psychological health and living a worthwhile life – one that is successful for them, however they choose to define this beguiling word.

We begin in Chapter 8 by suggesting that it is not sufficient to love our children, we must also respect them as well, not least their right and responsibility to create their own destiny.

To respect a child means to provide time and space for them to find their own way while you protect them from risks they cannot yet handle on their own. As a parent you can advise, coach and encourage but be wary of taking over so that their life becomes your project which is more about meeting your needs than theirs.

In particular, we explore the differences between respecting a child and loving them, taking them seriously or being concerned for them, something even the best parents may confuse.

The need for family rules is discussed in Chapter 9. Rules are necessary so that families can live in relative peace and harmony while, at the same time, provide opportunities for each member to pursue their own path with a minimum of disruption to and from others.

However, rules are only of value if parents, firstly, are prepared to observe those which apply to them (as well as their children) and, secondly, when necessary, implement agreed consequences for infringements. Consistent, fair and compassionate discipline, which is the true core of positive parenting, is discussed in Chapter 10.

Discipline provides the boundaries children need to find the safety and security they crave, and within which they learn to become confident, autonomous adults.

If you are serious about discipline, you must be prepared to have 'difficult' conversations with children. Difficult conversations occur when a parent intervenes to address unacceptable behaviour, or applies a consequence when a child infringes or ignores a family rule. Often a child will be querulous and not inclined to accept their penalty, which may discourage a parent from 'stepping in', even when they know they should. Chapter 11 looks at how to use 'difficult' conversations to discipline children calmly and effectively while building better relationships with them at the same time.

Talking about discipline leads naturally to a discussion of conflict. Conflict between people, as we shall see, is normal and inevitable when they spend time together. So it is with families.

The only strange thing would be if there was no conflict in your family!

Given that conflict between people is inevitable, it makes sense to understand how to use it to build stronger and happier families. In Chapter 11 we consider alternative styles of conflict management and recommend techniques of constructive conflict that will provide better outcomes for you and your children.

In Chapter 12 we consider children who are 'different', that is, those who seem quite unlike their more 'mainstream' peers and who may find growing up trickier as a result. If you have a child who is different, even odd or eccentric, this generally should be a cause for celebration, even if they are less easy to understand or live with. The danger, however, is that parents may react to difference in a child with disappointment or, label one who is merely unusual as a 'problem' to be 'solved', with potentially serious consequences for their future.

The final chapter offers a number of 'tools for the road', skills and knowledge children will need for their journey and which will increase their chances of building a worthwhile and rewarding life.

8

Respect Your Children as well as Love Them

"A person's a person, no matter how small."
Dr Seuss (Theodore Seuss Geisel, US author)

"He that will have his child have a respect for him and his orders, must himself have a great reverence for his child."
John Locke (English philosopher and physician)

Positive parenting begins with the imperative to respect children, no matter how young they may be, as persons who, while needing our support, have the same fundamental rights and responsibilities which are the birthright of every human being. This is the point Dr Seuss is making in the above quotation. If one day children are to become fully competent and mature adults parents must never lose sight of this essential truth.

It goes without saying that your children are not your property, that you don't own them. They are, as we have suggested, honoured guests in your home and like any other guest you afford them privileges as well as placing obligations on them as the 'price' of your hospitality. But they are also much more than guests, if only because they had no say in coming to live with you. For that reason alone you have duties towards them that you would not recognise or accept for anyone else. In particular, these are to provide them with the love, support and direction they need before leaving to forge a life for themselves.

The fact they are privileged visitors, who one day will depart, in no way diminishes our love for our children which, at times, can be overwhelming, or the unique bond which exists between every parent and their child.

Therein lie two traps for the unwary parent. Too much, or rather misguided, love can mean you fail to genuinely respect them, particularly their need to become independent of you, and hence you may fall into the error of overprotection. Alternatively, you may omit to pay them proper respect by failing to place on them, in age related stages, the responsibilities that every adult member of society must ultimately shoulder, in particular to respect the rights and needs of others.

Parents may indulge their children in either way because they believe they are 'special' – which they are – so the 'normal' rules should not apply to them which, of course, they must. But love is not the same as respect; mistreating children either through overprotection or misguided tolerance for behaviour you would not accept from others, are not the acts of a respectful or loving parent.

So yes, children are born with the same rights as everyone else but, as every parent knows, these cannot be bestowed in full until they are mature enough to understand and exercise them wisely. Similarly, you don't insist they immediately meet all the expectations you place on an adult guest in your home.

At the heart of positive parenting is a duty to socialise your children so that ultimately they can exercise their privileges responsibly and meet their duties to society easily; in other words become socially competent adults.

For this reason alone they are, once again, much more than merely guests or visitors to your home. You would never attempt to 'socialise' any other guest. The difficult ones are simply not invited again, but you can't 'disinvite' your children, they are bonded to you for life.

Social competence means that not only are children welcomed and supported by adults and peers outside the home – what we have called social desirability – but also that they have the personal qualities and skills required to take advantage of the opportunities offered by others. But a responsibility to render children both socially desirable and competent in no way moderates a basic truth – children are born autonomous souls and should always be respected as such.

Failing to socialise children to live up to their inheritance as members of society – with all its benefits and burdens – means to fail as a parent. Genuine reverence for children (John Locke's term for respect in the quotation at the beginning of this chapter) means to accept this sometimes onerous task and the pain and heartache it can entail. But this is what it means to respect as well as love your children (see Story: Art Lessons).

Story: *Art Lessons*

Most young children like to draw and paint, while a smaller number continue to study art more formally through their school years. Our son Rory was one of these.

He clearly enjoyed art, and certainly some of his teachers thought they detected a degree of talent. His father, however, was less sure. Rory's school reports were not encouraging and he was regularly in trouble in Art class. His father's concern was that he was using Art to avoid subjects that would be more 'useful' for his future.

Fortunately, his mother was wiser. Whenever it was suggested that he swap subjects she counselled to let him be.

When he left school, he studied Economics and Finance and appeared to have left Art behind. Subsequently, he pursued a successful career in business consulting but he was not happy. He almost ceased being the considerate, cheerful person we had known for 20 odd years. He became morose, argumentative, and less pleasant to be around.

Finally, after a few years, he told us his heart was not in consulting and what he really wanted to be was an architect, interestingly like his great-grandfather. He moved back home, completed five further years of undergraduate and postgraduate study, and today is happy and successful in his chosen career.

He has found his calling.

This is a quite a common story. After a false start, a young man finds his true vocation.

However, it is worth noting that, without his mother's respect for him – reflected in her acceptance of him as *who he was* – it is quite possible Rory would not have continued with Art. In this case the vital stimulus it gave him, to develop the ways of seeing and thinking which are essential to architecture, would have been lost.

Unlike his father, in this regard at least, she respected him as a person and was less concerned about him accumulating prizes. She could look past his indifferent school reports and sense his preference for thinking in three dimensions and genuine fascination with images, expressed in an obsession with 'rubbish' TV – much to his father's chagrin.

Rory may have become an architect regardless, but it is less likely. To us, this story underscores the importance of respecting children as well as loving them; to acknowledge them as individuals in their own right and treating their interests and preferences with deference – even if these do not accord with ours.

An additional benefit for parents, as John Locke notes above, is that if we truly respect our children they are more likely to respect us, an important accomplishment of character.

And, if they respect us, it is much easier for us to like and love them.

In addition they will respect themselves, a further accomplishment of character.

Taking Children Seriously

We agree that to say we should respect our children is rather trite and obvious. We are sure that you, like most parents, would argue vehemently that you do regard your children and the business of parenting very seriously indeed. Why else would you be reading a book on that very subject?

But there is an important difference between respecting a child and loving them, taking them seriously, or being concerned for their welfare.

Concern for their children's future leads many parents to make significant sacrifices in time, career opportunities and income to assist them succeed in a competitive world. There is no doubting their commitment.

These children enjoy the best education available, complete a regular schedule of extra-curricular activities, and pursue a busy social life, all the while being monitored by watchful parents anxious for them to 'keep up'. The current expression 'helicopter parents' springs to mind once more.

But there is a line between providing opportunities for children and turning them into a project which may reflect more of your aspirations than theirs.

Respect for children doesn't simply mean treating them with courtesy at all times, although you should. It also means giving them time and space to develop in their own way and resisting the temptation to impose too many of your own expectations – in terms of what their future should look like – onto them (see Story: *Playing Matchmaker*).

Story: *Playing Matchmaker*

Another further example of the importance of treating children with respect comes once again from our own family.

When our elder son Hugh was a teenager, he appeared to have no close friends and spent a lot of time on his own. Concerned for his welfare we consulted a colleague who is a psychologist. He simply asked us if we thought Hugh was unhappy. We said we didn't think so but argued that surely it would be better for Hugh if he had more friends and spent more time with people his own age.

Our colleague disagreed.

His sage advice was to leave Hugh to make friends in his own time and his own way rather than try to conjure them up for him. Fortunate-

ly, we listened and, as an adult, Hugh has formed his own family and a wonderful group of friends without any help from his parents.

How he would have reacted to us playing 'matchmaker' does not bear thinking about!

ঌঌঌ

To our mind this story highlights the critical difference between loving or being concerned for children (or taking them seriously) and treating them with respect.

We were clearly concerned for Hugh's welfare but did not necessarily respect his autonomy as a person when we were contemplating taking a more active role in his social life. The critical difference between respect and love is that, by being too concerned for a child's welfare, parents may fail to give them the time and space they need to find their own way; in other words, they may be tempted to 'step in' more often than is desirable.

ঌঌঌ

Once again we are confronted with the dilemma of stepping in vs holding back; how much to engage and how often to stand aside?

As we already know, there are no obvious answers to these questions and sometimes you will get it wrong. All parents do. But if you remain aware of the difference between respect and concern (or love) you are less likely to take over your children's lives, thus preventing them from becoming the people they want and need to be.

It is too easy for parents to assume that they always know what is best for children because they often do, particularly when they are young.

Acting on their behalf can be a habit that is hard to break. If extroverted parents have an introverted child, it can be difficult for them to understand quite how he or she interacts with the world (quite differently than an extrovert by the way) or 'what is best' for them. Simply applying what worked for you to your own children, and leaving it at that, is not a good idea.

If they are not unhappy and getting along reasonably well at home and school, it is probably best to leave them in peace to find their own way. There will still be a lot of parenting for you to do.

Practising Respect for Children

Genuine respect for children requires a degree of deference towards them which recognises their prerogative to ultimately live their life as they see fit, within the constraints placed on every member of society. It also requires parents to accept them for who they are rather than be disappointed because they are not, perhaps, what you wished for.

This does not mean, however, that you should accept any and all behaviour from your child without comment or intervention. But it is important at all times to maintain a rigid distinction between their behaviour, some of which you may seek to influence for the better, and the child as a person who demands and deserves your respect and love.

Conscientious parents place constraints on children, particularly when they are young, to protect them from risks they are not yet able to manage on their own. They also insist on adherence to family rules in order to teach them how to live successfully with others; that is, to be socially desirable and competent.

But you should never lose sight of the fact that your children are autonomous individuals, even if temporarily they need your guidance and protection.

How can parents ensure they don't lose this focus? Well there at least four things you can do:

First, remember that your purpose as a parent is not to dictate ends or outcomes for your children. Positive parenting is about creating a family environment, built with love, affection, routine, rules and discipline, within which children learn to feel secure, develop their own identity, and create a quality life for themselves. Your concern should not be their destination but how they conduct themselves along the way, so that ultimately they can claim their full birthright as human beings (see Story: *The Aussie Rules Star*).

Second, include children, as early as possible, in all discussions about them and the decisions you make on their behalf. Parents should still have the final say until their children are in late adolescence, but you should endeavour to meet as many of their preferences as possible.

Third, as we emphasised earlier, provide them (even toddlers) with a sphere of autonomy, which expands with age, in which they can exercise their own discretion. This allows them to plan their own 'work', learn from their errors and, at the same time, to come to understand 'what is generally best'.

Fourth, use discipline as a tool for encouraging children to take responsibility for their own behaviour and the consequences which follow. This can be done, for example, by emphasising that if they decide to ignore a family rule then they, and no one else, trigger the penalties this may entail.

You can agree with a teen that she/he has the option of staying out later than arranged but you should also emphasise that, if they do break their curfew, then they, not you are responsible for what happens next. Teenagers will naturally blame their parents if they are 'grounded' but it is important they learn personal responsibility. Recognising that they, and not others, primarily determine most of what happens to them is essential if they are to acquire maturity, positive identity and resilience as accomplishments of character.

By adhering to these four fundamentals of positive parenting you will display genuine respect for your children from the very beginning. You will also place them on a path to psychological health and adult success.

Story: *The Aussie Rules Star*

Jeremy was a childhood Aussie Rules prodigy, stronger and, initially at least, more talented than his classmates. He excelled with minimal effort, won many awards, and was mentioned in the local newspapers. His family schedule revolved around his sport while his coach and parents kept reminding him that he was a special player with a golden future.

Unfortunately, in the process, he became a rather arrogant and unpleasant boy who neglected his education and his friends. As he got older it became clear that he would not succeed at a professional level. His contemporaries quickly surpassed him, and he became an average player in the amateur leagues.

Without an aura of sporting success, he ceased to be the centre of attention. He struggled at school and eventually left before completing his high school certificate. His life as a young adult since then has been marred by periods of unemployment, mental disorder, drug use and poor relationships with his parents and siblings.

⚘⚘⚘

Several things are worth noting from this rather unfortunate story.

A talented boy was defined almost exclusively in terms of his sporting ability, which meant his other talents may well have been neglected. He was fed a regular diet of praise for largely unearned success (i.e., for what he would achieve in the future), which led him to assume that success was his by right rather than by effort, which was reflected in his disdain for school.

In addition, both his parents and coaches, possibly basking in the reflected glow of his success, tended to overlook his less appealing behaviours or made excuses for them.

As we discussed in Chapter 5, an undiluted diet of indiscriminate praise puts children at risk of developing a narcissistic personality. Perhaps not surprisingly, Jeremy learned to interact with others from a position of assumed superiority which prevented him forming solid friendships. Arrogance and a lack of empathy became key features of his character. And when his football career went into decline, he was ill-equipped to deal with failure.

Little wonder then that his life after school has been unhappy.

Respectful Relationships

An even more obvious demonstration of respect for children (or lack of it) can be seen in the way parents interact with them on a daily basis and the relationships they develop with them as a result. Manners and courtesy are important, but they are not the whole story.

The most useful tool for building respectful relationships between people that we have come across is the Emotional Bank Account in Steven Covey's bestselling book *The 7 Habits of Highly Successful People*.[1]

Covey suggests that, in one sense, a relationship with another person is not unlike a bank account, albeit one that trades in trust rather than money. And as with a financial account, you can invest in a relationship to increase your balance of trust with another person or make withdrawals to reduce it, and potentially put the relationship at risk.

By investing in their relationships with their children on a daily basis, parents create a surplus of trust which they can draw down on, when necessary, without damaging these to the point of no return. With children, examples of drawdowns include when you intervene to modify their behaviour – with or without a disciplinary consequence – or deny them an opportunity they desire but which you believe is premature.

Despite your best efforts, they may feel disappointed or possibly even 'betrayed'. Drawdowns can also occur when circumstances outside your control (like unforeseen work commitments) mean you must break a promise or fail to keep an arrangement you have made with them. Events of this kind, as long as they are infrequent, will not harm your relationship with your children, provided you maintain a solid working balance of trust between them and you.

Using the Emotional Bank Account model, Covey identifies six ways of investing in a relationship, as well as six types of withdrawals:

Investments	**Withdrawals**
Listen to understand	Don't listen
Attend to the others' needs	Ignore the other's needs
Keep commitments	Break promises
Be loyal	Gossip, betray confidences
Be honest – clarify expectations	Be dishonest – set false expectations
Apologise sincerely (when you make a withdrawal)	Be arrogant – never apologise

These lists are self-explanatory and, indeed, common sense. Used consistently, behaviours listed in the right-hand column, and others like them, are guaranteed to damage and ultimately destroy any relationship. Those in the left-hand column provide easy to use tools for keeping important relationships on track, in particular, attending to another's needs.

What this means is that, particularly in the case of children, parents should regularly recognise and respond to their need for attention and approval. Every conversation with a child provides an opportunity to pay them a compliment, to recognise their progress and positive qualities, even if you are speaking to them for disciplinary reasons. This an easy way to bring them closer to you and encourage the behaviours and qualities of character you wish them to display.

When we first came across the Emotional Bank Account it seemed too simplistic and mechanical to adequately encompass the complexities of interactions between human beings. But, as long as we understand that its primary purpose is to build and sustain trust – which forms the foundation for relationship success – and no more, it works!

From the perspective of this chapter, you will also note that the behaviours in the left-hand column are also external markers of the respect which we have emphasised should characterise relationships between children and their parents. Using these in every interaction you have with a child and avoiding those on the right will achieve two things. Firstly, your respect for your children will be demonstrated publicly to them and others on a regular basis. Secondly, the behaviours in the left-hand column, together with targeted praise for the accomplishments of character you wish them to acquire, will ensure you build and maintain enduring relationships with them.

A relationship with a child based on solid trust will make everything else in your interactions with them easier, including the use of discipline. They know that you will respond to their needs and concerns in a positive way and hence are more likely to ask for help when they need it. They are also more likely to listen when you offer advice or ask them to stop or change what they are doing.

John Gottman, a psychologist, used the Emotional Bank Account to research the likelihood of married couples staying together. He found that simply to maintain an existing relationship required a daily 5:1 ratio of 'investments' to 'withdrawals'. That is, we have to work hard just to keep the show on the road![2, 3]

What is even more interesting is his finding that to *influence* the behaviour of others requires a regular ratio of 8:1 of investments to withdrawals. In other words, to successfully change your children's behaviour requires an intensely supportive relationship between you and them, characterised by very high levels of trust. Influencing children's behaviour and personality development is, of course, the essence of positive parenting and daily use of this powerful little tool will make your task a lot easier.

Using the Emotional Bank Account is not difficult. It is relatively simple (and time free) to make 'investments' during every interaction you have with your children and your partner on a daily basis.

Remembering someone's birthday is far more important than giving them an expensive gift (particularly if it comes late). As with all the other accomplishments of character you seek to pass on to children, teaching them relationship management starts with *your example*, particularly how you interact with your partner – which is constantly on display and which your children observe closely.

It goes without saying, and the research supports this, that the better the relationship between parents the better it is for children.[4] Regular use of the Emotional Bank Account will ensure you enjoy rewarding relations with your partner as well as your children.

Another benefit of the Emotional Bank Account is that, once internalised, it is a daily prompt to keep relationships with family and friends up to scratch. These won't survive without regular reflection on whether we are pulling our weight, notably in the small things, which others notice and remember. Therefore, to say, "Well I earn all the money so my family should be grateful and accept that I am often disinterested and grumpy", is a 'copout' which will inevitably end in tears all round.

Don't Make Your Children a Project

Two of the pleasures of being a parent are encouraging children to develop their talents and celebrating their successes with them. But be sure you are doing this for them and not yourself.

The story of Jeremy, the Aussie Rules star, reminds parents to ensure that their children engage in a range of pursuits rather than focus too early on one or two obvious strengths. Encouraging children to 'spread their net' in this way is important for four reasons.

First, it gives them more options to fall back on in the future if their initial career plan comes unstuck; second, they become more stimulating, better-rounded characters with more interests to share with others; third, it helps them learn to manage failure more comfortably because they are not focusing exclusively on their strengths where success comes relatively easily.

Finally, by experimenting early with a variety of activities, they are more likely to acquire competence as an accomplishment of character which will provide a lifetime of professional and personal satisfaction.

Encourage each of your children, regardless of how proficient they may be in one talent, to tackle and stick at things they find more difficult (remember they are antifragile) as well as those which they find comparatively straightforward.

In this way they will learn to persist, to remain cheerful and confident, even when they are failing and, most important, to lose with grace. These accomplishments of character will be easier to develop if you and your partner are less concerned with how high up the leader board they are and more interested in how they handle success (however limited) and failure (however great).

Turning our children into a project or living our dreams through them is a seductive and, dare we say, lazy thing to do, simply because it is easier than realising our own aspirations. It also reflects a lack of respect for them.

In Australia today, there are too many young people at university, who would prefer, and be better off, doing something else except for the pressure of parental aspiration reinforced by social expectations.

Deciding that your child will be 'the first one in our family to go to university', however laudable an ambition, may not be in their best interests. Also, statements like this always sound as if they are more about meeting a parent's needs than a child's.

To us this is a perfect example of the 'accumulation of prizes' approach to parenting that we warn against in Chapter 2. It also displays a lack of respect for the child; by the time they have left school, they should be making career decisions for themselves. You might advise and encourage them to seek advice from mentors and professional counsellors, but they should be steering the ship. .

In 2019 the Australian Productivity Commission reported that 60% of school leavers attended university by the time they were 22 years old. Unfortunately, only two out of three finished their course within six years.[5]

It is hard to believe that university style training is the next best step for nearly two-thirds of high school leavers, since a third of these don't graduate. So it is worth asking how many of these students were there as a result of parental as much as personal ambition?

Completing a degree is not the only reason to attend university, of course. Nevertheless, these numbers suggest that too many young people are being channelled straight into a career path that does not suit them, not to mention that they are running up a HECS debt they may struggle to repay.

In fact, some concerned educators are now calling for a compulsory 'gap' year between Year 12 and further learning (university enrolment in particular) to allow school leavers a chance to consider their next steps more closely. Your own experience will tell you that a majority of high school graduates are not ready to plunge into three or more years of further academic study and that it makes sense to encourage them to explore the many alternative career tracks available. University education might be appropriate some time in the future, but maybe not immediately.

The final point to make about the dangers of turning your children into a project is that they won't be around forever. When they are gone you still have your own life to lead, which is just as important as theirs. Don't lose your identity in your children.

Saying you should resist the temptation to impose your preferences on children does not mean you should have no expectations of them. Quite the contrary. But, as we emphasised in Chapter 2, your focus should be not so much on *what* they do but *how* they do it – this is what it means to focus on character development rather than on achievement for its own sake.

If they prefer competition (i.e., structured) skateboarding to soccer, no problem, provided you attend their skateboarding as you would their soccer and that their language and behaviour on the skateboard ramp is no different from what you would expect on the soccer pitch.

If skateboarding (or soccer) means they drift into unsavoury company, that is more your fault than theirs if you have not monitored their behaviour and the people they are mixing with on and off the skateboard ramp (or soccer pitch). If you still want them to play soccer, even though they express a clear preference for skateboarding, ask yourself, "Whose needs am I seeking to satisfy?"

True respect for children means accepting who they are, although not necessarily everything they do or how they do it. It also means focusing your efforts on assisting them to acquire the character they will need to create their own life, rather than trying to dictate a future for them.

With time, space, opportunity and encouragement, children will find the path they wish to pursue. Helping them follow their star, the one they choose for themselves, is our privilege as parents.

As Well as Love Them

The title of this chapter reminds parents to respect as well as love their children.

We have discussed the need for respect, and how to practise this on a daily basis, and we have met many parents who need to practise more respect for their offspring. Less often we have also encountered those who have got the respect thing right, in the sense of giving children time and space to be themselves, but who also seem to be unaware of their need for affection, attention and support – which are the outward signs of parental love.

Love at its most basic is a biological bond which is almost impossible to break. Even those who hate their parents will profess to love them at the same time (and vice versa) and we believe them. But for love to work its magic it must be expressed in daily demonstrations of your care, concern, physical affection and time for your children. When this is missing or, more likely, inadequate, the implications for them can be ominous (see Story: *Amelia*).

Story: *Amelia*

Amelia was 13 years old when she developed anorexia nervosa. Anorexia nervosa is a potentially life threatening eating disorder characterised by a distorted body image and unwarranted fears of being overweight.

Sufferers obsess about their body size and what they eat. They also will often report elevated anxiety and depression. Binge eating followed by vomiting to avoid weight gain (bulimia) may also be part of the picture.

Amelia displayed all of these symptoms and was eventually hospitalised because of genuine fears for her life. Naturally she became the focus of her family's concern. Her parents visited daily and her classmates arranged a roster so that she would see a friendly face from school every day.

A follow up interview revealed that her parents were both highly accomplished and successful professionals who were often absent interstate or overseas on business. While they were genuinely concerned for their daughter, one sensed that her ill health was also an inconvenience, pre-

venting them from getting on with the real business of life, pursuing their careers.

There is no doubt they loved their daughter in an abstract sense but their attitude towards her was almost the same as one might adopt towards a professional colleague; respect, certainly, and a positive regard for their welfare, but little of the warmth, intimacy, and affection that one would expect to see between two parents and a teenage daughter.

Fortunately, Amelia recovered and finished school and university. However, she remains an anxious, emotionally fragile adult who is chronically concerned about others' opinion of her and hypersensitive to what she perceives as criticism. She also continues to consult mental health professionals, something she has been doing since she was first admitted to hospital as a young teen.

⁂

We have suggested that children who receive insufficient positive attention from parents, in the form of praise and recognition, will seek to attract it via other less appropriate and, at times, unhealthy ways. This certainly seems to have been the case with Amelia.

Her pleasant, but also preoccupied, parents, appear to have been an uncertain source of love and affection. As noted, they treated her with the same respect they would afford any professional colleague, but seemed unaware of her need (like every child) for active friendliness, physical closeness, time together and ongoing support as they make their way through childhood and adolescence.

Her parents had married later than many couples and when she arrived they were already deeply embedded in their respective careers. Given this, it is possible to speculate that Amelia failed to achieve secure attachment to a primary care giver during the critical period of 0 to three years, particularly if her mother was frequently absent.

In Chapter 1 we stressed the importance of secure attachment to children for promoting a bedrock sense of security and a fundamental trust in their world and those around them.

If Amelia's early circumstances meant that attachment was compromised, then research suggests she would already have been at greater risk of developing mental illness in adolescence. If this were the case, her essential lack of security would appear to have been translated into a severe eating disorder, which at least attracted the parental concern and support she was missing.

Whether or not inadequate attachment was involved, while Amelia recovered physically, unfortunately she was left with a legacy of chronic anxiety and insecurity.

Amelia's story highlights every child's need for both respect *and* love.

Respect Cuts Both Ways

In this chapter we have been at pains to make the case for respecting our children. But it is also worth noting that, for a relationship to endure, respect between people must be reciprocated.

If parents are to fully respect their offspring, children must extend the same courtesy and consideration towards their parents, that we are suggesting parents should display towards them.

It is not pleasant to sit with a parent and their child while the latter treats their mother or father with little more than contempt.

They may interrupt with rude comments about their parents, or the consultant, ignore requests to answer questions, or refuse to turn off their screen. Either way they present a good example of a child who has failed to learn social desirability and competence (see story: *Douglas*).

Story: *Douglas*

Douglas (eight years old) and his mother came to see one of us because, according to his mother, he was anxious and difficult to discipline at home.

He was an intelligent boy who was keeping up at school but resisted, and indeed resented, attempts by his parents to get him to shut off his screen, clean his teeth, or go to bed as well as follow pretty much any request made of him to cooperate in family life.

He was also frequently verbally aggressive towards his younger sister. In contrast, however, he was compliant at school and received generally positive reports from his teachers.

The defining feature of Douglas's behaviour was his absolute disregard for his mother. He was openly rude to her, frequently contradicted what she said and, from time to time, stood up and waved his hand in front of her face to prevent her from talking.

In short, much of his behaviour, in our sessions anyway, was extremely unpleasant which his mother, a gentle and sensitive person, seemed incapable of dealing with. The poor lady was in tears as she described her daily battles with her son whenever she tried to get his cooperation.

She had grown up in an extremely strict household where her father's word was law and any disrespect for him or her mother unthinkable. Not surprisingly, she found her own son's behaviour inexplicable. She concluded that the root cause of his behaviour was anxiety which needed treatment.

Douglas's father, who attended a later session, appeared relatively disinterested in his son's behaviour and seemed to think that it was his wife's problem to sort out. He was a busy business owner who was frequently absent from home.

We discussed the need for agreed rules and consistent discipline to enforce them but, perhaps predictably, without both parents' engagement, this came to nothing and Douglas and his mother discontinued their sessions.

We heard later that he had been diagnosed with an anxiety disorder but no outcome other than that.

❧❧❧

A couple of points can be made here.

It is quite likely that anxiety was one of the drivers of Douglas's behaviour at home. But if so it was caused by a lack of boundaries and reliable discipline. In Chapter 10 we discuss children's need for clear boundaries if they are to feel secure in any situation.

The fact that he was getting along quite well at school suggests that there, at least, these were in place. At school he also had an added incentive to fit in so as to attract the approval of teachers and peers. In this regard children's behaviour can be quite situation specific; they may behave quite differently at home than at school or when visiting a friend.

Douglas's parents' unwillingness, in the case of his father, and inability, in the case of his mother, to discipline him left him flailing out to find firm boundaries in his home life. In addition, a lack of positive attention from a frequently absent father, appears to have led him to get noticed in less appropriate ways.

You might argue that, because he seemed to know how to get along with others when away from home, he would find his way to adulthood more or less successfully. But you will have met many adults, who, although successful in their careers, have a disastrous home life because they seem unable to afford their partner and children the same respect they display towards colleagues and clients.

In this sense the behaviour of adults can be just as situation specific as children's.

Ironically, while we should afford the greatest respect to those closest to us, and on whom our happiness ultimately depends, too often the reverse is true.

If we are not careful, we will display more courtesy towards casual acquaintances such as the 'postie' than our own family, with predictable consequences for us and them.

Role Modelling

"Children need models rather than critics." Joseph Joubert (French essayist)

In Chapter 3 we recommended eight techniques for bestowing accomplishments of character on children. While these are all important, the good news is that they can learn a lot of what they need to know simply by observing their parents; if your children are to acquire the personal qualities you value then you must display them first.

The easiest way for a parent to guide children to become the people you want them to be is to *be that person yourself.* Copying those around us, and especially those in authority, is in our DNA. For millennia our survival depended on conforming to the behaviour of our band or troop, principally its senior members. For better or worse, children automatically observe and imitate their parents.

When our son Hugh was in junior primary his teacher was once asking his class about the work their parents did. When Hugh was asked about his father he confidently replied that his father was a psychologist. His teacher then asked, "What do psychologists do?" Hugh paused for a moment, as he pondered this question, and then just as confidently said, "Drink wine." Today, you probably won't be surprised to learn, Hugh is just as keen on wine as his father!

More seriously, if we want sons to be kind, gentle and respectful towards the opposite sex then fathers need to behave the same way towards their female partner. Similarly, if we want our daughters to be confident, capable women, then mothers, supported by fathers, must provide a suitable example.

The bad news is that, as they get older, children quickly begin to see the gaps between what parents say and what we do, and to confront us with these discrepancies. This is understandable – none of us is perfect – but it is important to remain as consistent as possible for your own benefit as well as your children's.

Role modelling or providing an example to children is critical, but not enough on its own. We have already mentioned that watching someone else perform a skill is quite different from doing it yourself. Your own experience learning to drive will tell you this.

You may have sat in a car for years while your parents drove, but nothing really prepares you for your first time behind the wheel!

So while the example provided by parents is important, children will not learn all they need to know by simply watching and listening. They also need hands on training and practice.

Successive Approximations

We have already referred to the common lament of parents: "I know what I want my kids to do, I just can't get them to do it!" A major reason to be frustrated by a gap between your children's behaviour and what you wish it to be is to assume that they could, if they were prepared to make the effort, close this gap in a single jump or at least in a few large steps.

If this is the case you may find yourself gritting your teeth and muttering under your breath "Why won't they just do it!" The reason is, of course, that they can't. They don't have the knowledge, skills, and confidence required. And if you become frustrated or criticise them then they will become even less inclined to try.

It is interesting that while most parents are unlikely to expect children to display a reasonable level of sporting or musical competence, for example, without coaching, some assume that they should be able to do precisely this in the social sphere – to 'be responsible' or 'do the right thing' – without help other than a simple, sometimes barked, instruction.

Leading children to social competence requires the same approach as training them to hit the basket in basketball; that is, by helping them achieve successive approximations to the final goal of independent marurity.

If your 8-year-old daughter wants to play basketball for the Australian Opals, or at least become an accomplished player, you would approach her goal via a series of measured steps, each designed to reflect her current size and capacity.

Each week you would demonstrate and then coach a specific skill you believe she can manage at her current level of competence, with ball and equipment suited to her physical size. You would then move with her gradually towards genuine expertise. At the same time you would praise her efforts as well as *any* evidence of improvement, however small.

What you wouldn't do is go out and buy an 8-year-old an Olympic sized basketball and net and expect her to play with them. In this case you would be setting up a gap between where she is and where you want her to be, which is impossible for her to bridge. Common sense tells you that this will be to expect too much too soon and the quickest way to kill any interest she has in the sport at the very beginning. If you become grumpy because she can't do what you expect, you will put her off basketball for life.

True respect for a child means to value their effort and commitment at any level of performance; don't wait until they become recognised by others for their skills and success.

And so it is for social competence.

Children are not born ready socialised in the same way that ducklings automatically follow the first moving object they see after they hatch (generally their mother). Humans need to be taught how to live together amicably, to interact graciously, and to make wise decisions in the best interests of themselves and others.

When they are young, in particular, there is a generally yawning gap, in terms of their social desirability and competence, between what you want to see from your children and what you generally get. You can either become frustrated or teach them what they need to know.

The best way to achieve this is by using the same methods described above; firstly, by example, and secondly by taking them through a series of successive approximations to the final version of the behaviour you are looking for.

Parents can apply the technique of successive approximations to social behaviour using the following: observation of your child to determine their current level of competence, demonstration, direct coaching and *praise for effort as well as results.* If you observe your toddler reluctant to share their toys, for instance, you will first show them what to do. You then recognise their efforts, however rudimentary, to do the same and continue to praise in the future whenever you see them at least trying to share with others. Relatively quickly you can expect them to share regularly, preferably without being reminded. If they flat out refuse we advise you to apply the disciplining techniques discussed in Chapters 10 and 11.

The key point here is to look for *any* evidence in your child's behaviour that they are trying to meet your expectations and praise accordingly. Don't wait until they produce a perfect example of social competence. If you do you will be waiting a long time.

Children, as we already know, crave our attention. Your children will respond positively to any sign of your approval and whatever a parent praises or responds to they will do more of in the future. Carefully targeting your public praise to promote those behaviours and accomplishments of character you wish to see in your children is a potent tool of positive parenting.

Teaching social competence, the capacity to operate independently in society, is to teach children how to exercise their rights and meet their obligations as independent human beings so that they can deal on equal terms with whomever they meet. This is the essence of respect for children, namely preparing them so that in the fullness of time they can leave home and successfully take their chosen place in the world.

Conclusion

Respecting a child is not the same as loving them, taking them seriously or feeling concern for them. It is to recognise that, from the very beginning, they have the same rights and responsibilities as every other human being, even if, initially, they are unable to exercise these in full. In particular, they have the right, and obligation (albeit with their parents' support) to find their own way to their own future while extending the same courtesy to others.

Just because they cannot immediately claim their full birthright does not alter the fact they are autonomous individuals who ultimately must accept their share of the benefits and burdens of adult life.

Too much or rather misguided love or 'concern' may lead parents into overprotection, which can infantilise a child, or to take over their children's lives and turn them into a 'project'. It may also mean that they neglect to insist that a child respects others and/or accepts responsibility for the consequences of his or her own actions and decisions.

Parents demonstrate genuine respect for their children in four ways: by focusing on how rather than what they achieve; by involving them in discussions about their future; by providing an ever widening sphere of autonomy within which they can learn to be themselves; and by teaching them the vital lesson that much of what happens to them is the direct consequence of their own decisions and actions.

How you regard your children is also very apparent in every contact you have with them, particularly whether you invest in or withdraw from the balance of trust you have established with them. Over time, the quality of your interactions will determine the quality of the relationships you enjoy with them, particularly when they are adults, and, ultimately, the quality of their character as well.

Sincere respect also means to accept a child for the person they are rather than be disappointed because they are not the one you might have preferred. This, as we have emphasised, does not mean tolerating their unacceptable behaviour. Rather it requires parents to clearly distinguish between their child as an autonomous individual and those aspects of their conduct which may derail their future and which, for their benefit, need to change. In seeking to modify a child's behaviour, however, you should never lose sight of their right to be treated as sovereign individuals.

Respect your children as well as love them.

Summary

- Respect for children is an important principle of positive parenting and is very different from loving them, being concerned for them, or taking them seriously.

- Respect for children begins by recognising that they are born with the same rights, privileges, and responsibilities as every other human being. The fact that they cannot fully exercise these immediately does not negate or dilute their birthright in any way.
- Misplaced parental love can override the need to respect children which may result either in overprotection, which runs the risk of infantilising them, or a failure to insist they meet the obligations they owe to others.
- Respect also requires a genuine acceptance of your children for who they are, rather than being disappointed that they are not what you hoped for or trying to turn them into someone quite different.
- Respect for children, however, does *not* mean accepting behaviour which is inappropriate or harmful to them or others without intervening to address it.
- Parents demonstrate respect for children by (a) focusing on character development rather than defining their future for them; (b) providing a sphere of autonomy which teaches them independence; (c) including them in discussions about their future; (d) teaching them to accept the consequences of their own actions.
- Parents also demonstrate respect for children by how they interact with them on a daily basis; a relationship not characterised by respect and trust will inevitably fail.
- Don't turn your children into a project to satisfy your own needs or inject your own life with relevance and purpose. Pursuing your own life is just as important as assisting them to live theirs.

9

Living Together – The Need for Rules

"Children are born with an innate sense of justice."
Edward Abbey (US author)

Steve Biddulph suggests that boys want to know three things:

1. Who is in charge?
2. What are the rules?
3. Will those rules be fairly applied?

He continues:

> Boys feel insecure and in danger if there is not enough structure in a situation. If no one is in charge, they begin jostling with each other to establish a pecking order. Their make-up leads them to want to set up hierarchies, but they can't always do so because they are the same age. If we provide structure, then they can relax. For girls this is not so much of a problem.[1]

If you have observed children (and particularly boys) at play particularly without adult supervision you will recognise the jostling and search for a pecking order. You will also know that both boys and girls will, when playing together, not only make and follow their own rules, but also complain bitterly if they believe these have been broken or unfairly applied. This reflects their innate sense of justice referred to by Edward Abbey in the quotation above.

Children's preference for structure and fairness is of great value to parents trying to run a reasonably orderly and happy household, provided – and this is very important – children themselves are involved in creating rules for their family and establishing the consequences which follow any infringement.

It is fascinating to watch how seriously children engage in discussions about rules and consequences and their insistence on fairness or equity in their application. All of us display more commitment to rules we have a hand in setting than those arbitrarily imposed upon us.

Why are Rules Important?

Why are rules important? Well, without agreed standards or expectations which are reliably applied no one feels secure or confident. We are all familiar with the uncertainty we associate with new situations where we don't understand what 'the rules' are. (Our first day at school or in a new job for example). Rules in the home, consistently applied, promote routine and contribute to the sense of security growing children need if they are to flourish.

Rules also teach children to live successfully, to cooperate with others and later to navigate the wider world of laws and regulations with relatively few mishaps. In this way family rules gently introduce children to the reality that trying to live without reference to the rights of others, and their own obligations as a citizen, is not an option. Failure to acknowledge their responsibilities to society can have unpleasant consequences for them in the future.

Finally rules also assist them to thrive in a world full of other people, people who have their own preferences and priorities, just as they do. Even motorcycle gangs have rules even if these don't necessarily lead to the good life. Nevertheless, they set and enforce them because they know the alternative is chaos in which very little of value can be achieved.

As we have discussed children are not born knowing how to live with others. Initially they are only aware of their own immediate needs and desires. Left to their own devices they will pursue these at the expense of anyone else and, in the process, create a great deal of mayhem around them.

This is perfectly normal by the way; young children literally don't know anything better but to express their frustration vocally or physically. Don't be concerned if, for example, your two-year-old starts to hit out at you or others or is rough with a younger sibling. Understanding such behaviour as normal, of course, is not the same as tolerating or accepting it. You may need to gently restrain your child and explain why what they are doing is not appropriate and that, although they may be unhappy, hitting or hurting others is not a solution to any problem.

Nevertheless, despite their apparently 'selfish' behaviour – and their response if anyone tries to stop them – we already know that children, small ones in particular, crave the structure and security provided by routine. One function of family rules, which are reasonably and consistently applied, is to create routine and the order and predictability that come with it. They also provide a clear set of behaviours which, through targeted praise from parents, children learn will be recognised and appreciated.

Useful rules provide a balance between their own and others' priorities and, at the same time, create enough independent safe space in which they can grow and become the person they wish to be. Rules, like routine, are also a source of external control which ultimately provide a path to self-discipline.

Reasonable rules, reliably applied, provide external constraints with which children eventually become familiar and comfortable. Rules place limits on their conduct – the need to respect others' possessions for example – and specify accepted ways of behaving. As they grow these restraints become internalised as personal habits, characteristic of a mature adult, without them fully realising what is happening.

Children acquire bad habits in the same way. Families characterised by disorganisation, disrespect and selfishness, for example, will bestow similar behaviours on children growing up in them.

By learning to follow family rules children will also develop many of the accomplishments of character presented in Chapter 2. These include respect for others, emotional control, empathy and maturity.

What Children Learn from Rules

By setting rules for a family and applying measured consequences for infringements, you will teach your children at least three important lessons: how to live in the wider world of legislated laws; how to pursue their ambitions without infringing the rights of others; and how to relate effectively with all manner of people – including those they may not particularly like.

As we have already emphasised (in Chapter 1), this does not mean turning children into 'pushovers' or 'doormats' to be bullied or exploited by the unscrupulous.

Rather it is to teach them the following (as well as encourage associated accomplishments of character):

1. They, like others, have rights which should be respected (grace and respect).
2. Rules enable every individual to exercise their own rights – and live as independently as possible – without infringing on those of others (maturity, grace, respect and empathy).
3. Rules inevitably place some restrictions on freedom of behaviour – this is the price we pay to live in a crowded world – but they also maximise personal space to operate freely while allowing others to do the same (maturity, grace, respect, emotional control and empathy).
4. They have a responsibility to stand up respectfully for themselves and others when they believe their rights are being infringed in an arbitrary fashion; that is, not according to the rules – say by a bully (self-confidence, personal identity, emotional control and resilience).
5. Being respectful of rules and, by extension, of others, is generally the best way to get along with people and to *get more of what they want from others* (maturity, grace, respect and empathy).
6. Just as there are rules at home and school governing the behav-

iour of children, so are there laws governing the behaviour of adults in the wider community. Furthermore adherence to the law is obligatory and infractions are punished whether we like it or not (maturity).

(This last point is included as a reminder that, once in place, rules at home and school are also obligatory, and must be followed or consequences will occur. Children should never have the option of either declining to follow agreed rules or 'cherry picking' the ones they prefer).

7. As in the adult world, so it is at home. Some rules are imposed on children (who may well disagree with them) for their own benefit, such as the requirement to attend school or share in household chores (maturity).
8. Most importantly, consequences following a breach of a family rule are the direct result of *individual choice*. If a child is sanctioned within agreed rules, this is the result of *their* decisions and behaviour, no one else's. Under these conditions a consequence is not something that is 'unfair' or arbitrarily imposed by a third party – in this case a parent – or beyond their control to avoid. Rather it is something they have *chosen* for themselves even if, initially, they don't see it that way (maturity and positive identity).

Rules and the use of discipline to enforce them are central to positive parenting. And both will make a lot more sense to both parents and children – and are more likely to be observed – when they are presented within a broader explanation of why rules are in place and why there are consequences for infringing them.

Having an explanatory framework of the type presented above, will give you more confidence that appropriate discipline is in the best interests of your children. Thus, when disciplining a child, you can explain what is happening and why, by reference back to the above points as well as the rules developed by your family.

These discussions should commence very early, even before your child fully understands what you are talking about. Over time, provided you are firm, fair and consistent, they will come to know not only how to behave appropriately towards others, and why it matters, but also that they are primarily responsible for most of what happens to them, good and bad (see story: *Kylie*).

Story: *Kylie*

By 10 years of age it is fair to say that Kylie was out of control. She was frequently in trouble at school, often for physical aggression towards other children, and came and went as she liked from home without reference to her parents' wishes. Her teachers had effectively given up trying to teach her and her parents were gravely concerned for her safety when she stayed out late on many nights of the week. Not surprisingly her behaviour was also beginning to 'rub off' on her younger sister and brother.

Her parents came to one of us for help.

Our advice was to immediately develop rules (with input from all their children) to describe how they wanted their family to function and each member to behave. We also discussed the use of disciplinary procedures including time out and removal of privileges, such as access to smart phones and pocket money.

These suggestions, thanks to the parents' commitment, proved remarkably successful. They and their children developed a set of rules governing chores, meal times (which previously had been haphazard), and appropriate behaviour, as well as curfews, bedtimes and use of screens.

Even more impressive was that the children themselves instituted a procedure whereby the number of minutes each child spent in time out, when it was required, was equivalent to their age! (This, by the way, is not a recommended practice, but reflects the level of their children's engagement. The use of time out is discussed in Chapter 10).

At their next appointment the parents described the almost miraculous impact that applying agreed rules had had on the whole family. While Kylie was still by no means a model citizen, she was happier at school and relations between everyone at home, especially between her and her siblings, had improved significantly.

Both parents agreed that home life was far more harmonious than it had been for a long time.

ক্ষক্ষক্ষ

Three points can be taken from this story.

Firstly, the mere fact that parents set rules, discussed (even if not agreed) with children, can make a big difference to family functioning.

Why exactly this is so may be unclear, but to us underscores the point that we all feel insecure in situations where 'the rules' are not apparent and prefer at least some structure which clarifies what is expected of us and others.

The second point is that setting rules is the easier part; applying them consistently requires a considerable effort from parents, not least if you are trying to restore a family that is in danger of sliding into chaos.

The last and most important point is that having rules gives you a solid place to start from, even if your application of them is not always consistent. Persistence rather than perfection is the key.

Family Rules

Any family, large or small, is an organisation and needs rules to function effectively. Once your children are old enough to understand (and that's often a lot younger than you might think), involve them in a discussion about rules. Ask them why rules are important, which ones are needed at home and what should happen if they are not followed.

While parents exercise final authority, because they carry ultimate responsibility for a family's welfare, as much as possible rules and consequences should be the result of a genuine whole family discussion. It is important that the views of the youngest member are listened to with the same respect as those of the eldest.

Some rules will apply to everyone, such as apologising if you have been rude. Others will apply only to children and these will vary according to age, including coming home times and use of social media (although some parents choose to match their use of screens at home with the limits they place on their children). It is also wise to review family rules regularly to ensure they remain age relevant and to discuss them immediately if one or more is not working as required.

In this sense treat your family as a 'mini' parliament operating according to an agreed set of rules, which no one can ignore on a whim and where, although some people have more authority than others, everyone has a say.

Your rules will not be perfect and, as is the case in other parliaments, there will be protests of unfairness and untidy compromises made to deal with specific circumstances. But this is infinitely preferable to the alternative which is anarchy, where the interests of the strongest are imposed by force alone. Without dependable rules no one feels safe and very little is achieved.

Children need to feel secure, most importantly at home, and family rules consistently applied are an important tool for achieving this. In addition, you practise respect for your children when you engage them in discussion about why rules are required and encourage them, regardless of their age, to contribute to framing these. A discussion like this also emphasises to them that they, like everyone else, have rights which should be recognised.

The advantages of agreed family rules are significant, provided – and this can never be overemphasised – they are implemented reliably and fairly. When used in this way, they work because they appeal to children's innate need for structure and equity.

Earlier we discussed what children learn when parents discuss the need for rules.

Once they have become accustomed to reliable rules and consistent discipline, they will learn another set of important lessons (which will also reinforce key accomplishments of character). These include:

1. The world need not be random, unpredictable, or capricious (self-confidence, positive identity and resilience).
2. They can interact effectively with a range of people, even those they do not particularly like, provided they respect others' right to live as they choose within agreed boundaries, which apply to everyone (maturity, grace, respect, competence and empathy).
3. While structure and order can be irksome at times, they are invaluable for allowing a maximum number of people to pursue their own interests simultaneously, with minimal impact on others (maturity, grace, respect, emotional control and empathy).
4. Absolute power should not determine how family affairs are managed; in other words, might is not right (maturity, grace, respect, positive identity and empathy).
5. There are consequences for infringing agreed rules, but these should be established beforehand and be proportionate to the breach (positive identity, maturity and resilience).
6. Rules are not sacrosanct; they can be challenged and changed by the people who made them. But they should be followed while they are in place (self-confidence, maturity, positive identity and competence).

Teaching your children an understanding of rules as a set of personal boundaries, within which a group of people can live, learn, and work successfully, is an important preparation for the road they have ahead of them, and for living successfully as an adult.

Let's face it, children will either learn these life lessons in the home, where the people who love them can shield them from the worst consequences of their conduct; or, more painfully, as adults, when they confront the more formal world of laws and regulations, and the penalties for ignoring these.

You may well observe that no matter how often you discuss rules you can't get your children to agree with them. This is very common but while you may never achieve complete agreement at least they are more likely to understand what rules are for, why they are in place and the reality that there are consequences for ignoring them. Understanding even without agreement introduces order and structure into their lives which is crucial if they are to feel secure and ultimately achieve responsible self-discipline.

How Many Rules?

Aim to keep your family's rules as short and simple as possible, remembering that the focus should be not so much on what people do but how they do it. A coach of our acquaintance ran a highly successful sports program with three rules only:

1. Do what's right.
2. Do your best.
3. Treat others the way you wish to be treated.

Notice that these rules are geared towards teaching children how to behave so that they gain maximum benefit from their involvement while allowing others to do the same. Learning to live and work successfully with others, while pursuing one's preferred life, is critical because it promotes accomplishments of character which lead to genuine success and happiness: respect, empathy, grace, emotional control and maturity.

At a minimum, any list of rules should expect every family member to contribute to the daily household workload, and to treat other members with respect and consideration.

Here are some suggestions:

1. We respect others; if we are rude or lose our temper, we always apologise (grace, respect, emotional control and empathy).
2. We always tell the truth, even when it hurts us or others (maturity and positive identity).
3. We take responsibility for our own mistakes and don't blame others (maturity, positive identity and empathy).
4. We complete our chores (listed separately) on time and without complaint unless we and others have agreed to changes (maturity, grace, respect and empathy).

5. If we make a mess we clean it up straight away (respect and empathy).
6. We never borrow another's possessions without permission and we return them when agreed (maturity, respect, positive identity and empathy).
7. If we damage or lose something that is not ours we make good (maturity, respect, positive identity, and empathy).
8. We always come home at the agreed time; if we are running late, we call (maturity, respect, and empathy).
9. No drugs, no pornography, no motorbikes – our favourite, especially for boys (maturity, respect, positive identity and empathy).
10. Screen time is restricted to two hours use per day (excluding school work) without special permission from either parent. (This is the current recommended maximum for children and teenagers and is probably a good rule of thumb for adults as well. Many parents restrict recreational screen time to less than this. See 'Screen Time' below).
11. If we take up something new, such as a sport or musical instrument, we stick to it for at least a year. This means going to training/lessons and being available for selection for every game/concert, regardless of what else we could be doing (persistence, maturity and resilience).
12. We never upload or share inappropriate messages, images or video of ourselves or others; we are very cautious about the information we share (maturity, respect, positive identity and empathy).*
13. We are responsible digital citizens; we demonstrate respect in posts and when sharing content; if it's not OK to say or do something face to face, it's not OK online (maturity, respect, positive identity and empathy).

---

* Rules 12 and 13 are taken from the Australian website Raising Children.net.au 2020.

While your family's list may contain some of the above it will also differ. This is obviously fine. The important thing is that your list addresses issues of relevance to your family. A mother, following our advice, once told us that her children had come up with three separate rules for using the bathroom. Apparently in her family this was a major source of concern!

We are aware our 13 rules contradict our earlier suggestion to keep these as few as possible, but they cover many if not all of the issues of concern to children and their parents. Something like these can either stand alone as the family rules or, if you prefer, provide explanatory detail for a more basic list- such as the three rules listed earlier. (Another example of a simple set of rules – Guide for Living – is provided below).

A parent knows what they mean by, "Do what's right", a small child may not. Rules 1, 2, 3, 8, 9, 12 and 13 above clarify exactly what we mean by this. "Do your best" is explained in Rules 3, 4, 5 and 11 and Rules 1, 3, 6, 7, 12 and 13 cover "Treat others as you wish to be treated".

So your three or four basic rules, which should be on the fridge door, can be expanded in another document, including something like the 13 points above, which is kept handy for easy reference and, as necessary, used as a guide when discussing or applying rules.

Guide for Living

For many years, having not come across the three basic rules listed earlier, we had the following Guide for Living (author unknown) on our fridge door, which captured, succinctly and eloquently, most of what we wanted, and still want, for our children:

1. Love tenderly (respect and empathy).
2. Walk humbly (grace, respect and positive identity).
3. Act justly (maturity, respect, positive identity and empathy).
4. Speak truthfully (maturity and positive identity).

These, together with some discussion as to their precise meaning, seemed to do the trick for us and them.

Screen Time

Rule 10, above, addresses the critical issue of screen time. Given the compelling evidence of the potentially malign impact of excessive screen time (particularly devoted to social media) on teenage mental health (see Chapter 4) we believe a rule like this should feature in every family's primary list or their supporting 'explanatory' document.

Find out how much screen time your children average each week at school, including accessing social media, and adjust your rule accordingly. Many parents we know ban social media and video gaming at home completely during the school week. This is probably not a bad starting point – when in doubt go for less screen time rather than more.

TV, for example, can be restricted during the week to one or two programs which your children particularly enjoy. Similarly time spent playing video games and other screen based activities should be carefully monitored, including on the weekends.. Also children and young teens should never have a TV in their bedroom and should not go to bed with a phone or tablet.

Leaving children alone at night with a screen means parents have little or no influence over what or how much they are viewing or how much sleep they are getting. They are vulnerable to the mental health risks associated with too much screen time discussed in Chapter 4 as well as at risk of cyber bullying. In addition, they almost certainly will not be getting the 8 to 10 hours of uninterrupted sleep per night recommended by the Australian Department of Health, as necessary for healthy physical and psychological development.

If you are concerned about what your children are doing with social media follow the advice of Jean Twenge (author of iGen discussed in Chapter 4) and only allow them access to these applications via your computer for a short period each day.

Other alternatives for managing what children are doing online include placing their screen so you can see what they are viewing, as well as the application of a parental lock on selected sites.

Screens and Mental Health

Our clinical experience has taught us that reducing screen time of all kinds can have an immediate and positive effect on the behaviour of children diagnosed with Attentional Deficit Hyperactivity Disorder (ADHD) regardless of whatever other treatment is recommended.

Many of these children, some as young as five years old, have almost unlimited access to screens and their parents regard this as normal. Screens literally deluge us with information, much more than we can hope to process or remember. Most we ignore or forget immediately but for a child (or adult), who is already struggling to focus their attention and effort, the effect of additional doses of data via a screen is to exacerbate their symptoms and make successful management of their behaviour even harder.

If you have a child who has been diagnosed with ADHD then permanently reducing screen time of all kinds is something we strongly recommend.

The research clearly suggests that excessive screen time, particularly time devoted to social media, promotes poor mental health in young people, which means that parents need to be alert to its impact on their own children. And, as we mentioned earlier, we also recommend that any patient who is suffering from anxiety or depression, whatever their age, give up social media for good.

Buying smart phones for children is popular among parents (and, of course, children themselves) because it is easier to 'stay in touch' with them which for many parents is code for 'keeping them safe'. But exactly when a child should receive their first personal device should be the subject of careful consideration between parents and their offspring. Before the advent of the internet many millions of children were successfully raised without 'smart' devices. They walked, rode and caught the bus to school alone in times significantly more dangerous than today. So it is hard to argue that today a phone is an essential item for any child.

Certainly primary school children don't need one and maybe not until they are well into high school. If they must have a phone, consider giving them one they can use to text and call, but with no internet function so that social media is not an ever present temptation.

If your children must have an internet profile, insist that they 'friend' you so that you can see what they are posting. If they are reluctant to do this, maybe it tells you that what they are planning to post should not be seen by anyone.

The plea that "I need an iPhone because my friend Maria has one" is hardly a clinching argument for putting one of these devices in a young person's hand.

Back to Rules

Agreed rules and consequences that follow for infringements are essential for any community, including a family, to function successfully. Also, as discussed in Chapter 7, settled rules are most important when children divide their time between separate households. If their parents, even though they are separated, can agree on basic guidelines – and stick to them – it makes life easier for everyone.

Will the fact that your family has agreed written rules ensure that they are always followed without exception? Of course not! But this is no reason not to have rules.

As suggested above, children have an innate need for the structure and security that fair and consistent discipline, based on agreed rules, brings to their lives. While having rules won't guarantee that they are always followed, the mere fact that they are up on the fridge will bring a degree of order into a household that may be in danger of losing its way.

If there is no prior agreement on who should be doing what and how people are expected to behave, be ready for endless and fruitless arguments with your children and your partner about pretty much everything that happens at home and elsewhere.

Family Functioning and Children's Mental Health

We have already argued that the recent and significant increases in mental disorder among children, and especially adolescents, observed in Australia and overseas, can only be explained in terms of environmental factors, particularly by how they are raised and schooled.

There is further evidence to support this conclusion from the Young Minds Matter Report which we reviewed in Chapter 1.[2] This study examined links between the quality of family functioning and the incidence of mental disorder in children and adolescents.

The authors used an assessment tool to measure the quality of five fundamentals of family functioning:

1. Communication
2. Planning
3. Conflict management
4. Emotional support
5. Practical support

Using these they assessed the quality of family life in terms of four categories: very good, good, fair and poor.

The results clearly indicate that the incidence of mental disorder in children and adolescents increases as the quality of family functioning declines; more than a third (35.3%) of young people in families assessed as functioning poorly were diagnosed as having a mood or behavioural disorder. The comparable numbers for the three higher levels of functioning were 19.7% (Fair), 15.3% (Good) and 10.9% (Very Good). Similar ratios were observed for girls and boys.

According to these results, any child, *regardless of their innate nature*, is more than three times as likely to be diagnosed with a mental disorder if they live in a home in which family functioning is assessed as poor rather than very good.

These findings suggest that homes in which parents provide emotional and practical support, and in which family members interact respectfully, according to a few agreed rules, are more likely to provide children with the fundamental security they need for positive identity development and sound psychological health.

In contrast, disorganisation (minimal routine and rules) and a lack of care and empathy for others, create a fertile ground for the development of child and adolescent mental disorder.

It is also worth noting that while a dysfunctional family is more likely to produce children diagnosed with mood, behaviour and conduct disorders, the behaviour of these children will further contribute to the disorganisation which characterises their homes. Disorganised family functioning and the disruptive behaviours this encourages are likely to exacerbate and reinforce each other to create a vicious cycle which ensures that both become progressively worse.

If this is the case perhaps it is not surprising that the prevalence of conduct disorder, or chronic misbehaviour, is effectively *seven times higher* in poorly managed homes than those rated as very high functioning.

We would argue that an absence of agreed rules, reliable routine and consistent discipline are the primary reasons for this last finding. What these data strongly suggest is that the conditions prevailing at home, created by parents, exert a defining influence on the mental health and behaviour of children growing up in them.

This is a perfect example of Dorothy Nolte's comment (quoted earlier) that children "learn what they live". Dysfunctional homes produce dysfunctional behaviour and mood disorders in children.

These findings also strongly support our argument that, even if a child has an inherited predisposition towards anxiety or depression, or any other non-organic mental disorder, whether he or she displays any of these is primarily determined by how they are raised. As noted earlier, this is confirmed by other research which demonstrates that, among children genetically vulnerable to depression, only a proportion – those exposed to particular environments – display symptoms of the disorder.[3]

Happy and psychologically healthy children are more likely to emerge from families in which communication is conducted with care and respect, where reliable routine is provided via agreed rules, conflict is managed in a constructive fashion, and parents provide consistent practical and emotional support.

The practical and emotional means for achieving high and very high levels of family functioning are generally agreed and understood: the practical tools are routine and family rules applied using fair, reliable and compassionate discipline; the emotional tools are love, affection, empathy and respect for children of all ages.

Rules, of course, are only half the story, discipline is the second and more difficult part.

To be of lasting value, rules must be backed up with consequences which are applied impartially and reliably. Despite any number of rules, you are still likely to have many conversations with a child about why they have neglected their chores, or why they were fighting with their sister. This is quite normal and to be expected by the way, we have already agreed that children are not born ready socialised.

Managing such discussions, what we call 'difficult' conversations, is explored in detail later. While they may be difficult, like anything hard, they get easier with practice. Most importantly, conversations of this kind are a valuable opportunity for parents to reinforce the values, attitudes and behaviours (or the accomplishments of character) children need to prepare them for a successful future.

Even more encouraging, you will also learn that a well-handled conversation like this with your child can strengthen your relationship, leaving you both feeling better about yourselves and each other.

We look at the broader challenge of discipline in the next chapter before turning to the management of difficult conversations in Chapter 11.

Conclusion

Children have an innate need for structure and order which is provided by (preferably) agreed and equitably administered rules. Like adults, they feel apprehensive in situations which lack apparent order, and in which the consequences which follow actions are unpredictable and seemingly unfair.

Routine, backed by rules, provides the security they need to develop self-confidence, grace, respect, a positive identity and empathy, as accomplishments of character.

Rules also afford an external source of direction which, when implemented consistently and impartially, set children on a path to self-discipline, independence and personal maturity.

This is especially true if they also learn that they, and no one else, are responsible for most of the consequences which follow their actions, including infringements of rules.

Summary

- Children need structure in their lives to feel secure. Parents can provide this by using routine and agreed rules as well as reliable application of agreed consequences for infringements.
- Consistent and equitable application of rules provide a source of external regulation which ultimately, with encouragement, children internalise as self-discipline. The 'habits' introduced through rules eventually become their own.
- Understanding that they can choose to follow a rule or not, and that they – and no one else – are responsible for the consequences that follow, is truly liberating for children. It gives them the confidence they need to take responsibility for their own lives.
- Family rules, and the need to observe them, introduce children gently to the expectations that school and, ultimately, the adult world of laws and regulations will place on them.
- Aim to keep the basic rules of your household as short and simple as possible. These can be supported by an explanatory document, which develops each rule in more detail as well as include a list of regular chores.

- No set of rules, no matter how well crafted, will guarantee peace and harmony in your home, but they are an important first step. The alternative, no rules at all, is a guarantee of chaos, characterised by endless arguments, unhappy children and exasperated parents.

10

Discipline Your Children Or the World Will Do It for You

"You can discipline your children, or you can turn that responsibility over to the harsh, uncaring, judgemental world – and the motivation for the latter decision should never be confused with love."

Jordan Peterson (Canadian psychologist)

"Children need love, especially when they do not deserve it."

Harold Hubert (US author)

Story: *Party Outfits*

Some years ago we observed an interaction between a nine-year-old boy and his mother. She had brought two alternative outfits for him to wear to a party they were both attending. The plan was that he would change when they arrived at the party and his mother had obviously gone to a great deal of trouble to prepare his clothes.

She presented the two colour coordinated outfits to her son who proceeded to tell her that he liked neither and, for good measure, didn't like her either!

So far so predictable, but it was the mother's response that caught our attention. Instead of physically dressing him herself (or better still taking him home immediately, if he did not apologise and comply), she proceeded to plead with him to make a choice and became upset when he continued to refuse.

She appealed to her husband, who thought the whole thing funny, but did nothing. In the end she gave up and her son wandered off smirking to join the party dressed as he was.

What can we learn from this story? More importantly, what did the boy learn?

Primarily that he could be rude to his mother – and by extension to women in general – when he felt like it and that this was perfectly acceptable to his father and, by extension, to men in general. Not only were there no negative consequences – neither parent made any attempt to discipline him – he was actually rewarded for his discourtesy by being allowed to stay and enjoy the party.

He also learned that there was no need to display gratitude to someone who had tried to help him, even if her taste in clothes was not his.

This story illustrates the point, made elsewhere in this book, that in every interaction with our children, whether we like it or not, they learn important lessons about how to live. Repeated interactions between a mother and her son of the type described will produce a young man who does not respect women. Moreover, it is possible to speculate that, when he's 18, he will be telling her that he can't find a young lady whom he likes, who is willing to go out with him more than once or twice.

It may appear that we are exaggerating the likely consequences of recurrent interactions of this kind, but we think not.

Our professional and personal experience of decades of observing young people growing up tell us we are not. In every interaction you have with your child, for better or worse, you are teaching them how to be an adult.

True, this incident may have been relatively minor and unimportant. It may have been an uncharacteristic example, of otherwise exemplary parents, omitting to discipline a child's rudeness because they were busy at a social engagement. Alternatively, if it was typical of how both parents consistently responded to his disrespect, it had profound implications for his future.

Unfortunately, it was the latter, as his later history confirmed. This talented little boy, through initially no fault of his own, grew

into a rather unpleasant man whose abrasive interpersonal style resulted in stormy relationships with women, a failed business, once his clients became weary of his manner towards them, and acrimonious relations with every family member.

Worse still, he continues to consult mental health services to address self-destructive behaviours, including abuse of alcohol and prescription drugs.

❧❧❧

To us the story *Party Outfits* is a perfect illustration of the point made in the title of this chapter, inspired by Jordan Peterson's striking discussion of raising children in Chapter 5 of his "12 Rules for Life".[1]

If parents don't discipline their children when they have the chance, so that they learn social desirability and social competence, the world will do it instead. In addition, as this story demonstrates, the punishment the world dishes out is generally a lot more brutal than most parents would ever contemplate, for even the naughtiest child. What is worse, as we shall see, is that by the time children are adults it is often too late for discipline, no matter how harsh, to change their ways.

We have emphasised that parents can and do influence children's behaviour at any age, but there is no doubt that this is easier when they are younger and the impact of school and peers are less significant. If you make the effort in their first few years you will not only get your children on track socially, but will also have done much of the hard work of disciplining early, before they move out into the wider world. This, in turn, makes the subsequent years of raising them much easier.

This was certainly our experience. Because our children, more or less, had learned to behave themselves and interact reasonably easily at home when they were small, taking them out for meals and to other social events as they grew older was generally a pleasant experience.

For most children, after the age of five or six, peers increasingly become an important source of socialisation. This being the case – and certainly after this age they begin to spend almost as much time with peers as parents – then the imperative to teach them how to live successfully with others as early as possible is even stronger.

Recidivism in Australia

There is evidence to support the argument that if children don't learn to live comfortably with the requirements of society in their formative period, between 0 and 10 years, they may struggle to do so more or less indefinitely.

In 2019, the rate of recidivism or re-offending for Australian prisoners released in the period 2016-2018 was just under 55%. What this means is that, within two years of their release, more than half of ex-prisoners had either returned to prison or been placed on community service orders.[2]

There are many reasons why an individual may not 'go straight' following a term of imprisonment, such as unemployment, mental illness or addiction. But this statistic highlights the fact that many adults struggle to abide by societal expectations even after severe punishment for an earlier offence.

This can be partly explained, at least, by poor socialisation; children who acquire an asocial or anti-social temperament early in life growing into adults who struggle to meet the minimum expectations of their community.

Fortunately, we can avoid consequences of this kind for our own children provided we are prepared to exercise appropriate discipline over their behaviour when they are young. This is not merely beneficial for children; parents also have a duty towards their community to discipline rather than release half civilised little monsters into the world.

This being the case, it is important to establish exactly what we mean by the word 'discipline'.

Disciplining is not something we do with children because we do not love them, or because we are 'cruel' or 'uncaring'. On the contrary, we discipline our children precisely because we do love and respect them, and want them to thrive. We intervene and, if necessary, penalise, when we observe unacceptable behaviour or infractions of agreed rules, because we know that if we don't our children will suffer much worse punishments in the future for similar conduct.

Neither is discipline something done from anger or spite or simply to hurt, possibly as a result of personal unhappiness, no matter what the provocation. Quite simply, discipline is a gift of love parents bestow on their children without which they will never develop the accomplishments of character they need if they are to find their way to their preferred life.

This is the meaning of Harold Hubert's comment, quoted at the beginning of this chapter; it is precisely when they "do not deserve it" – when they are misbehaving – that children need their parents' love in the form of consistent, impartial and compassionate discipline.

Discipline of this kind teaches children to contribute to their family and community and to live comfortably within reasonable boundaries. It also instils many of the accomplishments of character they require to become well-adjusted adults and achieve genuine happiness and success.

Through consistent and compassionate discipline they learn some basic realities of life, that rules apply to them as much as anyone else and that they can't always have things their own way or do what they would prefer, at least immediately. They also come to accept this cheerfully and uncomplainingly.

Discipline is indispensable to positive parenting and for raising psychologically healthy children. It is as important for children's development as good nutrition and regular exercise.

Learning Personal Responsibility

"The greatest gifts you can give your children are the roots of responsibility and the wings of independence." Denis Waitley (US author and speaker)

In the previous chapter we discussed what children learn when they become accustomed to living within a framework of rules which are fairly and consistently applied.

The last lesson we suggested was:

> … consequences following a rule breach are the direct result of *individual choice*. If a child is sanctioned within agreed rules this is the result of *their* decisions and behaviour and, no one else's. Under these conditions a consequence is not something that is 'unfair' or arbitrarily imposed by a third party – in this case a parent – or beyond their control to avoid. Rather it is something they have *chosen* for themselves.

This point is crucial and goes well beyond a simple understanding of rules and consequences.

As soon as possible children need to understand and accept their personal responsibility for creating the life they want for themselves. This means to learn that every choice they make – to act or not, to speak or not – will trigger outcomes for them, good, bad or otherwise. It is far better that they learn this in the security of their home, where negative consequences will always be milder, than to learn it in a rather more ruthless fashion when they are older.

They need to understand that most of what happens to them, especially the 'bad' things, are the result of choices they make themselves.

A parent teaches this vital lesson when they say to a teenager something like, "Well you may choose to stay out later than we have agreed but if you do you will not be allowed out to social functions for the next two weeks, a consequence we have also discussed. *It's really up to you and not me*." The last sentence puts the responsibility for what happens next – what time they come home and the consequences of this – fairly and squarely where it should be, on the teen.

Statements of this kind demonstrate your genuine respect for your child as an individual who is capable of making decisions and deciding outcomes for themselves. In addition, by giving your child responsibility you build their self-confidence and a sense of positive identity. They feel respected and trusted because you are not simply imposing arbitrary restrictions on them, whether as a result of a bad day at work or for some other reason.

Because of this, they are more likely to conform willingly. Similar conversations can be had with two-year-olds: "I need you to wear your hat while playing outside. If you won't we'll have to go back inside; you decide." It is never too early to begin helping a child to understand that when they act they are, in effect, selecting outcomes in the form of consequences good or bad for which they, and no one else, can take the credit.

In the process you will teach them maturity as an accomplishment of character: their conduct will become characterised by prudence and thoughtfulness for others and they will come to accept personal responsibility for the consequences of their words and deeds.

Understanding and then accepting personal responsibility is truly liberating for children. They become aware that they are not powerless objects at the mercy of external, random forces, but rather independent people who can exercise genuine agency or control over the course of their lives. In this way parents bestow the gifts of responsibility and independence referred to by Denis Waitley in the quotation at the beginning of this section.

In Chapter 3 we noted that research and clinical experience confirm that children's psychological health is directly linked to feelings of personal control or mastery.

A sense of personal control gives them confidence to pursue their own path in the face of what otherwise may appear to be an intimidating and capricious world. They may still choose to break a rule, to avoid doing something which goes against their conscience, but they will do so in the full knowledge that they have chosen this option. This, in turn, provides self-assurance to face any penalties calmly without the added burden of debilitating emotion.

And no matter how serious these may be they will manage them a lot better if they accept them as self-inflicted rather than regard them as random persecution imposed by others.

By accepting personal responsibility, and calmly accepting the consequences of their choices, children will acquire self-confidence, maturity, personal identity, emotional control and resilience as accomplishments of character.

They acquire these priceless personal qualities when parents emphasise that *they and no one else* trigger a penalty when they break an agreed (or at least previously discussed) rule. They will also learn to stand up for what they believe in and that personal values (central to a positive identity), while important, sometimes come at a price. You can also use the techniques of emotional control, discussed in Chapter 6, to encourage them to accept cheerfully any consequences they bring on themselves with a minimum of resentment or anger.

Effective and Efficient

Disciplinary techniques should be both effective and efficient: effective because otherwise they will fail to modify a child's behaviour, and efficient so that they are not too time consuming or overly complex to apply consistently.

Physical punishment may have been efficient (getting 'six of the best' didn't take too long!), but we have come to understand that it is not particularly effective. Similarly, supervising a child while they write 100 times, "I must not use my brother's iPad without asking" (à la Bart Simpson) might be an effective deterrent, and this is debatable, but it is time consuming and very frustrating for all concerned.

Generally, the most effective and efficient methods are those which deprive a child of something they value, generally of a social nature. Time out, of which more later, deprives the young child of their parents' and siblings' attention – something they value highly. Missing out on social or sporting events, access to social media, or shared computer gaming, similarly constitute a significant deprivation for most teenagers because the attention of peers is so important to them.

Consequences for rule breaking should be considered carefully and, once again, discussed with those for whom they are designed. When they are relaxed children will happily discuss what is important to them and what they least wish to lose, if only temporarily.

Children should also have the opportunity to avert a consequence, even following an infringement, if they are prepared to make amends immediately and properly. This might be, for example, by apologising sincerely for rudeness or cheerfully accepting someone else's right to have their 'fair turn' at a game. Being given a chance to quickly redress a lack of courtesy in this way encourages at least two accomplishments of character: grace and respect.

They will also learn the benefit of forgiveness between reasonable people and, even if they have erred, that it is often possible to quickly rectify an offence to minimise the damage done and avoid a worse outcome. In this way they learn how to manage their mistakes and maintain relationships with others despite the inevitable, if only occasional, incidents of thoughtlessness which occur in any busy household. And during this process they will strengthen two other accomplishments of character, in this case, maturity and empathy.

Learning to take active responsibility for addressing their own errors also means they can avoid feeling miserable when they brood over, say, rudeness to others. We are all familiar with the relief that comes when we apologise for our mistakes and make appropriate amends.

Furthermore, apologising when one is at fault is a hallmark of adult maturity.

Consistent and Impartial

In addition to being effective and efficient, your approach to discipline should also be consistent and impartial.

Consistency means that parents are reliable disciplinarians; for your efforts to be fully effective your children must understand that you mean what you say and that you will always apply previously discussed consequences, regardless of what else is going on in their lives.

Impartiality means that household rules are applied in the same way to each of child in a family. We don't have to remind you that 'playing favourites' with your children will deliver you (deservedly) into a world of pain.

Consistency and impartiality reassure your children that their world can (and should be) predictable and reliable when it comes to paying a price for misdemeanours, large or small (see Story: *Kung Foo Fighting*).

Story: *Kung Foo Fighting*

Many years ago one of us returned home on a Friday evening from interstate to learn (via a recorded message!) that Rory, our second son, had been suspended from primary school for fighting.

When we questioned him we learned that he and a friend had been practising 'kung fu' moves they had seen in a movie and that things had got a bit out of hand, resulting in a fight between them.

Rory was relaxed about being suspended, no doubt looking forward to a few days extra holiday, but what did concern him was that his friend had not received a similar punishment and was to remain at school.

Apparently his friend's father had gone in to school on the previous Friday, the day of the fight, and demanded that his son's 'assailant' be removed from the school. So far so predictable.

What did surprise us, however, was that the principal had agreed to this without demur and without discussing the events with us first.

On Monday morning we saw the principal and pointed out the fundamentally inequitable nature of his response, given that neither boy had deliberately initiated the fight. To be fair, he agreed with us but the father was a large, rather testy man who seemed to have intimidated him. We suggested that, in the interests of equity, either both boys be suspended, or neither, and another consequence be applied for both of them.

Our friendly principal agreed to this and lifted Rory's suspension. Both boys eventually spent a Saturday morning at the school cleaning windows, ably assisted, to his eternal credit, by their form teacher!

Later, at a cricket match we tracked down the father, who was very uncomfortable about the whole affair, and spoke to both boys together. We asked them to shake hands and asked both for their commitment that this would be the end of the matter (which it was).

ঔঔঔ

The point to note here is that it was not the suspension itself which upset Rory, but rather the obvious inequity of him being suspended while his friend was apparently going to walk away 'scot free'. This is another example of the innate sense of justice children seem to carry with them from birth.

Children are not silly; they generally know when they have overstepped a limit and will accept their punishment provided they can see that it is fair.

We could comment a great deal about this story, particularly the rather hysterical response from the school to two boys of similar size fighting. Small boys (and sometimes girls as well) as you are well aware have been scuffling since Cain and Abel and will continue to do so until the end of time.

As we discussed earlier, free play, including 'play' fighting which occasionally can escalate, is one of the ways youngsters turn inherited potentialities into practical skills. We also noted how children appear to deliberately expose themselves to moderate degrees of risk in order to learn how to manage the fear that comes with it.

The primary point to make, however, is the critical importance of being equitable and consistent, and to be seen as such, when disciplining children.

We are not suggesting, by the way, that you encourage your children to fight, rather to put scuffling between young children into a proper perspective. As they grow towards maturity two of the qualities we must teach them are respect for others and emotional control, as well as how to resolve differences in a civilised manner without resorting to violence.

They will learn to do this primarily by watching their parents;

if you use corporal punishment when they are young, don't be surprised to see them use physical aggression to sort out their differences when they are older. If, on the other hand, you seek to resolve disputes with them and others respectfully but assertively they are more likely to follow suit.

Compassionate not Coercive

If, as we have suggested, disciplining children is an act of love, this implies that parents should seek to influence their behaviour in positive ways, rather than resort to criticism and condemnation, or worse, abuse of some kind. This suggests you should approach the business of disciplining children in a compassionate rather than coercive manner.

The sole purpose of discipline should be to encourage children to modify their behaviour in directions you believe will be better for them and others. That is all. Neither the intent nor outcome of discipline should ever be to humiliate or distress children through threats or intimidation. Nor should the exercise of discipline ever be an attempt to establish parental superiority (as distinct from authority) or to try and 'make' children do what parents want them to do, through the use of physical force, verbal abuse or psychological blackmail.

Disciplining children should rarely require raised voices or anger (at least on your part) unless you see someone genuinely at risk of harm or when you observe obvious and intentional abuse or bullying of a weaker party.

If you truly respect your child you will recognise their right to make their own choices. Therefore, you can calmly accept their decision to *not* follow your requests without becoming angry or disappointed. Similarly you can, just as calmly, impose whatever consequences you and they have already agreed on, without resorting to sarcasm or hostility. True you may get an unhappy response but, just because a child or adolescent becomes grumpy or distressed, there is no need for a parent to do the same. In fact try to keep any conversation of this kind as relaxed, positive and respectful as possible.

At no time during the disciplinary process (once people are no longer at risk) is there a need for raised voices; and there is never a case for abuse or humiliation. You (like most parents) may prefer your children to 'follow the rules', but just because they choose not to, this is no reason for you to criticise or denigrate them in any way. This will simply alienate them from you and make it even harder to influence their behaviour in the future.

Certainly, parents need to indicate what aspects of their child's behaviour are unacceptable and why there will be a penalty, particularly if the child is not prepared to apologise or otherwise make amends. But as we point out elsewhere (Chapter 12), commenting on one aspect of a person's behaviour in measured language is quite different from 'labelling' the whole person in negative terms, especially if this is done in an aggressive or insulting manner.

How you intervene to discipline in many ways is more important than *why* you 'step in', in the first place. Your children will quickly forget the content of most of the 'difficult' conversations you have with them but they will retain lasting memories of how they have been treated during these interactions.

Are you quiet, respectful and low key when disciplining children or angry, anxious and discourteous? The answer to this question is important because it describes probably the most lasting impression they will have of their parents and one they will take with them to adulthood; that is, how you conducted the 'hard' or 'difficult' talks you inevitably had with them, while they were growing up. In addition, the approach you adopt to discipline may well be the one that they use with their own children.

Avoiding a combative or coercive disciplinary style, however, is not just about leaving a better reputation behind you. Over time, how you approach matters of discipline can have a direct and lasting impact on your children's mental health. Research in Australia suggests that children raised using a coercive disciplinary style are more than three times as likely to display symptoms of mental disorder than those whose parents adopt a more encouraging approach.[3]

Coercive parenting is reflected in harsh behaviour, including hitting, yelling, scolding, rejection and psychological control to enforce a child's compliance. Parents who use this approach tend to be authoritarian, rigid and inconsistent in terms of how they respond to a child's behaviour.

An authoritarian or coercive parenting style has been associated with the following outcomes for children:

- Unhappy disposition
- Insecurity and lowered self-esteem
- Behavioural problems and conduct issues
- Lower academic performance[4]

It would not be surprising if a sustained series of hostile and stressful interactions with one or both parents regarding their behaviour left an adolescent or young adult with raised anxiety and lowered self-confidence. This will be particularly true if, as a child, they have been fed a regular diet of negative criticism focused on their 'undesirable' personal attributes, behaviour and achievements.

A more positive approach to disciplining children recognises that it is unwise to expect 'perfect' behaviour from them all or even most of the time, simply because, as we noted earlier (see Chapter 8), social competence, or 'doing the right thing', is a complex set of skills and knowledge which children only acquire over time with the help of others, usually parents. If we accept this we can *expect* children to 'misbehave' – that is, to *not* do what we wish them to do – at least occasionally.

Consequently, parents need not be very concerned when children 'play up' or regard this as 'deliberate' or 'offensive'. It is important to recognise that 'misbehaving' children are simply normal children behaving normally as they explore the limits of their world, even if their behaviour fails to accord with your wishes. This doesn't mean ignoring what they are doing but rather to intervene in ways which are less stressful for you, avoid traumatising them, and are also more effective in terms of modifying their conduct.

In Chapter 8 we discussed a model of successive approximations for assisting children to acquire required skills, including social competence – the capacity to mix effectively with others and integrate successfully into broader society. This approach to raising children accepts that they are not born fully socialised and require assistance to become successful friends, partners, employees and citizens.

Once we accept that children need to learn how to "comply gracefully with the expectations of civil society"[5] and will not come to it on their own, we can use the model of successive approximations to guide them there. Because we understand that they need our assistance to become successfully socialised, we are less likely to become angry or anxious when their behaviour is not what we would wish and we will avoid falling into the trap of trying to coerce or force them into change.

Time Out

Time out, or time away from parental attention, is generally considered to be the most effective technique for disciplining youngsters.[6]

As we have seen, the years 0 to 5 are an important window of opportunity to decisively socialise our children, to turn them into people who are attractive to and welcomed by others. Time out, correctly applied, is a potent tool for achieving this.

Also, as we shall see, it teaches children very early in their life to take responsibility for their own behaviour, that they have choices and that the choices they make have consequences; in other words, to acquire maturity as an accomplishment of character.

When a child refuses to share or pack up their toys, for instance, you should point this out and give them the opportunity to make good their lapse. If they then share or clear up their mess, simply thank and praise them and move on. Similarly, if they are being rude to you or a sibling, ask them to stop and apologise, and if they comply thank them and praise their courtesy.

If, however, they refuse to apologise, or do what you ask, then time out becomes an option.

Even then you can still give them a chance to briefly reflect before placing them in time out. We did this by warning our children that time out was coming if they chose to ignore our request to do what we asked. The warning was simply, "1, 2, 3". If by "3" nothing had happened, then time out was on! After a while, simply saying the numbers was often enough to produce the desired outcome; they would apologise, or do what they were asked, because they knew what was coming if they didn't.

Time out may occur on a chair in the same room as the parent or in another room. We favoured the laundry because it was a boring place to be with a hard floor and nowhere to sit down. If you select the laundry, however, make sure the washing machine, etc., are safely secured. (Rory once climbed into the dryer!) In contrast, their bedroom is comfortable and likely to offer them a wide range of enjoyable distractions.

If you are concerned your child may damage something, put them in a room where this can't happen. Using a separate room also avoids the tedium of trying to keep a small child on their 'time out' chair. And if your child won't stay in the time out room lock the door.

As you put the child into time out you say, "As soon as you are ready to apologise (or pack up your toys or whatever), you can come out. You decide when you are ready." These comments emphasise to your child that they are in control of the situation and responsible for what is happening. As soon as they decide to change their behaviour, their circumstances will change also.

For this reason, you should not put a set period on the time out process; children, even toddlers, should decide when they are ready to come out, not their parents. They will learn that they control the time out process and, because they prefer to be with others, will seek to end it as soon as possible by complying with your wishes.

Once you have explained what is happening, close the door or leave them on the 'time out' chair, and *ignore* whatever they are saying or doing, including kicking the door. After a minute or two –

once they understand the time out process, even 30 seconds may be enough – you say to the child, from outside the door, if they are in a separate room: "Are you ready to come out and apologise? It's up to you."

If you get a negative response or silence, wait and repeat this after a minute or two. Going to the door regularly reassures the a child that they have not been abandoned. It will also generally decrease the amount of time the whole process takes because small children genuinely do not like being on their own. As we have seen, they have a fundamental need for the attention of others, not least parents.

In contrast, sending a child to their own bedroom 'for an hour' is pointless. As noted, they will find something to amuse themselves with, and the reason they have been sent will be forgotten or confused by the passage of time.

If your child starts crying, ignore this for a short while before going to the door and repeating the earlier question, while adding that they will need to stop crying as well as apologising if they are to come out. It is important to remember that small children cry as often because they are angry as for any other reason.

If you persist the first few times you will find that time out is very effective in quickly modifying a child's behaviour. If you use the 1, 2, 3 technique mentioned above, you will also find, with practice, that the mere threat of time out is often sufficient.

What is critical is that you *don't* engage with a child in a lengthy discussion about their transgression and or the 'fairness' or otherwise of time out; provided, of course, the process has already been explained to them at another time when they are relaxed and prepared to listen.

Remain calm and simply state precisely what they have done and why there must be consequences. Try to avoid simple generalisations like, "You are a naughty girl, I've had it with you!" She is not a 'naughty girl', merely one small aspect of her conduct is undesirable. Aim to replace this kind of comment with something like, "You are generally pretty good, but (state what they did) is unacceptable." This allows you to praise your child while simultaneously addressing the behaviour you wish to change.

Then give him/her a chance to immediately apologise and/or make amends, as discussed above, and go straight to time out if they refuse to comply. At the same time, continue to emphasise that they are responsible for what is happening and can stop time out as soon as they wish.

Arguing with a young child (or anyone else for that matter) is unlikely to change their behaviour and merely threatens to damage your relationship with them. Also, as Jean Kerr points out in her bestselling *Please Don't Eat the Daisies*, the danger of arguing with an angry child is that very soon you begin to look and sound like one yourself![7]

Why is time out so effective? Because, as we have already discussed, children of all ages, particularly younger ones, crave parental attention and their affection. They also want to please their parents despite their occasional misdemeanors. The more praise and attention a child gets for being socially desirable and competent, the more likely it is that these will become established habits.

This is the essence of the psychological concept 'reinforcement'. Any behaviour a child displays which is praised, acknowledged or, indeed, *criticised* by a parent – that is, any act or word which receives *parental attention of any kind* – is likely to be repeated more often. Conversely, *ignoring* a behaviour will *reduce* the chance of it recurring.

Time out, preferably in another room, deprives them of attention for misbehaving; in effect you are ignoring them and their misdeed. This is especially true if it is imposed quickly with a minimum of fuss and discussion. By removing your attention from your child for a short while you will reduce the chance of a misdemeanour being repeated. In contrast, arguing with a child about what they are doing or criticising what they have said, perversely has the *opposite* effect.

While you are arguing or shouting about your child's misdeed, they are receiving a massive dose of just what they desire, your attention, which, in turn encourages more of just the behaviour you are trying to eliminate. While you think you are training them to behave, they are literally training *you* to 'bark' on command!

Anyway, we know from our own experience as children that they are paying little or no attention to what you are saying so why bother? It certainly won't change their behaviour. By calmly and quickly instituting time out you minimise any argument between you and them which is a lot less wearing on your nerves and the harmony of your home.

Time out is over once a child (with your encouragement) apologises and does what you originally asked them to do. What happens next is most important. You should first thank them and praise their willingness to comply and then *never refer to the incident again*. They have apologised and conformed with your wishes and that should be the end of it. Avoid harping on about something that they will have already forgotten; reminding children (or anyone else) of their past transgressions is a stale and pointless exercise. In addition, as noted above, this will merely serve to undermine their confidence as well as reinforce or increase just what you are trying to eliminate.

If another incident arises in the next few minutes or hours, it should be treated entirely separately, but in the same way. Children need to quickly learn that, in this regard, you are implacable, that in matters of discipline you will always do what you say.

It should also be said that any form of discipline, including time out, is more effective when it occurs within an environment of obvious respect, love, and affection for children. Using public praise frequently when they are behaving in ways you wish to encourage, such as helping their younger siblings, will ensure they continue to demonstrate more of the same.

As we now know, if children are 'misbehaving', they are simply telling you that they need more of your attention. It is up to you to ensure that this is mostly positive attention for preferred behaviours and accomplishments of character, rather than angry or exasperated personal criticism in response to their latest adventure.

Through frequent recognition of their efforts to cooperate and contribute, as well as enjoying time with them, you will build close relationships with your children which they will be less willing to disturb by 'playing up'.

Regular and targeted public praise for desired behaviour is an automatic habit of positive parenting and with practice it can be for you as well. When we praise our children warmly and appropriately they respond positively towards us. And when they like us they will regard our displeasure much more seriously and be more likely to listen and conform when we ask them to stop or change what they are doing.

It should also go without saying that discipline is a responsibility of both parents and should not be allocated solely to only one or the other. If discipline is Dad's job only ("You just wait 'till your father gets home!" was commonly heard by children of our generation), this not only makes his relationship with his children that much trickier, but they are also more likely to lose respect for their mother who leaves this, admittedly challenging, task to her partner.

If both parents apply agreed disciplinary techniques consistently they are more likely to occur when they should – immediately following an infraction – and quickly become an accepted part of children's lives.

Reluctance to Discipline

Some parents are reluctant to discipline their children for fear of losing their love or affection. This is because they regard any form of discipline as an act of hostility towards their child which he or she will resent, possibly indefinitely, and damage their relationship irreparably.

In response to this it is worth reiterating that disciplining a child in the manner we have described is an act of love or, as we suggested above, a gift. You are preparing them for the future when they will have to manage on their own in the adult world, with all its attendant rules and restrictions. Failure to discipline is to fail as a parent and may well expose children to much harsher punishments when they are older.

In the previous chapter we suggested that the existence of consistent rules, and reliable consequences for ignoring them, provide children with the structure and security they need to make sense of their world and find their own place in it alongside others – exactly what loving parents want for their children. And, as we also argued earlier, a strong sense of who they are and where they fit in are powerful defences against the risk of future mental disorder.

The alternative is for children to inhabit an unpredictable environment. One in which they are subjected to random and, possibly coercive, discipline, which they don't understand and which is applied by frustrated parents trying to make them behave. This is not helpful for children or their parents.

A second reason why parents may avoid a consistent approach to discipline is because they regard their children as 'special', and are concerned that any form of restraint may impair his or her development, thus preventing them from realising their true potential.

The first part of this statement is fine, children need to feel special, but the second is misguided.

While we want children to have every opportunity to find their own path and become the person they wish to be, the simple fact is that they can only do this with the cooperation of others. They need to learn social desirability and competence as soon as possible; that is, to be welcomed by others and to interact successfully with them so that they get the support they need.

Raising a child as if the normal rules of life do not apply to them is unlikely to achieve either of these. In addition, it is to leave them at risk of conflict with more formal authorities when they are older (see story: *The Artist*).

Story: *The Artist*

Oscar (16) was the eldest son of two adoring parents. He was a tall, good looking and quick witted boy who made friends wherever he went. He was also a reasonably talented artist.

Unfortunately, his chosen 'canvas' was the walls of other people's buildings; in short he was a graffiti artist. It should also be noted that his parents were impressed with his skills, including the risks he took to illegally put his 'tag' on spaces which did not belong to him.

One school night, quite late, he was observed at work by a police patrol which proceeded to apprehend him. He escaped their first attempt so they called up the dog squad to track him down. It began to rain and Oscar was eventually located hiding under a neighbourhood hedge, very wet, very cold and very scared.

Police dogs are trained to pull down someone who is running away, but not to attack a person lying relatively motionless. So Oscar was not physically injured, but it is fair to say that he was extremely distressed by being pursued and cornered by two large Alsatians.

He was taken to the watch house where his father arrived to collect him after he had been charged with defacing public property. He was eventually fined, but the magistrate recorded no conviction.

What is interesting about this story is the response of Oscar's parents. They were outraged by the way he had been apprehended and terrified by two dogs in the middle of the night. In their opinion the police had used excessive force and should be censured.

This came to nothing but they continued to criticise the way he had been treated while regarding the reason he had been apprehended in the first place as something of an afterthought. They regarded graffiti as a legitimate art form and thus, where it is placed, inconsequential.

Oscar, in turn, was treated as something of a hero by his family and, eventually, by his friends as well.

❧❧❧

Oscar's story highlights two things: firstly, the dangers of treating a child as 'special' in the sense that the rules and regulations which apply to everyone else should not apply to them; that these should be disregarded in their case so they can 'express' themselves.

The issue is, of course, that too much of this will lead them to

believe that other rules which govern the rest of us should also not apply to them, with obvious and likely painful consequences. The second point to note is the much harsher discipline which the world provides for children when we neglect to provide a more benign alternative at home.

As far as we know, Oscar has stayed out of trouble with the police since then. Perhaps his parents changed their ways, but it is more likely that his taste of flouting the law was enough to teach him to change his. We hope so anyway.

ঌঌঌ

A third reason why parents are reluctant to discipline appears to be that too many of them lack the confidence to use appropriate disciplinary techniques, or to recognise that they have the authority to do so. Some seem to require 'permission' from someone else, such as a doctor or school teacher, before they are even prepared to try.

In response to this we urge all parents to accept and use the legitimate authority they have to exercise appropriate discipline (as described in this book) for their children's benefit. We acknowledge that managing unruly children can be distressing, not least for first time parents. However, the calmer and more matter of fact you can be about it, the less upset they and you will become.

We have already argued that discipline should be applied by parents in a relaxed, encouraging manner, for a number of reasons. These include happier households, better relationships between you and your children and, most importantly, improved psychological health for them.

It simply requires a quiet comment to point out an indiscretion to a child and remind them of the consequences that you and they have agreed to, if they choose not to stop or comply with your wishes. Provided you are consistent your children will be well aware that you mean what you say without the need for you to raise your voice or become anxious or angry.

The emotional responses you display when you are having a 'difficult' conversation with a child will be mirrored in theirs. If you are polite and pleasant (even though you are determined to modify their behaviour), they will certainly be calmer and more receptive to the whole process as well. In this way the business of 'discipline' can become easier and less of a 'big deal' for all concerned.

Why Do Children 'Misbehave'?

Perhaps we can feel easier about the need for discipline if we understand why children 'misbehave' in the first place.

We might regard them as 'naughty' or 'disobedient' but they don't! As we have suggested, they are merely trying to work out what is possible – where the boundaries are – in the alarming but also exciting world into which they have emerged. (This is not a conscious process but it's what 'misbehaviour' amounts to).

A rowdy child, or one who frequently hits his parents or other children, generally has no particular animosity towards anyone. He or she is simply following a natural impulse to dominate the space around them. We have emphasised that this behaviour in a toddler is quite normal and no reason for parents to become alarmed, even though it should be addressed. The response their aggression elicits from others, albeit negative, is often powerful enough to encourage them to go on doing it unless parents intervene.

If we approach the management of 'misbehaviour' in a calm, relaxed but focused manner, children will quickly come to accept it as a normal part of life and to understand and acknowledge the requirements for living successfully with others. Ideally, disciplining children is never a source of anxiety or distress for parents or, indeed, their children.

Consistent and impartial discipline administered with empathy and respect is the central pivot which positive parenting revolves around. It is a normal part of a well-functioning family – not something that is 'bad' or 'unusual' – but rather something which happens as a matter of course from time to time because normal healthy children are driven to explore their world.

Indeed having a boisterous or noisy child should never be a source of embarrassment for parents, provided they are prepared to manage them firmly and consistently. Children like this are generally lots of fun. Their enthusiasm for life will occasionally spill over into unacceptable conduct, but their high spirits should be celebrated, nonetheless.

Regarding disciplining of children in this way will dramatically reduce its potential to upset you or them, or damage your relations with them.

As suggested, if you persist in their early years, you will find the need for disciplinary action, including the use of time out, declines quite rapidly. Children quickly become accustomed to reasonable rules consistently applied and, for the most part, learn to live quite happily within these.

Provided you persevere, your children will become well aware of three things: firstly, that there are predictable consequences for anti-social behaviour or a failure to observe agreed rules; secondly, that they – and no one else – are responsible for these outcomes and that they can avoid them if they wish; and, thirdly, that there will be no exceptions. This last point is important; if children believe you are not serious they will simply ignore you.

Learning each of these lessons is critical for their future mental health. Consistent rules and reliable consequences at home provide a path, as we have suggested, to self-discipline and personal responsibility which are at the core of adult maturity. In addition, a 'no exceptions' approach provides essential security by reassuring children that their world can be a (relatively) predictable and reliable place.

Boundaries

We place expectations or boundaries on our children's behaviour (in the form of rules) because we know that, if we don't, eventually they will run in to conflict with similar boundaries at school and elsewhere, with almost certainly more serious results. If they have not learned to live relatively comfortably within these at home they will experience the more painful consequences of not doing so when they move out into the world.

As already discussed, children naturally explore boundaries to find out what is and isn't possible, in just the same way that they will test a rope to breaking point by swinging on it. For children to test boundaries is *desirable*; it is one of the ways they experience the struggle their antifragile nature needs for them to thrive physically and psychologically. When they push against constraints, this should generally be a source of satisfaction rather than concern for parents, even though it can be irritating at times.

Gravity quickly teaches children the physical boundaries of their world, that there are, say, limits to how much weight a rope will stand. In future they are more likely to respect the the restrictions imposed on them by gravity without requiring a painful reminder. They don't resent gravity, but come to simply accept it and learn to adhere uncomplainingly to its requirements. This is because it places dependable restrictions on what they can and cannot do and also delivers predictable outcomes for disregarding these. In this way their understanding of physical reality becomes internalised. The same is true when reliable limits, and penalties for ignoring these, are placed on their social behaviour.

Behavioural boundaries created by parents are more complex and the limits less obvious, but children will push on them, nonetheless. When they reach a limit imposed by their parents, they may be unhappy in the same way they are unhappy when a rope breaks and they 'skin' an elbow.

However, over time they become comfortable with social boundaries formed by firm, fair and consistent discipline based on love and respect. These make it easier for them to learn and practise acceptable behaviour which, in time, becomes internalised as self-regulation; having worked out their boundaries, they learn to live happily and securely within these.

Once boundaries have been established, give them as much autonomy as possible, subject to sensible precautions, to set their own targets and manage their own lives.

The importance of 'holding back' rather than 'stepping in' for parents has already been emphasised. The self-discipline children acquire through positive parenting will actually reduce the number of times you will need to step in, giving both of you more time to get on with your lives.

Outside the Home

A major benefit of successful discipline at home is that children are much more likely to conduct themselves reasonably well elsewhere. However, if they have not learned the basics of rules and consequences beforehand, then even preschool may come as a nasty shock when, possibly for the first time in their lives, an adult insists that they change their ways and is willing to apply a penalty if they do not.

Even finding friends may be tough, which means their experience of preschool is an unhappy one. This, in turn, may create difficulties the next time they are due to go.

In contrast, children who are accustomed to having reasonable constraints placed on what they do, and to being asked to modify or forgo their preferences from time to time, will find their first experience of interacting with strangers much easier. In effect, they will have already begun to internalise the lessons of home and acquire the self-discipline required to navigate the wider world on their own.

When they do infringe a rule, which inevitably happens with spirited children, the application of (again reasonable) consequences will be familiar to them and not regarded with fear or as an unwarranted affront to their right to do as they please. Repeated tussles with teachers, or quarrels with peers, are not conducive for young people gaining the maximum benefit from their time in kindergarten, school or college.

Children who are familiar with considered and consistent discipline at home are also easier to manage when you are out with them at a restaurant or a party. Often a quiet word or warning will be enough for them to modify how they are interacting with others.

We found that a soft tap with two fingers on their hand followed by a quick word was a very effective combination. The soft tap served to unobtrusively get their attention in a social situation so that we could quietly remind them of what we expected. This can be done without disrupting others' enjoyment of the occasion. After a while, merely a tap accompanied by a shake of the head or a stern look will be enough.

If, however, your child refuses to quickly stop what they have been doing, they should be removed immediately and your car used as a substitute for a time out room. Using the same time out procedure she/he is given an opportunity to modify their behaviour while you wait outside – they should never be left in a car alone – and if they refuse they should be taken home immediately and put in bed. In addition, they may be required to decline the next party invitation they receive.

Once again, perseverance is the key, but if you are persisting at home you will have fewer problems when you are out (see Story: *Out To Dinner*).

Story: *Out To Dinner*

A mother of our acquaintance told us this story about a dinner party she recently attended with her partner and their two boys, who were the only children present. The boys sat happily at the table conversing with the adults and generally being 'socially desirable'. When the adult conversation became boring they simply talked to each other.

Finally, one of the adults said, "Where are their devices to keep them occupied? I haven't seen a kid out for dinner without a tablet or a phone at the table in ages!"

ஃஃஃ

The only reason for mentioning this story, apart from paying a compliment to the two parents for the way they are raising their boys, is to note the comment of the other adult.

Clearly, seeing two well behaved children enjoying adult company without a 'smart' device to occupy them was a revelation to him. His statement alone suggests that too many parents are relying on technology to distract their children rather than make the effort required to teach them to socialise comfortably with others.

This is a reminder to parents to accustom children to sitting down most evenings to dinner with the family without a device (this rule should obviously apply to adults also) and to teach them the basics of common social intercourse: to respect and engage with others and to hold a normal polite conversation, even when they may not feel like it.

If we assume children will learn these skills and qualities elsewhere, from friends or school, without assistance at home, we are likely to be disappointed.

Reflecting on Misbehaviour

We have emphasised that once a consequence, such as time out, is satisfactorily completed, the event which provoked it should not be referred to again, if only to minimise unpleasant and unnecessary conversations with your children. As we have suggested, nothing is more tedious than dragging up old quarrels.

However, having said that, sometimes it will be necessary to reflect on a particular incident with your a child, usually as they grow older and their interactions with others become more complex.

These conversations should take place after the episode is over and initial consequences administered, rather than in the heat of the moment when their emotions, at least, may still be running high. The purpose of reflecting on misbehaviour is to ensure that your child understands the reasons why what they did was wrong, and your requirement that they not repeat it in the future.

Discussions of this kind also allow you to acknowledge and validate what your child was feeling at the time. You might agree that losing at tennis can be frustrating, but emphasise that being rude or refusing to congratulate the winner because, say, your daughter lost a tennis match, is not acceptable. You can also review and suggest alternative ways of expressing or dealing with frustration. This type of conversation will reinforce grace and respect in their character – a capacity to remain cheerful and respectful of others even though things are not currently going their way.

You can point out that feeling frustrated is okay and can be a spur for improvement, to practise harder for example, but should never be an excuse for ill manners. In this way your son or daughter learns that you respect their feelings and point of view, even if their behaviour in this instance did not reflect your expectations of them.

We use the word discussion here advisedly. A discussion is a two way conversation which gives your child the chance to express their version of events and suggest how they might handle the situation differently in the future. It is not a lecture in which the parent simply 'lays down the law' without reference to the child's understanding of what occurred or their feelings about it.

You can start this type of discussion by asking them a series of open questions like, "What do you think happened?", "Why did you respond in the way you did?" or, "How could you deal with the same situation differently if it happens again?" Once they have answered, you can explore their comments further with follow up questions before expressing your concerns.

Choose your words carefully when discussing their behaviour with children. We have already emphasised the importance of remaining calm and avoiding inflammatory generalisations such as "You really are stupid!" or "You'll never amount to anything!" Rather, you should be very specific by pointing out exactly what was unacceptable about what your child said or did.

In another situation you might say, "I understand that Mary was rude to you and that you felt angry, but this does not excuse what you did when you broke her iPhone. If people are rude to you, ask them to apologise and if they refuse ignore them until they do. Becoming aggressive towards them simply makes things worse. I need you to apologise to Mary and offer to pay to have her phone repaired." (A refusal to do this should result in a teenager losing their phone and all access to the internet at home until they change their mind).

By focusing precisely on the specific behaviours you would like your child to change you reduce to the bare minimum the extent of any disagreement. This lowers the emotional temperature of the discussion and encourages a solution that both parties will find easier to support.

It also preserves their self-esteem as you focus on specific behaviours rather engage in a wide ranging critique of them as people. By participating in conversations of this kind children learn over time how to discuss awkward or unpleasant subjects, without losing the respect or friendship of others – a useful skill to take with them on their journey to adulthood.

With assistance, mainly in the form of open questions and careful listening from you, your child will come to understand why the situation unfolded as it did and how they might avoid or defuse it next time. Also, if they were at fault, they will also learn why their response was unacceptable and how to make amends thereby reinforcing maturity as an accomplishment of character.

A discussion of this kind also allows you to broaden their understanding of what will happen, when they are older, if they engage in activities deemed offensive or unlawful by more formal authorities than yourself. You can then move to a discussion of further consequences if necessary.

For instance, you may have had to pick your child up early from a party because of their conduct. If their behaviour was particularly egregious, you may decide that they must also miss a social event scheduled for the following weekend.

Similarly, if your child has been disciplined for misbehaviour at school, you will also need to discuss this with them, to ensure they draw enduring lessons from the incident. Generally no further penalty should be warranted; the school has identified the issue and determined the outcome and that should be the end of it. Sometimes, however, you may decide a further penalty is warranted.

Once again, encourage your child to contribute to this conversation, but if further consequences are required don't allow their protests to deflect you. We discuss how to manage 'difficult conversations' like these and the conflict they can entail in the next chapter.

Rights and Privileges

We have discussed the use of the time out technique with younger children, those say between two and eleven years old. As children get older the principle whereby they are disciplined – temporary deprivation of something they value – remains the same, but the means for doing this tend to change.

From school age onwards they become familiar with spending less time with parents because, ideally, their social life has broadened to include a network of friends and social activities outside the home. The value they place on these allows parents to continue to exert a beneficial influence over their behaviour.

It is important that children and teens are aware that spending time with friends and enjoying other benefits provided by their family, including use of their possessions, are privileges that they must earn every day, not merely inviolate 'rights' due to them as a matter of course, regardless of how they behave.

This is analogous to the adult world in which adults are expected to meet community expectations in order to enjoy their rights as citizens and to pay their way in order to enjoy the privileges of a comfortable lifestyle. The familiar expression, "The world does not owe you a living", comes to mind here and our children need to learn this sooner rather than later.

By all means give your children possessions and opportunities but ensure they understand the link between rights and privileges on one hand and their social responsibilities, particularly towards their parents and siblings, on the other. These require them to contribute to the life of their family, at a minimum by doing their chores and participating in regular family meals without a phone or screen, as well as conducting themselves with courtesy towards others.

Other expectations ideally include participation in important family events. It is disappointing when teenagers begin to absent themselves, with their parents' permission, from family occasions where they would otherwise meet older and younger generations. It is not unreasonable to expect teenagers and young adults to spend an hour or two once in a while with their wider family in return for what their family has done, and continues to do, for them.

As we have already discussed, by attending such events they come to understand that, although they are individuals, they are also embedded in a network of relationships that contains a unique place for them and which only they can fill. The importance of a sense of 'biological' identity or belonging for children was explored in Chapter 7.

This point is not simply about them being polite to their grandmother or kind to their young cousin, although these are desirable for their own sake. Learning, at first-hand, that they are part of a chain of humanity which includes the dead, the living and the yet to be born, is important for them knowing more about where they came from and hence who they are.

In this book we have emphasised the importance of a strong sense of self or positive identity as essential to enduring mental health. Spending time with and learning more about their wider family is one of the ways in which children acquire this fundamental component of psychological wellbeing.

We are not suggesting that your children will necessarily understand or value this immediately, but the benefits will accrue nonetheless, particularly if they see you and your partner genuinely engaged with your wider family. In addition, while they may be reluctant to attend, devoting some time to others – even while they would rather be elsewhere – is a useful discipline for children and reinforces respect and empathy for the needs of others. And, who knows, they might enjoy themselves!

As adults they will attend many functions which they would prefer to avoid and, although of limited immediate social value, may be very useful in terms of longer term career and other opportunities.

The fundamental lesson for children here is that if they are prepared to contribute to the support of others then others are more likely to reciprocate and take a greater interest in them. Parents the world over have learned the efficacy of promising a reward in return for a child's cooperation with activities they dislike. Personally we found that a trip to the ice cream or lolly shop, and/or the bookstore, was ample reward for almost any amount of inconvenience we inflicted on our children.

In our view this is perfectly reasonable. In return for cheerfully accepting that, for a while at least, our preferences were more important than theirs – accomplishments of character which include grace and empathy – they were rewarded with something they valued. This is no different from a great deal of what happens in the adult world.

At any age we need to learn to delay gratification of our immediate wishes until those whose support we need are willing to help. Similarly, as employees we know that we will only continue to get paid if we make the required effort. This is true even though we may find some of our work boring and repetitive and possibly even unpleasant.

Self-Discipline

So back to the business of disciplining pre-teens and adolescents. As noted, if you are successful in your efforts when your children are young, it will be much easier to help them manage on their own as they grow older.

This is the period when they need to acquire self-discipline, necessary for them to successfully pursue their own lives as independent adults. Self-discipline is also integral to the accomplishment of maturity; the capacity to make wise decisions and do 'what is generally best' when parents are not around.

To do this they first need to accept that some restrictions on individual behaviour are necessary, so that everyone can get on with their lives with minimal disruption, and then become accustomed to living within these reasonable limits. This is much easier for children with firm, consistent and loving parents. In other words, children who are the product of positive parenting.

Bessel Van der Kolk, introduced earlier, makes the point:

> Children whose parents are reliable sources of comfort and strength have a lifetime advantage – a kind of buffer against the worst that fate can hand them.[8]

Children achieve successful independence and autonomy by internalising guidelines first introduced by parents and later reinforced by teachers and others. External rules become internal habits for self-regulating their behaviour. Self-management acquired in this way forms the foundation of character children need to face an uncertain future with confidence.

A key question is what can parents do to promote self-discipline? Well, you can nurture this quality in your child by avoiding giving instructions or issuing orders but rather by reminding them that they have choices. You will recall the earlier conversation between parent and teenager about returning home on time from a party. The wise parent doesn't bark commands (which invite resistance) but reflects with their daughter or son on previously agreed rules and consequences. They also stress that the decision to conform is entirely the child's and not theirs.

The point is made that if they choose to stay out later than agreed there will be consequences – which they, not their parents, have chosen – unless their delayed arrival home is genuinely through no fault of their own.

A conversation of this kind respects a child as an autonomous human being who has options regarding how they choose to act. It also promotes the broader lesson that the choices they make *always* produce outcomes of some kind, which ultimately determine much of what happens to them, good and bad. Understanding that they each exert substantial influence, if not total control, over the progress of their lives by the choices they make, is essential for life-long mental health in children.

People who know they have options and make choices which promote their own welfare and others' are more content. Why? Because they know they have selected their life in preference to other alternatives and they also know they can act to improve or change their situation if they wish. Thinking in this way is reflective of self-confidence, maturity, positive identity, emotional control and, in particular, resilience.

The Guiding Principle

Depriving children of something they value – generally of a social nature – remains the guiding principle for disciplining them throughout adolescence. Occasionally time out may still be of value but, increasingly, the temporary removal of prized social activities (virtual or real), becomes more effective.

Most adolescents are attracted to the opportunity to interact with friends electronically or face to face, and these can be (relatively) easily withdrawn following infractions of agreed household and (increasingly) school rules. We know children will not always agree with 'the rules' and may argue vehemently against loss of privileges. But, once established, both rules and consequences, must be rigorously adhered to.

For your children's welfare you must be firm in this regard. Haphazard and impulsive disciplining is confusing for everyone, generates unnecessary argument, and breeds justifiable resentment on the part of children. It also will produce little long term change to their behaviour; it may, in fact, make it worse.

Deprivation of privileges need not be draconian or excessive. In using their judgement parents need to assess what has occurred and what would be a reasonable response from them.

Losing the use of an iPad for a week will be no more effective for disciplining a young person than losing it for a for a day or just an evening. Even fifteen minutes loss of screen time (from the daily amount agreed to in family rules) can be sufficient to encourage future improvement.

Provided your approach to discipline is consistent, so that your children understand what is happening and why, they are more likely to accept the consequences of their misbehaviour. It is the arbitrary imposition of penalties, which appear mismatched to their misconduct and are unaccompanied by earlier warnings or discussion, that upset children and leave them feeling 'victimised' or unfairly 'punished'.

A childhood of vague and chaotic discipline will leave a young adult sceptical of any authority, including that which their community regards as legitimate, because they have learned that it is random, vindictive and genuinely unfair. This is not a useful preparation for living in the adult world of laws and penalties for transgressing these.

By all means encourage your children to question authority and test its legitimacy in appropriate ways, but don't leave them believing that all authority is innately random and hostile, imposed on the weak by the strong for their own benefit or pleasure.

As they grow, review, with their input, the restraints you have placed on their behaviour. Be prepared to progressively loosen and remove these as they demonstrate increased self-discipline and a capacity for responsible independence. This will establish the link between freedom and accountability. It will also signal that you recognise they are acquiring maturity and trust them with increased responsibility.

Approaching disciplinary conversations in a calm, encouraging manner – while avoiding a coercive style – becomes even more important with teens who can have a flair for the dramatic. Your example will cool their emotions. making talks about constraints easier for everyone. It also reduces the likelihood that they will feel any lasting resentment towards you provided you display a consistently positive regard for them and avoid unhelpful labels such as, "You are stupid, hopeless!" etc., which are insulting and untrue.

Similarly, impartiality and reliability continue to be critical when disciplining teenagers.

Impartiality means to apply rules in the same way regardless of which of your children is involved. Playing favourites, we have already suggested, can unleash a storm of adolescent fury.

Reliability means that rules and consequences are applied whenever necessary, regardless of what else is going on. Erratic or irregular discipline will actually make things worse, causing yourself and your children unnecessary grief with no redeeming benefit for them.

When temporarily removing privileges, briefly explain why a teenager's behaviour is inappropriate and why you are imposing a penalty. Also, where appropriate, give them a chance to avoid this by apologising and immediately complying with your request. When an apology is insufficient, such as when they have ignored agreements to be home at a certain time, or not drink alcohol at a party, then you should follow through with the planned penalty as a matter of course.

Story: *Not Cricket*

Pedro was an indifferent scholar but a budding athlete. A large part of his modest academic progress, however, was due to his difficulty in getting on with his teachers. He chaffed against many of the requirements imposed on him by his school, including the need to complete homework and other projects.

Unfortunately, his wealthy professional parents were active accomplices in this.

They afforded 'mere' school teachers little respect and encouraged him to regard them with a similar disdain. They retained their admiration exclusively for those as or more materially successful than themselves and tended to look down on everyone else. Pedro, of course, followed suit.

Not surprisingly, as he grew older he gained a reputation among the teaching faculty as a rather unpleasant boy, which spread from the academic staff to his sports coaches. Teachers are, after all, only human too and it is fair to say that some at least developed a distinct prejudice against him.

This became apparent when he was dropped from the his school's best cricket team, not because of his form, but because of his offensive attitude towards his coach and others. Instead of enjoying the distinction of being a 'Captain of Sport', which he was quite capable of achieving, he spent his last year at school bitterly resenting his demotion.

There is no doubt that in one sense he had been unfairly treated, as on balance he was a better player than the boy who replaced him. What he failed to learn, and on last contact with us, had still failed to learn, were the skills and temperament required to be a successful team member. The people who could have helped him develop his talents, teachers and coaches, were simply not interested.

Worse than that, some of them actively impeded his progress.

ஃஃஃ

Like many other stories in this book, the importance of this one lies not in the actual events at the time but in the legacy they created. Respecting legitimate authority and working effectively with people at all levels in any organisation are essential for success as an adult. Treating your staff with care and respect is just as important as managing effective relations with your colleagues and the 'boss'.

It is quite possible that Pedro will have continued to resent figures of authority and regard their requests with suspicion, while treating those he considers to be beneath him with condescension.

Because of this he will struggle to manage a team successfully and his relations with any superior are likely to be more difficult than they should be, with obvious implications for his career.

All the management training in the world is unlikely to change these well-established character traits.

Once again we are not suggesting that you raise your children to be subservient 'tools' of authority who will do whatever they are told without murmur. Every organisation and business needs people at all levels prepared to contribute their own thoughts and, when required, voice their disagreement respectfully.

If, however, when your child is an adult, he or she fundamentally disagrees with the values of their employer, they should find another job.

The Role of Schools

It is unreasonable and an abrogation of the responsibilities of parenting to expect a school alone to discipline children's behaviour. At best the school has a secondary responsibility for this which is well behind that of parents.

Once you (with input from children as they get older) have selected a school, it is important to respect its authority in any discussion about the fairness or otherwise of discipline. This includes recognising the legitimacy of school rules and reinforcing their application at home when required.

You may have some misgivings about certain school rules or requirements, and you may even raise these with a senior teacher, but denigrating what their school is trying to do is not helpful for a child. At best, they will become confused about their relations with authority and at worst they will actively rebel against it (see Story: *Not Cricket*).

This, as we have seen, may lead to unnecessary difficulties for them in the future. If both you and your children genuinely believe that their school is misguided in its approach to rules and discipline it is time to go elsewhere.

Teachers, employers, colleagues and, of course, social workers, police officers and prison warders, easily identify children, adolescents and adults who have received inadequate or inappropriate discipline.

These unfortunates overlook commitments, miss deadlines, disregard conventions and break rules with little or no awareness of the impact that this has on others, not least those who are relying on them. This in turn can lead to failed relationships, generally fatherless children, serial unemployment, and mental disorder, as well as wasted opportunities for a better life.

More ominously, such young people may also interact uneasily with formal authority and continually run up against restrictions that their more fortunate peers take for granted as a normal condition of civilised coexistence.

Too many of them break the law and have their lives disrupted or worse by periods, possibly repeated, of imprisonment or community service. What makes these dismal outcomes even sadder is that many of those involved often have little understanding of what is happening to them or why.

To many of them, the world appears to be inherently hostile and unjust, randomly administering punishment and 'unfair' outcomes. Not surprisingly, they struggle to change their ways.

Can you guarantee that none of the above will ever happen to your children? Unfortunately, no. We have already agreed there is no road map to the perfect life. But compassionate and dependable discipline, from the early years on, will skew the odds liberally in their favour.

We have already emphasised that positive parenting revolves around the appropriate application of discipline – to 'step in' to modify children's behaviour when required. This is because the primary purpose of parents is to prepare children to thrive in the wider community, to successfully navigate the rules and regulations of civil society as they create a worthwhile life for themselves. A lack of appropriate discipline will make it less likely that your children will succeed in finding genuine success and happiness.

Conclusion

Disciplining children is an act of love; it not only teaches them self-regulation, but also liberates them in the sense that they know that they have choices. Through discipline they learn that the world is not random or capricious, and that most of the consequences they experience are the result of decisions that they, rather than others, make.

In this way discipline imparts a sense of personal control or mastery to children, an exhilarating sense that they are free to choose the right life for them. Furthermore, as noted earlier, being aware that they can control much of what happens to them is a critical requirement for sound psychological health.

Discipline which is effective, efficient, equitable, reliable and compassionate provides boundaries or limits within which children learn to feel secure, to explore their potential and to prepare themselves to succeed in a future where parents will not be there to guide them.

Rules, laws and constraints are integral to human existence. Accepting this reality and voluntarily, for the most part, living within the restrictions they create, is necessary for enjoying the full fruits our world has to offer.

Unless they learn this during their early years, children are at risk of living a diminished existence, punctuated by painful interactions with formal authority, with potentially unpleasant outcomes for them and those they love. Teaching this fundamental truth is the work of parents rather than schools, which can only reinforce but not replace the lessons learned at home.

Discipline your children or the world will do it for you.

Summary

- Providing reliable, fair and compassionate discipline is the central pivot around which positive parenting revolves. It makes possible the achievement of personal maturity and resilience, indeed all the accomplishments of character covered in this book.
- Positive discipline is an act of love, a gift bestowed by parents on their children, one which is critical for their future psychological health, happiness and success. It is just as important for their development as regular exercise and sound nutrition.
- Disciplining children should rarely require you to raise your voice or become angry or anxious, and it should never involve intimidation, humiliation or abuse of a child.
- Consistent discipline backed by agreed rules and reliable consequences teaches children three important lessons: how to thrive in the wider world of laws and regulations; how to pursue their ambitions without infringing the rights of others; and how to relate effectively with others, including those they may not like.

- Discipline also teaches children the fundamental truth that the consequences of their actions are generally the result of decisions that *they* and not others make. In this way they learn self-regulation and the liberating possibilities of accepting personal responsibility for their own lives.
- Neglecting to discipline your children, either through misguided love or a fear of losing their affection, is to fail them badly. If they don't learn the fundamentals of living in a community and respecting the rights of others while they are still at home, they will suffer the far more painful consequences of neglecting these when they are older.
- For their own benefit children need to learn that privileges are earned. It is a mistake to let them believe that prized possessions and freedoms are automatically theirs by right, rather than a recognition of their contributions to family and their wider community of friends and school.
- It is the duty of parents to respect and support the rules of the school your children attend. Similarly, you and they should respect their teachers, the school's custodians of authority.

11

'Difficult' Conversations

"The real menace in dealing with a five-year-old is that in no time at all you begin to sound like a five-year-old."

Jean Kerr (US author)

This book is based on the premise that parents can and should seek to positively influence their children's development in order to enhance their chances of living successful lives free of the menace of mental illness. In Chapter 2 we defined 'success' for children as accomplishments of character or personal qualities, rather than goal achievement per se, and suggested that the task of parents is to teach children how to live, rather than what to live for.

We believe this approach to raising children confers at least three important benefits: firstly, it clarifies how parents should conduct themselves; secondly, it provides clear expectations for how they wish their children to behave; and, thirdly, it avoids dictating to children what their lives should look like.

Pretty much every advisor on raising children rightly stresses the importance of the example or role model parents and other adults provide for children. We have done so ourselves in this book. Our children copy us whether we like it or not.

When people speak of certain qualities 'running in families' – like a 'short fuse' – they are referring specifically to habits children have learned from parents rather than inherited characteristics, whether they are aware of this or not.

We should aim to consistently demonstrate the personality traits and behaviours we wish to see in our children and encourage them to follow suit, through targeted praise and recognition. But there will be times when their behaviour does not meet our expectations and we need to discuss this with them. These discussions – what we call 'difficult conversations' – go to the heart of positive parenting because they make effective discipline possible.

'Difficult' Conversations

In addition to role modelling and targeted praise, it is through discussions about their behaviour, in particular behaviour which is likely to derail their progress, that parents shape a child's character.

These, sometimes trying, conversations become easier if parents have previously established expectations, reflected in family rules, regarding the behaviour of both yourself and your children. These will never be exactly the same, as parents will always have more autonomy until their children become adults themselves. But the same rules should apply regarding how all family members are expected to conduct themselves and interact with one another.

As we have emphasised, it is reasonable that everyone, regardless of age, is treated with respect and that their point of view is listened to as carefully as anyone else's. Similarly, everyone should keep their promises except in very unusual circumstances. The important thing is that all family members are aware of shared expectations and that parents, in particular, live up to these.

Many of the expectations you have for each other can be captured in family rules. The remainder will be found either in an explanatory document which expands on the rules or in the ten accomplishments of character presented in Chapter 2.

As an example, let us consider our definition of grace as an accomplishment of character: we are modest when we succeed, we acknowledge the efforts of those less fortunate than us, and we are cheerful in defeat.

This may not appear in the family rules but is a useful guide for handling winning and losing in a way which maintains good relations with others, while minimising the disappointment of loss.

Having established this as your family's preferred approach to success and failure is clearly useful if you later need to intervene to address behaviour which is inconsistent with this. For example, when your daughter is rude to an umpire and storms off the hockey pitch after being penalised.

Using this as a guide you would intervene immediately and insist that she apologises to the umpire and her coach. A clear understanding of what behaviour you are seeking from your children and why lends clarity to your own thinking and behaviour when you need to act to modify theirs. It will also give you confidence that intervening is worthwhile and will be of lasting benefit to them.

Having said this, no one enjoys arguments, accompanied sometimes by tears and recriminations, something most of us have experienced. What parents need is a tool which allows them to start and finish a difficult conversation quickly, while remaining calm themselves, but which also is effective in promoting real change in our children's conduct. This tool is known as the 4Is.

The 4Is

The 4Is is a simple but powerful communication tool for speaking with children and teenagers (as well as adults) when you need to intervene to modify their behaviour. It is also useful when you wish to praise and encourage. (We have searched for the original author without success). The four steps for using this tool are:

1. "I just noticed … " (You identify the specific behaviour you wish to change)
2. "I'm concerned …" (You express concern for your child)
3. "I need to understand …" (You ask your child why they behaved the way they did)
4. "I need your commitment …" (You ask for a commitment from them to change)

The best time to address a behaviour you wish to modify is immediately after it has occurred, when memories are still fresh and there is less chance of disagreement over what actually happened. Even at a social gathering you can quietly take a child aside and have a short conversation using this tool.

Its great strength is that it focuses on observed behaviour – what a child actually did – rather than what you believe or assume they were thinking or feeling at the time. This means there is less room for disagreement and avoids fruitless discussion about intentions or motivation which can only be inferred (and argued about) on the basis of behaviour anyway.

Another key benefit of this tool is that it avoids labelling your child in some way. Labelling is generally non-specific; such as, "You are a thoughtless girl" or "You are a bad boy". Applying a generic negative label to a child in this way distracts everyone's attention from the specific behaviour you wish to address.

In addition, apart from being rude and inaccurate, labelling a child in this way lowers their confidence and reduces their willingness to even listen to you, much less change their behaviour. Labelling adds no value to a conversation. By antagonising the child, it invites the retort, "No I'm not!", or "She's just as bad!", or words to that effect.

Very soon you can find yourself involved in a juvenile argument about the relative 'goodness' or 'badness' of your son or daughter compared with others, which has no relevance to why you started the conversation in the first place. This is precisely the point made by Jean Kerr, whom we mentioned earlier, and quoted at the beginning of this chapter; you begin to look and sound like an angry child yourself.

Crucially, to ensure it remains short, calm and tightly focused, a 4Is conversation should address one piece of behaviour only. It is important not to introduce multiple examples of unsuitable conduct which only contributes to the confusion you should be trying to avoid. In this way the 4Is targets only the particular act which you wish to discuss, thus reducing the size of any disagreement between you and your child. At the same time it eliminates any need for raised voices (on your part at least).

Using the 41s allows you to get into, and out of, a difficult conversation quickly and relatively painlessly. You do this by sticking to the point – what your child actually did – and avoiding a discussion about their motives, opinions, or attitudes, or what others may or may not have done, all of which are fertile topics for disagreement.

Using the 4Is

Let's look at how the 4Is tool works, using a situation experienced by many parents.

1. Firstly, you commence a conversation with a child by referring to the specific behaviour you wish to alter: *"I just noticed that you refused to share your toy cars with your brother/sister even though you weren't actually playing with all of them at the time"*.
2. Secondly, you express your concern about the possible negative consequences for *them*, if they continue to behave in this way, *not* for their siblings who missed out on playing with the toy cars. You can point out that a failure to share may mean others are less likely to play with them in the future.

   At this point you also have an opportunity to pay them a compliment. By praising, and expressing your concern for them at the same time, you are far more likely to get them to engage in the conversation in a positive way. *For example, "You are normally pretty good at sharing your toys" (or "You're generally nice to others). I'm concerned that people will think less of you or not want to play with you when you don't share/be kind."*
3. Thirdly, give them an opportunity to explain their actions by asking them why they chose not to share. It is possible that their brother or sister was being unkind, or that they were anxious that a toy car of particular value to them would be damaged. This question allows them to introduce issues that you may be unaware of.

By asking an open question you achieve two other things as well: you encourage them to engage in the conversation and demonstrate respect for their point of view which should, at least, be considered. For example, "*Can you tell me why you are reluctant to share your toy cars? I need to understand why you wouldn't share.*"

4. Finally, you ask them for a commitment that, in future, they will share their toys, except possibly for one or two of special importance to them. You might say, "*Will you promise me that now, as well as in the future, you will share your cars and other toys, except for the red truck that Granny gave you? If for some reason you would prefer not to share will you promise me that you will speak to me or Mum/Dad first?*"

Generally, children, particularly younger ones, will give you their commitment and commence to share their toys. If they refuse point blank this should be the subject of a time out process and, later, a conversation about the need to share and the possible consequences for them if they won't.

Once you get a commitment, that should be the end of the conversation. It can be finished in a matter of minutes without the need for raised voices, threats or accusations – from your side at least. In fact, it is most important, as we emphasised in the previous chapter, that parents set an example by remaining calm, pleasant and polite in the middle of a difficult conversation.

It is also important that there should be no recriminations. As with time out, once a 4Is conversation is finished it should not be referred to again. Your child has made a promise to change and you should respect their commitment unless you need to comment on the same issue in the future.

In this way, children learn that disagreements between reasonable people can be managed courteously and quickly and do not need to be prolonged or unpleasant. With this in mind, try to avoid saying something like, "If I ever see you not sharing again I'll …!"

Will their commitment fix the issue of sharing for good? Probably no. Will you need to address it again in the future? Probably yes. But you will have influenced their thinking and approach the next time they are playing with others.

If you persist, the 4Is, backed if necessary with further discipline, will gradually produce the changes you wish to see in your child and encourage the development of desired accomplishments of character.

This is especially true if, in the future, when you see them sharing, you praise them publicly and warmly. This is absolutely critical. We have already emphasised that the alert parent is ready to praise briefly but sincerely those specific behaviours, or personal qualities, they desire their children to acquire as habits.

A simpler version of the 4Is can be used for this purpose, such as, "*I just noticed you sharing your toy cars with Mary without being asked. I am really impressed and very proud of you*". Once again you will note that the parent's comments are clearly focused so that the child knows precisely why they are being recognised and how they can attract similar approval in the future.

Praise and recognition, as we have already discussed, are key tools of positive parenting because they reinforce desired qualities and behaviours; that is, they increase the likelihood these will be repeated in the future.

In summary, the 4Is process allow you to have rapid and focused conversations about undesirable language or actions without raising your voice or labelling your child. Also, because it targets observable behaviour that all can agree on, and includes concern and praise for children, it is less likely to start an argument.

Your praise and concern will generally get a child quickly onside once they realise they are not simply going to get a 'telling off' for doing the wrong thing. Their engagement also increases when you ask them for their side of the story, rather than simply assuming you know exactly what happened.

Finally, asking for their commitment to change achieves three things: firstly, it encourages them to take personal responsibility; secondly, it puts them on notice that you are expecting a different approach in the future; and, thirdly, it increases the likelihood that they will comply.

If they continue to ignore the needs of others, you can remind them of their earlier commitment(s) and then proceed to use time out or a deprivation of privileges as appropriate. With practice you will find the 4Is rolling off your tongue almost before you have started to think consciously about what triggered them

The Nature of Conflict

The 4Is is one important tool for managing difficult conversations successfully, but there are many others. Before looking at these it is important we understand why conflict between people occurs in the first place. We can start this discussion by making the following observations:

1. Conflict is normal.
2. Conflict is inevitable.
3. Conflict is healthy.
4. Conflict is desirable.
5. Conflict may be a sign that change is required.

It is not possible for any group of people to live or work together for any period of time without some conflict occurring between them. Conflict is inevitable, and therefore normal since potential sources of conflict are all around us. Because people are different they will inevitably disagree about what is important, how things should be done or how limited resources should be distributed.

Conflict is also inevitable because people's needs and preferences often differ and because their demands for time and attention will always exceed the available supply. This means that disputes are unavoidable, solutions must be reached, and alternative points of view reconciled as much as possible.

In the absence of successful conflict resolution no group of people, including a family, can continue to interact effectively.

You will recall the research reviewed earlier (in Chapter 9) which linked mental disorder in children to low quality family functioning. This research identified that badly managed conflict is a major contributor to family dysfunction and associated with significantly higher levels of behavioural and mood disorders in children.

When conflict is not resolved reasonably amicably it can be destructive of relationships, encourage abuse of others and foster an atmosphere of permanent hostility. No wonder it contributes to a greater prevalence of psychological distress in children who are invariably the weaker party in any dispute.

In contrast well-handled conflict is both healthy and desirable, particularly because it assists children develop a number of accomplishments of character. Firstly, it encourages respect for others; all family members are aware that they can raise concerns, confident in the knowledge that these will be listened to calmly and respectfully. This increases the likelihood that inevitable friction will be identified and resolved, rather than becoming a lingering source of resentment which continues to sour relationships.

Well managed conflict also promotes empathy or awareness of the needs of others. For parents it highlights the changing needs of growing children and that the constraints placed on their autonomy should be regularly reviewed and expanded.

Finally, successful conflict management, led by a calm and thoughtful parent, is desirable because it leads children towards maturity. By observing their parents they will learn to practise prudence in what they say and do as well as thoughtfulness for others. They will also come to recognise that there will always be some, unavoidable – that is, normal – disagreements between people.

While conflict may be normal and healthy, what is clearly not normal, inevitable, healthy or desirable is raised voices, anger, tears or abuse of any kind, whatever the circumstances. In other words, there are two types of conflict: constructive conflict which leads to improvement for all parties and destructive conflict, which initiates no worthwhile change but damages relations between those involved.

Conflict is positive when all parties understand three things: firstly, that some differences are part and parcel of everyday life; secondly that it does not need to be accompanied by discourtesy or unpleasantness of any kind; and thirdly, that it is simply a means for resolving sometimes inevitable differences rather than an opportunity for hurting others.

Like so much else in family life it is the example set by parents which will ultimately determine how everyday disputes are managed. If routine arguments between parents are characterised by a lack of respect and bad manners it would be naive to expect something different from their children.

Five Responses to Conflict

Psychologists Thomas Ralph Kilmann and Kenneth Thomas identify five different responses to conflict:

- Avoid – refuse to discuss an issue or problem.
- Accommodate – give in to the other's demands.
- Compete – one party 'wins' and the other 'loses'.
- Compromise – haggle about how to 'cut the pie'.
- Collaborate – cooperate to find a satisfactory solution for both parties.[1]

The first three of these approaches to conflict are essentially destructive. Perhaps avoidance is the most common of the these: for parents whose own childhoods were distinguished by regular 'screaming matches' between family members, avoidance is a very attractive option. They, understandably, associate disagreement with unpleasantness and, being unaware of any alternative, seek to minimise it by pretending it doesn't exist.

Alternatively, they may respond using more clandestine means. For example, a parent may simply ignore a child whose behaviour they can't manage or commence a campaign of low grade hostility characterised by hurtful or sarcastic comments. This, of course, achieves nothing, other than to undermine a child's confidence. It also guarantees further animosity, and more damaging confrontations in the future, because the original causes of conflict continue to fester.

If they can't avoid it, parents with an unhappy personal history of disputes at home may simply give in by accommodating all the demands of the other party without reference to their own. The consequences of this approach, when dealing with an angry teenager, for instance should be obvious.

The teen gets to do or have whatever they wish without reference to the needs and preferences of others. Worse they may come to learn that this is the way life should be, and that they will always get their own way using verbal abuse or worse. Until, that is, they meet formal authorities outside the home, which not only refuse to submit to their demands but also insist, using coercion if necessary, that they do what they are told.

A lifetime of conflict with schoolteachers, employers, and even the police, is almost guaranteed. Such adolescents are literally at war with the world.

A 'winner take all' or competitive approach to conflict is likewise destructive because, once again, one party's needs are ignored; the 'loser' is unhappy because the 'winner' is sufficiently powerful to impose their preferred 'solution'. Any child will resent a parent who simply uses their superior strength to impose an 'agreement' and will seek to evade it anyway.

In this case children learn that force is all that matters. An aggressive, authoritarian parent teaches them to impose their will on those weaker than them and to be wary of those who are more powerful. The bad feelings generated by a 'might is right' strategy can lead to permanently damaged relationships between parents and their offspring as well as dysfunctional personality development in children. It can also risk leaving a young adult distrustful of legitimate authority elsewhere.

Alternatively, a child who grows up with aggressive parents may shrink away from conflict of any kind. This can leave them unable to stand up for themselves when they should, and thus vulnerable to exploitation by the unscrupulous. It will also inevitably lead them into relationship difficulties as an adult because they will be unable to express themselves confidently and assertively during a dispute.

Looking for a compromise between two opposing views is an improvement. But it still places people on the opposite sides of an argument trying to maximise their 'winnings' with minimum reference to the needs of the other side. Inevitably, one side or another will feel they have been 'short changed'.

Constructive Conflict

A truly constructive approach to conflict requires genuine collaboration. This is harder because it takes more time and effort; it also requires both sides to walk away from their (sometimes strongly held) position in order to cooperate with the other party to search for a solution. In addition both must put aside any negative feelings they have about the other while they explore why a conflict has emerged in the first place, and how it might be resolved to everyone's satisfaction.

And while total agreement may not always be possible, a genuine attempt to achieve it will preserve and even enhance relationships, while increasing the commitment of all parties to making any outcome work.

When effectively managed, conflict is a great tool for resolving problems, achieving improvement in how people live and work together and, most importantly, building better relations between them.

When a child or teen is listened to respectfully, has their concerns acknowledged and their ideas incorporated into a solution, they are more likely to feel well disposed towards the parent they have just been 'arguing' with. Clearly the reverse will be true if they are 'labelled' in some way, or if their ideas are simply criticised.

When you engage seriously with your child's concerns, in order to find a resolution that recognises their needs and interests, as well as your own, they are more likely to engage cooperatively with you. Alternatively, by ignoring their views and insisting that they simply conform to your demands – which they may well disregard anyway – you will create bitterness and resistance, further damaging family relationships.

Conflict management is not merely about resolving disputes at home or elsewhere.

We have already suggested that how parents approach discipline is the defining characteristic of their parenting style, as well giving children some of their most lasting memories of growing up. Conflict management within a family is part of this process; how disagreement is managed reflects how parents have chosen more broadly to raise their children, which, in turn, determines the adults they eventually become.

In this context it is worth repeating that research into family functioning reviewed in Chapter 9 confirms that poorly managed conflict within families is associated with higher levels of mental disorder in children and adolescents.

Conflict and Antifragility

Children, as we know, are antifragile; they thrive by addressing challenge. Having their conflicts resolved for them is actually harmful. It is essential for their current and future wellbeing that they learn to grapple with the inevitable disputes that arise in any family and learn how to resolve these respectfully. When they are younger parents will be more involved but as they grow children should be encouraged to stand up for themselves and resolve their own disagreements.

They will not always get this right and may lose some friends along the way. But they will learn 'what is generally best' when managing the inevitable quarrels which arise between human beings and, in doing so, acquire maturity and self-confidence as accomplishments of character.

So, as much as possible, children should be encouraged to sort out childish squabbles on their own; parents should only intervene when such conflicts becomes destructive or physically dangerous.

Even then how you intervene is important. Your focus should be on how they are behaving, not that there is a dispute in the first place. Yelling at children "Will you lot stop arguing!" is not helpful. It will not make the quarrel go away nor will it teach them how to resolve it amicably.

If you do intervene make sure you use the opportunity to coach them in how to resolve arguments in a respectful manner. In particular, explain that when it comes to differences of opinion, it's okay to agree to disagree; that they can acknowledge another's point of view without supporting it themselves, or losing the respect or friendship of the other person. A failure to grasp this basic point, that we don't have to agree on everything in order to be close, mars too many adult relationships.

Conflict will be an inevitable part of children's lives at school and work, the sooner they understand that it is normal and learn to deal with it successfully by themselves the better.

Time for Change?

Wise parents also recognise that conflict may also be a sign of a need for change. This is especially true of disagreements with growing children.

For example, if you and your teenage daughter are at loggerheads about the time she is expected to return home from a weekend party, this may (not must) be a sign that it is time to relax the constraints placed on her movements outside of home.

Certainly her (quite natural) push for more freedom indicates a need to talk and, if possible, create a suitable solution. Even a small alteration to her 'be home by' time may be enough to satisfy her request and confirm her sense of being a responsible individual with her own interests and needs that deserve to be recognised. It will also increase her self-confidence as it demonstrates you trust her to behave sensibly. Even if you conclude that she is not yet ready to stay out later, merely talking with her about it at least confirms that her views are of value and should be listened to.

It is both normal and desirable that children seek and, indeed, demand, greater autonomy as they grow. Desirable, because it gives you a chance, while they are still with you, to assist them grow into independence successfully; in the not too distant future, they will be facing the challenges of adulthood on their own.

A cooperative approach to conflict will encourage them to consider the potential consequences of what they wish to do and allow them, with your help, to develop strategies for achieving more freedom without unnecessary risk. In effect you will be teaching them how to successfully navigate the world as an independent adult (See Story: *Either/Or*).

Story: *Either/Or*

Maria (16) and her father were having their usual argument about what time she should arrive home from her Saturday night social engagement. As far as he was concerned, a girl her age should be home by 11.00pm at the absolute latest. She, on the other hand, was pushing for 12am because, according to her, that was when her friends were expected home.

Both were adamant that they were right and their weekly tussle was not only exasperating, but also threatening to create lasting resentment between them. She resorted to generalisations such as, "You always treat me like a child!", while he replied, "That's because you are behaving like a child!", and kept insisting that she would come to harm if she came home any later.

On this occasion, he finished the argument by stating that, as her father, he would decide what time she would come home and, if she didn't like it, she would be permanently 'grounded' until further notice.

Perhaps, not surprisingly, the following Saturday night she failed to appear at the agreed location when he arrived to collect her. When he finally tracked her down, she was drinking alcohol with a group of older adolescents.

It is common for two sides of a dispute to get stuck in what Edward de Bono calls the "Either/Or Trap".[2]

This occurs when either party insists on their preferred outcome and can't see, or refuses to contemplate, any other, despite the fact that there are always multiple solutions to any disagreement.

In the above story, her father insisted on 11.00pm while Maria was adamant that 12am was appropriate for a young woman her age. In this case, de Bono's point would be that, by each sticking to their preferred outcome, both are missing the opportunity to build a shared solution that may be preferable to either of these alternatives.

By refusing to discuss alternatives, the father runs the risk of (a) harming his relationship with his daughter, (b) setting the scene for future arguments, and (c) provoking even more inappropriate behaviour from Maria.

The way out of the Either/Or Trap, de Bono explains, is to explore the concerns behind the positions people adopt. Why is Maria's father insisting on 11.00pm? Because he is concerned for his daughter's safety; he reasons that the later teenagers stay out the more likely they are come to harm and, on balance, he is probably right. Hence his insistence on an earlier time.

Why does Maria want to stay out until 12am? Because it is evidence to both her and her friends that she is an independent person and no longer a little girl.

So the time Maria comes home is not the real issue for either of them!

Her father is concerned about her safety and she is seeking greater freedom. If this dispute really was about the right time to come home it would be impossible to resolve because there is no 'right' time. (Disputes framed in these terms may explain why parents and adolescents/young adults sometimes become locked into irreconcilable differences).

The real issue for both is how does Maria gain more independ-

ence while remaining safe? Once the disagreement is expressed in these terms there are numerous solutions.

For example, she could commit to going to – and staying at – agreed locations and ringing at 11pm as well as just before she is heading home at 11.45pm. Her father could also escape the Either/Or Trap by introducing a time frame into the discussion; she may agree to keep coming home at 11.00pm, for the time being, provided this is extended to 12am once she reaches her next birthday. The important lesson from de Bono is that we need to look behind the positions adopted by each party in a dispute to understand their true needs.

ꕥꕥꕥ

Using the Either/Or technique gives both parties a reasonable chance of reaching a satisfactory resolution provided – and this is important – they conduct the conversation in an atmosphere of mutual respect and civility.

This means that they, and parents in particular, remain calm and courteous, ask open questions (i.e. "How," "Why" and "What") and listen respectfully in order to understand each other's needs. Obviously both should also refrain from name calling or sweeping generalisations about the other's motivation or intentions (e.g. Father: "You simply don't understand the dangers!," or Daughter: "Why can't you ever trust me?").

Parents, as we have noted, set the example in this regard. Respectful disagreement is much easier when both parties understand, or parents at least, the true nature of conflict; that it is a normal part of family life which should not be avoided, and can be resolved (reasonably) amicably. Furthermore, that constructive conflict leads to stronger and more mature relationships between child and parents, fewer quarrels, and happier families. But it requires skills which must be learned, children will not come to these on their own.

The Conduct of Conflict

It is the responsibility of parents to ensure that conflict in their household is constructive by demonstrating how to do this on a daily basis and teaching their children to do the same. This starts by including a reference to conflict in your family rules.

In this case, we have suggested the following rule: we respect others; if we are rude or lose our temper, we always apologise.

Adherence to this rule is the foundation of constructive conflict. No issue or disagreement, however pressing, is more important than the fundamental requirement to treat others with respect; the subject of a disagreement is less important than how it is resolved. Children quickly forget what a difference of opinion was about, but will have lasting memories of how they were treated by a parent.

The legacy of conflict management in your household will be twofold: the quality of the relationships you have with your children when they are adults, and the approach to conflict they adopt in their own families.

Conducting disagreements in a respectful, constructive fashion requires the following skills:

1. Remain calm, regardless of the behaviour of your child. By remaining calm and avoiding raising your voice or losing your temper you encourage them to do the same. This is the essence of role modelling which we have already mentioned.
2. Ask open questions: Open questions commence with the words "Why", "What" or "How". Their purpose is to encourage your child to explain their desires and preferences. By using open questions you demonstrate that their opinions have value and are important to you. You will also come to understand the real needs behind their position – provided of course you listen to their answers.
3. Listen carefully: Once you have asked a question, *listen without interrupting*. Otherwise, you are sending a clear message that your child's point of view and, by extension them, are of little importance. Careful or active listening also involves, when necessary, asking further questions to make sure you understand the other's 'take' on the topic.

4. Remember that listening is *not* the same as agreeing: Once a child starts talking be careful not to interrupt. Let them say their piece. The temptation to interrupt when we hear something we disagree with can be immensely powerful, but listening does not imply agreement. Interrupting, once again, sends the message that we really are not interested in their version of events but merely wish to impose our point of view. Wait until they have finished before you respond.
5. Agree with a child as much as possible. Finding common ground is a powerful tool for resolving conflict because, in the middle of a disagreement, it reminds you both that what you share far exceeds your differences. Agreeing where possible also tends to get children 'onside'; they become more willing to listen and collaborate. It also clarifies the relatively few points in dispute thus making resolution easier.

   For example, you can agree with the facts (e.g. "Yes, you will be seventeen on your next birthday") and with the balance of probabilities (e.g. "Yes, I believe your friend John is a reliable person") even if you still don't want your daughter hanging out with John in the mall.

   It is worth repeating that by agreeing that John is dependable does not necessarily mean you are also agreeing to a meeting in the mall. As noted when we agree with children they tend to calm down and feel more positive towards us. Agreeing with them where possible also shows them that you are listening and want a solution that incorporates as many of their preferences as possible.
6. Avoid insults, name calling or 'labelling'. This has been mentioned before and should be self-explanatory since rudeness will merely exacerbate any quarrel. In addition, as we have mentioned, labelling is invariably inaccurate (e.g., "You are just hopeless!") and undermines a child or teenager's confidence in themselves.

It is easy to list these tips for managing conflict, but much harder to practise them, and even tougher when a child declines to play by the same rules. Nevertheless, it is important to try because they reduce the chance of any dispute degenerating into an irrelevant exchange of unpleasant words which you and they will quickly regret.

A constructive approach to disagreement is much less stressful and less likely to lead to hurt feelings and lingering resentment. With practice you will get better. And remember if you do get it wrong you should always apologise.

The techniques discussed above are primarily about how parents should behave towards children, especially during an altercation.

You can also encourage them to display preferred similar behaviours *towards you* by *always* modelling these yourself as well as applying the following techniques:

7. Reinforce desired behaviour: We have already noted that to pay attention to a specific behaviour displayed by a child, through praise or acknowledgement, is to encourage more of it. Reinforcing desirable behaviour, even during a disagreement, increases the likelihood that it will be repeated. It will also increase their willingness to engage constructively.

   The trick is to look for *any* sign of, say, cooperation in your child and highlight it: "Thank you for listening to what I have said" or, "I really appreciate your willingness to make suggestions that might suit us both."

   This is a powerful technique for influencing your children and, over time, their character development as well, particularly if you make it a habit. By carefully observing what your child is saying or doing you can use any conversation, even the 'difficult' ones, to reinforce those behaviours which reflect the accomplishments of character – including grace, respect and empathy – you wish them to develop.

   Targeted praise and acknowledgement will also mean that both a parent and their child finish a difficult conversation with increased respect and appreciation for the other which strengthens rather than weakens the relationship between them. A child warms to a parent who actively highlights the positive aspects of their personality and behaviour and the parent develops a greater appreciation of a child's strengths and individual qualities.

8. Ignore inappropriate behaviour: It is perhaps inevitable that children will say and do things to hurt their parents, especially during an argument, such as the old standbys, "You don't love me, you've never loved me!" or "I hate you!"

   As much as possible try to ignore this type of comment or behaviour. Ignoring, or not responding to a behaviour, as we know, has the *opposite* effect to reinforcement; it *reduces* the likelihood it will be repeated. Put simply, if you react to a comment like, "I don't love you, or "You hate me", you are encouraging more of the same. You are literally teaching your children what your 'hot buttons' are!

   Of course some comments or behaviours cannot be ignored and should be addressed immediately using a 4Is conversation and, if necessary, the imposition of a penalty of some kind. In this situation, the current dispute should be put on hold until your child apologises and agrees not to use certain expressions or gestures when addressing you. Until they do, and can demonstrate it, you should refuse to deal with this or any other issue that concerns them.

Finally, to conclude our discussion on conflict management, there are two further techniques which will help you resolve disagreements with your children as painlessly as possible:

9. Focus on facts not opinions: When discussing behaviour with your child it is important to discuss the facts – in this case, what you, or others, *observed* them doing. In other words, try to focus on *what* they did rather than make assumptions about *why* they did it or how they were feeling at the time.

As an illustration, consider the statement, "You were unfair to Peter because you don't like him". This contains your assumption that what your child did was unfair as well as your opinion of how they feel towards Peter.

Both assumptions and opinions are open to dispute and likely to provoke vehement denials from a child. They also unnecessarily prolong the conversation and risk distracting you from why you intervened in the first place. Have you ever tried to end a conversation quickly with a child about what is fair or not fair?

Offering an opinion about another's feelings is to invite a fruitless debate about what they were thinking as well as risking counter accusations of a similar kind. Concentrating on the facts – observed behaviour that is causing us concern (e.g., "I notice you took Peter's ball away from him"), allows you to get into and out of a difficult conversation quickly and relatively easily by keeping you on topic and focused on improving your child's conduct. We have already presented the 4Is as a useful tool for doing this.

10. Attack the issue *not* the other person: When you see a child being rude, or selfish or doing something dangerous, it is easy to slip into non-specific criticism or labelling (e.g., "You idiot!") rather than focusing on the real issue – what they were actually doing or saying. By labelling you fail to maintain a clear distinction between the child as a person (who should always command your love and respect) and one small aspect of their conduct which is not acceptable. Also you know from your experience, as both a child and parent, that generic criticism from a parent is either ignored or simply hurts feelings.

    This point reminds us that constructive conflict management is a *joint* process in which both parties *collaborate* to resolve their differences. You can encourage this by 'attacking' the problem (by searching for a shared solution) rather than your child. You do this by always displaying courtesy and respect towards them while asking open questions to find out what the interests are behind the dispute, and making suggestions to benefit you both.

Conclusion

While 'difficult' conversations with children are necessary they can also be upsetting and exhausting for all concerned. The good news is that, with practice, you can use the tools of constructive conflict to resolve differences while building stronger families and better relationships with your children.

By exploring their position – and the interests behind it – and creating shared solutions, you demonstrate that their feelings and opinions are important, thereby strengthening their self-confidence and sense of positive identity. Repeated experiences like this will bring them closer to you now and forever.

Also, by understanding that conflict with growing children is to be welcomed, you can resolve it with more confidence. It is simply a sign that their natural desire for freedom is bumping up against the constraints or boundaries you have put in place to shield them from risk that, in the past at least, they couldn't manage on their own.

Recognising this allows you to withdraw gracefully, which demonstrates your trust in them. In this way they will become self-assured and autonomous adults, whom you not only admire, but are confident will build the rewarding life you desire for them.

Summary

- Difficult conversations with your children become inevitable the moment you set out to discipline them with expectations, rules and consequences.
- Discipline sets boundaries which children naturally test, which in turn may create conflict with their parents.
- Conflict in any family is normal and inevitable because people have differing interests, needs and priorities. It is also often a

reminder to adjust boundaries as your children become older and need to take more responsibility for themselves.

- Avoiding conflict for the good reason that you have only experienced the damaging variety, is quite common. Unfortunately this merely postpones an inevitable confrontation. Issues which are left unresolved grow bigger and uglier and eventually erupt, while, at the same time, breeding antipathy between you and your children.
- Destructive conflict, characterised by bad feelings, labelling and cruel language, rarely succeeds in resolving problems but permanently harms relationships and leaves lingering resentment in its wake. Constructive conflict, on the other hand, not only resolves disputes with children (relatively) amicably, but will bring you and them closer.
- How you handle conflict with your children will create many of their most lasting memories of childhood and their parents.

12

All Children are Different But Some are More Different than Others

"I think it ill advised to attribute pathologies to healthy people. It doesn't help normal, healthy, thriving children to be viewed as pitiable and fragile." Christina Hoff Sommers (US author and philosopher)

"All animals are equal, but some are more equal than others." George Orwell (English author, *Animal Farm*)

Every child is different because each is unique, but, to paraphrase George Orwell, some are more different than others!

It is true that many children grow up smoothly and happily. They pass all their developmental milestones on time and progress through childhood and adolescence with a minimum of difficulty for themselves or others. They make friends easily, meet the expectations of their teachers, and create successful families and careers for themselves with little or no angst. These kids make parenting look easy!

Others however are different. Their lives, if not exactly a struggle, are much less serene.

They may be unhappier as babies, have more frequent altercations with parents, siblings and peers and experience more difficulty finding a satisfactory life for themselves as adults. They may be noisier or quieter than their peers or seem more or less motivated, they may learn faster or slower or they may simply not be interested in the same things as other children. Less often some may also be diagnosed with a psychological disorder, developmental delay or cognitive disability of some kind.

Either way they are different.

Because each child is unique from the beginning some will be better equipped to manage their world from birth. But we know that DNA is only part of the equation. Their genetic potential will flourish, change or remain dormant, depending on the environment they grow up in, particularly the family home.

Research into child development, reviewed in Chapter 1, suggests that their genetic profile and how children are nurtured interact in an ongoing, reciprocal, process to produce physical, neurological and psychological change, which, in turn, determines the adults they become.

These interactions place each child at various locations on a range of distributions of behaviour and temperament; locations or, if you like, preferences, which constitute the greater part of their personality. Such preferences determine, for example, whether they are shy or extroverted, or whether they are more or less empathic towards others.

Children also come to reside on other distributions or continua of aptitude and capability, locations which are reflected in their preference and capacity for academic, creative, sporting and other activities. Because of this they will display more or less facility when learning to speak or read, playing a musical instrument or riding a bike and so on.

Similarly, some children will always be more comfortable in their own company and are perplexed by those who prefer time with others. Again others will struggle to express themselves clearly, while envying those with more fluid language skills, or remain mediocre at sport while their friends continue to improve.

It is important to note that a person's pattern of preferences or aptitudes (and a child's in particular) is never permanent. Over time their pattern or profile changes making each the unique person they are and always will be. The ongoing nature of the interactions between nature and nurture means no human being is ever a completed project; we continue to change, develop or regress throughout our lives. This is particularly obvious in children, and not merely in a physical sense, but is also true of adults.

The child you see today will not be the same person tomorrow and may, in fact, change beyond recognition. This observation should caution parents, teachers and health professionals against making definitive statements about the nature or capabilities of a child or adolescent as they grow.

From time to time aspects of their behaviour, what they say and do (to themselves and others), or their failure to meet developmental milestones on time, for example, may cause parents grave concern and require specific intervention. But, as already pointed out, assessing a child's behaviour or performance is quite different from judging the child as a whole person; some of their behaviour may warrant criticism or require special attention, but as people they should always command our love, care and respect.

The simple truth is that if you don't respect and accept your children as who they are as people, at every stage of their development, regardless of how they are currently 'performing', they will struggle to respect themselves, a key accomplishment of character.

Talking about Children Who Are 'Different'

"Children usually live up to our expectations." Steve Biddulph (Australian author)

We have already noted the power of language to influence a child's capacity to manage their emotions (Chapter 6). In that discussion we emphasised that parents must be careful what they think and therefore say to their children, as well as to themselves and others.

A parent who regularly comments in earshot of a child, "Oh she's no good at Math", can expect him or her to mirror that expectation in their performance at school. Children don't know any better; as Steve Biddulph notes (see above) they can only accept their parents' assessments of them and aim to live up or down to these.

The language and beliefs we use to describe children go a long way in determining their self-image as well as the expectations they set for themselves.

Consider these contrasting responses to a child who receives three marks out of ten for a spelling test: "Yes, that figures you can't spell, you're just like your father", versus, "Well you still have some progress to make but I know if we work together on your spelling you can still improve a lot." Regardless of a child's innate capacity, the second comment – repeated often enough and backed by assistance – will produce a far more competent and confident speller than the first.

We recently met a mother who at a social gathering publicly described her adult son as a 'train wreck.' Now admittedly this young man is struggling with some personal issues, including anxiety and drug use, but it is unlikely that language like this is helping him, or her, to successfully come to grips with these. Also if this comment is typical of the way he has been described to himself and others while growing up, perhaps it is not surprising that his life has turned out the way it has.

How we talk about our children (to them, to others and to ourselves) will significantly influence any aspect of their development. Describing a child to their face as 'difficult' or 'impossible' will, once again, create a self-fulfilling prophecy. It also inflates the size of the 'problem' created by the child's behaviour in the parent's mind, making it even tougher to address. Alternate descriptors like 'busy', 'boisterous' or 'feisty' create different, and more positive, images and expectations in the mind of both child and parent.

Similarly, a parent or teacher who says "There's no point talking to Juan because he just doesn't listen" is at risk of condemning a boy who struggles to concentrate to miss just the conversations he needs, to know that he is loved, cared for and respected by the important adults in his life.

If anything, of course, he needs more of these than most children if his disruptiveness, which is alienating his peers and irritating adults, is to be resolved. Which it can be with love and affection as well as consistent and compassionate discipline.

The issue here is that such a child may be denied much of the standard or mainstream socialisation that they need just as much, or more, than their less troublesome peers. And if this means that they fail to acquire the accomplishments of character necessary for success as an adult then their future prospects will be diminished even further.

None of the above is meant to underestimate the challenging business of managing children on the far ends of the 'shy', 'moody' or 'disruptive' spectrums of behaviour; or those who have been diagnosed with a behavioural, mood or personality disorder, or indeed who are simply very different from most of their peers.

We are merely emphasising that these children are best raised using exactly the same methods we have recommended for all those who are closer to the middle or mean of any particular continuum, and therefor appear to be 'more normal'. It may require more effort and determination by parents but their need for love, respect, affection and discipline remains the same.

Label Behaviour not Children

We can agree that despite their parents' best efforts, some children will experience a tougher journey through childhood and adolescence than their siblings or friends.

They are different and may always be in ways which, as we have suggested, means navigating the world is a much trickier business for them. People who are unusual, or more different if you like, can find it harder to fit in, to make friends, and attract the support and care they need to benefit from the opportunities that life has to offer.

If the fact they are different means they fail to meet the expectations of others, including parents, this may create confusion, disappointment and unhappiness around them. Depending on how their particular personality is expressed other people (teachers and coaches for example), may come to regard them as not merely as different but 'difficult' or even worse a 'problem' with all the implications this may have for their future.

Whatever else is going on always try to maintain a rigid distinction between your child as a whole person and those aspects of their progress which concern you. Yes, some of their habits or behaviours may be difficult, or need to be addressed, but a child themselves is never a problem and should not be labelled in this way.

The previous discussion highlighted the power of language to promote or impede a child's progress. This becomes particularly apparent when we use a simple description to define a whole child.

In practical terms, when we apply a negative label in this way, there is nothing left to praise or admire; the child's mere presence may trigger an unpleasant response from us.

This might be okay if they are the neighbour's son or daughter whom you rarely see but clearly isn't for your own with whom you interact every day. If you are unhappy about some of the things your children do, their performance at school, or the people they hang out with, then all the more reason to highlight, to yourself and them, what it is about them that you appreciate and respect even if currently you are finding it difficult to warm to some of features of their conduct or personality.

Genuine recognition of the strengths or positives which reside in every child will make it easier for you continue to love and respect one who is 'different'. This in turn provides some shared space between you and them from which you can seek to influence them in ways you believe to be beneficial for them and others.

A relationship in which there is no common ground of mutual respect and admiration, let alone liking, will fail. Love alone, which will generally persist through the worst possible scenarios, is insufficient to sustain a rewarding relationship between parent and child.

It is not merely impossible, but also inappropriate for us to have no expectations for our children. Indeed, in Chapter 2 we presented ten accomplishments of character which we recommend parents should encourage in every child.

However, parents need to exercise care not to condemn their children as people, even when they believe a son or daughter would be happier if they changed in some ways. Some may simply take longer to develop while others may always display characteristics which parents find awkward or 'difficult' and differ from those they would prefer.

This should not mean you stop seeking to influence and encourage them to change. But all parents need to be careful to not allow a gap between what they hoped for and what they see in their children to become a disappointment or 'problem' for either.

This may occur if a son or daughter chooses not to follow you into a career or sport you love, for example, but perhaps is more likely if you find them irksome in some way or their lack of progress in some area(s) is distressing you.

If this happens a parent may lose interest in their child's development or stop liking them, as well as neglect to make the wholehearted efforts on their behalf that they deserve.

Worse still they might 'write them off' using labels such as 'useless' or 'hopeless'. Labelling a whole child can create a self-reinforcing feedback loop; as they become aware of your disappointment or disinterest they are less inclined to listen to or comply with your requests. This then serves to increase your displeasure which, of course, encourages them to be even less agreeable. Failing to obtain your approval or attention in socially desirable ways they become increasingly disruptive and unpleasant to live with.

The implications of this for their future mental health should be obvious. Parental disapproval lowers their self-esteem and self-confidence. They become prey to feelings of worthlessness, which reduces their motivation to tackle the challenges of growing up as well as leaving them vulnerable to developing anxiety and/or depression.

We have both consulted parents where it was quite apparent that their active dislike of their child was the major driver of his or her self-destructive behaviour (see Story: The *Chef*).

Story: *The Chef*

One of us consulted a couple who were wrestling with one of the worst possible scenarios one could imagine for a family. Their only cherished daughter had become an intravenous drug user.

She was a very clever, inventive young woman with a passion for cooking who had a range of very practical interests and pursued hobbies completely different from those of her parents who were both successful professional musicians.

When she became an apprentice chef, it is safe to say she disappointed her parents who had much grander plans, as they saw them, for her to become a concert pianist. As is often the case, there was a long back story which began when she started getting tattoos and smoking marijuana while she was still at school.

The more her parents expressed their displeasure with her lifestyle, the more enthusiastically she embraced it.

When she won a national award for apprentices her father was unable to conceal his contempt. Her mother's response was more muted, but her attitude was not dissimilar. Relations between daughter and parents became increasingly strained so that the next development, intravenous drug use, was only a short step away.

❧❧❧

There is no doubt that these parents loved their daughter and devoted a considerable effort to her upbringing. But because she didn't turn out the way they expected they became increasingly disenchanted with her. They were unable to put their disappointment to one side and encourage her to become the person that she had to be.

Essentially, they lost faith in her and her future. No matter how much they continued to be engaged as parents, it was impossible for them to conceal their dissatisfaction with who she was.

She, in turn, sensing their displeasure, used increasingly inappropriate means for gaining their attention and approval, which she,

like all children, still craved. Fortunately, her career success provided the confidence and self-esteem she required to give up drugs.

For us this is a clear case of failure to respect and accept a child for who they are, as well as honour their need and responsibility to make their own life. In this sense, our love for our children should be genuinely disinterested regarding *what* they chose to do, while, at the same time, quite prescriptive in terms of *how* they do it.

The irony is that in most cases children will go their own way, regardless of our preferences, so why fight about it? What we should 'fight about', or rather seek to influence, is the type of person they become in the process.

❧❧❧

Labelling children may not only occur if one is behaving 'badly'. It can also happen as their personality and pattern of aptitudes begin to emerge.

For example, you may regard one of your children as 'studious', who is expected by you and themselves to perform well at school and generally they will. So far so good, but you may also contrast him or her with their siblings and regard the latter as 'frivolous' or 'lazy' or 'only interested in clothes' or 'sports mad' and so on.

If you are not careful you can end up with only one child in the family who is interested in school, even though they may be all equally capable of academic excellence. Why can't we have children who are both studious and frivolous, as well as interested in clothes and good at sport?

The point is not to place children in very narrow pigeonholes, which end up defining who they are, and will be to themselves and others. Perhaps it is inevitable to have short-hand identifiers for children (e.g., "He's always been clumsy") but, as we have emphasised, the danger is that these may come to define the whole child to a parent, and hence to the child.

This, obviously, is not a good development. You create a child's expectation of themselves when you might say, "He/she is 'lazy', 'thoughtless', 'slow'", or whatever. They will come to believe this and turn what may have started as a harmless comment into a self-fulfilling prophecy, with consequences you may both regret.

The way to prevent this is to be aware of the inherent dangers in labelling and develop habits to counteract these. Thus, you might observe, "She loves fashion but she is very smart and could make a career of it someday", or, "He certainly does bounce around the furniture a bit but once he gets a little older I expect he will be a great athlete." Or yet again, "School is certainly a challenge for her, but with our help she will succeed".

The trick is to avoid using the same statement regularly to describe your child and eliminate negative ones altogether. You can influence their future for the better by 'prophesising' good things for them in the way you speak about your children, to them, to yourself and to others.

Don't Play Favourites

It is not uncommon for parents to have a favourite child. To an extent this is inevitable; because the personalities of the 'favourite' and one or both parents are more compatible, relations between them may be easier than those either parent has with their other children.

This need not be an issue, provided both parents are scrupulous in ensuring each of their children is treated equally in terms of receiving their affection and attention, as well as how they are disciplined and rewarded, and the opportunities offered to them. But you need to regularly review your approach to all your children to ensure this is happening.

Unfortunately, and less creditably for parents, preferencing one child over others can also occur because the favourite is an 'achiever', while the others are less so. If this is the case, you should do all you can to eliminate, or at least reduce, your prejudice in favour of the one who, for the moment at least – it probably won't last – is winning all the prizes (see Story: *The Favourite Son*).

Story: *The Favourite Son*

Some years ago we knew a father with two children, a boy and his younger sister. The teenage son was successful at sport and schoolwork while the daughter much less so. The father would relate his son's achievements with obvious pride and enthusiasm, which was understandable.

Unfortunately he would also compare his daughter with the son in disparaging terms, criticising not only her lack of achievements but also her physical appearance and personality. Both children were well aware of the father's preference for his son. Occasionally he would acknowledge that this was unfair to his daughter, but seemed unwilling to stop.

Not surprisingly, his daughter was a shy, anxious and overweight girl, uncomfortable in company and struggling at school; her father's criticism had become a self-fulfilling prophecy.

Tragically, the son later died in a motor vehicle accident leaving his father devastated, unable to continue living his previous life, and without a solid, affectionate relationship with his daughter to assuage his grief when he most needed it.

❧❧❧

We are aware that this (true) story makes for painful reading but it highlights the dangers of playing favourites between your children and the potentially disastrous consequences for the less favoured child and, in this case, following subsequent events, for a parent also.

The fate of the son could not repair the damaged relations between daughter and father or restore her permanently diminished personality. It did, however, tragically exacerbate his grief because in the process of idolising one child he had sacrificed the other.

Whatever the circumstances, playing favourites not only harms a less favoured child but can *also* damage the one who attracts more of their prents' affection and/or admiration.

A favourite can become accustomed to unadulterated praise from an adoring parent, regardless of their conduct. This, as we have already noted, can lead to the development of narcissistic elements in their personality.

Consequently, the favoured one may find it difficult to adjust

to a wider, more discerning, world which is less willing than an indulgent mother or father to tolerate their less attractive traits.

If this is the case a favourite child is left with a positive disadvantage when it comes to interacting with others; he or she may be unaccustomed to recognising their obligations to others, or in extreme cases, even fail to recognise that these exist.

The result can be a traumatic transition from being at the centre of positive attention to difficult, indeed stormy, relationships with others (including their siblings), who are less inclined to accept a favourite's expectation that whatever they do is not merely appropriate, but deserving of others' support and encouragement.

The future of a family 'favourite' may be very difficult indeed.

Understanding Children Who Are 'Different'

As we have suggested, all types of behaviour and performance, including, for example, boisterousness and distractibility, sit somewhere on a range between a great deal and little, or none at all. The majority of children – those who can concentrate, and be (reasonably) quiet, when necessary – are closer to the centre of this continuum while their less common or 'different' peers can be found towards either end. Easily distracted and/or unruly children – who might attract a diagnosis of ADHD – will be found on the far right hand end of this particular spectrum while their more passive peers – who might be regarded as shy – will be located towards the far left.

Just as children come to reside (at least temporarily) at different points on the alternative dimensions of preference and character which make up the 'pattern' of their person, they will also, as we have suggested, display varying aptitudes for different types of cognitive and physical performance.

Towards the lower (or left) end of a particular scale, intelligence for example, a child may be assessed as being 'below normal' and in need of specialist teaching to assist them proceed academically as far as they can go. These children display significantly lower levels of (some types of) cognitive processing than their same age peers, a competency necessary for them to flourish as adults. Targeted intervention can improve their performance significantly by moving them further along to the right of the particular dimension of skill or capacity in which they are 'below par'.

In the absence of a genetic abnormality or an acquired intellectual disability (through illness or injury), there is no organic difference between children diagnosed with below normal intelligence and those who are not, other than that their scores are lower on a number of standardised tests of cognitive functioning.

Certainly they have less aptitude for certain types of thinking than their more able peers (which may always be reflected in lower levels of academic functioning) but the severity of their condition will be significantly influenced by how they are raised and schooled (See Story: *Angela*).

Story: *Angela*

Angela was nine years old when she came to see one of us because she was academically well behind her peers at school. She was quiet but pleasant and interacted quite well although without saying too much.

She also obviously had a warm relationship with her parents who adored her.

Surprisingly her assessment revealed that she had a moderate to severe degree of intellectual disability. We say surprisingly because it was not what we anticipated, following our initial interaction with her in which she presented as a quiet but alert and well socialised girl.

From discussion with her parents it was clear that they had suspected for a long time that she was intellectually less able than other children. This became clear during her assessment when she struggled with tasks, like general knowledge, simple arithmetic and reading, which the vast majority of her same age peers would handle with ease.

On the surface, however, she did not display many of the behaviours which identify an intellectually disabled child, since she could follow straightforward conversations and was aware of the need to recognise and interact with those around her.

Listening to her parents it became clear why she performed socially so well despite her disability.

As soon as they began to suspect that she was behind her peers, they had emphasised the importance of her taking her full place in the family, including contributing to daily chores and participating in dinner table conversation. Importantly, their other children actively supported their sister in this regard.

The result was that she had grown up in a home where clear expectations for her social behaviour and involvement in family life were set and reinforced by her parents. The consequences were extremely impressive to say the least.

Of course her future was likely to be curtailed in some ways but her parents were obviously giving her the best possible preparation so that she could be as independent as possible and live as full a life as she was able.

One outcome of this consultation was to change forever our own expectations of children with an intellectual disability.

🙠🙠🙠

We are pleased to record this story in recognition of the work of two remarkable parents.

It also emphasises the critical difference which parents can make to the lives of children who are 'more different' than their peers, including those who may be diagnosed with a 'disability' of some kind.

Even a child who is diagnosed as being 'below normal' or 'disabled', in some respects is still normal in the sense that they require the same upbringing we recommend for their more fortunate counterparts. This remains true even though they may require more support and special programs of one kind or another. It also remains true even if they are less likely to achieve full adult independence.

Angela's parents were determined from the very beginning that

she would develop as far as she could go in as many directions as possible, especially in her capacity to interact effectively with and be independent of others.

As well as extra academic coaching, she participated in dancing and pony riding, both of which she loved. She also regularly contributed to family shopping expeditions and cooking at home.

The results of her parents' commitment were astonishing in terms of the quality of Angela's relations with others and the calm she displayed even when baffled by parts of her assessment.

We believe that the best conclusions to draw from this story are, firstly, to never accept any diagnosis of your child as a definitive statement of what they may become in the future and, secondly, to never stop trying to promote their chances of living a life that is as full and rewarding as possible.

Angela's story reminds us that even the impact of significant disability can be ameliorated, relative to its severity, by how a child is raised.

ꕥꕥꕥ

To diagnose 'below normal' intelligence is simply to draw a line on the continuum of 'intelligence'; that is, to identify two groups of normal children – those who require individual assistance in academic activities versus those who can be expected to manage successfully in a mainstream school environment.

That the extent of an intellectual disability may be rated as severe, moderate or mild, further highlights that diagnosis is not a clear cut business in the sense that it divides children into two groups who are, always have been, and always will be, organically or physically different. To reiterate, children diagnosed with a non-organic intellectual disability (and these are the vast majority) are normal kids who happen to display less of a particular skill set than their same age peers.

The good news is that most of these children do respond positively to support and individual instruction in the same way as any other child, even if they never progress as far in terms of intellectual or scholastic attainment. Targeted support, delivered by skilled teachers and committed parents, can be expected to realise at least some performance improvement in those areas where they are struggling. Experience and research tell us that this is so.

This is important to know because it reinforces a key point we wish to make about raising children: just because a child attracts a diagnosis which confirms that they are behind – sometimes well behind – their same age peers in significant aspects of their development, or they are different in other ways, they remain fundamentally normal children. The principles of positive parenting used to guide their growth should be exactly the same as those we are advocating for their 'less different' counterparts.

These are:

1. All children should be encouraged to travel as far as possible (in every direction) as they are capable, regardless of where they currently are on their developmental journey.
2. It can never be over emphasised that an assessment of a child at any point in time is merely a 'snapshot' of where they are today, not a dependable guide to the person that they can, with help and encouragement, become tomorrow.
3. Relative to their level of 'disability' or 'delay' parents should place similar expectations on a child, in terms of their character development (particularly personal maturity), as their non-diagnosed peers, even if they continue to be behind in some areas.
4. Parents should also continue to raise their aspirations for every child, subject to their progress, to encourage them to keep striving for further improvement.
5. All children need a family environment created by love, respect, affection, routine, rules and discipline, even if they also require individual support or specialist intervention. And if they are indeed 'different' their need for acceptance, respect and love will be that much greater than it is for their 'mainstream' peers.

6. Parents should avoid defining or labelling a child in terms of 'disability', 'disadvantage' or 'delay'. Ideally they accept and respect all their offspring for the people they are, while continuing to assist them progress as far as they can go.
7. If a child does display less of a particular capacity, necessary for achieving adult independence, then their need for positive parenting, particularly the expectation that they will travel as far as possible towards an independent life, is, if anything, that much greater than it is for others.
8. Every child is different, unique in fact; we wouldn't expect or want them all to behave or perform in the same way. From this perspective differences should be accepted and respected rather than become a reason for disappointment (see Story: *On the Farm*).

Story: *On the Farm*

Early in Harry's life it became obvious that his speech was delayed, in fact he appeared unable to speak at all. His grandmother insisted that he was like his father and would start speaking 'when he was ready'. His mother, however, was not so sure.

She had him assessed, which confirmed a severe language delay, and organised speech pathology for him. Unfortunately this had minimal impact and his speech remained extremely rudimentary.

Nevertheless his parents learned that he could hear and understand what they were saying and he has been taught to communicate using sign language and sign boards. Just as important they encouraged him to take a full role in the life of the family including taking responsibility for his share of chores on the farm. Today he competently operates all the farming machinery and helps his father while attending the School of the Air.

Time will tell whether Harry will achieve full independence as an adult but his parents are giving him every chance. What is more important is that, with their support and encouragement, he has grown into a happy boy, with a range of employable skills, who loves life on the farm.

Harry's story highlights the relevance of positive parenting for children who have a severe disability or developmental delay of some kind, specifically the importance of parents accepting and respecting a child for who and what he/she is, while assisting them to develop their talents as far as possible.

Harry's parents have defined him in terms of what he can do, rather than the reverse, and expect him to use the strengths and capacity he does display. Because of their love and support he has the same privileges and responsibilities as his siblings and continues to grow in competence and confidence, even though he may never learn to speak like most adults.

When necessary, they also use discipline to insist he conducts himself appropriately and to teach him to not use his communication difficulties as an excuse for rudeness or hostility.

In short they are giving him the best possible chance of reaching full adult independence or of getting as close to this as he is capable. If parental commitment and persistence count for anything Harry will succeed.

Raising Children Who Are 'Different'

We argue strongly that positive parenting – the approach to raising, managing, nurturing and disciplining children as recommended in this book – remains appropriate even if your child has been diagnosed with a behavioural, personality or mood disorder, a Specific Learning Difficulty (SLD), a developmental disorder such as speech delay, or ASD (Autism Spectrum Disorder) or, indeed, an inherited physical or cognitive disability of some kind.

Why? Well because all children are the same – including those less capable, in some ways, than their more blessed peers – in the sense that they all have the same needs for love, care, attention, discipline and respect. What is more, those considered 'less able' still have to grow up and live an independent life when their parents are no longer there to support them. Which, in the majority of cases they will, with extra assistance, be capable of doing.

Believing that a child who has been diagnosed with a mood, behavioural or developmental disorder is somehow abnormal or a problem is of no help to them. And taking a fundamentally different approach to raising them, even though you may provide specific intervention or additional support, is the worst thing you can do.

We have met parents who tolerate quite appalling behaviour from even adult children, that they would not accept from anyone else, simply because he or she has been diagnosed with a mood or personality disorder, for example. Instead of insisting that they display ordinary respect towards others, which in the majority of cases they can do, their anti-social behaviour is enabled by anxious parents who accept their discourtesy, because of their 'condition'. By lowering their expectations in this way parents can make it even harder for children to thrive in the wider world; in effect they are adding to the difficulties which these unfortunates are already facing as a result of their diagnosis.

An adult child who refuses to demonstrate appropriate respect to parents or stepparents, regardless of what else is happening in their lives, should no longer be welcome in the family home until they apologise and display the common courtesy they owe to any human being. Adolescents and children who behave like this should be disciplined using the techniques discussed in Chapter 10.

This rule (as well as other family rules) should apply regardless of what diagnosis they may have attracted. The only exception to this is if they have a cognitive impairment, inherited or acquired, which is sufficiently severe to prevent them from effectively managing their own behaviour.

It can be difficult to deal with an adolescent or young adult who is angry and abusive or moody and withdrawn for example. And it is very tempting to make allowances for them because they are experiencing genuine difficulties. But placing different, that is lesser, expectations on them than their siblings, will simply encourage them to remain at a lower level than they are capable of and further disadvantage their development.

In the case of a child diagnosed with ADHD you may need to use disciplining techniques more often and have more difficult conversations with them, and they may always be something of a contrary individual. Similarly a child diagnosed with a learning difficulty or speech delay needs additional training and support. But, to reiterate, just because they require special intervention in no way changes their need for the same love, respect, affection, attention, rules and discipline which every child deserves.

Although they may require individual assistance, the vast majority of children who are 'different' nevertheless have the capacity to make their way to their preferred life. To do this, even more than their more mainstream peers, they need an upbringing which equips them with the accomplishments of character required for adult success; and they won't receive this if they are treated quite differently for much of their childhood.

In contrast to regarding a child who is different as a 'problem' to be 'solved', there is another trap parents can fall into; that is to regard them as 'special' who, because of their diagnosis, should not be required to meet all, or at least some, of the expectations they place on other children.

This might occur with a child whose difficulties quite naturally arouse our compassion, for example one diagnosed with an inherited disability of some kind, which does restrict their potential in a number of ways.

In this case understandable sympathy for a child like this may lead parents to set lower standards for how they manage themselves than they would otherwise be capable of. This can mean that they unwittingly disadvantage their children even further through misguided love.

It can be heartbreaking as well as inspiring to raise a child with severe disabilities but they need and deserve parents who expect them to progress socially and cognitively, as well as in terms of personal independence, as far as they can go. They are still antifragile and wrapping them in cotton wool because you feel sorry for them is not the act of a conscientious parent.

ADHD

The danger of regarding a child who is different as a 'problem' and hence something of a burden or a disappointment becomes more acute if their behaviour aggravates those around them or they are obviously lagging behind their peers in developmental terms.

This is especially true for those who have been diagnosed with a behavioural or conduct disorder of some kind, such as ADHD (Attention Deficit Hyperactivity Disorder).

ADHD is defined as a pattern of inattention and/or impulsive behaviour, both of which are sustained over time, and significantly more marked than in peers at the same age/developmental level.

Children (and adults) with ADHD are distractible, they struggle to concentrate and complete set tasks. They may also fidget, chatter a lot and have trouble keeping still or quiet when required.

In 2015, the Young Minds Matter survey of mental health of children and adolescents in Australia, (reviewed in Chapter 1) reported that in the previous 12 months some 7.4% of children and adolescents (11-17) displayed symptoms consistent with a formal diagnosis of ADHD, approximately 298,000 young people. Boys are more likely to be diagnosed than girls (1 in 10 males compared with less than 1 in 20 females), and older adolescent girls least of all.[1]

You will recall the research, reviewed in Chapter 9, which found that the incidence of behavioural, conduct and mood disorders (including ADHD) is significantly higher in children from dysfunctional households. In response to this data, we argued for a causal link between how well a family functions and the mental health of children growing up in it.

These findings (and others like them) confirm that, in the absence of inherited or acquired cognitive impairment (such as foetal alcohol syndrome), disorders of this kind are largely learned or acquired as children grow.

It is not unreasonable to expect that any child, regardless of genetics, is more likely to be distractible, attention seeking and unhappy if they grow up in a home characterised by disorder, erratic discipline and destructive conflict, and where too little attention is paid to their emotional and practical needs.

These conditions are precisely those that will encourage symptoms commonly observed in children diagnosed with ADHD: personal disorganisation, inappropriate attention seeking, low impulse control and disregard for the needs of others, as well as anxiety and sometimes depression.

In other words, these are *normal* children responding *normally* to the chaotic environment in which they live. And the longer such conditions persist, the more likely it is that such behaviours and emotions will emerge and become permanent features of their personality.

If we are not careful, we may regard such children as categorically different, as if they had an abnormality of some kind, when in actual fact they are simply further along the same continuum of 'acting out' behaviour than their quieter peers. And the risk of regarding them as 'different' will be even greater if they have attracted a diagnosis of ADHD.

There is no organic test for behavioural disorders such as ADHD, or indeed for conduct, mood or personality disorders as well. Diagnosis can only be made on the basis of a specialist's assessment as well as reports from parents and teachers about a child's behaviour at school and elsewhere.

How might a child who is diagnosed with ADHD have learned to be hyperactive or distractible? We have already suggested that misbehaviour in children is their clumsy attempt to receive the attention from parents, teachers and peers that they crave and need if they are to be successfully socialised.

Their very unruliness is unambiguous evidence of their need for more interest, input and warmth from others. And if, as is likely, they are also more anxious than their better behaved peers, their need for loving engagement is even greater.

But if they have fallen into a learned a pattern of unruliness, excitability or distractibility as their method for gaining attention – and others have come to expect and accept this – then there is a real danger that this will be progressively reinforced until it is impossible to change.

Because they are disruptive they may be expected to be disruptive. Those around them may then respond to them and their disruptiveness as 'problems' to be managed, rather than an indication of their very normal need for closer involvement, firm and consistent discipline, and better relationships with family and friends.

These children need a lot more attention in the form of praise and encouragement for even the tiniest signs of improvement in their behaviour. At the same time there will be the necessity to engage them in 'difficult' conversations (of the kind described in the previous chapter) backed up, if necessary, with appropriate discipline, when their behaviour becomes unacceptable.

Unfortunately, the very reverse of what is required may be happening if their unruliness or distractibility is regarded as a 'medical condition' and thus being reinforced and exacerbated. And if this goes on happening until the child becomes an adult, who knows no other way of interacting with the world, it will trigger a train of inevitable and mournful consequences which are likely to include mental illness.

So it is for mood disorders, such as anxiety and depression, as well. A child may be withdrawn and interact less with those around them due to anxiety or sadness. In this case their behaviour and underlying unhappiness may be reinforced by parents who expect them to be quiet and undemonstrative or, alternatively, become angry because of their 'lack of interest' in others. These children require even more love, affection and attention than their more outgoing peers, even though they may fail to respond to, or even reject, the kind overtures of friends and family.

Rather than ignore them or become frustrated because they are quiet, it is important to draw them into the family circle with with acknowledgement and praise. Their essential behaviour may not change, but they are less likely to become prey to debilitating anxiety or depression.

Diagnosing ADHD

The Australian Commission on Safety and Quality in Health Care reports that in 2013-14 the dispensing rates for prescriptions for ADHD medication for patients 17 years and under were *seventy-five times greater* in some parts of Australia than others.[2]

Prescription rates were assessed on a state by state basis as well as between smaller local areas. To take one example, the average number of prescriptions varied from 5,541 per 100,000 children seventeen and under in South Australia, to 13,588 in New South Wales.

Even when the areas of highest and lowest prescription rates for ADHD medication were removed (to allow for a lack of access to medical services in remote areas or the presence of large hospitals in others) prescription rates were still up to 7.3 times greater in some parts of the country than others.

Between 2013-14 and 2016-17 diagnosis and medication of ADHD continued to increase across Australia although the magnitude of variation between the highest and lowest dispensing areas declined to 17.4. Nevertheless, in 2016-17 the differential between dispensing rates in SA and NSW remained essentially the same – 7,001 and 16,813 (per 100,000 children, 17 years and under), respectively.[3]

Given that prescription rates reflect diagnosis it is clear that there is significant variation in specialist assessment of ADHD across the country.

What to make of these findings? It is hardly likely that South Australian youngsters are significantly less distractible or hyperactive than their counterparts in NSW or anywhere else for that matter. There must be another explanation for the substantial differences across Australia in the diagnosis and medication of ADHD reported above.

Certainly diagnosis and dispensing rates will be influenced by a range of factors, including how individual specialists approach the diagnostic process as well as variation in parents' decisions to medicate their children or not. Nevertheless, the significant disparities across Australia in prescription rates tells us something about the condition itself, in particular that diagnosis of ADHD is an uncertain science at best.

Given that diagnosing ADHD relies on observation based assessment and parent/teacher reports, this alone leads to widespread differences in opinion between specialists, reflected in varying rates of diagnosis and medication.

While DSM IV (the global standard for diagnosing mental disorders including ADHD) requires certain criteria to be met for a diagnosis to be made – whether relevant behaviours occur both at home and school for example – there is still plenty of room for disagreement between individual specialists.[4] The fact that a diagnosis may be 'mild', 'moderate' or 'severe' further highlights the absence of a clear dividing line between children who might be diagnosed with ADHD and those who clearly should not.

Thus there is a large 'grey area' between behaviours which can be clearly categorised as hyperactive or inattentive and those which should not be – a grey area that captures an awful lot of boisterous and/or easily distracted children!

This is why diagnosing a behavioural disorder like ADHD is so difficult because a paediatrician or child psychiatrist is drawing a (somewhat) arbitrary line on a range of normal behaviour and, in doing so, places normal children into two separate groups (in the same way as 'below normal' intelligence is identified). How much unruliness or distractibility is enough to justify a diagnosis?

Well that decision, rightly or wrongly, depends a great deal on a specialist's training and experience, as well as the (second hand) information they have available, all of which will inform their diagnosis. This is not a criticism of paediatricians or child psychiatrists – there is no denying that the behaviour of some children requires particular intervention – it merely highlights the challenges in making a diagnosis.

The danger is that the parents of children with ADHD may regard them as categorically different from their non-diagnosed peers, rather than simply being further along a continuum of normal behaviour. If this is the case there is a risk that they will be socialised quite differently as a result (in the manner described in the previous section) thus compromising their future.

The same is true of mood disorders, a central concern of this book. As with ADHD there is no organic test for these conditions; diagnosis is based on patient self-report as well as parent and specialist observation. Once again, a specialist draws a line across a dimension of normal behaviour (in this case 'moodiness') which divides normal children into two groups. The risk here is that, once more, children who are regarded as anxious or depressed will, to their detriment, be raised differently in ways that may exacerbate their condition. As with ADHD, we are not suggesting that for some children assessment and treatment are unnecessary. We are simply highlighting the importance of parents not losing sight of these children's need for exactly the same approach to parenting described in this book as their non-diagnosed or less 'different' peers.

Unfortunately, in our experience some parents regard a diagnosis of a behavioural disorder (like ADHD) or a mood disorder (such as anxiety or depression) as some sort of solution. To them it 'explains' a child's behaviour which, of course, it doesn't (a diagnosis is merely a description) and therefore resolves it, which, once again, is clearly not the case. For these parents there may be nothing more to be done except ensure that a child takes their medication in the same way if he or she was diagnosed with an organic condition of some kind.

Medications, such as Ritalin, commonly prescribed for ADHD, can be highly effective in calming a child and reducing their impulsiveness or distractibility. But medication can't directly assist a child to interact more successfully with others or teach them how to read. Similarly medication prescribed for depression will often assist a teen to stabilise their feelings but, on its own, does not teach them how to feel more comfortable with themselves or learn how to manage their emotions effectively.

Medication can provide an opportunity for conscientious parents to assist a child to address these conditions but only if they are prepared to make the necessary effort using the tools of positive parenting described in this book. If anything, these children require more love, respect, affection, discipline, rules and routine than their less 'different' peers, not an upbringing which is quite dissimilar, and which may well exacerbate the condition which caused concern in the first place.

While children who are 'different', including those diagnosed with ADHD, may always be different to some extent, the severity of any condition they display, and its impact on their future, can be significantly reduced through positive parenting.

Specific Learning Difficulties

Specific learning difficulties (SLDs) refer to a range of information processing issues which can slow a child's academic progress, making it difficult for them to keep up with same age peers. It is estimated that between 5% and 15% of children have an SLD of some type.[5] Dyslexia and dyscalculia – problems associated with reading/writing and numeracy respectively – are common examples of an SLD.

It is important to note that children with an SLD are not intellectually disabled and can often be highly intelligent and gifted in other ways. Steve Jobs, Muhamad Ali and Walt Disney all suffered from dyslexia. An SLD can be highly specific, impacting a child's spelling only, for example, but not their reading, while other children with SLD may display a cluster of information processing issues.

The term SLD is often interchanged with others such as, learning disorders or learning disabilities. In Australia and the UK the term specific learning difficulty is used in order to distinguish between conditions that can be overcome – children with dyslexia can and do learn to read – and disabilities which present lifelong challenges (see story The Engineer).

When it comes to cognitive processing all of us display relative strengths and weaknesses. Some are poor at reading maps, or mental arithmetic, while for others distinguishing left from right is a genuine challenge. An even more common processing disorder is difficulty in putting names to faces.

The issue with SLDs, of course, is that they impact how well children acquire the literacy and numeracy skills required for further learning and which they will need for pursuing a career in more and more occupations in the future.

Story: *The Engineer*

Many years ago one of us consulted a young boy (11 years) and his parents because of severe problems he was experiencing with his schoolwork.

Assessment revealed that he had significant symbolic processing issues and he was diagnosed with moderate to severe dyslexia.

However, we were able to reassure his parents that he was of well above average intelligence, which is not uncommon among children with an SLD, and that with extra coaching there was no reason he should not successfully complete high school and, indeed, attend university.

Imagine our surprise and pleasure when we received a letter from his mother some 15 years later to tell us that he had just successfully graduated as an engineer!

It was heart-warming to read that what they had learned about their son all those years before had provided the stimulus they needed to support him through the difficult years of high school.

His graduation was a testament to their love and determination that, just because he was different, this was no reason for him to be deprived of a successful future.

❧❧❧

We include this story to emphasise to all parents whose children are 'more different' than others, the powerful impact that love, respect, sustained encouragement and appropriate intervention can have on the quality of a child's future.

It also reinforces the point, made in the main text, that a diagnosis of a child is simply a 'snapshot 'of who and where they are at a single point in time. It should never be regarded as a definitive statement about who they are today or what they are likely to be in

the future. The people they become will primarily depend on how they are supported, educated and socialised as they grow.

We have already suggested that any diagnosis of psychological, behavioural or developmental disorder is a picture of some aspects of a child or adolescent's behaviour or performance at a particular moment. It is never a conclusive statement about them as a whole person or the adult he or she will become. Your own experience will tell you that many people can and do overcome significant personal disadvantage in the form of mental illness, addiction or problems at school and go on to lead happy and rewarding lives.

However, if parents are not careful any such diagnosis may indeed become a self-fulfilling prophecy.

Many disorders, including anxiety and depression, are, as we know, primarily learned and should never be considered to be permanent conditions which condemn a child to a life sentence of unhappiness, mental disorder or under achievement. And because they are learned, with love and instruction from their parents children can, in many cases, unlearn them or, at least, reduce their severity and impact. Mood disorders need not be a permanent feature of any child's character. Some may well remain quieter and more withdrawn than their more extroverted peers, or more sensitive to stressors, but these need not be associated with chronic depression, unreasonable anxiety or psychological distress.

The evidence is clear cut that how children are educated and socialised – and the character they develop in the process – are critical in two ways: firstly, whether or not inherited predispositions (to anxiety say) emerge in the first place; and secondly, if they do appear how they influence a child's subsequent development and behaviour. A child who does experience elevated levels of anxiety, for example, will manage this much more effectively if they have been taught emotional control as an essential accomplishment of character.

No diagnosis of your child, however grim, is the end of the story. It is, in fact, only the beginning, provided you remember that from the moment of their birth you can significantly influence the people they eventually become. A parent's focus should be on the people who, with care and encouragement, their children *can* become tomorrow as well as on the people they are today.

Moreover, we firmly believe that this is also true of children diagnosed with a permanently disabling condition of some kind. In this case, they may never reach the same level of adult autonomy as their more fortunate peers, but the people they eventually become and how far they travel towards independence can be significantly influenced by their parents.

Autism Spectrum Disorder

Autism Spectrum Disorder (ASD) is a neurodevelopmental disorder which can seriously compromise a person's capacity to socialise with others and to communicate effectively. ASD may also include repetitive, stereotyped motor movements, ritualised behaviours and restricted or fixated interests that are unusual in their intensity or focus. While signs of ASD may be detected in early infancy, a categorical diagnosis is not typically made until at least three years of age. Currently, 1 in 70 Australians are diagnosed with ASD, with males four times more likely to display this condition than females.[6]

A recent Australian study demonstrated the impact of trained carer intervention during the second year of life – during which the infant brain is rapidly developing – on the social development of infants considered at risk of developing ASD.[7]

Video feedback of infant behaviour was used to train a group of parents and carers to become more aware of and responsive to their child's individual communication style and to learn how to encourage greater infant-adult engagement. Training took place over a six-month period (from 12 months) and the psychosocial progress of children in the study was tracked from 12 months to three years of age.

The progress of two matched groups of infants, both considered to be at risk of developing ASD, were compared, one whose carers had received intervention training and one whose carers did not. The progress of each experimental group was also compared with that of a control group of infants assessed as not being at risk of developing ASD.

Intervention training was designed to assists parents and carers to 'tune in' to their babies and get on their 'wavelength' in order to encourage their responsiveness and facilitate two-way communication. Training of this kind appears to promote the attachment process discussed in Chapter 1. It may well be that, for infants who are at risk of developing ASD, attachment is a more difficult process, since these babies are typically less responsive to others. Attachment may be impaired unless carers are trained to attend more closely to their verbal and non-verbal cues and actively encourage their engagement.

The twin purposes of the study were, firstly, to determine whether intervention training for carers of at-risk infants would reduce the severity of any ASD symptoms they later displayed and, secondly, whether such intervention decreased the chance of such children being later diagnosed with the condition at all.

The results of the study demonstrated a small but lasting (and statistically significant) reduction in the severity of ASD type behaviours in the intervention group (those with trained carers) when compared with similarly at risk children in the non-intervention group. The rate of subsequent diagnosis of ASD in the intervention group (6.7%) was also significantly lower than that in the non-intervention group (20.5%).

These findings, although limited, are supported by the results of similar research and more generally by the growing evidence (reviewed earlier) that the care a child receives during the early years of life will permanently change their neurology and hence their subsequent cognitive and psychosocial development.

For us these results also reinforce our argument that parenting style can directly improve the social and psychological development of all children, including those diagnosed with a significant developmental disorder such as ASD. Even in those cases where a diagnosis is made the ultimate severity of a child's symptoms can be reduced by parent/carer engagement (see Story: *Reggie*).

Story: *Reggie*

Today Reggie is 32 years old. When he was born, much less was known about ASD than today and he was not formally diagnosed with the condition until he was well into his teens. However, his parents were well aware that even as a young boy he was behind his peers in terms of his social development and at risk of getting 'lost' in a large suburban primary school. His teachers were less convinced and, perhaps, because they were busy, had little time for a boy with special needs.

Concerned for his future, his parents moved him but found that little was different at his new school. Desperate, they home schooled him for 18 months until they found a small private school which, although not specifically catering for children like Reggie, provided a warm, compassionate environment in which he felt secure.

Reggie continued to receive extra coaching and support, including lessons to develop his obvious musical talents. As a result, he made sufficient progress to successfully finish his schooling in a mainstream high school. He has gone on to play in two bands, hold down a full-time job (for which he is never late or absent) and lives independently two suburbs over from his parents.

On Anzac Day at dawn he plays the Last Post on his front lawn and the whole street turns out to listen and applaud.

❧❧❧

There are two points to be made in response to this story.

Firstly, as with other stories in this chapter, this one confirms the vital impact which engaged parents can have on the future of any child regardless of how 'different' they may be and whatever diagnosis they attract.

But, more importantly, it highlights how Reggie's parents, while responding to his particular needs, were also able to identify and encourage his innate strengths, in this case musical talent. They did not define their son in terms of him being 'autistic', but as a normal little boy with gifts to be realised as well as some skill sets which needed further improvement, just like any other child.

Respecting and accepting children for who they are, while encouraging them to become all they can be, are, as we have emphasised, critical elements of positive parenting.

Make Sure You Understand Your Child

Unless they are properly supported, children with an SLD, for example, can have an unhappy time at school where they may struggle to keep up or be victimised by peers. This can lead to withdrawal or disruptive behaviour in the classroom, which further impairs their confidence and progress.

This highlights a broader point; the need to gain a full understanding of why a child may be 'causing trouble' at school (or elsewhere), or failing to keep up, before coming to any conclusion about the reasons. There are many possible explanations.

A disruptive child in the classroom may simply be bored because she is significantly more intelligent than her peers and the learning material being offered does not excite her. Alternatively, while still bright, she may have an undiagnosed SLD which is currently holding her back.

Yet again she may have poor eyesight, cannot see the whiteboard, and hence is losing interest. An adult would bring this to our attention, children often do not.

If your son or daughter is struggling or 'playing up' at school the very first thing we recommend you do is to have them physically assessed, including having their eyesight and hearing tested.

On one memorable occasion one of us was considering whether a little girl had a learning difficulty or not only to learn that she was partially deaf in her left ear!

Her problem was 'fixed' by having her moved from the right to the left the side of the classroom (facing the teacher) so she could hear what was going on!

This taught us a valuable lesson about fully exploring all the reasons why children may be unhappy or underperforming at school before coming to any definitive conclusions about their behaviour or academic performance. We urge you to do the same if you have a child who is 'different' and for whom school is a trial.

Conclusion

Because of the unpredictable interaction between biology and environment every child is different, unique in fact. At any point in time as they develop they will reside at various locations on a range of dimensions of behaviour, personality and aptitude, which constitute the unique pattern of their person.

However, these locations are not permanent. Parenting, socialising with peers and schooling all continue to influence a child's development as they interact with their environment. The child we see today will be quite different in a few years' time.

While some children enjoy a relatively easy progress through infancy, childhood and adolescence, others are 'different' in that they find growing up more difficult. Some may display a psychological disorder, learning difficulty or developmental delay of some kind. Others may be eccentric or unusual, or require support to strengthen some aspect of their cognitive or psychosocial performance. Unfortunately, a minority will never reach full adult independence.

However, the key point made in this chapter is that no matter how 'different' a child may be, he or she will still benefit from positive parenting. *All children* need and deserve a family environment characterised by love, respect, affection, routine, rules and discipline if they are to travel as far as possible towards a fulfilling life for themselves.

Summary

- Each child is unique therefore they are all different. As a rule differences should be celebrated but there is no doubt that some children have a harder passage towards adult maturity than others.
- Children are a work in progress; the child you see today will not be the same tomorrow and may, in fact, change beyond recognition. This means parents should exercise caution when

tempted to assess, judge or describe a child at any given point in time. Any assessment of a child is a 'snapshot' of where they are now and may well tell you little about the person they will be in the future.

- A gap between who your children are and who you would prefer them to be should not lead parents to regard a child as a 'problem' or 'disappointment' or lose interest in their progress. True respect for a child means to accept and love them for the people they are even though you may need to work hard to encourage them to change in ways beneficial to them and others.
- Labelling a whole child, rather than aspects of their behaviour or performance which are of concern, can set up a self-reinforcing loop which only serves to increase their difficulties and further undermine their progress.
- Having a 'favourite child' may be inevitable. What is not inevitable or healthy, for them or their siblings, is that he or she is treated differently or more advantageously. A family 'favourite' may well face tough times in the future.
- Wherever a child is in terms of their development, conscientious parents can significantly enhance their social and intellectual development through structured interventions and a sustained expectation that they will travel as far as they are truly able towards successful independence.
- There are many reasons why children struggle at school or elsewhere and these should all be checked before a definitive diagnosis is made.
- *All children*, regardless of their specific circumstances, require positive parenting; that is, they need to grow up in a family environment characterised by love, respect, affection, rules, routine and discipline.

13

Tools for the Road

"The road to success is always under construction."
Arnold Palmer (US golfer)

To complete our discussion of positive parenting, we consider what we have called tools for the road.

Before going on a bush walk you pack a rucksack with food and water and hiking equipment, as well as all the other kit you need to camp out for a night or two under the stars. Some of what you take you hope you will never need, but you bring it anyway in case things don't work out as planned – like emergency rations and a two-way radio. The longer the trek and the more remote the terrain the more 'emergency' gear you are likely to need.*

* We have already referred to camping and bushwalking, accompanied by an adult as well as alone, as desirable activities for children and adolescents. Many of our conversations with young adults highlighted how much they enjoyed family camping holidays when they were young and, in many cases, have continued with their own children. Why camping is so attractive to many children is unclear. Perhaps it is the fun of setting up their own 'home' in their tent, which gives a feeling of independence from parental supervision, or simply the sense of adventure that arises from going to new places and trying new things, like swimming under waterfalls or climbing hills to look at the horizon. It may also be because they are living more closely with their whole family than is usual when they are at school, or simply the attraction of not having to wash properly for a few days! Whatever the reason, there is no doubt that it has a special significance for them and certainly for parents as well who also get to see a lot more of their children than they normally would. This being the case we strongly recommend camping holidays for the whole family for bringing you closer together and providing your children with many opportunities for learning new skills and taking on new responsibilities.

So it is for children on their journey to adulthood. They too will need tools or, if you prefer, knowledge and skills as well as accomplishments of character, if they are to successfully negotiate the uncharted road in front of them.

Some of the tools discussed below we have already touched on and develop in more detail here while others are new:

Tool 1: Circle of Competence

Tool 2: Learning to Concentrate

Tool 3: Managing Failure

Tool 4: Do the Thing You Fear Most

Tool 5: Managing Relationships

Tool 6: Learning to Love

Tool 7: Learning to Laugh

The tools we discuss obviously do not cover everything a child will need to know or learn for their journey but, for us, they are some of the more important ones. You will discover others with your children as they grow and reveal their capabilities – this is part of the fun of being a parent and a child.

Tool 1: Circle of Competence

We know that there are many skills children will need in the future, some of which are yet to be invented. So where to start?

It is not possible to cover everything they will need to know. But what parents can do is assist them find their 'circle of competence' as early as possible. We understand that this nugget of wisdom originated with Warren Buffett, the legendary investor, but we first came across it in Rolf Dobelli's lovely book, *The Art of the Good Life*, first introduced in Chapter 2. He describes it thus: "Inside the circle are skills you have mastered. Beyond it are things you only understand partially or nor at all."[1]

By mastered he means something at which you genuinely excel, which makes you stand out from the crowd; you are not merely better than others, you excel sufficiently to be a recognised expert. Identifying our strengths and honing these to the point where we truly shine takes time and effort.

Dobelli notes that many successful people begin to do this in childhood. Apparently Warren Buffett began investing his pocket money when he was 12 years old. Dobelli also makes the point that even for the most talented their circle of competence will necessarily be limited. He suggests that smart people, like Buffett, work out where their gifts lie as early as possible, develop this small skill set to the highest possible level, and then stick with what they know and are good at.

Interestingly, Dobelli argues that achieving a circle of competence is necessary, not only for career success, but also emotional wellbeing. Certainly being a recognised expert, the accomplishment of character we have called competence, is handy when looking for a job, but there is more to it than this.

Dobelli points out that developing a circle of competence creates 'an invaluable feeling of mastery', which echoes our earlier suggestions that a sense of personal control or mastery is integral to psychological health and essential for achieving positive identity as an accomplishment of character.[2]

Dobelli emphasises the value of a circle of competence for managing an uncertain future. He makes the point, already familiar to readers, that 'the idea that you can make life stick to a plan is an illusion. Chance tears through everything with the force of a hurricane'.[3] Genuine expertise gives anyone, he argues, a much better chance of surviving, financially and emotionally, unforeseen and calamitous change in their life. In effect it promotes personal resilience, a further accomplishment of character.

By encouraging, indeed insisting, that children explore a range of activities and experiences in and out of school you can encourage them to search for their own circle of competence. Whether it lies in artistic, scholastic, sporting, IT or technical domains, or somewhere else, may not be initially clear, but everyone can have one if they are prepared to explore.

It makes sense for children to search and experiment as much as possible when they are young and have the time, and parents are there to encourage their early steps. During this process they will also learn the value of persistence and that 'failure' – finding out what doesn't work – is integral to ultimate success.

We recommend that, in addition to their schoolwork, all children engage in at one least one structured physical/sporting activity in winter and summer as well as a hobby of some kind. And as a rule of thumb they should continue any new activity they take on for at least 12 months to determine their aptitude as well as to instil persistence in their character.

Opportunities for physical activity are almost limitless and can range from salsa dancing through gymnastics, orienteering, golf and rugby union to weightlifting. A hobby can also encompass almost any imaginable pursuit, including a part time job, which is the best way for children to prepare for adult employment and to learn the value of money.

And even if, by the time they leave home, your children have yet to find their true circle of competence, they will be a lot closer to it and will also have absorbed a lot of useful things along the way. More importantly, with your help, they will have acquired qualities of character including the pleasure of testing themselves, to 'fail' with confidence, to persist with a smile, and to handle the joy of winning as well as the disappointment of loss with grace.

Tool 2: Learning to Concentrate

It is a truism to say that before a child can learn they must learn to concentrate. The capacity to focus long and hard on the unfamiliar and intractable is a requirement for successful achievement in any sphere.

Isaac Newton attributed his discovery of gravitational force to his capacity to sustain extended periods of intense concentration. He said, "I keep the subject constantly before me and wait till the first dawnings open slowly little by little into the full and clear light".[4]

Obviously only a tiny fraction of people can ever be an Isaac Newton and it should be noted that his willingness to wrestle with a problem not merely for hours, but for days, weeks and months as well, was dangerously obsessive. At times he compromised his physical health in search of an answer.

Nevertheless, he provides an object lesson in the value of concentration for the rest of us mere mortals, who must also be able to focus for lengthy periods to the exclusion of most other things, if we are to turn our potential into genuine achievement.

While small children will focus on activities which temporarily catch their interest, they need to learn what is called 'directed attention', the sustained concentration required to remain at a task and complete it, even when it is losing its appeal. Like so much else, directed attention is not a capacity with which they are born.

However, no one learns to concentrate directly, we acquire it while pursuing one or more challenging activities.

Learning to read is a case in point; children are born with the potential for symbolic processing – attaching sounds and meaning to printed symbols – but not the skill itself.

As with spoken language, they need external input from adults. But, unlike learning to talk, which most do automatically, to learn to read successfully requires structured practice. Left with a pile of books few children would learn to read on their own.

Parents can teach their children to read and concentrate at the same time by breaking this complex task into small easily managed segments. Children love to be read to and you can use this to introduce them to reading for themselves.

Begin by reading to babies and toddlers while asking them questions about the pictures accompanying the text. You can also encourage them to 'sound out' individual words. Then teach letter recognition by linking each letter with its sound and asking them to copy you before moving on to whole words. Later you teach them to read simple sentences by repeating each a number of times while tracing the words with your finger. Then suggest they read along with you as well as on their own while you praise their efforts.

Like learning any other skill children are more likely to persist if their early efforts, however rudimentary, are recognised and encouraged. This reassures them that they are on the right track and inspires them to keep going.

Initially, any sound they make in response to a printed letter or word should be encouraged, before you repeat the correct sound and ask them to do the same. This is the same model of successive approximations for coaching children discussed in Chapter 8.

Don't wait for a perfect result before you praise their efforts; any attempt at all to sound a letter or word should be recognised, however inaccurate it may be. At this stage the child is learning an important lesson – that sounds and symbols go together. The next step is for them to associate each symbol with its appropriate sound.

As they become more proficient share the reading with them word by word and then sentence by sentence. In return for them persisting with this for say 10 minutes each evening offer to read to them for a further 20 minutes. As mentioned children are neurologically preprogrammed to read, write and spell; with help and encouragement from parents, most will come to these relatively easily.

Needless to say frustration or criticism on your part will only inhibit this process. Each child sits somewhere on the 'reading' continuum of behaviour, some will love to read and pick it up easily, while for others it will always be more of a challenge; their preferences will always lie in other directions. But your approach to coaching should remain the same if you wish your children to progress with reading, or indeed any other skill, as far as they can go.

And it is important to persist, particularly with reluctant readers, because, needless to say, symbolic processing of all kinds is central to modern culture and critical for their employment prospects. It also lays the foundation they will need to exploit many of the other genetic possibilities they inherit so that they can pursue their preferred life.

We may not be able to predict too much about the future but we do know that an increasing number of careers that children will pursue as adults will require this crucial capacity.

In the process of learning to read, write, type and calculate they will also learn to concentrate; they will become comfortable persisting with tasks which initially, at least, are complex and frustrating, while remaining confident that they will eventually succeed.

In addition, an important part of 'directed attention' or sustained concentration is to properly complete a job which may have lost its attraction but which nevertheless must be delivered to a teacher or manager tomorrow.

Once again children will acquire this through practice and praise. Initially you can work with them to design, prepare and complete a piece of work on time. Then, as with reading, increasingly pass more of the responsibility over to them. In this way, with help, they will acquire persistence and competence as accomplishments of character.

Barring a specific cognitive impairment, concentration is just another skill which with practice and perseverance can become a lifelong habit for a child, even though some will always be able to concentrate longer and harder than others.

You may know adults who progressed through school without too much difficulty but in later years have neglected to retain the habit of reading and working intently for extended periods of time. Their capacity to concentrate deteriorates because, like any other skill, it declines through lack of practice.

Tool 3: Managing Failure

"Success is the ability to go from one failure to another without the loss of enthusiasm." Winston Churchill (UK statesman and author)

The more they try the more they will fail but if children don't try they will never know what they are truly capable of, find their circle of competence, or live a life which is truly fulfilling for them. What is implied in this statement is that if they are to succeed they must first learn to shrug off successive failures in the manner prescribed by Winston Churchill.

Teaching children to manage failure successfully starts, as with much else they need to know, at home. By applying rational or adaptive thinking to your own life (see Chapter 6) – particularly how you respond to setbacks and failure – your beliefs will become theirs.

If a parent loses their job they may rage at the 'injustice' of the world and blame others (e.g. the boss) for their situation. In this case their children will learn that the world is unfair and full of people out to 'dud' them. This will obviously colour their own view of employment and the people in charge.

Alternatively, the same parent may respond to being unemployed by saying to themselves and their children: "I'm disappointed this has happened; I'd have preferred to keep my job but I'm OK with it. I realised the company was struggling and was expecting something like this. It is what it is and I will immediately start looking for another and better job".

The contrasting lessons learned here are that setbacks do sometimes occur despite our best efforts, and when we can't change what has happened, accepting the facts cheerfully is the best way forward. Listening to this parent, a child will also learn that the future is always full of new possibilities.

The second thing you can do to encourage children to think adaptively about 'failure' is to gently challenge their language when you hear them practising one or more unhelpful beliefs. For example, you may hear one of them say "The coach hates me, that's why she never picks me for the top team. I've always said she is biased!" You can assist by suggesting an alternative way of approaching the situation by asking "Have you spoken to the coach? Do you know why you haven't been picked? Maybe she thinks the other players are better than you, at least at the moment".

You can also ask "What can you do now to improve your chances of being selected?" If your child persists in believing that the coach genuinely doesn't like them – and it could be true – you can also ask what they can do to influence her opinion of them, rather than simply condemning her as a bad person.

For example, you could suggest they attend every training session on time with all their gear, try their best and follow instructions as well as volunteer to pack up afterwards. The key point is to encourage them to think and behave differently about what has happened so that it no longer arouses unnecessary and painful emotions, which may distort their subsequent behaviour. Until they learn this, an initial 'failure' may be sufficiently unpleasant or humiliating to make them reluctant to persist or to try anything else for fear of 'failing' again.

And, as mentioned before, if a child genuinely believes they have been unfairly treated this is something that you can raise with their teacher, when they are younger, or they can do themselves. This is a potentially difficult conversation which you can coach and practise with them before they see their teacher on their own.

Six Lessons About 'Failure'

Children need to learn six important lessons if they are to handle set-backs with confidence now and in the future:

1. The first is, as noted above, that the more they attempt and the harder they try the more likely they are to 'fail'; in fact, they are guaranteed to experience 'failure'.
2. This leads to the second (discussed in Chapter 4): 'failure' is merely a stepping-stone to success, a tool for learning how to succeed next time. Parents teach children to use this tool by encouraging them to ask themselves "What could I do differently in the future to avoid this happening again?"
3. Thirdly, once they have extracted all the lessons they can from a temporary or even permanent failure, they need to know how to 'put it to bed', that is, to leave it in their memory, until they forget about it completely. This ensures that it won't keep coming back to taunt and upset them. They can do this by using the magic words: "While I would have preferred the outcome to be different, it is what it is and I'm OK with that."

These words may not sound like magic but, applied consistently, they are a powerful tool for assisting children come to terms with even the worst of unavoidable traumas. Why this works is because, repeated regularly, these words replace the old unhelpful or irrational beliefs or 'frames' regarding failure and loss which reside in the subconscious, with a healthier alternative which is acceptance. Irrational beliefs generate negative feelings – humiliation, or self-loathing for instance; genuine acceptance, on the other hand, produces milder and more moderate emotions. (If you are not sure about this try it for yourself, and remember the secret is persistence).

4. A fourth lesson is to understand that a single or even multiple instances of failure do not mean that they are a 'failure' or 'a 'worthless' person. For a child to believe that minor or even major failure negates their value as an individual is a classic example of irrational thinking.
5. The fifth lesson for children to draw from all of this is to accept that sometimes, regardless of what they do, the world is not always just or fair. Unfortunately, sad things sometimes do happen to good people. Accepting this does not mean suggesting that they 'roll over' and accept any unfairness or injustice. On the contrary we advocate that parents should encourage their children to stand up for themselves and others, for example if they are being bullied at school.

   What we are saying is that sometimes, despite their best efforts, life will not always go the way they planned and that unfortunate events can and sometimes do happen. When this occurs children need to accept the consequences with grace, however unfair these may be and press on.
6. This brings us to the final lesson about failure. Like it or not, as we have already emphasised, children need to learn that they are primarily responsible for what happens to them, not others. Yes, there are some events, a bout of illness for ex-

> ample, which may be entirely beyond their control, but they need to know that they can influence most of what happens to them through the choices they make. As a case in point Peter and Robert could both have decided to reject drugs and hence avoid gaol (see Chapter 6).

As we have already emphasised failing to learn personal responsibility has profound implications for children's mental health. If they can't accept accountability for their own choices – and the consequences of these – they will feel trapped in a chaotic world over which they believe they have little control.

If this is the case they will assume that they are at the mercy of external forces and that their happiness depends on the whims of others or pure chance. Such a child lacks a sense of personal identity and is prey to debilitating anxiety and depression – mood disorders associated with the twin destructive beliefs that bad things can happen without warning and that there is nothing they can do about it.

Children need to integrate each of these lessons in 'failure' into their thinking if they are to establish many of the accomplishments of character we have used to define success:

- Self-confidence
- Persistence
- Maturity
- Grace
- Positive identity
- Emotional control
- Resilience

Acceptance of some inevitable bumps along the road is necessary for them to remain reasonably contented and enjoy a stable emotional life. The alternative is for them to become focused on the 'bad' event and the 'bad' people who are responsible and to keep reliving their unhealthy reactions to both.

These will include anger about a perceived 'injustice' or 'loss' –

imposed 'unfairly' by others who should be punished – followed by sadness when they realise that they can do nothing to change the past. Chronic sadness becomes depression which may last months or years and seriously impair a child's capacity to live a worthwhile life.

We have put the words bad, injustice, loss and unfairly in inverted commas to indicate that these interpretations are not inevitable and not necessarily correct. Alternative interpretations (driven by different beliefs) will produce other healthier and more adaptive emotional and behavioural responses.

When discussing disappointment with a child it is important to acknowledge how they are feeling at that time and offer your support. But it is also essential to help them understand why they are feeling the way they do, which is caused by what they believe about what happened. At the same time you can encourage them to consider other ways of 'reading' – by applying different beliefs – the same event.

And Success…

Before concluding this discussion, we should emphasise that success, as well as disappointment or loss, also provides valuable opportunities to influence children's character development.

When they succeed acknowledge their effort and persistence and enjoy the moment with them. But also remind them that any success is always the work of more than one individual, and that a gracious winner will recognise the contribution of others which includes acknowledging those who have been less fortunate than them. At the same time, you can use their success to encourage them to continue to develop their talent. In this way you will assist them to develop the accomplishments of character of grace, competence and persistence.

And if they are envious of the success of others point out that any achievement, while requiring some aptitude and luck, is primarily the product of patience, persistence and courage – qualities available to us all

Tool 4: Do the Thing You Fear Most

"Do the thing you fear most and the death of fear is certain."
Mark Twain (US author)

We have already mentioned a number of times that mood disorders, including anxiety and depression, are essentially learned rather than innate or inherited conditions; that is, they are primarily the product of socialisation or how children are raised.

This, as we have also suggested, is encouraging; if we can understand why children become anxious or depressed then we can do something about it while they are growing up.

A minimum resting level of anxiety or arousal is normal and healthy, it is a genetic endowment which allows humans to react quickly when threatened, sometimes before they are consciously aware of danger. Moderate but temporary spikes in anxiety are also normal, they occur in response to a perceived threat, real or imagined.

Unfortunately it is possible for anxiety to become semi-permanently elevated so that some people remain hyper-alert even when there is no need; they overreact to minor disturbances and experience at least mild symptoms of raised anxiety much of the time. Chronic anxiety is neither normal nor healthy.

Babies and young toddlers display remarkably little fear. They will pick up anything and taste it. They will also play with dangerous objects and put their hand on a hot surface unless prevented; all new parents are familiar with the need to 'toddler proof' their kitchens.

Most of the time babies will laugh when raised high in the air and interestingly a majority will swim, even underwater, with little concern even if a few years later they are 'afraid to get in the water'. True they are startled by a sudden loud noise and distressed by pain or if left alone for too long – these are instinctive reactions.

Nevertheless, they start life with few of the fears and anxieties that can emerge later and may persist into adulthood. Despite this it is not uncommon for young children to develop – or learn – anxiety or fear as they grow, including fear of failure, fear of being laughed at or simply fear of trying something new.

Helping children understand and manage fear or anxiety is clearly an important task for parents. Two things are worth noting when considering how to do this: firstly, as we have already argued, most fear is learned, and secondly, as we shall see a majority of fears are either misplaced or artificial.

Fear of heights is a good example of misplaced anxiety. What sufferers are really – and rationally –concerned about is a hard collision with the ground which can be easily avoided with proper care. However, a reasonable fear of pain and injury can quickly morph into irrational anxiety associated with high places, regardless of any real danger involved.

It is physically impossible to fall by accident from a properly constructed building, yet some people struggle with a fear of heights when standing on a balcony, or debilitating anxiety when required to travel by aeroplane – even though most know that commercial air travel is much, much safer than driving a car.

Even more anxieties are artificial, that is a fear of something that contains no inherent danger at all, for example, a crowded shopping mall, meeting new people, or sitting an exam. But to say that most anxiety is either misplaced or artificial does not mean that it is not real to the sufferer or that it should be ignored.

And anxiety is insidious. If anxiety about a specific issue, say fear of meeting new people, is not addressed it can generalise to impact on other areas of a person's life to the point where life itself becomes the source of their anxiety. Thus smaller childish fears can grow to the point where they become a major impediment to future success and happiness. Needless anxiety has ruined many lives.

It makes sense to ensure children and teens can distinguish between those things which are genuinely dangerous, such as skateboarding on a busy suburban road, and the vast majority which are not; for instance, going on their own to ask a pizza shop owner for part time work.

It is right and proper to protect children from danger, but it is most important that parents clearly distinguish genuine danger from the misplaced or artificial variety. If you are not careful, as we observed earlier, your own misguided or misplaced fears for your children will lead you to doing things for them, particularly as they grow older, which they need to be doing for themselves.

In this way you may find yourself explaining to a teacher why homework is unfinished or making their apologies when they wish to decline an invitation. It may even extend to explaining to an employer why they can't come to work (except if they are ill). If you are still doing any of these or similar for your adolescent or adult child it is time to stop.

An HR (Human Resources) colleague of ours regularly receive calls from anxious parents with questions about their (adult) children's employment, questions which their children are reluctant to ask for themselves.

Apparently this practice is widespread. It is also consistent with our concern that young adults have become less confident about facing up to the challenges of independent living.

The evidence suggests that we – parents, carers and educators – are primarily responsible for the unhealthy anxiety displayed by too many adolescents and young adults. We are enabling their anxiety by neglecting to insist that they take responsibility for their own lives in age related stages as they grow. And where does this leave them? Clearly less able to navigate their world confidently and to achieve the success and happiness we so fervently desire for them.

It is important to note here, however, that comforting a child, teenager or young adult who is feeling upset or hurt is not the same as protecting them from emotional harm by shielding them from potential sources of anxiety in the first place.

The first is necessary and desirable to help them resolve their immediate distress. The second is not because it leaves them unprepared to manage anxiety when they are confronted by the normal stressors of life and have to deal with these on their own.

Potential stressors or triggers for anxiety are everywhere. They are the stuff that much of life is made of. They can include going to a party alone, giving a speech at a wedding, addressing an unpleasant neighbour or disputing an invoice with a plumber. The list of potential stressors in anyone's life can be as long as you like.

But it is important to note that just because everyday events can trigger unreasonable anxiety, this is not inevitable; stress or anxiety are not beyond a child's control.

The job of parents is not to insulate children from stressors – hence our emphasis on their need for 'free' play and exposure to risk in age related doses – but to teach them to manage these effectively. Positive parenting will assist them to minimise their apprehension when confronted with something new or challenging, as well as to eliminate unnecessary anxiety altogether, by the addressing the source of fear itself.

In Chapter 6 we discussed how to coach children to think adaptively about past, current or likely future events in order to remove their power to generate anxiety and other negative emotions.

Learning how to 'read' their world adaptively, that is to think differently, teaches children that bad feelings – including stress or anxiety – are not the product of external events but something they create for themselves by how they choose to interpret what happens to them. Adaptive thinking is the essence of emotional stability or control, a key accomplishment of character and central to adult maturity (see Story: Seema).

Story: *Seema*

In February 2021 a BBC online news story, which reviewed the sometimes disastrous impact of the coronavirus pandemic on children's mental health, reported the following:

"Seema [not her real name] attempted suicide and started self-harming when exams were cancelled last summer.[5]

'We tried very hard for our exams – you're taught that your entire future revolves around these exams, but that crumbles right in front of you and it's really shocking. It has a huge impact,' she says.

'I felt like stabbing myself … I was in a constant state of anxiety.'"

ꕥꕥꕥ

Fortunately, 'Seema', who is now 17 years old, recovered, but her comments demonstrate what happens when a negative event, in this case an exam cancellation, impacts a person who is applying maladaptive beliefs ("… your entire future revolves around these exams") to a normal challenge facing every teenager.

The cancelling of her exams – a minor event in the broader scheme of things – was sufficient to drive her to self-harm and attempted suicide. You might respond by saying that this was not a 'minor' event for her and we would reply by asking, "Why?" It is simply absurd for a young person to seriously believe that her 'entire future' revolves around a single set of exams.

Seema's unhealthy beliefs about examinations must have been *taught* to her by others, teachers and parents, no doubt, who really should know better.

Even in the absence of a pandemic, comments like, "I hate exams! I get so nervous! I know I'm going to fail and that will be awful!" will inevitably trigger a cycle of anxiety and distress which unfortunately increases the likelihood of failure; the young student is so focused on 'failing' and the consequences that they are unable to concentrate or revise properly.

Alternatively, the same student, coached by a parent, might choose to apply a different 'frame' or set of beliefs which will reduce their 'exam anxiety' to a healthy level so that they can prepare properly. This might sound like: "This exam could be pretty tough but that's OK; if it's tough for me, it will be the same for everyone else. I've covered most of the material and I'm feeling fairly confident. Anyway the absolute worst thing that could happen is that I do fail and have to try again. That's not the end of the world, I'll be fine. Either way I'll be okay and I'm going to learn quite a bit."

In this case the student will approach the exam with more confidence, better preparation, and fewer sleepless nights.

Interestingly, before last year's Year 12 exams our local council erected road signs stating that "Year 12 results are not a marker of future success." Maybe adaptive thinking is going mainstream.

❧❧❧

Failing to teach children how to manage negative emotional responses to the new, the unusual or the challenging is to leave them permanently disadvantaged. Their fears will become a standard feature of their personality and increasingly generalise to other parts of their life.

This, in turn, will ensure that they will avoid anything which they feel even slightly apprehensive about and anxiety, accompanied by depression – caused by feelings of being unable to cope – will become chronic. This is not a recipe for future success or happiness.

It is true that a student facing an exam may still have a few 'butterflies' but that's fine. A little apprehension is no bad thing when facing a challenge, it promotes a proper focus. Make sure your children understand the following: that some 'butterflies' are normal in this situation, nothing to be concerned about and will disappear once they have started; and most importantly, that cheerfully accepting the challenge and completing the exam is the best way to eliminate 'exam anxiety' for good. In other words, overcoming fear requires action as well as thought.

Mark Twain, quoted above, suggests that to banish fear means to tackle something we would prefer not (but need or want) to do rather than simply reneging or letting someone else – a parent for example – take over. Teaching this truth to children should commence at an early age. There are a myriad of ways parents can do this; for example, by insisting they go to school unless they are genuinely unwell, asking them to hand out snacks at an adult party or go next door to deliver a message to a 'grumpy' neighbour.

As they grow older and more capable parents should increase a child's responsibilities to include everything they will need to know and do as adults. This can be difficult, particularly in the face of protests and tears. But you can make it easier for them when you break a demanding task into smaller segments and coach them in how to perform these one at a time.

When children are young parents generally organise a birthday party for them but as they get older you should aim to increase their contribution; designing, making and sending invitations as well as helping prepare food and decorations etc, until, as teens, they can do it all themselves.

Another useful way to assist is to 'role play' activities which worry them, particularly those that are new. These might be acting in the school play, asking for a discount from a retailer, or inviting someone to go on a first 'date'.

First, ask what they think is the best approach in each case and make suggestions where necessary. Then encourage them to practise what they plan to say or do with you taking the part of the other person. In the case of inviting someone to a movie remember to practise handling refusal gracefully in case they say 'No'!

While we do not advocate pushing a child in 'at the deep end' (hence our focus on coaching) we do believe there are times when parents need to firmly insist that children take responsibility for things, handled by Mum or Dad in the past, but which they are now ready and able to do on their own.

This includes refusing – except in exceptional circumstances – to help them with anything they should be doing for themselves even though they don't like doing it.

For example, planning, purchasing and preparing meals for the whole family, writing job applications, making phone calls, accepting or declining invitations, paying bills and dealing with neighbours and tradespeople as well as random visitors to their home. The list goes on but ideally by the time they are in their late teens they should be comfortable with doing most of what is required to live and work independently.

It is fair to say that parents are the major obstacle to children overcoming their anxieties and learning to stand on their own feet. If we are apprehensive about them taking on something new they will also be reluctant and if we doubt their capacity so will they. We must manage our own anxiety about giving them more responsibility before we can help them to manage their own about taking it on. Worrying that 'they might get it wrong' is counter-productive; they will make mistakes and that's fine. Fixing errors is part of the struggle anti-fragile children need if they are to become resilient, mature adults.

Tool 5: Managing Relationships

We have referred frequently in this book to relationships and their importance, particularly those children develop with their parents and their wider family. We have emphasised the necessity of children learning social desirability and competence so that they can comfortably engage with others and benefit from their support. And we have discussed how parents can communicate with children, especially when there are disagreements between them, so that they strengthen rather than impair their relations with them.

In Chapter 8 we introduced Steven Covey's Emotional Bank Account which parents can use to build loving and respectful relationships with children. This handy technique is very useful for maintaining trust between people, despite the inevitable misunderstandings and normal conflict that will occur from time to time in any busy household.

Obviously it is a mistake to assume that, once established, important relationships will take care of themselves. Dr Johnson, creator of one of the very first English dictionaries, once observed, "Friendships are like houses, both must be kept in constant repair."

A strong social network, made up of high quality relationships with a partner, colleagues and friends, and of course children, is a principal requirement for mental health. It also primarily determines the quality of much of the rest of our lives. Therefore it is important that children know how to create and maintain one for themselves.

We know this cannot be done by 'sucking up' to people and tolerating their unacceptable behaviour just to keep them as friends. We achieve long term, rewarding relationships by investing in them, using the behaviours advocated by Covey:

- Listen to understand
- Attend to the others' needs
- Keep commitments
- Be loyal
- Be honest – clarify expectations
- Apologise sincerely when necessary

If these are reciprocated we have a friend, maybe for life. If not, then after a while we shrug our shoulders and move on.

Children need to understand that persisting with any relationship, in which there is an unequal balance of trust, respect or power, is not only a sterile experience but can damage them psychologically as well. If they are the ones 'on top' there is a danger of them becoming arrogant and dismissive of others and, if they are being taken for granted, staying 'friends' with another will lower their self-confidence and bring them needless unhappiness.

Every group of children will have an 'in crowd' which, unfortunately, outsiders may be desperate to be part of. Teenagers, particularly, are often very anxious to be included in the 'cool' group. Unfortunately non-members may be treated with indifference when they seek to join, or worse, be subject to abuse and humiliation.

If your child is included well and good, provided they don't develop a superior attitude to the rest of the world and remain clear eyed regarding the ephemeral nature of their status. As the saying goes, 'Cock of the walk this week, feather duster the next!'.

Whatever their status they would also do well to maintain a wider circle of friends and acquaintances so that they are not dependent on the uncertain goodwill of the 'cool kids'. Those who are not members may still prefer to join but can be helped to manage their disappointment using the adaptive thinking tools discussed earlier.

Either way, whether your children are 'in' or 'out', it is crucial that they recognise that true and lasting friendship is based on mutual trust and respect which lay the ground for subsequent liking and affection and sometimes love. By teaching them this fundamental truth you will assist them to acquire empathy as an accomplishment of character as well as set them up for a lifetime of rewarding relationships. (See Story: *The Party Crashers*).

Story: *The Party Crashers*

Some years ago our daughter Megan, who was about 15 years old at the time, went to spend a Saturday evening at the home of a friend, according to her to stay in and watch TV. We knew her friend and her parents well so dropped Megan off with her assurance that they would bring her home.

Later in the evening we were surprised to get a call from a lady we barely knew (she was a mother from the same school that Megan attended) to say that Megan and her friend had tried to attend a party to which they were not invited using fake identities!

Her father's first response was to laugh, but her mother was less impressed!

In discussion with Megan the next day, after a trip with her friend to apologise to the lady whose party they 'crashed', we discovered that they wanted to attend, even though they hadn't been invited, because all the 'cool kids' would be there.

What we learned, and should have known already, was Megan's fervent desire to be accepted into the 'in crowd' in her year at school.

This was a sobering lesson; we simply did not appreciate how strongly adolescents feel about being accepted by people they admire. It also prompted a number of conversations with Megan about the nature of true friendship vs the transient alternative offered by the unreliable camaraderie of 'popular kids'. Interestingly, her fellow 'party crasher' is still her best friend today.

ॐॐॐ

This experience was a wake-up call for us to be more aware of how Megan was travelling socially. In retrospect this is something we, as parents, could have done better.

Unfortunately, we assumed that she and her brothers would be just as alert as us to the dangers of trying to be friends with people who weren't inclined to reciprocate. But, as noted in the story, we were not really aware of how strong an adolescent's desire can be to be accepted by peers they regard as high status.

It also warned us that, while we wanted our children to stand on their own feet, adolescence is a time of powerful physical and emotional change during which they need help if they are to navigate it successfully. Teens want and need to talk about what is happening to them but, as our conversations with young people have revealed, they are often reluctant to raise the subject themselves – parents have to make the effort to get the ball rolling.

We also learned from these conversations that adolescents who are going through puberty are not necessarily looking for solutions but reassurance that their parents appreciate, and, to some extent at least, understand what is happening and are there to support them. Keeping communication going can be tricky, however, if the only answer you get from the question "How was school?" is "Fine" or "OK". It is more likely that these topics can be broached in the course of other activities and conversations, particularly when one parent is alone with one of their children.

The closeness and camaraderie that comes when there are just two of you provides an opportunity to ask a few delicate questions about their emotional life, if only to reassure yourself and them that all is well. We return to this topic in the section Learning To Love (see below).

For now, let us just note the importance of setting aside regular times for parents to get together alone with each of their children. This is extremely rewarding for both parties and something we have continued with success even though our children are now adults.

Tool 6: Learning to Love

Understanding the emotional and physical changes associated with puberty and integrating these successfully into their personal lives are two of the trickiest hurdles faced by adolescents and among the most difficult for parents to assist with as well.

It is fair to say that many adolescents (and parents) find it awkward to talk about these changes. Our own experience was not dissimilar, and you will probably need to initiate such discussions if they are to take place at all.

Conversations about the emotional aspects of romantic involvement, as well as the practical details of sexual health, safety and hygiene, are mandatory – you can't leave this up to their school. Even if you have very firm views about the sanctity of sex within marriage, you can't simply assume that your children will follow your lead.

You need to ensure they understand what is involved, why a decision to have an emotionally and/or physically intimate relationship with someone needs to be considered carefully, and to be postponed if they have any doubts at all. In addition, remember to discuss the potential consequences if, as is quite likely at this age, it doesn't last.

Intimate relationships are special and should be treated as such. And sex, in particular, should not be something which is expected, by either party, as a normal part of a casual date. Your teenage children need to be well aware that a desire to be included or liked may lead to them or their friends being exploited by unscrupulous peers. Similarly, they need to understand that a temptation to exploit others will damage them as well.

How conversations like this go will depend of course on the quality of the relationship you have developed with your child over many years. As we have seen, deep trust between parents and children is an absolute necessity for them to seriously engage and listen to what you are saying, particularly when you express concerns for them. And the level of trust between you will also determine the extent to which any conversation influences their subsequent behaviour.

They are going to engage in intimate relationships anyway, if not tomorrow then at some point in the future, so there is no point avoiding the subject even though both of you may feel uncomfortable about it. And, as noted above, parents will generally need to take the lead.

In any such conversation it is important to acknowledge that the physical and emotional changes they may be experiencing can feel frightening and, often overwhelming at times (all the more reason for them to tread warily before becoming someone's girlfriend or boyfriend) but also quite normal and desirable.

At the same time, it is important to emphasise the deeply joyful and satisfying aspects of the sensual side of human nature. A fulfilling physical relationship with someone we care intensely about is one of the gifts which life has to offer and should be celebrated.

Certainly, the majority of children today receive far more formal instruction in 'sex education' than their parents or grandparents and this is a good thing. But it is fair to say that 'sex ed' is of limited value when it comes to teens understanding the psychological and emotional dimensions of puberty.

William Galston and Stephen Goldsmith make this point when they observe:

> Teens hear about biology and body parts, they are instructed on how to reduce the risk of pregnancy and sexually transmitted diseases, but rarely are they given guidance about how to successfully negotiate the minefields of teen and young adult relationships. In short, young people are often told what to avoid, but hardly ever told how to achieve responsible and respectful relationships.[6]

Yet, finding a life partner with whom they achieve a long-term loving and satisfying connection is an important requirement for their mental and physical health, happiness, and contentment. Some of us may have found this problematic ourselves and feel ill-equipped to help our children as a consequence.

Among the accomplishments of character which we believe parents should aim for when raising a child, we have included empathy: a capacity to respond to the feelings of others, and to develop strong friendships and lasting relationships – most importantly with an intimate partner – characterised by love, respect and trust.

Assisting your children to establish empathy as part of their character is critical to their future capacity to find and keep loyal friends as well as a partner for life.

But while your partner may well be your best friend, she/he is obviously a lot more than that. An intimate relationship, while encompassing friendship, is a more profound experience and one which transforms you and your partner in a way no friendship ever will. True intimacy means that you reveal and express yourself with few or no inhibitions, leaving you vulnerable to hurt and humiliation.

To do this successfully requires courage and intense trust from both parties. There are no guarantees, and sometimes one or more of your children may be badly wounded by a failed relationship. As parents, you can't guarantee success for them in affairs of the heart, but you can help them develop the courage and self-confidence to try, as well as the emotional control and resilience required to manage failure.

Sexual Behaviour in Adolescents

In 2019 the AIFS (Australian Institute of Family Studies) reported that two-thirds of Australian teenagers 16-17 had already been in a romantic relationship and that around one in six had engaged in sexual intercourse. Even more concerning, of those in this age group who were sexually active, about 20% admitted that they had done nothing to prevent sexually transmitted infections and one in twelve said that they had done nothing to avoid pregnancy the last time they had sex.[7]

This data should prompt us to begin talking about sex with teens earlier than we might think is necessary. Interestingly, however, and consistent with our earlier argument that today's young people are growing up more slowly than previous generations, there is evidence that they are having less sex than their parents were at the same age, and indeed than their parents are having now.

US research suggests young people born in the 1980s and '90s are more than twice as likely to report having no sexual partners as adults when compared with those born in the 1960s and '70s.[8] A major reason for this is that fewer Millennials and iGen'ers are in long term stable relationships.

The Second Australian Study of Health and Relationships (2014) found that the proportion of adult respondents in an ongoing heterosexual relationship had fallen from 87% to 74% in a decade.[9] Many young adults lament that despite the preponderance of dating apps it is getting harder to find someone who is seeking a long-term stable partnership. This to us is further evidence that young people today are taking longer to reach maturity than their parents and grandparents.

In 2020 the *Daily Mail Australia* ran the following headline: "Young Australians in their prime are now having half as much sex as their PARENTS – and the explanation for the bedroom drought is even more disturbing". The article reported that a survey of 50,000 Australians had found that 40% of those between 18 and 24 have never had sex, while 15% per cent had sex once a month compared with 30% per month for 40- to 49-year-olds.[10]

One explanation put forward to explain this difference was that young people have become more comfortable communicating online and may be losing the ability to communicate easily face to face. Another theory is that the presentation of perfectly proportioned bodies and ideal sexual performance on the internet is causing teens and young adults to be more anxious about their own physical appearance and less eager to engage in sex themselves.

Neither of these suggestions will surprise you if you have read our earlier discussion of the impact of the internet and social media on teens and young adults. It would be no surprise that young adults who have had limited experience interacting face to face with others while growing up, and for whom excessive screen time has been a way of life, will encounter difficulties establishing 'normal' adult relationships. For parents to expect otherwise is wishful thinking.

But even if young people are having less sex than previous generations, they are still exploring their feelings about intimacy and discussing these with friends. This should remind parents to begin addressing these issues as soon as they become important for their children, which, as noted above, may be earlier than you think. And the AIFS report, mentioned above, emphasises the key role parents play in supporting their children as they manage their emerging sexuality.

To underscore the need to engage early with your children it is also worth noting that in this report approximately 15% of children aged 14 to 15 years said that they had a boyfriend or girlfriend at the time they were interviewed. In addition, one in 15 (7% of boys and 6% of girls) reported having had sex for the first time at age 14 years or younger.

To complete these findings one in 10 (9% of boys and 10% of girls) said they first had sex at age 15, and one in six (17% of boys and 16% of girls) had engaged in intercourse for the first time at age 16 or 17.[11]

Conversations with Young People

Our own conversations with young people about this topic have revealed what we believe are some useful tips for parents when approaching the issues of puberty and intimate relationships with youngsters.

Firstly, we were impressed by how serious they were; they already knew more than we expected, but wanted help to understand and manage the intensity of their feelings and physical reactions. We also learned that they want to talk about these things very much, but tend to wait for parents to take the initiative. They are also concerned that their parents don't necessarily understand what they are going through.

Perhaps this is predictable, as most adolescents recoil in horror at the thought of their parents 'making out', much less having sex!

Our young interlocutors appeared to be well aware of the significance of being attractive or attracted to other boys or girls and the importance of treating intimate relationships with care and respect. They don't necessarily want to be told what to do but to be listened to as they work out for themselves the best way forward.

One young lady of our acquaintance lamented that parents tend to 'overthink' their adolescent children's behaviour, which made it harder to have a simple conversation about what is admittedly a complex subject.

She wanted to be able to discuss relationship issues with her parents when she needed to without them trying to 'psychoanalyse' (her word) her motives and desires. She was also aware of her parents' concerns and shared some of these. Her comment was, "I wish they would sometimes just listen and not necessarily try to understand everything."

If we are not careful, our natural concern to protect our children from harm may prevent conversations of this kind from being as beneficial as they could be. In summary, we learned that young people want to talk about the physical and emotional aspects of adolescent relationships but, more often than not, will need our help to get the conversation(s) started.

We also learned that listening and asking a few questions, usually when one parent is alone with a teen – to highlight your concerns and help them clarify their thinking – is the way to go. When they are ready they will specifically ask for your advice, provided they trust you.

Tool 7: Learning to Laugh (At Ourselves Mostly)

"*Life is too important to be taken seriously.*"
Oscar Wilde (Irish poet and author)

We have decided to finish this chapter on a lighter note. We have made many references in this book to mental illness, notably mood disorders such as anxiety and depression, because we want you to raise your children so that they never have to grapple with these curses. But we also want your experience of parenting to be a happy and joyous one, which it can and should be.

One way of ensuring this is to remember the wise advice of Oscar Wilde, a man who had more than his fair share of hardship in his own life. Like many others he coined, this quip is self-contradictory. How can something that is important not be serious at the same time?

A way out of this conundrum may be found in 'Sturgeon's Law'. This rule of thumb was originally coined by the sci-fi author Ted Sturgeon who, when told that 90% of all sci-fi literature was rubbish, replied that the same was true of all types of literature, as well as music, movies and TV.

Rolf Dobelli in *The Art Of The Good Life* (introduced in Chapter 2) argues that Sturgeon's Law can be applied more broadly and quotes the following observation: "90% of everything is crap. That is true whether you are talking physics, chemistry, evolutionary psychology, sociology, medicine – you name it – rock music, country western."[12]

The point Dobelli is making is that a great deal of what happens in life is hardly worth thinking, much less worrying, about. From your own experience you will know Sturgeon's Law applies to a majority of meetings, emails, reports, conversations, products for sale and so on. Whether the true figure is more or less than 90% is not important. The key point, as Dobelli says, is that "Precious few things are valuable, first rate or essential and applying Sturgeon's Law will save you plenty of time and frustration."[13]

This is what we think Oscar Wilde is referring to in his famous aphorism; by not taking most of what happens in life too seriously, we can reserve our time, attention and emotions for those few things that are truly important.

While you may have to wade through a lot of dross to find what is "valuable, first rate or essential", it is important to keep in mind two things and to pass these on to your children. These are, firstly, that most of what happens is hardly worth responding to, much less being anxious about, and, secondly, the importance of maintaining a focus on the small number of things that really matter, in particular their relationships with their partner, their friends, their parents and, of course, their own children.

"I wish I had stayed in touch with my friends."

In this context it is interesting to reflect on the final regret of dying people (see Bronnie Ware, introduced earlier) we have yet to discuss: "I wish I had stayed in touch with my friends."[14]

For many people counselled by Ware, the realisation that relationships are, not only more important than material wealth and achievement, but one of the keys to happiness and fulfilment, came too late. But this need not be the case for you and or your children.

By keeping your mind uncluttered by the passing parade of nonsense you will have time and energy to appreciate and enjoy your life, especially your family. Those precious years, when your children are growing up, when you are still the centre of their world, and adulthood, with all its challenges and uncertainties, is still a long way away.

The Importance of Laughter

"Parenting without a sense of humour is like being an accountant who sucks at math." Amber Dusick (US author)

If we do agree, as Dobelli suggests, that "In short, ninety percent of all the material and intellectual things put into the world are bullshit.", then there is something we can do about this and that is laugh.[15]

Laugh at all the pompous silliness we see every day around us, as well as on TV and social media, laugh at the affected airs and graces of self-important narcissists, laugh at the feverish efforts people make to 'keep up' and, most of all, laugh at ourselves when we are at risk of getting caught up in the 'bullshit' that clogs and blights too many lives.

Laughing at the world, and at ourselves in particular, helps us manage the inevitable disappointments we will encounter. Just as important, laughter is a potent source of physical and mental health.

If you can laugh at yourself and the world, your children will automatically learn to do the same and reserve their emotional resources for what is really important – the people close to them.

Conclusion

Without a road map we know that, in the future, our children will have to work out a lot of things on their own. It follows then that we should provide them with tools to assist them on their journey.

In a sense this whole book has been about equipping children with skills, knowledge and personal qualities – accomplishments of character – to aid their search for a life which is rewarding and fulfilling for them. This is the true purpose of positive parenting.

In this chapter we have expanded on some of the ideas we have already mentioned earlier in the book, as well as discuss a few new ones which they and you may find useful. No set of tools of this kind will ever be complete, many they will create as they go, but we hope those we have covered will make their and your task a little easier.

Summary

- Encourage your children to find and develop a circle of competence which will provide both financial and emotional support when unpredictable change threatens them or their family.
- Teaching children to concentrate provides a gateway to all the other learning they will need for a successful and rewarding future.
- Ensure your children understand that some failure is inevitable when they tackle something new, but also only temporary, provided they are prepared to persist.
- Help children understand that some fear is normal, particularly when they accept a challenge, but can be overcome through adaptive thinking followed by action.
- Mutual respect and trust are the foundation of all lasting and worthwhile relationships, whether these be with a partner, friends, colleagues or children.
- Teens want to talk about love, relationships and physical in-

timacy, but generally will need parents to start the conversations. They don't necessarily want answers, but rather help to understand the powerful physical and emotional changes that accompany adolescence.

- If 90% of what goes on around us is 'bullshit', then the most appropriate response is to laugh, most of all at ourselves, when we are in danger of taking too much of life too seriously. Encourage your children to preserve their concern and emotions for what matters – their relationships with family and friends – and to laugh at the rest.

Summary

Raising Psychologically Healthy Children

"My philosophy is I'm raising future adults, not children."
Usher Raymond (US musician)

At the beginning of this book we asked the question: "Why is it that in a world which is safer, healthier, more prosperous and provides more educational and career opportunities than ever before, are so many young people struggling psychologically?"

To answer this question we have pointed to some dramatic changes in our world. These include a rising culture of safetyism, 'paranoid' parents who are reluctant to let their children grow up, a decline in the amount of 'free' play afforded to children, family dysfunction, increasing marriage breakdown and the genuine revolution which 'smart' technology has wrought in the lives of children born since 1995.

Whatever the precise causes of the current epidemic of mental illness in adolescents and young adults in Australia and elsewhere, the good news is that we now know a lot about raising psychologically healthy children. And most of this, of course, concerns the behaviour of parents and carers. In fact, we have argued that the mental health of adolescents and young adults, and the likelihood of them leading a fulfilling and worthwhile life, are primarily determined by how they are raised.

This is good news because it means parents can do something about the ominous trends threatening young people. You don't have to stand by and simply watch your children become more miserable and less able to face the future. You can act to assist them avoid these threats in the first place as well as manage them more effectively if they do emerge.

While we acknowledged that there is no guaranteed formula or road map for taking children directly and safely to an 'ideal' future, we have recommended some aspirations parents should have for their offspring to maximise their chances of successfully making the journey.

We concluded that our best option is to focus on a child's personality development – what we have called accomplishments of character – rather than emphasising an accumulation of prizes or achievements. And we argued that while character may well lead to material success, the obsessive pursuit of wealth or status, for its own sake, will never deliver genuine feelings of happiness and contentment.

We have reflected that much of what we call positive parenting – raising psychologically healthy children – has been known for a long time. Some (but not all) of the methods our parents and grandparents used to raise us remain valid. These include 'free' play, family rules, daily routine and compassionate discipline.

We reprised the often quoted saying "Prepare the child for the road, not the road for the child' to emphasise the critical role parents play in preparing young people to successfully manage an uncertain future. The alternative is to make their current life unnecessarily easy while leaving them woefully ill equipped to prosper on their own.

To prepare children for the road, we have recommended providing, from an early age, an ever widening sphere of autonomy within which they make their own plans, correct their own mistakes and learn to be comfortable with sometimes failing. In the process they will develop a positive identity – a strong sense of being an autonomous individual – reflected in powerful feelings of personal control and mastery.

We have also argued that affording children genuine discretion, within their sphere of autonomy, will lead them to personal maturity as they deal with the consequences of their own actions and decisions. In this way they come to understand 'what is generally best', that is how to act in the best interests of themselves and others when parents are not there to guide them.

Along with the wisdom of generations we also reviewed findings from current research into child development. These included striking new insights into what is required to raise happy, confident and resilient human beings.

We commenced by exploring the concept of antifragility. Children are antifragile, they need the stimulus of challenge, indeed adversity, and the strain and stress associated with these, in order to become physically and psychologically resilient. In the absence of moderate degrees of pressure, qualified by aged, their psychological, social and physical development will be permanently impaired.

We also argued that, while some children may have a genetic predisposition to mental disorder (including mood, conduct, behavioural and personality disorders), whether these conditions emerge as they grow is significantly determined by how they are raised and the type of families they grow up in. In other words, the symptoms associated with non-organic psychological disorders are primarily learned and not solely the result of genetics, and therefore they can be unlearned as well.

DNA is not destiny. Parents, whatever their situation, can significantly minimise children's experience of negative emotions including anger, envy, depression, anxiety and resentment. And if a child is unfortunate enough to experience a mood disorder, how seriously this impacts their life will be determined by the personality or character they develop on their way to adulthood. Accomplishments of character, particularly self-confidence, positive identity, emotional control and resilience, will go a long way to insulate them from the worst impact of mental illness.

To assist them acquire emotional control, and avoid a mood or personality disorder altogether, we have emphasised that children must learn two things: that feeling is preceded by thinking, and that they create their own emotional experience via the language and beliefs they choose to interpret or 'read' what happens to them. These techniques, taken from Cognitive Behavioural Therapy, are incredibly powerful and will equip any child to ride out, relatively comfortably, whatever bad times they may encounter in the future.

The core of this book has focused on positive parenting – what it takes to raise psychologically healthy children. First we emphasised the primary importance of respecting children for who they are as well loving them. Love for our offspring is an innate biological bond which is almost impossible to destroy. But love alone is not enough to ensure an enduring and rewarding relationship between a child and their parents, respect and trust are also essential.

We suggested that parents respect a child when they acknowledge that they are endowed from birth with the same rights and obligations as every other human being even if, temporarily, they are unable to fully exercise this birthright. And we recommended a range of techniques to ensure you practise respect for them on a daily basis. However, we also emphasised that true respect includes a responsibility to intervene, with discipline if necessary, when a child's behaviour is disrespectful or harmful to themselves or others.

Respect for children becomes particularly important when they are clearly different from their more 'mainstream' peers. They may be quite shy, 'misbehave' more, be slower to talk, or less intellectually able and so on, or simply eccentric; either way they are not the children parents expected or perhaps wished for. If this is the case you must be careful to avoid labelling them as a 'problem' of some kind which needs to be 'solved' even though they may need extra support or professional intervention.

Children themselves we have argued are never a problem although at times aspects of their behaviour or performance may be. By maintaining a rigid distinction between the child as a person, whom you always love, respect and accept, and those aspects of their progress which trouble you or them, you can ensure they get the help they need while continuing to raise them in the same way as their 'less different' peers.

Teaching children social desirability and social competence we suggested begins with family rules which help them learn to live comfortably in a world filled with other people who also have rights, needs and priorities. Rules together with routine introduce structure and order into young lives and replace what otherwise would be chaos with predictability and security. In time external 'habits' imposed by rules become internalised as self-discipline.

We identified compassionate, consistent and equitable discipline as the central pivot around which positive parenting revolves. Discipline of this kind teaches children how to live successfully in an adult world of rules and regulation. It also gives parents the confidence to override a child's wishes when they believe this to be in his or her best interests.

Most importantly, we emphasised that consistent or reliable discipline teaches children that they and no one else are predominantly responsible for what happens to them; that the choices they make primarily determine what happens to them, good or bad.

This knowledge is liberating for a child. It enables them to become an autonomous adult who can make choices regarding the person they want to be and the life they wish to lead. In doing so they will avoid most if not all of the regrets recorded by Bronnie Ware's patients.

In the final chapter we discussed a number of 'tools for the road' which you and your children may find useful during those delightful, exhilarating and sometimes painful years when you are the rock they rest on as they prepare themselves for their future.

It is during this period that all your hard work when they are young will pay off.

There is nothing more inspiring than to spend time with cheerful, confident and motivated young people as they talk about their lives today and their aspirations for the future. To say that this is life affirming for parents and carers is a genuine understatement. It is to reassure us that our own lives have meaning and purpose, that we will live on through the accomplishments of character we have bestowed on our children and which ensure their future will be bright.

Postscript

Your Children Are not Your Children

Your children are not your children.

They are the sons and daughters of Life's longing for itself.

They come through you but not from you,

And though they are with you yet they belong not to you.

You may give them your love but not your thoughts,

For they have their own thoughts.

You may house their bodies but not their souls,

For their souls dwell in the house of tomorrow, which you cannot visit, even in your dreams.

You may strive to be like them but seek not to make them like you.

For life goes not backward nor tarries with yesterday.

You are the bows from which your children as living arrows are sent forth.

(*The Prophet*, Kahlil Gibran, Penguin, 2010)

It is difficult to finish a book on parenting without reflecting on the timeless words of Kahlil Gibran. His 1923 classic, *The Prophet*, is replete with insights for living wisely and well but it is his few lines about children (part quoted above), which have particular resonance for us.

What is he saying? For us his words encapsulate – far more eloquently and economically than ours – the core message of this book: that children are unique individuals deserving of our respect as well as our love.

Although we create them, they do not belong to us; they are not our project. They are honoured guests in our home but they are always more than guests as well. They are on their own journey and, while we nurture and protect them, we must allow them to become the person they need to be and whose destiny we cannot foresee.

It is our privilege, which we gladly accept, to start them on their way, to launch them if you like. But we should never try to make them in our own image; they must be free to find their own way to their own future, one that is meaningful and rewarding for them. So that when they leave us, as they must, while we may be sad we will also be proud. Proud of who they are and who they are yet to be, as well as proud of ourselves for a job well done.

Endnotes

Introduction

1. Australian Institute of Health and Wellbeing website 2020.
2. Jean M. Twenge, Brittany Gentile, C. Nathan DeWall, Debbie Ma, Katharine Lacefield, and David R. Schurtz, "Birth Cohort Increases in Psychopathology Among Young Americans, 1938–2007: A Cross-Temporal Meta-Analysis of the MMPI," *Clinical Psychology Review*, 30, 2010.
3. J. Twenge, "iGen: Why Today's Super Connected Kids Are Growing Up Less Rebellious, More Tolerant, Less Happy – And Completely Unprepared for Adulthood and What that Means for the Rest of Us," *Atria International*, 2017, 77.

Part 1

1. A. Storr, *Churchill's Black Dog and Other Essays*, Harper Collins, 1997, 17.

Chapter 1

1. N. Segal (2017), "Twins together and apart: The science behind the fascination", Proceedings of the American Philosophical Society, 161(1), 1-17.
2. S. O. Lilienfeld, S. J. Lynn, L. L. Namy and N. J. Woolf (2010), *Psychology: A Framework for Everyday Thinking*, Boston, MA: Pearson Education, Inc.
3. D. G. Thomas, E. Whitaker, C. D. Crow, V. Little, L. Love, M. S. Lykins and M. Lettermman (1997), "Event-related potential variability as a measure of information storage in infant development," *Developmental Neuropsychology*, 13, 205–32.
4. D. Cicchetti & D. Tucker (1994), "Development and self-regulatory structures of the mind", *Development and Psychopathology*, 6, 533–49, 538.
5. J. Twenge, op. cit., 118.
6. N. Segal, (2017) op. cit.
7. R. Plomin (2011), "Commentary: Why are children in the same family so different? Non-shared environment three decades later", *International Journal of Epidemiology*, 40, 82–592.
8. US National Institute of Alcohol Abuse and Alcoholism website 2020.

9. W. A. Collins, E. E. Maccoby, L. Steinberg, E. M. Hetherington and M. M. Bornstein (2000), "Contemporary research on parenting: The case for nature and nurture," *American Psychologists*, 55(2), 218-32.

10. W. Meeus, M. Helsen and W. VoUebergh (1996), "Parents and peers in adolescence: From conflict to connectedness – Four studies" in L. Verhof-stadtDeneve, I. Kienhorst and C. Braet (Eds.), *Conflict and Development in Adolescence* (103-15), DSWO Press, Leiden University.

11. L. Steinberg (2001), "We know some things: Parent-adolescent relationships in retrospect and prospect", *Journal of Research on Adolescence*, 11, 1-19.

12. D. Baumrind (1989), "Rearing competent children" in W. Demon (Ed.), *Child Development Today and Tomorrow*, San Francisco: Jossey-Bass.

13. D. Baumrind (1991), "The influence of parenting style on adolescent competence and substance use," *Journal of Early Adolescence*, 2, 56-95.

14. E. E. Maccoby and J. A. Martin (1983), "Socialization in the context of the family: Parent-child interaction" in P. H. Mussen (Ed.), *Handbook of Child Psychology* (Vol. 4), 1-101, New York: Wiley.

15. E. Scabini (1995), "Psicologia sociale delta famiglia. Sviluppo dei legami etrasformazioni sociali" (Social Psychology of the family. Development of bonds and social transformation). Torino: BoUati Borinmghieri.

16. Steinberg, op. cit.

17. Mission Australia/Black Dog Institute. Psychological Distress in Young People in Australia, Fifth Biennial Youth Mental Health Report, 2012-2020.

18. T. A. Furukawa, R. C. Kessler, T. Slade and G. Andrews (2003), "The performance of the K6 and K10 screening scales for psychological distress in the Australian National Survey of Mental Health and Well-Being," *Psychological Medicine*, 33 (2), 357-62.

19. J. J. Prochaska, H. Y. Sung, W. Max, Y. Shi and M. Ong (2012), "Validity study of the K6 scale as a measure of moderate mental distress based on mental health treatment need and utilization," *International Journal of Methods in Psychiatric Research*, 21(2), 88-97.

20. Australian Bureau of Statistics 2012, "4817.0.55.001 – Information paper: Use of the Kessler Psychological Distress Scale in ABS health surveys, Australia, 2007-08 – K10 Scoring".

21. Mission Australia/Black Dog Institute op. cit.

22. Ibid.

23. D. Lawrence, S. Johnson, J. Hafekost, K. Boterhoven De Haan, M. Sawyer, J. Ainley and S. R. Zubrick (2015), "The Mental Health of Children and Adolescents," Report on the second Australian Child and Adolescent Survey of Mental Health and Wellbeing. Canberra: Department of Health (Young Minds Matter Report).

24. American Psychiatric Association (2000), *Diagnostic and Statistical Manual of Mental Disorders*, fourth edition, text revision. Washington, DC: American Psychiatric Association.

25. Young Minds Matter, op. cit.

26. Ibid.

27. In 2010 it was reported that 19.9% of young people (11 to 17 years) in WA had experienced high or very high levels of psychological distress in the previous 12 months but for females aged 16 to 17 years this was significantly higher (36.2%). (Commissioner for Children and Young People WA. (2015). Our Children Can't Wait – Review of the implementation of recommendations of the 2011 Report of the Inquiry into the mental health and wellbeing of children and young people in WA, Perth: Commissioner for Children and Young People).

28. Presentations to NSW Emergency Departments with Self-harm, Suicidal Ideation, or Intentional Poisoning, 2010-2014, Jayashanki Perera, Timothy Wand, Kendall J Bein, Dane Chalkley, Rebecca Ivers, Katharine S. Steinbeck, Robyn Shields and Michael M. Dinh. (MJA 208 (8) 348-353, 2018).

29. J. Twenge, op. cit., 108

30. Ibid., 109-110.

31. Janet Albrechtsen, *The Weekend Australian*, 10 October 2020.

32. Young Minds Matter, op. cit.

33. Australian Government Institute of Health and Welfare website, 2020.

34. Australian Bureau of Statistics website (2019), Causes of Death, Australia, 2018.

35. In 2018, the suicide rate for Aboriginal and Torres Strait Islander young people (15-24) was 40.5 deaths per 100,000, more than three times the rate for non-Indigenous children (11.7%), Australian Bureau of Statistics (2019), Causes of Death, Australia, 2018.

36. P. Dudgeon and C. Holland (2018), "Recent developments in suicide prevention among the Indigenous peoples of Australia," *Australasian Psychiatry*, 26 (2), 166-9.

37. Mission Australia/Black Dog Institute Report, op. cit.
38. J. M. Twenge et al., "Age, period, and cohort trends in mood disorder indicators and suicide related outcomes in a nationally representative dataset, 2005-2017," *Journal of Abnormal Psychology*, 128(3), 14 March 2019, 185-99, https://doi.org/10.1037/abn0000410
39. Australian Institute of Health and Welfare website 2021.
40. Between 2001 and 2017, the proportion of men aged 18 to 29 living with one or both parents increased from 47% to 56%. The increase for women in the same age group was even more marked, up from 36% to 54%. Staying at home for longer is particularly true of women in their early to mid-20s; in 2001, 30% of women aged between 22 and 25 were still living at home, while by 2017, this proportion had almost doubled to 58%. (Housing Income and Labour Dynamics (HILDA) Survey, University of Melbourne).
41. Between 1998 and 2018 the median age at marriage in Australia for females rose from 27.7 years to 30.5 years. For males it increased from 29.8 to 32.4. The 'crude' marriage rate (marriages per 1,000 estimated resident population) fell in the same period from 5.9 to 4.8. (ABS website 2019).
42. Although the proportion of 15-24-year olds who were employed increased from 57% to 60% between 1983 and 2003, this was mainly attributable to a rise in part-time employment among this age group. For young Australians aged 15-24, full time employment declined by 47% for teenagers and 13% for young adults between 1986 and 2005 (ABS 2005).
43. The percentage of women having their first child over the age of 30 has risen from 23% in 1991 to 43% in 2011 and 48% in 2016, Australian Institute of Family Studies website 2020.
44. In Victoria, for example, in 2009 some 55% of 18-year olds held a driver's licence. By 2014 this figure had fallen to 40%. For 19-year olds the comparable numbers were 65% and 58%, Update on Australian transport trends: Charting Transport website, December 2019.
45. Jordan Peterson (2018), *12 Rules For Life: An Antidote To Chaos*, Penguin/Random House, UK, 134.
46. John Bowlby (1969), *Attachment*, Penguin.
47. Allan N. Schore, "Effects of a Secure Attachment Relationship on Right Brain Development, Affect Regulation, and Infant Mental Health" (15), *Infant Mental Health Journal*, Vol. 22 (1–2), 7–66 (2001).
48. Ibid., 14.
49. Bessel Van der Kolk, *The Body Keeps The Score*, Penguin, 2015.

50. Ibid., 110.
51. Quoted in Anthony Storr, op. cit., 100.
52. Ibid., 100.
53. Bowlby, op. cit.
54. Schore, op. cit., 9.
55. M. H. van Ijzendoorn, C. Schuengel and M. Bakermans-Kranenburg, "Disorganised Attachment in Early Childhood: Meta-analysis of Precursors, Concomitants, and Sequelae," *Development and Psychopathology*, 11 (1999) 225-49.
56. D. W. Winnicott, *Primary Maternal Preoccupation*, London, Tavistock 1956, 300-5.
57. Storr, op. cit., 18-19.
58. Cooper, Hoffman and Powell, circleofsecurity.net
59. Van der Kolk, op. cit.
60. Ibid., 121.
61. S. Greenspan (1981), *Psychopathology and Adaptation in Infancy and Early Childhood*, New York: International Universities Press.
62. Schore, op. cit.
63. Allan N. Schore, "The Right Brain Is Dominant in Psychotherapy", *Psychotherapy*, 2014, Vol. 51, No. 3, 388–97 © 2014 American Psychological Association.

Chapter 2

1. Zero to 3/Bezos Family Foundation, 2016.
2. Peterson, op. cit., 123.
3. Bronnie Ware (2012), *The Top Five Regrets of the Dying: A Life Transformed by the Dearly Departing*, Bolinda Publishing Pty Ltd.
4. Steve Biddulph (2018), Raising Boys in the 21st Century, Simon Schuster, 208.
5. Rolf Dobelli, *The Art of the Good Life*, Sceptre, 2017.

Chapter 3

1. I. Macdonald, C. Burke and K. Stewart, *Systems Leadership: Creating Positive Organisations*, 2nd ed, Routledge, 2018, 15.
2. Ibid., 15-16.
3. Sigmund Freud, *Civilisation and Its Discontents* (1930), Norton and Co., 2010.

4. Macdonald et al, op. cit., 16.
5. Ibid.
6. P. Gray (2011), "The decline of play and the rise of psychopathology in children and adolescents," *American Journal of Play*, 3(4), 444.
7. J. E. Black, T. A. Jones, C. A. Nelson and W. T. Greenough (1998), "Neuronal Plasticity and the Developing Brain," in N. E. Alessi, J. T. Coyle, S. J. Harrison and S. Eth (Eds), Handbook of Child and Adolescent Psychiatry, Vol. 6, 31-53, NY, John Wiley.
8. J. B. Rotter (1966), "Generalized expectancies for internal versus external control of reinforcement," *Psychological Monographs: General and Applied*, 80(1), 1–28. https://doi.org/10.1037/h0092976.
9. I. Costantini, A. S. F. Kwong, D. Smith, M. Lewcock, D. A. Lawlor, P. Moran, K. Tilling, J. Golding and R. M. Pearson (2021), "Locus of Control and Negative Cognitive Styles in Adolescence as Risk Factors for Depression Onset in Young Adulthood: Findings From a Prospective Birth Cohort Study," *Frontiers in Psychology*, 12. DOI: 10.3389/fpsyg.2021.599240.
10. Gray, op. cit., 450.
11. Mission Australia/Black Dog Institute. Youth Mental Health Report: 2012-2020, op. cit.
12. Ellen Beate Hansen Sandseter and Leif Edward Ottesen Kennair, "Children's Risky Play from an Evolutionary Perspective: The Anti-Phobic Effects of Thrilling Experiences," *Evolutionary Psychology*, 2011, 9(2), 257-84.
13. Ibid., 257.
14. I. Macdonald (1990), Identity Development of People with Learning Difficulties through the Recognition of Work, PhD Dissertation, Brunel University.
15. Sandseter and Kennair, op. cit., 275.
16. Macdonald et al, op. cit., 19.

Chapter 4

1. Martin Seligman, *Learned Optimism*, Alfred A. Knopf Inc, 1991.
2. Ibid.
3. Housing Income and Labour Dynamics (HILDA) Survey, University of Melbourne, 2017.

4. Greg Lukianoff and Jonathan Haidt, *The Coddling of the American Mind*, Penguin, 2018.
5. Ibid, 29.
6. Ibid, 30.
7. Twenge, op. cit.
8. Ibid, 5.
9. Pew Research Centre website, 2020.
10. Lukianoff and Haidt, op. cit., 249.
11. Australian Government Department of Health website, 2021.
12. Twenge, op. cit., 116.
13. Mission Australia Youth Survey, 2021.
14. VicHealth, 2018.
15. Australian Government Department of Health website, 2021.
16. Twenge, op. cit., 51.
17. Australian Bureau of Statistics, Household Use of Information Technology, Australia, 2016-17.
18. Twenge, op. cit., 112.
19. A. Joshi and T. Hinkley (2021), "Too much time on screens? Screen time effects and guidelines for children and young people," Australian Institute of Family Studies, Canberra.
20. N. Stiglic and R. M. Viner, "Effects of screentime on the health and well-being of children and adolescents: A systematic review of reviews," *BMJ Open*, 9 (1), 2019.
21. X. Wang, Y. Li and H. Fan, "The associations between screen time-based sedentary behavior and depression: A systematic review and meta-analysis," *BMC Public Health*, 19(1), 2019, 1524.
22. Ibid., 84
23. Ibid., 77
24. S. Tang, A. Werner-Seidler, M. Torok, A. J. Mackinnon and H. Christensen (2021), "The relationship between screen time and mental health in young people: Systematic review of longitudinal studies," *Clinical Psychology Review*, 86: 102021.
25. Ibid.
26. J. Nesi and M. J. Prinstein, "Using social media for social comparison and

feedback-seeking: Gender and popularity moderate associations with depressive symptoms," *Journal of Abnormal Child Psychology*, 43(8), 2015, 1427-38.

27. Twenge, op. cit., 82.
28. Lukianoff and Haidt, op. cit., 249.
29. Jean M. Twenge, Brittany Gentile, C. Nathan DeWall, Debbie Ma, Katharine Lacefield, and David R. Schurtz (2010), "Birth Cohort Increases in Psychopathology among Young Americans, 1938–2007: A Cross-Temporal Meta-Analysis of the MMPI," *Clinical Psychology Review*, 30.
30. Gray, op. cit., 449.
31. Ersilia Menesini and Christina Salmivalli (2017), "Bullying in Schools: the state of knowledge and effective interventions," *Psychology, Health and Medicine*, Vol. 22, 240-53.
32. Bullying No Way! Australian Education Authorities / the State of Queensland website © 2020.
33. US National Centre for Education Statistics website, 2020.
34. K. L. Modecki, J. Minchin, A. G. Harbaugh, N. G. Guerra and K. C. Runions (2014), "Bullying prevalence across contexts: A meta-analysis measuring cyber and traditional bullying," *Journal of Adolescent Health*, 55, 602-11.
35. S. Hymel and S. M. Swearer (2015), "Four decades of research on school bullying: An introduction," *American Psychologist*, 70, 293-299.10.1037/a0038928.
36. Young Lives Matter Report, op. cit.
37. Bullying No Way! website, op. cit.
38. Ibid.
39. Data from the U.S. Department of Justice, Bureau of Justice Statistics, School Crime Supplement (SCS) to the National Crime Victimization Survey, 2017.
40. D. S. J. Hawker and M. J. Boulton (2000), "Twenty years' research on peer victimization and psychosocial maladjustment: a meta-analytic review of cross-sectional studies," *Journal of Child Psychology and Psychiatry*, 41, 441–55. doi:10.1111/1469-7610.00629.
41. C. Cook, K. R. Williams, N. G. Guerra, T, Kim and S. Sadek (2010), "Predictors of bullying and victimization in childhood and adolescence: A meta-analytic investigation," *School Psychology Quarterly*, 25, 65-83.10.1037/a0020149.

42. S. T. Lereya, M. Samara and D. Wolke (2013), "Parenting Behaviour and the risk of becoming a victim and a bully/victim: A meta-analysis study," *Child Abuse and Neglect*, 37, 1091-1108. 10.1016/j.chiabu.2013.03.

Chapter 5

1. Nassim Nicholas Taleb, *Antifragile: Things that gain from disorder*, Random House, 2012.
2. Lukianoff and Haidt, op. cit., 23.
3. Ibid., 31.
4. R. B. Cairns and D. M. Stoff (1996), "Conclusion: A synthesis of studies on the biology of aggression and violence" in D. M. Stoff and R. B. Cairns (Eds), *Aggression and Violence: Genetic, Neurobiological and Biosocial Perspectives*, 337-51). Mahwah, NJ: Erlbaum, 349.
5. U. S. Spitzer and W. Hollmann (2013), "Experimental observations of the effects of physical exercise on attention, academic and prosocial performance in school settings," *Trends in Neuroscience and Education*, 2(1), 1-6.
6. S. J. H. Biddle, S. Ciaccioni, G. Thomas and I. Vergeer (2019), "Physical activity and mental health in children and adolescents: An updated review of reviews and an analysis of causality," *Psychology of Sport and Exercise*, 42, 146-55.
7. Australian Institute for Health and Welfare, Australia's Health 2018, Chapter 4.
8. Ibid.
9. Taleb, op. cit., 5.
10. Ware, op. cit.
11. Van der Kolk, op. cit., 115.
12. K. Lyons-Ruth and D. Block (1996), "The Disturbed Care Giving System: Relations Among Childhood Trauma, Maternal Care Giving, and Infant Affect and Attachment," *Infant Mental Health Journal*, 17(3), 257-75.
13. Lorna J. Otway and Vivian L. Vignoles (2006), "Narcissism and Childhood Recollections: A Qualitative Test of Psychoanalytic Predictions," *Personality and Social Psychology Bulletin*, 32, 104-16.
14. Jean M. Twenge and Joshua D. Foster (2010), "Birth Cohort Increases in Narcissistic Personality Traits Among American College Students, 1982–2009," *Social Psychological and Personality Science*, 1, 99-106

Chapter 6

1. William James (1890), *Principles of Psychology*, New York: Holt.
2. Daniel Day, Steven Jay Lynn and Albert Ellis (Eds) (2010), *Rational and Irrational Beliefs: Research, Theory and Clinical Practice*, OUP.
3. Ware, op. cit.
4. Viktor Frankl (1946), *Man's Search for Meaning: An Introduction to Logotherapy*, Beacon Press.

Chapter 7

1. William Robinson (1845), *The Philosophy of Human Happiness*, Simpkin Marshall and Co, London, 91.
2. Peterson, op. cit., 18.
3. William James, op. cit.
4. Australian Institute of Family Studies website, 2020.
5. .id Consulting Pty Ltd website, 2020.
6. Ibid.
7. Australian Bureau of Statistics website, July 2020.
8. Australian Bureau of Statistics, Marriages and divorces, Australia, 2010.
9. Kevin Andrews (2012), *Maybe I Do: Modern Marriage and the Pursuit of Happiness*, Connor Court, Ballarat, Victoria.
10. .id Consulting Pty Ltd website, 2020.
11. Andrews, op. cit., 49.
12. D. Allen, "High School Graduation Rates Among Children of same Sex Households," *Review of Economics of the Household*, 2013, 635.
13. Scholars of marriage, Amicus Curiae brief, Supreme Court of the USA, Obergefell, 2015.
14. D. Popenoe (1996), *Life Without Father: Compelling New Evidence That Fatherhood and Marriage Are Indispensable for the Good of Children and Society*, The Free Press, New York, 197.
15. K. Moore, S. Jekielek and C. Emig, "Marriage from a Child's Perspective: How Does Family Structure Affect Children and What Can Be Done About It?" *Child Trends*, 2002.
16. Gunilla R. Weitoft et al (2003), "Mortality, severe morbidity, and injury in children living with single parents in Sweden: A population-based study," *The Lancet*, 361 (9354) 289-95.

17. M. Regnerus (2012), "How different are the adult children of parents who have same-sex relationships? Findings from The New Family Structures Study," *Social Science Research*, 41, 752-70.

18. The National Centre for Fathering (2000), *A call to commitment: Fathers' involvement in their children's learning*, Washington DC, US Department of Health and Human Services.

19. Ware, op. cit.

Chapter 8

1. Steven Covey (1989), *The 7 Habits of Highly Successful People*, Free Press.

2. J. M. Gottman and L. J. Krokoff (1989), "Marital interaction and satisfaction: A longitudinal view", *Journal of Consulting and Clinical Psychology*, 57, 47-52. doi: HYPERLINK "https://doi-org.proxy.library.adelaide.edu.au/10.1037/0022-006X.57.1.47"10.1037/0022-006X.57.1.47

3. J. M. Gottman, J. Coan, S. Carrere and C. Swanson (1998), "Predicting marital happiness and stability from newlywed interactions", *Journal of Marriage and Family*, 60, 5-22.

4. Laurie Tarkan, "Fathers Gain Respect From Experts (and Mothers)," *New York Times*, 2 November 2009.

5. Data from *SBS Report*, 29 November 2019.

Chapter 9

1. Biddulph, op. cit., 52.

2. Young Minds Matter Report, op. cit.

3. Twenge, op. cit., 118.

Chapter 10

1. Peterson, op. cit., 113.

2. Australian Productivity Commission, Steering Committee for the Review of Government Service Provision, Report on Government Services 2020, Part C, Table CA.4 2020.

3. WA Child Health Survey, "To Have and to Hold," 1998.

4. D. Baumrind (2012), "Differentiating between Confrontive and Coercive Kinds of Parental Power – Assertive Disciplinary Practices. Human Development," 55(2) 35-51. doi:10. 1159/000337962.

5. Peterson, op. cit. 134.
6. Mark R. Dadds and Lucy A. Tully (2019), "What is it to discipline a child: What should it be? A reanalysis of time-out from the perspective of child mental health, attachment, and trauma," *American Psychologist*, 74(7), 794-808.
7. Jean Kerr (1957), *Please Don't Eat The Daisies*, Doubleday, New York.
8. Van der Kolk, op. cit., 110.

Chapter 11

1. Ralph H. Kilmann and Kenneth W. Thomas (1977), "Developing a Forced-Choice Measure of Conflict-Handling Behavior: The 'Mode' Instrument," *Educational and Psychological Measurement*, 37(2), 309-25.
2. Edward De Bono (1967), *The Use of Lateral Thinking*, Penguin.

Chapter 12

1. Young Minds Matter Report, op. cit.
2. Australian Commission on Safety and Quality in Healthcare (2018), "ADHD medicines dispensing 17 years and under 2013-14" in *The Australian Atlas of Healthcare Variation.*
3. Ibid.
4. American Psychiatric Association (2000), op. cit.
5. J. L. Skues and E. G. Cunningham (2011), "A contemporary review of the definition, prevalence, identification and support of learning disabilities in Australian schools," *Australian Journal of Learning Disabilities*, 16(2), 159-80.
6. Autism Spectrum Australia website, July 2018.
7. A. J. O. Whitehouse et al (2021), "Effect of Preemptive Intervention on Developmental Outcomes Among Infants Showing Early Signs of Autism," *Journal of the American Medical Association (Paediatrics)*, 175(11), p.e213298-e213298.

Chapter 13

1. Dobelli, op. cit., 54.
2. Ibid., 54.
3. Ibid., 56.
4. Quoted in E. F. King (1858), *A Biographical Sketch of Isaac Newton*, 2nd ed. Grantham: S. Ridge, 66.

5. BBC, 2021.
6. William Galston and Stephen Goldsmith (2008), "Making a love connection," *Threshold*, 93:32.
7. Australian Institute of Family Studies, 2019.
8. Jean M. Twenge, Ryne A. Sherman and Brooke E. Wells. (2017), "Sexual Inactivity During Young Adulthood Is More Common Among U.S. Millennials and iGen: Age, Period, and Cohort Effects on Having No Sexual Partners After Age 18," *Archives of Sexual Behavior*, 46, 433-40.
9. Australian Institute of Family Studies, 2019.
10. Claudia Poposki, *Daily Mail Australia*, 22 January 2020.
11. LSAC Annual Statistical Report 2018 Chapter 5. Published by the Australian Institute of Family Studies, November 2019.
12. Dobelli, op. cit., 198.
13. Ibid., 201.
14. Ware, op. cit.
15. Dobelli, op. cit., 199.

Index

www.ingramcontent.com/pod-product-compliance
Lightning Source LLC
LaVergne TN
LVHW020039110826
845155LV00029B/559

* 9 7 8 1 9 2 2 8 1 5 1 9 4 *